The Sign New and improved for 2015!

DOWNLOAD ALL YOUR CONTENT VIA OUR BRAND NEW WEBSITE!
www.the-sign.co.uk

Are you a parish magazine editor looking for good quality well written content to supplement and enhance each issue you produce?

If the answer is yes, then we can help... we are delighted to announce that The Sign has been refreshed and improved for 2015 to give you even better articles, ideas, reviews, puzzles and the lectionary for the month - all to add to your local content. Our BRAND NEW website will allow you to download all the material you need from one place. And even better, our introductory subscription prices start from just £10 – a saving of 83% on the full price of £60!

Simply visit www.the-sign.co.uk for more information and to start your subscription straightaway.

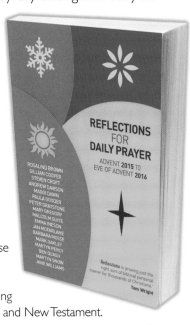

Resources for a Changing World

Multi-Congregation Ministry
Malcolm Grundy

Local church life is changing radically. Multi-congregational groupings are increasingly the norm with fewer stipendiary clergy and greater reliance on self-supporting and lay ministry.

As ministry increasingly becomes the responsibility of the local congregation, Malcolm Grundy explores the theology of this and how it works in practice, drawing insights from rural ministry which has pioneered advances in this area.

978 1 84825 791 7   £18.99

Creative Ideas for Ministry with the Aged
Sue Pickering

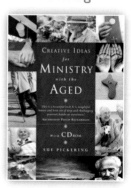

This handbook meets the urgent need for resources for ministry among the elderly. It offers a wide range of ideas and material for use in both individual and group settings, during home visits or in residential care.

It includes: simple services outlines and special liturgies; ideas for spiritual activities using prayer, song, laughter, memory and touch; and resources for addressing the big questions of old age.

978 1 84825 648 4   £24.99

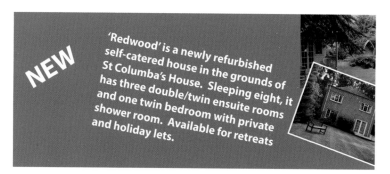

The Canterbury Preacher's Companion 2016

This book is also available on Kindle

The Canterbury Preacher's Companion 2016

Sermons for Sundays, Holy Days,
Festivals and Special Occasions
Year C, the Year of Luke

Michael Counsell

CANTERBURY
PRESS
Norwich

© Canterbury Press 2015

First published in 2015 by the Canterbury Press Norwich
Editorial office
3rd floor, Invicta House
108–114 Golden Lane
London, EC1Y 0TG, UK

Canterbury Press is an imprint of Hymns Ancient &
Modern Ltd (a registered charity)
13a Hellesdon Park Road
Norwich, NR6 5DR, UK

www.canterburypress.co.uk
www.norwichbooksandmusic.co.uk

British Library Cataloguing in Publication data

A catalogue record for this book is available
from the British Library

Scripture quotations are mainly drawn from the New Revised
Standard Version Bible © 1989 by the Division of Christian
Education of the National Council of Churches of
Christ in the USA
Readings are from *Common Worship: Services and Prayers
for the Church of England* (with later amendments), which is copyright
© The Archbishops' Council 2000: extracts and edited extracts are
used by permission.
Readings for days not covered by that book are from
Exciting Holiness, second edition 2003, edited by Brother
Tristram, copyright © European Province of the Society of
Saint Francis, 1997, 1999, 2003, published by Canterbury
Press, Norwich; see www.excitingholiness.org

ISBN 978 1 84825 748 1

Typeset by Manila Typesetting Company
Printed and bound by
Ashford Colour Press Ltd, Gosport, Hants

Contents

SUNDAYS

Unless otherwise stated, the readings and the verse numbers of the psalms are taken from *Common Worship: Services and Prayers for the Church of England* (Church House Publishing, 2000), with revisions, and are for Year C.

vii

ix

xi

SERMONS FOR SAINTS' DAYS AND
SPECIAL OCCASIONS

Readings are from *Common Worship*, or from *Exciting Holiness* by
Brother Tristam SSF, second edition, Canterbury Press, 2003.

Preface

I am privileged to be allowed, once a month, to sit near the entrance to my local cathedral wearing a badge which gives my name, with my position as 'Visitors' Chaplain'. I have a most interesting time, because all sorts of people, from different parts of the country and all over the world, come in. I approach them and say, 'Welcome to the cathedral. Where are you from? Have you been here before?' Sometimes a local resident says to me, 'I lived in this city ever since I was born, and often passed this building, but this is the first time I've come inside. Isn't it beautiful? Such a sense of peace!' Then I offer each visitor a short welcome leaflet, with a brief history of the cathedral and a plan. If they speak a foreign language that I happen to know I will say a few words of welcome in their own tongue.

One day a young Chinese woman spoke to me; she was a student. After a brief pause to sum me up, she suddenly said, 'I have never said this to anyone before, but please tell me, how do I become a Christian?'

I was so astonished I was lost for words. All my life in the ministry I have been praying that some of the people I meet might give their hearts to Jesus, if they have not already done so. Or at least make a deeper commitment to our Lord. But never before had anyone come up with the vital question out of the blue like that. I was so amazed and unprepared that I made a complete mess of my answer, may the Lord forgive me!

What I should have done was put her in touch with one of the cathedral clergy to welcome her into the congregation there, find the dates of the next adult baptism classes, and give thanks with her that she had found her spiritual home.

Instead, I asked where she was studying, and when she told me it was at a university some distance away, I thought that was too far for her to come to classes in this place. I suggested she see the university chaplains, or a church near where she was living. She should choose between a Roman Catholic church, or a Protestant church, or the Church of England, which is a bridge between the two. I told her there are now more Christians in China than in Western Europe – which was news to her – so she should decide whether she wanted to attend an 'open' church, an 'underground' church, or a Roman Catholic church when she returns, but she appeared to be hoping to settle in England. So then I told her that she would have to be baptized, and explained the difference between churches that baptize adults by sprinkling and those that practise immersion, and that she would need a course of preparation classes whichever church she chose. By this time she seemed a little confused, and soon she left to digest what I had told her. I can only pray that God moved in her heart to overcome my blunders, and that she has now found a warm welcome into some lively Christian fellowship.

But I hope that other people do not find themselves lost for words as I was. I think similar situations will become increasingly common all across Britain, not only from the increasing number of foreign students, but from other visitors, immigrants and from members of our own increasingly secular population, who suddenly realize what they are missing by never having learnt what it was that Jesus taught, which makes these Christians so happy.

So I suggest that every church ought to have a supply of New Testaments readily available, or at the very least copies of St Luke's Gospel. A modern translation will be easier for those who are not familiar with seventeenth-century English, the simpler the better. Then you could give it, free, to any enquirers, together with a paper on 'How to become a Christian'. I have written a draft which comes next in this book, which you could print off without needing special permission or paying any copyright fee; or, better, you could rewrite it in your own words, and keep a supply available free at the back of the church for enquirers, and some more near your front door. I have tried very hard not to use theological terms which will be unfamiliar to those whose English is not too good, and ancient language which is never used these days; if I use technical terms I give a simple definition.

So I continued the same policy in the brief introduction to the various seasons in this book, in the hope that it will help preachers to bear in mind that many who listen to them will be very ignorant of the traditional words we use when saying that we are in the Advent or Epiphany seasons and so on. These introductions were the last part of the book to be written, so I haven't yet explored many of the ideas I propose in my own sermons. But I am always trying to put ancient ideas into modern language.

After all, that is what we are here for: to share the good news of Jesus and his love with those who have not yet met him, in words they understand. If you are well prepared, you will recognize the opportunities to do this, and will not make such a mess of it as I did.

Michael Counsell

How to Become a Christian

This is a simple summary, for those of any religion or none, of what it means to follow Jesus. Most Christians are welcoming, and happy, because we know that Jesus loves everybody. To find out why, get to know us better and read this leaflet.

God's plan for you

Here is exciting news: God has a plan for your life. Maybe you haven't yet decided whether there is a God. Read what follows, assuming that there might be a Spiritual Being at the heart of the universe, who wants you to know the plan that has been worked out for you. God wants everyone to have:

A full and fulfilling life

Do you ever feel that your life is dull and superficial, and wish it was deeper? God has a plan to make your life really satisfying.

Meaning, purpose and guidance

Do you ask yourself, 'Who am I? What am I here for?' God made this universe with a definite purpose, towards which everything is heading, and in which you have a part to play. Don't be afraid; God will give you all the guidance you need, for you to achieve your full potential.

Peace

Are you tense, worried, stressful or afraid? God wants you to have a secure calmness, because you trust God to bring you through your troubles to a happy conclusion. Believing in God will bring you a deep inner peace of mind.

Heaven

Do you wonder whether there is life after death? Many people have felt that, when their loved ones die, they are still invisibly present. Not as a ghost, but as a person who has found a better and happier life after they died. Wouldn't it be wonderful if, in a parallel universe perhaps, we could meet up again with those we love, in a world where our faults have been washed away, where all is love and peace, and there is no more pain and death? Jesus came to tell us there is such a world, which we call 'heaven'.

Jews

Since the first humans appeared on earth, people felt sure there was a spiritual world beyond this material one. At first they thought that there were many competing gods, but God chose the Jews to discover that there is only one God, in charge of everything, and who loves all races and nations equally. So we should all try to find out what God wants us to do, and follow the Maker's instructions.

Jesus

Jesus was born a Jew, some 2,000 years ago. At first sight he appeared to be a perfectly ordinary man, though kind and thought-provoking. Jesus said that anyone who wanted to could be his friend. He also taught that:

God is your loving father

Everyone was afraid of God. But Jesus told funny stories, to teach us that God loves each one of us as much as the best of human parents love their children. Jesus talked to God, calling him 'Abba', which means 'Daddy', and taught us to pray to God as our Father, too.

We should love God

God loves us, said Jesus, and wants our love in return. 'Stop ignoring me,' says God, 'stop being afraid of me, or being ashamed to talk to me; but trust me and enjoy feeling my invisible arms around you.'

We should love all those we meet

Jesus said that since God loves everyone as his children, then we should love our sisters and brothers for God's sake. That means working hard to achieve the very best quality of life for everyone we meet, and if they have wounded us, to forgive them, just as God has forgiven us.

Jesus is like God, as a son resembles his father

Nobody has ever seen God, because God has no physical body – and therefore no gender. But God wants to have a human relationship with us. So we should imagine God as a human being. We can do that, by believing that the tender compassion, which we see in Jesus, displays the character of God. Jesus is like God, as a son resembles his father. We call Jesus the Son of God, because God was in Jesus, trying to win our love and faith.

Jesus brought good news

Jesus said that he had come with good news for the whole human race, including you. The good news is of the promise of eternal life in heaven; the free gift of God's forgiveness; and the power to do good. In heaven we shall be close to other people, so we must learn to be companionable now. Religion teaches us to live together in fellowship 'on earth, as it is in heaven'.

The way to heaven

So how do we get to heaven? The first step is to admit we can never get there through our own efforts, because none of us is good enough. So we have to go through several steps:

Admit we are selfish

The first step is to admit that we are not as unselfish and loving as we should be. We do selfish things, which hurt us and other people, and our whole attitude is self-centred and unsympathetic.

Ask God to forgive us and 'wash us clean'

Next we must ask God to forgive us for our selfishness. Forgiving somebody does not mean saying that what they have done doesn't matter – it means that becoming friends again matters more than bearing a grudge. Forgiveness is like 'being washed clean'.

Ask God to help you change

Next you want to show your gratitude to God by becoming a better person. Obeying Jesus' commandment to love everyone should become the most important thing in your life. Ask God to help you to change, and God will give you help, free and undeserved, to be a good person. The technical term for this is God's 'grace'.

Make or renew your decision now

If you have never before made the decision to ask God's forgiveness, and give your life to Christ, talk to God and ask him now. Then write here your name, and when you made your decision. If you made it long ago but have got a bit casual since then, make it again:

Name:
Date: Time:

Christian life

The Christian way of life is centred on prayer, Bible reading, and worship:

Prayer

Prayer is simply talking to God – chatting with your Dad. But because you can't see God, or hear his answers, it takes practice. Set aside five minutes a day to start, and remember the letters 'ACTS', standing for ADORE (tell the depth of your love to God); CONFESS (tell God you are sorry for the selfish things you have done in the past 24 hours); THANKS (thank God for the good things that have happened to you); and SUPPLIES (ask God to supply other people with what they need in the next day or two, and finally ask for the strength you need to carry you through the days to come). If you ask God for specific things, remember that his answer may be 'YES', or 'WAIT', or 'NO, because I have got something much better in mind for you in a little while.'

Bible reading

Also set aside a few minutes each day for reading a few verses from the Bible, maybe starting with the Gospel of Luke. Buy a simple booklet to help you understand what you read. The Bible is a library of different types of books: some are history and some are fiction, but all of them have been told in such a way as to challenge you to trust God and be unselfish.

If the 'history' doesn't add up, God is telling you to look for the spiritual meaning of the words. Ask: **What does it mean *for me*?**

Join the club

It is not easy being a Christian. That's why we need to meet together, to support and encourage each other. We are trying to make the world a more loving place; nobody can do that on their own. Christianity is a community activity. Try to make friends of the people around you in church.

Making invisible love visible

The Church's task is to spread love. You can't see love, but a kiss makes love visible. God, too, uses symbols to show us that we are loved; they called 'sacraments':

Communion

To show us that we are part of the family, God invites us to a symbolic family meal, called 'Holy Communion', 'the Eucharist', 'the Lord's Supper' or 'the Mass'. We eat bread together and drink wine to remind us of the meal that Jesus had with his friends the night before he died.

Adult baptism

To convince us that God has forgiven us, we have a symbolic washing, called 'baptism', when we join the Christian family. In some churches this is done by a brief immersion in a special pool;

in others water is sprinkled on your head as a symbol of your cleansing.

Infant baptism and confirmation

But many Christians feel that it is wrong to exclude children from God's family. So in many churches, parents bring their children to church for infant baptism, or 'christening'. When children are old enough to understand, they confirm the promises that were made for them when they were christened, and the bishop confirms their membership in the church family. So this service is called 'confirmation'. Usually a series of meetings is arranged beforehand to explain the faith and answer questions.

It all fits together

So it all fits together. Life makes better sense if you assume there is a God than if you insist that there isn't. You thought you were searching for God, but actually God was searching for you. He has a plan for you, which will lead you to joy in this life and eternal life in the world to come. If you agree that following Jesus is the main priority in your life, learn all you can about him, and share the good news of his love with other people. God bless you.

[Write or print here the name and contact details of the appropriate minister in the church concerned.]

YEAR C, the Year of Luke

*(Year C begins on Advent Sunday
in 2015, 2018, 2021 etc.)*

ADVENT

All that many of our neighbours will know about Advent is that it is the time when we can buy Advent calendars, with a chocolate under each window for every day from the beginning of December to Christmas Eve. Some charities and traders, therefore, have introduced calendars where the chocolates are at least in the form of figures from the nativity story. So if we are to attract new members to our congregations, that is where we must start. Many people who never come at any other time of year will be in church for carol services, and most of those will contain Christmas carols, readings and even nativity plays. Christians have tried to say for many years now that Christmas begins on Christmas Day and continues until the eve of the Epiphany, twelve days, but we are fighting a losing battle. In very disciplined Christian homes it may be possible to resist putting up the Christmas decorations until Christmas Eve, but children will ask why we are out of step with all their friends, and with the shops which have been advertising Christmas goods since the beginning of November. So whatever we do in private, let us go with the crowd in public, and call this a season for getting ready for the coming of Jesus into the world at the first Christmas. If we can get that across, we shall at least have put Christ back into Christmas; statistics say a horrifying number of people in this country have no idea that Christmas has anything to do with Jesus. Then at the right time preachers may be able to introduce the idea that Jesus comes to us in various different ways still today: in answers to our prayers, in moments of inspiration, in bringing comfort when we are sad, and finally when we die; and

I

that is why we use the solemn purple colour and sing the solemn hymns. Whether or not you believe in the Second Coming of Christ, you would be a brave preacher to introduce the idea into a sermon without a great deal of explanation, as most of our secular neighbours think only nutcases believe in such bizarre theories. Far more likely, in their eyes, is that human life will come to an end on this planet in a few generations because we of this generation have so polluted our environment as to make it unliveable-in by humans, and many other species, in our children and grandchildren's time. A sermon on that theme would cause controversy!

First Sunday of Advent   29 November 2015
Principal Service   Fork 'Andles
Jer. 33.14–16 A King is promised; Ps. 25.1–9 Waiting for God;
1 Thess. 3.9–13 Prayer to be blameless at the coming of Christ;
Luke 21.25–36 The coming of Christ

> *'[Jesus said,] "Be alert at all times, praying that you may have the strength to escape all these things that will take place, and to stand before the Son of Man."' Luke 21.36*

Fork 'andles

Isn't it odd how just one joke in a long series of television pro-grammes catches the public imagination, so that there can be hardly anyone left in the country who hasn't laughed at it? You have only to say 'Fork 'andles' . . .? Well, you see what I mean? Ronnie Barker was a customer in Ronnie Corbett's ironmongery shop, and after a long time investigating handles for forks, Corbett realizes he is talking about a package of four wax candles. I thought I had better mention that before I start talking about the Advent candles, lit in many churches on the four Sundays leading up to Christmas. Four candles indeed, but nothing to do with handles for forks!

Advent wreath

The four Advent candles are usually placed in special holders on an Advent wreath. This tradition began in Germany, but nobody can agree how far back it stretches. Some say it is pre-Christian, and that the four candles represent the four seasons of spring, summer, autumn and winter. According to this theory, it was hung up in wintertime so that the greenery can remind us that the barren winter-cold does not last all year. Against this pagan-origin theory, it has been pointed out that although candles were known in China and Japan from an early date, in Europe, where olive oil for lamps was readily available, wax candles were unknown until the early Middle Ages. When the old translations of the Bible referred to a candle, they probably meant an oil lamp. So some people say that candles were introduced by Christians in the Middle Ages, or in the sixteenth century. Recent research, however, indicates that the Advent wreath, with four candles on it, was invented by Johann Wichern, a pastor in Hamburg, when schoolchildren kept pestering him to know, 'Is it Christmas yet?' In 1839 he hung up a wooden cartwheel, and placed round the rim four white candles to be lit on Sundays, and red ones for each of the weekdays in December. As the custom spread, the wreath was made smaller, and only four candles remained, usually coloured red. But when Roman Catholics adopted the custom in the 1920s they made them in the colours of the Advent vestments, purple because it is a solemn season for repenting our sins before Jesus comes, except on the third Sunday when the solemnity is relaxed a little and the candle is rose-coloured. There are usually no flowers in church, and the 'Gloria' is omitted, to mark the penitential nature of the season. Often a fifth candle in white is lit on Christmas Eve and Christmas Day. In the 1930s the custom spread to North America, and many people now hang a vertical wreath without candles on their doors.

Advent themes

In many churches, children are invited to light the candles, one on the first Sunday of Advent, two on the second Sunday, and so on. Special prayers are written to be said as they are lit, sometimes on the themes of the readings. Advent means 'coming'. So the themes are: the coming of Jesus to forgive those who repent; John the Baptist and the other prophets who prepared his way; the coming of justice on earth; and the announcement of the coming birth of Jesus.

Coming of the Light

There are other themes for the candle-lighting prayers, but for now let's concentrate on the idea of the coming of the Light. Before Jesus was born, people did not know that we shall go to heaven when we die; and they thought that God was a fierce judge who sent bad people to hell. It was like groping in the dark to find out where we should go. But Jesus brought the good news that God loves us and is only waiting for us to say sorry so that he can forgive us for anything unkind that we have done. God wants us to live with him in heaven, where we can meet those we loved who have died. Jesus said, 'I am the light of the world. Whoever follows me will never walk in darkness but will have the light of life.' So every time we light one of the – er – 'fork 'andles', we can think how much brighter and happier our lives have been since Jesus came to us.

All-age worship

Make up prayers to say when each candle is lit, and choose which children shall light them and which shall read the prayers.

Suggested hymns

Christ is the world's true light; In a world where people walk in darkness; The people that in darkness sat; Thou whose almighty word.

First Sunday of Advent   29 November 2015
Second Service   Morality

Ps. 9 The Lord judges the world; Joel 3.9–21 The valley of decision; Rev. 14.13—15.4 Blessed are the dead; *Gospel at Holy Communion*: John 3.1–17 Nicodemus

> *'Go in, tread, for the wine press is full. The vats overflow, for their wickedness is great. Multitudes, multitudes, in the valley of decision! For the day of the LORD is near in the valley of decision.' Joel 3.13–14*

Dawkins

Richard Dawkins, the atheist author of *The God-Delusion*, comes from a long line of determinist philosophers. They believe that when you say, 'I have chosen to do this', you are under a delusion. There is no such thing as choice, they assert; you are forced to do it by external pressures now and in your upbringing. To this, the philosophy of evolutionary psychology, to which Dawkins belongs, adds that you are compelled to act as you do because your remote ancestors who behaved in that way had more children than those who didn't. Now it is true that if a certain line of behaviour enables you to have many offspring, then by the law of the survival of the fittest their genetic line will continue to grow. But it is uncertain how many patterns of behaviour are inherited, and how many are copied by watching your parents, and deciding to behave as they do. The vast majority of the choices we agonize over have absolutely no effect on how many children we have. The theory of the selfish gene is not scientific, because it has never been proved, and never can be. The belief that there is no such thing as free will is only an illogical prejudice.

Moral choices

We all make dozens of moral decisions every day. To some we give the selfish answer, 'I shall do this because it will make me richer and everybody else poorer.' Most of us agree that such decisions are wicked. Or we may say, 'I cannot see that person suffering without trying to help them.' We call that virtuous, unselfish behaviour. Most people, when presented with a choice, will struggle for a while, and then decide that they couldn't live with themselves if they took the selfish path. So they choose the path of goodness. They are not forced; they are not made in such a way that this decision was inevitable. They have thought it out and made a free choice. We cannot prove scientifically that we were free to choose, but it certainly felt like that.

Religion

Does religion have any effect on the choices you make? For many people, it will not affect their conscious thinking; though religion may have shaped the culture within which we live. In other words, if your ancestors decided on religious grounds that murder is wicked, that may be the presupposition on which you start to think for yourself. But if you have chosen to belong to a certain religion, your faith will profoundly affect the choices you make.

Vietnam

I recently read a paper by an English clergyman who was a civilian chaplain in Saigon during the Vietnam war. Ministering to diplomats, workers for various aid agencies and charities, as well as a few soldiers and English-speaking Vietnamese, he was constantly being asked to help them decide what they should do. They did not want him telling them what to do; they wanted to know how to think out the right decisions for themselves. A few of their choices would result in life or death outcomes for other people; all of them would affect other people's well-being. After prolonged thought, he told them to 'educate their consciences'. By this he meant, 'get to know and listen to those whose lives would be affected by what they decided'. Second, he advised them to listen to God, by prayer and Bible reading, and applying what they read to their changed circumstances. For instance, Jesus said, 'If somebody strikes you, turn the other cheek.' But suppose someone strikes your dear old granny, should you pick her up and turn *her* other cheek towards the aggressor? Most people would decide, reluctantly, that to do nothing would be a greater evil than to use force to defend her. This is a difficult moral decision, to which the Bible gives no clear answer, but in which religion is a powerful motivating force.

Decision

The prophet Joel says there are multitudes standing in the valley of decision. There, the wickedness is great, therefore many must have decided against what religion tells us is unselfish good behaviour. But God will judge us on what decisions we have freely made. Actually Jesus tells us that we judge ourselves – because light has come into the world – if we prefer the darkness to the light. But you cannot plead that your selfish genes forced you to follow the wicked, selfish path. You must decide to follow Jesus, and then make the moral choice to do what he advises you to.

Suggested hymns

Hark, a thrilling/herald voice is sounding; Lo, he comes with clouds descending; On Jordan's bank the Baptist's cry; The Kingdom of God is justice and joy.

Second Sunday of Advent   6 December
Principal Service   **Reclaiming Advent**
Bar. 5.1–9 God will lead his people with joy, *or* Mal. 3.1–4 A messenger to prepare the way; *Canticle:* Luke 1.68–79 Benedictus; Phil. 1.3–11 Overflowing love; Luke 3.1–6 John the Baptist

'This is my prayer, that your love may overflow more and more with knowledge and full insight to help you to determine what is best.' Philippians 1.9–10

Consumption

This is the Second Sunday of Advent – four Sundays when Christians prepare themselves for the coming of Jesus Christ. You wouldn't think it, to look in the shops. There, December seems to be a month of massive consumption. Apparently, this month we munch 19 million pounds' worth of chocolate more than in any other month. Advent calendars have windows to open each day, and behind them are found not images of the birth of Jesus but chocolate models of the cast of the latest children's film. In some, the chocolate pieces get bigger the closer you come to Christmas Day. Where are the Virgin Mary and baby Jesus in all this? Missing, it seems, last seen in the pages of the New Testament!

Preparation for Christmas

It was not always like this. In earlier times, Christians spent the four weeks before Christmas – just as in Lent, the seven weeks before Easter – preparing themselves for the festival not by increased self-indulgence, but by a strict regime of self-denial and fasting. This was to help them concentrate on the spiritual meaning of the Christmas story. The Son of God chose to leave behind the glories of heaven and be born as a poor baby, so that you should know how much God loves you. He sacrificed his life for you, so that, through your love for him, he could take you to live with him and those you love in eternity. It doesn't help you to understand that in your mind, and feel it in your heart, if your body is bloated by four weeks of over-indulgence. Perhaps coming to church regularly – listening to the readings from the Bible, and discussing them with your friends – is a better preparation, and the explosive joy of Christmas Day will be all the greater because you haven't anticipated it in Advent.

Coming

Advent is a Latin word meaning 'coming'. Jesus comes to us in at least four ways:

- First, the Son of God came to us as a baby at Christmas.
- Second, Jesus taught us to pray that God's kingdom might come on earth, as it is in heaven. Jesus works through you and me to build his kingdom, righting the wrongs in society and building peace on earth.
- Third, Jesus comes to us in our daily lives when we pray. He comforts us in our sorrows, guides us when we pray, and shares in our joys.
- The fourth way in which Jesus comes to us is when we die. Please God, that may be many years from now. But whenever it happens, we don't want death to catch us unprepared. There is nothing morbid in making your peace with God now, and sorting out your relationships with other people, so that when Jesus comes to welcome you to heaven, you can put the past behind you, and enjoy your eternal future to the full.

Hope

So Advent is a season of hope. We look forward, not just to a few days of meaningless over-eating and drinking at Christmas, but to the fulfilment of God's plans for us and the whole human race. Scientists are undecided whether life on earth will end with a bang or a whimper; ecologists warn that the world might become uninhabitable in many areas in our own lifetime. Yet if our ultimate destination is heaven, we can look forward to death in hope, not despair. But the idea that the human race might die out makes all the more urgent our need to help the hungry, provide for the poor, and set up systems in society which lead to justice and peace. Then we must put right what is wrong in our own lives, by telling God we are sorry and will try our hardest not to do the wrong things ever again. Also we need to share with everyone on earth that the Christmas story is not a quaint old legend, but the true message that God made us to share the joys of eternity with him, then came to earth to tell us so. If we prepare in this way, and not by stuffing ourselves full of chocolate, we shall have a truly happy Christmas and a joyful year to come.

All-age worship

Borrow a globe and place a crown on it. Explain what this means about Jesus.

Suggested hymns

Come, thou long-expected Jesus; Hark, the glad sound! the Saviour comes; O come, O come, Emmanuel!; Thy Kingdom come, O God.

Second Sunday of Advent 6 December
Second Service Luke's View of Mission
Ps. 75 I will judge [76 To save the oppressed]; Isa. 40.1–11
Comfort my people; Luke 1.1–25 John's birth foretold

> *'Since many have undertaken to set down an orderly account of the events that have been fulfilled among us . . . I too decided, after investigating everything carefully from the very first, to write an orderly account for you, most excellent Theophilus, so that you may know the truth concerning the things about which you have been instructed.' Luke 1.1, 3–4*

Luke's Gospel

At this weekly service, beginning today, we have a series of readings each Sunday this year from the beginning of St Luke's Gospel. Luke was an ordinary doctor, but when Paul took him under his wing as his personal physician, Luke began to think, pray and write deep things about what they were doing together, spreading the good news of Jesus all over the then-known world. The story as Luke wrote it began, obviously, with the birth of Jesus at Christmas, but the prequel to that was the story of the birth of John the Baptist. Christ's work began after his cousin John had baptized him in the River Jordan, and continued, according to Luke's Gospel, in a series of banquets. The mission of Jesus didn't end when Jesus died and rose again, so Luke wrote for his friend Theophilus a second volume, which we call 'the Acts of the Apostles'. This describes how the message of Jesus spread to the ends of the earth, through the work of the missionary apostles, like St Paul. The ending of the book of Acts implies that the task of mission did not end with the apostles, but continues to be our task today.

Mission

The Five Marks of Mission, as defined by the Anglican Consultative Council, are:

1 To proclaim the good news of the kingdom.
2 To teach, baptize and nurture new believers.
3 To respond to human need by loving service.
4 To seek to transform unjust structures of society.
5 To strive to safeguard the integrity of creation and sustain and renew the life of the earth.

Community

That is a colossal task. It has to begin as a do-it-yourself job, but can never succeed if you try to make it a do-it-*by*-yourself job. Mission must always be done by a community. Luke tells us that Jesus was always at parties; so much so that he was described as a glutton and a winebibber. He told his followers, 'When you give a banquet, invite the poor, and people with disabilities.' This shocked the Pharisees: the Messianic Banquet had begun, but with the wrong guests. But God's kingdom must be open to all, including Samaritans, centurions and other foreigners. Then Jesus summed it up in the Last Supper, which continues in that grand communal eating and drinking that we call the Holy Communion.

Outcasts

Not only must our fellowship, like that of Jesus, welcome the outsiders – women, the poor, tax-collectors and foreigners – but we must learn to see things from their point of view. So the mission of the Church builds up a world community, because we are not fighting against those we disagree with, but trying to come to a common understanding. We have to respect those we differ from – the Church must be an open community, and open to all. So the mission of Jesus began with the Samaritan woman, and was continued after Pentecost with the Greek-speaking Jews like St Stephen, the Ethiopian Eunuch, Cornelius the Roman Soldier, the unorthodox Jews of Antioch, and St Paul's converts all over the Roman Empire. Christ's kingdom knows no boundaries.

The Spirit

This is only possible, says St Luke, if everything is centred in the Holy Spirit. Beginning with Christmas, right up to you and me, nothing can be done without praying for the power of God to work in our hearts by the grace of the Spirit. So to wish each other a happy Christmas, St Luke would have said, is only the beginning. It leads up to our mission, today, to the most unlikely people, by offering them our hospitality, through the power of the Holy Spirit.

Luke's Gospel

So Luke remained a doctor all his life, but he changed his speciality, and became a physician of the soul. It is the Church's task, working with the medical professions, to teach people to relax, through trust and confidence in God, so that they may more readily be healed. We are also responsible for healing the tensions of society, so that poverty and hunger may not make people sick. Like Jesus, we do this by our hospitality, making everybody, respectable or despised, welcome in our fellowship. Thus we support the worldwide mission of the Church, so that everyone may welcome Jesus into their hearts when he comes to us on Christmas Day.

Suggested hymns

I cannot tell why he whom angels worship; *Long ago, prophets knew*; *People, look East. The time is near*; *Thou didst leave thy throne*.

Third Sunday of Advent   13 December
Principal Service   **Teach Me, My God and King**
Zeph. 3.14–20 Sing, daughter Zion, God is in your midst; *Canticle*: Isa. 12.2–6 Great in your midst, *or* Ps. 14.4–10 Justice; Phil. 4.4–7 Rejoice in the Lord; Luke 3.7–18 The witness of John the Baptist

> *'Even tax collectors came to be baptized, and they asked [John], "Teacher, what should we do?" He said to them, "Collect no more than the amount prescribed for you." Soldiers also asked him, "And we, what should we do?" He said to them, "Do not extort money from anyone by threats or false accusation, and be satisfied with your wages."' Luke 3.12–14*

John's message

Jesus brought the good news of God's love. John the Baptist brought a message of terror, a proclamation of God's judgement. His fellow Jews were certain that God had a most-favoured-nation clause in his contract with the human race. They believed that God would never condemn them, simply because they were born Jewish. John declared that they were like slimy snakes slithering as fast as they could out of the path of an approaching forest fire. The only hope for them was to regard themselves as non-Jews, who were expected to wash away their sins as a sign of their repentance. Then baptized Jews and baptized Romans were schooled in the life of share-and-share-alike, which was expected of each of them in God's kingdom.

Daily work

Some Roman soldiers asked John to elucidate. Were they expected to resign from the army and become monks or preachers – for they sure as anything didn't feel drawn to a religious life. Tax-collectors, too, although they were Jewish, were hated because they collected money to pay the soldiers – should they hand in their notice and look for a different job? No, said John. Don't give up the day job; do the same work as before, only do it well and honestly. No bribery or corruption, and no cheating. It's surprising, even today, how many people in positions of authority make a little bit on the side, and think nothing of it. But provided you are willing to abide by the rules, you can glorify God in any occupation, by doing it well to the best of your ability.

George Herbert

The poet George Herbert knew about offering our daily work to God, and abiding by his moral laws in the way we do it, when he wrote the famous hymn:

> Teach me, my God and King,
> in all things thee to see,
> and what I do in anything
> to do it as for thee.
>
> A man that looks on glass,
> on it may stay his eye;
> or if he pleaseth, through it pass,
> and then the heaven espy.

All may of thee partake;
nothing can be so mean,
which with this tincture, 'for thy sake',
will not grow bright and clean.

A servant with this clause
makes drudgery divine:
who sweeps a room, as for thy laws,
makes that and the action fine.

This is the famous stone
that turneth all to gold;
for that which God doth touch and own
cannot for less be told.

Racing

So if we do our daily work well, and repent of our sins, Jesus will forgive us and welcome us into heaven when our time comes. What does it mean, to do our work well? A woman in hospital was unable to speak. Her family visited her regularly, but there's a limit to the time you can talk to a loved one who never replies. So they switched on the television and watched the Grand Prix motor-racing together. From the occasional smile which crossed her face the patient seemed to be enjoying this. But it created a problem for the chaplain when he came on his rounds, as he had no interest in motor-racing whatsoever. As he sat there with them, the chaplain came to the conclusion that racing-drivers need, if they are to succeed, four qualities which are important in any occupation. They are:

1 To concentrate every moment on what they are doing.
2 To ignore the pain.
3 To work hard.
4 To be self-critical, because one little slip can have dire consequences.

I think that would satisfy John the Baptist as a recipe for pleasing God by doing your daily work well. You don't need to be a 'Holy Joe'. And if you confess your sins and ask God to forgive them, I am sure a life spent pursuing any honest occupation in that spirit will please Jesus when he comes to you.

All-age worship

What recipes for success in your favourite sport can be applied to the rest of your life?

Suggested hymns

On Jordan's bank the Baptist's cry; Teach me, my God and King; 'The Kingdom is upon you!'; Ye servants of the Lord.

Third Sunday of Advent   13 December
Second Service   **His Life and Ours**

Ps. 50.1–6 Our God comes [62 Wait for God in silence]; Isa. 35 Here is your God; Luke 1.57–66 The birth of the Baptist [67–80 Benedictus]

> *'And you, child, will be called the prophet of the Most High; for you will go before the Lord to prepare his ways, to give knowledge of salvation to his people by the forgiveness of their sins.'* Luke 1.76–77

Proud parents

Proud parents are always thrilled at the birth of their children, and try to imagine what each of them will do with their life. It is good to dream that they will all become clever and famous, though the wise parent assures each of the children that their parents' love won't be any less if they only occupy a humble position. The old priest Zechariah, however, believed that his son John – later called 'John the Baptist' – would occupy a very special place in the history of the world. Every Jew expected that God would send a Messiah to rescue his people from all their troubles – John was not to fill *that* role, but to be the one who prepared the way for the coming of the Messiah. So Zechariah put his hopes and dreams into a song, which we know as the 'Benedictus'.

Four themes

'Blessed be the Lord God of Israel', begins the song. Zechariah praises God because John is to be the road-mender, who repairs the highway along which the Messiah will travel – metaphorically, of course. He lists four themes which will be at the heart of his son's message, when he says:

'And you, child, will be called the prophet of the Most High; for you will go before the Lord to prepare his ways, to give knowledge of salvation to his people by the forgiveness of their sins.'

The four themes are:

1 Preparation
2 Knowledge
3 Forgiveness
4 Peace.

Significantly, those four themes will also characterize the preaching of John's cousin, Jesus of Nazareth. And that is because they also define the life of every Christian. Watch carefully, and you will see that these four challenges form the outline of John the Baptist's life, the life of Jesus, and our life.

Preparation

Every fulfilled life needs *preparation*. Jesus needed John to prepare the way for him, by proclaiming the need for repentance, so that Jesus could preach the gospel of forgiveness. We travel along the ways defined for us by our predecessors, while simultaneously preparing ourselves for when the time comes for us to strike out in a new direction. You can never be sure in advance what that direction will be; but you can think about what the purpose of your life is, and pray for the insight to recognize the opportunity, and the courage to grasp it firmly when it arrives.

Knowledge

The second theme is knowledge. Everyone needs book knowledge, learnt at school; but more than that, we all need the *knowledge of God*. It would be no exaggeration to say that nobody knew what God was like before Jesus came to earth at the first Christmas. Greek philosophers believed that God was without passions or feelings, looking at the human race with total detachment, and so, of course, quite unable to help us in our troubles. The Jews proclaimed a God who controls us by constricting laws, and stands over us as a harsh judge. Our only relationship with such a tyrant could be one of fear. When Jesus proclaimed that God is love, everyone was astonished. They had no idea that God was like that – in fact, they had hardly known God at all, until Jesus revealed him as our loving heavenly Father.

Forgiveness

With this new understanding of God came the promise of *forgiveness*, and forgiveness is our third theme. This is not so much the remission of a penalty, but the restoration of a loving relationship with God, previously destroyed by our rebelliousness, and bringing with it a new relationship with the world and those who inhabit it alongside us.

Peace

Preparation, knowledge, forgiveness, and finally *peace*. When Zechariah promised that, as a result of the preaching of John and Jesus, God would 'guide our feet into the way of peace', he meant first of all an end to strife, and the violent struggle for supremacy which had marked the history of the world up till them. Yes, people were slow to learn that lesson, and still are. But the old priest also yearned for his son and his son's cousin to bring the reign of *shalom*, the life of wholeness, happiness and harmony for which we all long. Prepare yourself for this; come to know God as your Father; forgive those who hurt you; repent as John told you to; trust as Jesus showed us; and such a life will be for you and your children too.

Suggested hymns

Hark, what a sound, and too divine for hearing; On Jordan's bank the Baptist's cry; To Mercy, Pity, Peace and Love; Wake, O wake! With tidings thrilling.

Fourth Sunday of Advent   20 December
Principal Service   The Lord Will Come
Micah 5.2–5a A leader from Bethlehem; *Canticle*: Magnificat
Luke 1.46–55, *or* Ps. 80.1–8 Come with salvation; Heb. 10.5–10

When Christ came into the world; Luke 1.39–45 [46–55] Mary
visits Elizabeth

*'Blessed is she who believed that there would be a fulfilment of
what was spoken to her by the Lord.' Luke 1.45*

Coming

Advent means 'coming': the coming of Christ and his kingdom,
past, present and future. The Bible talks of his coming, and its
phrases are quoted in the hymns we sing at this season and the
prayers we use. But often it is unclear which a particular phrase
refers to – the past, the present or the future? Maybe it doesn't
matter. Yet sometimes, a misinterpretation of what Jesus meant
has disastrous consequences. Many Christians have believed that
Jesus would come again in their lifetime, bringing the end of human
history on earth. So certain were they, that some gave away their
possessions and sat on a mountain top, waiting for the so-called
'Second Coming'. Then, when it didn't happen, they had to beg for
their bread and looked like fools. Not only do the deluded believers
lose their faith, but others won't become Christians because they
think the whole thing is nonsense.

Past

Some of the prophecies foretell the coming of Jesus at Bethlehem, which
for us now is in the past. These mean a lot to us, as we prepare for
Christmas in a few days' time. Micah prophesies, 'You, O Bethlehem . . .
from you shall come forth . . . one who is to rule in Israel.' That fits,
because Jesus was born in Bethlehem in the past, though many people
still do not acknowledge him as their king. Mary sang 'Magnificat',
about the coming of Jesus at Bethlehem: 'He has shown strength with
his arm; he has scattered the proud in the thoughts of their hearts. He
has brought down the powerful from their thrones, and lifted up the
lowly; he has filled the hungry with good things, and sent the rich away
empty.' The birth of Jesus ushered in a process which is not yet complete. When the Psalmist cries out, 'Come to our salvation', that refers
to the birth of Jesus, whose name means 'Saviour'; but still, today,
there are many who eat 'the bread of tears'. The Letter to the Hebrews
states that 'when Christ came into the world . . . [he] offered *for all
time* a single sacrifice for sins'.

Present

So the process of our salvation *began* in Bethlehem, and many people obey God as king, yet the kingdom of God will not come in its fullness until everyone does. Jesus taught us to pray, 'thy kingdom come *on earth*, as it is in heaven'. In the present, there's work to do, building a new society based on universal love. Many of the sayings of Jesus, which we ignore because we think they refer to the distant future, challenge us to build up his kingdom here and now. Then, gradually, heaven will come down to earth, without waiting for all earth's people to be taken up to heaven. God's kingdom is coming to earth here and now through our labours on his behalf.

Future

The only thing we can be certain of *in the future* is that each of us will one day die, when Jesus will forgive us for our sins and welcome us to heaven. Whether that is tomorrow, or when life on earth ceases, doesn't matter; whenever he comes, we want him to find us busy making the world a better place.

Milton

A popular Advent hymn was written in the seventeenth century by John Milton, the author of *Paradise Lost*. He promises that 'The Lord will come and not be slow; his footsteps cannot err'. But instead of describing the last judgement in the future, he sings about building a just society in the present: 'before him righteousness shall go, his royal harbinger. Truth from the earth, like to a flower, shall bud and blossom then, and justice, from her heavenly bower, look down on mortal men.'

Come again

Phrases we use, like 'Christ shall come again', should be understood in context. The Bible nowhere uses the words, 'the Second Coming' – the people of his generation saw him 'coming on the clouds' when he came *to* God, at his ascension into heaven. The sufferings he warned people to expect were when the Romans destroyed Jerusalem. But he *is* coming to us, through the strength he gives us to build a just society, in the present; and he *will* come to us, with forgiveness, on the day we die, in the future. The message of Advent is urgent, because it warns us to be ready for Christ's coming, whenever he comes to us.

All-age worship

Make banners: 'Welcome Christ our king, past, present and future'.

Suggested hymns

O come, O come Emmanuel; The advent of our King/God; The Lord will come and not be slow; Thy kingdom come! On bended knee

Fourth Sunday of Advent   20 December
Second Service   The Handmaid

Ps. 123 As a maid looks to her mistress [131 My soul is like a weaned child]; Isa. 10.33—11.10 A shoot from the stump of Jesse; Matt. 1.18–25 Joseph and the angel

> *'As the eyes of servants look to the hand of their master,*
> *or the eyes of a maid to the hand of her mistress,*
> *So our eyes wait upon the Lord our God,*
> *until he have mercy upon us.'*
> *Psalm 123.2–3 (Common Worship)*

Ancestors

Ask your granny. Or research your family tree on the internet. Most of us don't have to go back many generations before we discover that one or more of our relations was 'in service', as they said then. The land around their birthplace could not feed the large families that were common in those days, so as soon as they were in their early teens, several daughters and a son or two were sent off to a large household somewhere to work as maidservants or footmen. They would stay in domestic service until they married, or for the rest of their lives if they didn't find a spouse. Life was hard for those 'below stairs', waiting on every whim of the family 'above stairs'. They rose early and went to bed late, in the attic, and had hardly any time off. They watched their employers' movements, trying to anticipate their needs, ready to leap to obey their instructions. Yet they were well fed, and many servants were deeply devoted to their masters and mistresses.

The Bible

The Bible tells us that our relationship with God ought to be like that of servants with their employers. Psalm 123 contains the lovely lines:

> As the eyes of servants look to the hand of their master,
> or the eyes of a maid to the hand of her mistress,
> So our eyes wait upon the Lord our God,
> until he have mercy upon us.

Simeon, the elderly priest, sang a song we call the Nunc Dimittis, beginning, 'Lord, now lettest thou thy servant depart in peace.' Israel is described as God's servant, and Jesus told his disciples that 'whoever wishes to be great among you must be the servant of all'.

Joseph and Mary

Joseph and Mary, when they were told that each in their own way must act as a parent to God's Son, gladly agreed to take on the role of a servant. Joseph, when he woke up from his dream, 'did as the angel of the Lord commanded him; he took [Mary] as his wife, but had no marital relations with her until she had borne a son; and he named him Jesus'. When the angel came to Mary, she said, 'Behold the handmaid of the Lord; be it unto me according to thy word.' Later, in the Magnificat, she sang, 'For he hath regarded the lowliness of his handmaiden.' 'Handmaiden' is an expressive word, meaning a girl who waits on her employers hand-and-foot, watching their smallest gestures, like the servants in the psalm.

Christmas

So, as we approach Christmas, we give thanks for the obedience of Joseph and Mary, who followed God's instructions to the letter, like servants carrying out the wishes of their employer. Also, we worship the baby in the manger, and acknowledge that he is one with his heavenly Father. If Jesus wants us to do something for him, it is because his Father wants us to do it. When Jesus says, 'This is my commandment, that you love one another as I have loved you', it means that God's will is for us to love. Can you say to God, 'Your wish is my command'?

Obedience

It is easy enough at Christmastime, when we are full of the spirit of goodwill, to say, 'Yes, I want to be God's servant and live the sort of life he'd like me to.' But that is a bit vague – it is too general. Have you realized that God has a fully worked out plan for what he wants you to do with your life? He will tell you if you will only stop and listen. But because we so seldom do that, and instead keep on trying to make our own plans and live life our way, God has to keep adjusting his plans accordingly. So let's promise, this Christmas, to be like Joseph and Mary, the devoted servants of the Lord, watching God's every hand movement to see what he wants us to do. His instructions may come in tiny things, a coincidence here, a word spoken by a stranger there, a verse from the Bible or a TV report on hunger in the Third World. Keep your eyes peeled and your ears washed out, to recognize the ways that God speaks to you. Then, as God's devoted servant, answer, 'Be it unto me according to thy word.'

Suggested hymns

Brother, sister, let me serve you/Will you let me be your servant?; Lo, he comes with clouds descending; People, look east; When we walk with the Lord.

CHRISTMAS, EPIPHANY AND CANDLEMAS

Christmas is a great opportunity for a church which wants to welcome visitors. The carols are beautiful, the nativity play is a laugh, and they meet old friends who have children of a similar age. And then what? What we are trying to tell them is that God loves you, me and the whole world, so much that he gave his only Son to come from heaven to earth in Bethlehem. He came to live a life of poverty among under-privileged people, to reconcile us to God and God to us. Yet that is far from obvious from the Christmas story itself, although it was to convey that message that the Gospels were written. But they were written for people who thought and spoke in Aramaic or Greek, and who would recognize the quotations from the Old Testament, and the custom of using legends to convey a spiritual truth. So somewhere along the line we have to persuade our hearers that, although opinions are divided as to how much of the Christmas story is historically true, it doesn't really matter, so long as we absorb the spiritual truths that lie behind it. Otherwise, by the time children no longer believe in Santa Claus, they will begin to think that everything they heard in church was an irrelevant fairy story. The Epiphany story of the wise men from the East was controversial when it was first written, for these were foreigners, of a different race, who were there at the beginning of the story of the Jewish Messiah, and who brought their own distinctive gifts to the history of Christianity. So Epiphany is, in a sense, a festival of race relations. Candlemas is popular, because everybody loves candles; the old man Simeon's word said the child was coming who would be 'a light to lighten the Gentiles' – which means 'the nations' – so this is another sign that the light of Christ is something Christians cannot hug to themselves, but must share with all who have not yet 'seen the light'.

Christmas Day   25 December

Any of the following sets of readings may be used on the evening of Christmas Eve and on Christmas Day: Set III should be used at some service during the celebration.

Set I   Children's Nativity Play

Isa. 9.2–7 A child is born; Ps. 96 Tell of his salvation; Titus 2.11–14 Salvation has come; Luke 2.1–14 [15–20] The birth and the shepherds

'In that region there were shepherds living in the fields, keeping watch over their flock by night.' Luke 2.8

Nativity play

I came across this delightful description of a Christmas play by the writer Rex Knowles. His children had dragged him out of the sitting room one Christmas to see the nativity play they had assembled. The baby Jesus was represented by an electric torch, switched on, to show that he is the light of the world, with a tea towel for swaddling clothes and lying in a shoe box as a manger. A six year old in an adult dressing gown and carrying a broomstick said nothing, but represented all the shepherds. His big sister announced that she was both Joseph and Mary. The youngest child had a pillowcase flapping on each arm to represent wings, and lisped that she was an angel. The procession ended with a girl hobbling along in a pair of high-heeled shoes, like somebody riding a camel, and announced that she was all three wise men, bringing gifts of 'gold, circumstance and mud'. Fantastic!

Understanding

We laugh at this story, as it is, indeed, very funny. And then we turn away, thinking that children are clearly unable to understand what Christmas means. I want to suggest to you that, on the contrary, many children understand the meaning of the story more accurately than most adults. Theologians tell you that the story of the birth at Bethlehem is an exposition of the incarnation. Humankind, they say, was intended to live in happy obedience to God, but we misused the freedom God had given us, to rebel against our creator, thus incurring the guilt of sin. So God sent his own son to be born as a human being. Then this God-Man, Jesus, submitted to death on a cross, as a sacrifice to spare us the punishment we all deserve as a result of our sin. We say those words glibly, and they enshrine a deep truth. But, frankly, many of them mean nothing to me, at least in that context. What was the relationship between Jesus and the God whom he called 'Father'? Self-sacrifice is a noble thing, but how does it wipe out the stain of guilt? Is God really so cruel that he cannot forgive us unless the best man that ever lived had been put to death? Not everyone is troubled in this way: many Christians accept the nativity story as

23

children do: a beautiful story, which relates to us at the deepest level, but a mystery which we shall never fully understand. And they, and the children, are right.

God's love story

Children, you see, go straight to the heart of the matter. It is not the details of this story which matter. At its heart, they realize, the Christmas message is a love story. It is a story about a father, who wants his children to understand that he loves them. So he takes time to come into their room to play with them. Only, the Father in this case is God, who comes right down to live with us and show us what love really means in terms of a human life. Love is a golden, precious thing; we come to church at Christmastime to hear the story of love, and share it with everyone we meet, by our loving words and our loving deeds.

Church

The Christian Church is a family, chosen to spread the message of God's love, and turn this world into a more loving place. At its best, the Church does this extremely well. But the circumstances of the life we live often distract us from this noble ideal. We become involved in the Church as an organization, the pomp and circumstance of our ritual, and the details of what people should do and shouldn't do. So the Christmas message of universal love gets all mired up in irrelevant details; people look at us, and see, not the children of God, but a muddy mess. We need to get back to the simplicity of the children's understanding of the Christian message of love, which is more precious than gold. Rex Knowles told his story of the children's nativity play to a friend; when he came to the child's description of the gifts of the wise men, the friend blurted out: 'Gold, circumstance and mud. What a brilliant description of the Christian Church!' My comment is, 'Never let that be said of this church.'

All-age worship

Make a model of a heart shape, cover it with gold wrapping paper and label it 'Love'.

As with gladness men of old; In the bleak midwinter; The first Nowell; We three kings of orient are.

Christmas Day   25 December
Set II   Isn't He Just Like His Dad?
Isa. 62.6–12 Prepare a way; Ps. 97 God comes to rescue his people; Titus 3.4–7 Salvation by grace; Luke 2.[1–7] 8–20 Shepherds go to Bethlehem

> 'When the goodness and loving kindness of God our Saviour appeared, he saved us, not because of any works of righteousness that we had done, but according to his mercy.' Titus 3.4–5

Like his dad

Before the nativity play, a schoolteacher told the children, 'I want you to look at the doll lying in the manger, imagine it is baby Jesus, then say whatever you think people normally say when they see a little baby for the first time.' One child looked hard at the face of the dolly, turned to the audience and said loudly, 'My, isn't he just like his dad?'

Sonship

He was right: that is just what people do say when they see a baby. But he was also correct in stating that Jesus is just like the God whom he always addressed as 'Abba', the word that Jewish children in those days used when speaking to their daddy. But what exactly do we mean when we say that Jesus is the Son of God?

Son of God

At the Annunciation, the angel said to Mary, 'The child to be born will be holy; he will be called Son of God.' The Hebrew language is short of adjectives; so to say 'a destructive man' you must say 'a son of destruction'; and a Jerusalemite woman is 'a daughter of Jerusalem'. The prophet Daniel wanted to describe a human-like figure, so he writes, 'one like a son of man'; in Psalm 2 God says to the all-too-human king of the Jews, 'You are my son, this day have I begotten you'; and the prophets refer to all human beings as 'children of the living God'. So calling Jesus the Son of God means that he was a godly man; and more than that, that he was 'just like his dad'. His disciples heard him talking about a God who is loving and forgiving, which was quite unlike the descriptions of the deity given by other preachers in his day. So they watched Jesus closely, to see whether he was qualified to give such an unexpected redefinition. They were amazed that Jesus spent his life loving people, caring for them, healing them, and building up their self-confidence; and he offered them God's forgiveness before they had even asked for it, speaking on God's behalf! The character of Jesus revealed the character of the God he spoke about.

Incarnation

That's probably as far as the disciples got during Jesus's lifetime. Don't worry if that's as far as you have reached in your thinking about Jesus, for it is quite a respectable starting place. But they saw his death as a supreme act of self-sacrifice, and his resurrection as a sign that he was not subject to the limitations of other mortals. Like Jesus himself, they asked God the question, 'Why did you abandon him?' Gradually they began to see that God the Father hadn't abandoned the Son of God at the crucifixion: he was right there *in him*, sharing in his Son's suffering. So God, too, must be a self-sacrificing lover, and there is no dividing line between the Father and the Son who resembles him. Then they started using new words about Christmas: words like 'incarnation', which means 'entering into the flesh'. On Christmas Day God entered into the flesh of a human being, and our Creator became one of us! You don't understand that? I'm not surprised; neither does anybody else. Anything we say about God must be a mystery; by which I don't mean it's contrary to reason, but it goes beyond our feeble human reasoning powers – you must have faith that it is true.

Faith

But don't worry – God will give you that faith, as a Christmas present, if you ask for it. St Paul says faith is the *fruit of the Spirit*, which means your faith starts small, but never stops growing if you keep praying. But Paul also calls faith the *gift of the Spirit*, and the word is exactly the same word used for a birthday present. Meaning we can never earn it or deserve it, but God gives us faith just because he loves us. Whereas *we receive* presents on our birthday, *Jesus gives* us presents at Christmastime, which is his birthday. The faith that Jesus, the Son of God, became a human being at Christmas, is all yours if you put it on your Christmas list. It comes labelled: 'Happy Christmas. The gift of faith from Jesus – who is just like his dad.'

All-age worship

Put under the Christmas tree empty parcels labelled 'God's gift of wisdom', '. . . knowledge', '. . . faith', '. . . healing', '. . . miracles', '. . . speaking for him' (1 Cor. 12.8–10).

Suggested carols

Angels, from the realms of glory; I cannot tell why he, whom angels worship; O come, all ye faithful; Once, in royal David's city.

Christmas Day 25 December
Set III Love Came Down to Earth
Isa. 52.7–10 The messenger of peace; Ps. 98 God's victory; Heb. 1.1–4 [5–12] God speaks through a Son; John 1.1–14 The Word became flesh

> 'The Word became flesh and lived among us, and we have seen his glory, the glory as of a father's only son, full of grace and truth.' John 1.14

Innkeeper

Imagine you are an innkeeper in Bethlehem, one winter's day 2,000 years ago. It's about the worst day you've ever had. The Romans have forced everyone to return to their birthplace to be counted, and there are about five times as many people clamouring for rooms in your inn than you have space for. There's even a man saying his wife is having a baby – of course, you'd like to help, but where can you put them? They'll just have to make do with the filthy little stable outside. You've almost forgotten about them, when about a dozen shepherds hammer on the door asking, 'Where is he? Where is he? Where's the little babba what's just been born?' You get rid of them by whooshing them off to the stable, thinking that all your troubles must at last be over, when three *kings*, of all people, turn up. Your inn's never had even *one* room that's fit for royalty, let alone *three*. Fortunately they mutter something about a star and make their own way down to the stable. You tell your wife that this has been the worst day in your whole life. But she's seen what's been happening in the stable. 'No,' she replies quietly, 'I actually think it may be the best day in the whole of human history. I think the universe may have been turned upside down today!' Huh! Women!

John and Paul

But she was right. St John, who wrote the Fourth Gospel, and St Paul who wrote all those letters, were very different people, but they said the same thing about Christmas Day. John wrote: 'The Word became flesh and lived among us, and we have seen his glory, the glory as of a father's only son, full of grace and truth.' In other words, God came down to earth that day. In one of St Paul's sermons, reported in the Acts of the Apostles, he said that the first Christmas Day was the end of history: '[God] made David [the king of the Jews] . . . Of this man's posterity God has brought to Israel a Saviour, Jesus, as he promised.' Through all the millennia of evolution, God had created creatures able to love, if they chose to, or chose not to if they preferred. Then he chose one people, the Jews, to learn that there is one God for the whole earth, who wants us to behave lovingly towards each other. God sent them prophets to warn them of the cost of their refusal, but also to promise that God had a plan to do something about it. Then, at the birth of Jesus, that promise was fulfilled, and God came down to earth. And God is love, so that Divine Love appeared on earth that day in human form – 'the Word became flesh and lived among us'.

Hard to grasp

Now that all sounds very complicated: not something you could expect an innkeeper to understand. What's all this about Word and flesh, prophets and saviours? Those aren't words we use every day. It's hard for ordinary people to grasp. So God simplified it and told us of his love in a basic winter's tale. When you talk about a baby, everybody knows what you mean. Everybody loves a baby, and babies love their parents. Babies thrive on love, and they remind us that love is the only thing that really matters. If there *is* a God, and he really wants to communicate with us, what better way can he show us what he's made of, than through a baby? So God puts his heavenly glory back into the cupboard, and appears to us as a humble poor baby, weak and defenceless, lying among the straw in a dirty old manger. What greater love could a god show than that? So God woos us with his love, by becoming a baby. If you run a mile when you hear people talking about the all-powerful, the almighty – just fall in love with the Baby of Bethlehem. Then, gradually, you will begin to realize that what we call love, with all its affection and caring tenderness, its vulnerability and its strength, is actually a description of what we mean by God. And love came down to earth on that first Christmas Day, asking us whether we would accept him and return his love, or reject him and break his loving heart. Surely even an innkeeper can understand that!

All-age worship

Make a Christmas crib. Instead of a baby, put in it a large red cut-out heart: ♥

Suggested carols

(Morning) Christians awake; (Evening) O little town of Bethlehem; Away in a manger; Hark, the herald angels sing; Love came down at Christmas (or It came upon the midnight clear).

Christmas Day 25 December
Second Service **Eternity and Infinity**
Morning Ps. 110 This day of your birth, 117 Steadfast love; Evening Ps. 8 Out of the mouths of babes; Isa. 65.17–25 A new creation; Phil. 2.5–11 Jesus emptied himself, *or* Luke 2.1–20 Shepherds go to Bethlehem (*if it has not been used at the Principal Service of the day*)

> *'I am about to create new heavens and a new earth; the former things shall not be remembered or come to mind.' Isaiah 65.17*

Crafts

If your hobby is making things, don't you sometimes wish, when it goes all pear-shaped, that you could throw your first attempt away, and start all over again? God must have felt like that, when he looked at the world he made. He meant it to be a world of love, happiness and peace, but instead everybody started disobeying him, and fighting each other to get what they wanted. Rather like naughty children on Christmas Day. God's raw materials were eternity and infinity. Within that he created time and space, and put human beings in it so that they could enjoy it. But they tore up the maker's instructions, and started doing whatever they pleased. Yet God is a master craftsman, proud of what he has made, and he wastes nothing. So instead of scrapping the whole thing, he set about *remaking* his creation from within. The prophet Isaiah imagined that God was saying, 'I am about to create new heavens and a new earth; the former things shall not be remembered or come to mind.' And when did God begin doing this? On Christmas Day!

Fresh start

What God needed was an example, a model of what he had intended the human race to be. Then other people could look at this, gasp and say, 'Oh, was *that* what you meant us to be like? Please can we go back to the beginning, and build our lives this time according to your plan?' And God would answer, 'No, you have to start where you are, and try to *remodel* your own personalities as I intended. But I'll be with you, and I'll help you whenever you ask me to.' So Jesus was born in Bethlehem. Of course not everybody could see him, and those who did, often failed to understand what Jesus was doing. So those who recognized his perfection were entrusted with the task of explaining this to the others. And that's why you and I are here.

God's tool

Yet Jesus wasn't just the model; he was the tool, through which God was going to rebuild the world from within. The only raw material Jesus has to work with is ordinary sinful human beings like you and me. St Paul wrote that 'God was in Christ, reconciling the world to himself, not counting their trespasses against them, and entrusting the message of reconciliation to us.' Jesus wasn't just a perfect human being – Jesus is God, hard at work remaking a world in which human beings will be friends with their Maker, and friends of each other.

Eternity

Jesus was a native of eternity, and came down from that unimaginable, timeless world, to inhabit Mary's womb. Eternity is not 'a very long time'; we mistranslate it when we talk of 'everlasting life', or 'for ever and ever. Amen.' *Everlasting* life would be incredibly boring. But *eternal* life means life where there is no time. As Spock would have said to Captain Kirk, 'It is life, Jim, but not as we know it.' God created time. So, for God, all times are present. It is as though God were the hub of a wheel, and what we call past, present and future are all points on the rim, and joined to him by spokes of equal length. If we are given eternal life, we shall be able to turn our attention to whichever moment of earthly history we please, and talk to people of the past whenever we choose. But the words that Jesus used for 'eternal life' translate literally as 'the life of the age', meaning the new age of the kingdom of God which Jesus is busy creating here on earth.

Christmas

On the first Christmas Day, when Jesus was born, eternity was brought into time, and infinity was brought to birth in a tiny child. So time and space were transformed at Christmas, and we can see eternity and infinity all around us. As William Blake put it in one of his mystical poems:

To see a world in a grain of sand
And a heaven in a wild flower,
Hold infinity in the palm of your hand,
And eternity in an hour.

That is the change in our appreciation of reality which Christmas has made; and into the fullness of that joyous life we shall come when Jesus welcomes us into heaven. Happy Christmas, everybody.

Suggested hymns

Ding dong, merrily on high; God rest you merry, gentlemen; Joy to the world! The Lord is come; Silent night, holy night.

First Sunday of Christmas 27 December

(St John, Apostle and Evangelist)

Principal Service **Christmas Carols**

1 Sam. 2.18–20, 26 Giving children to God; Ps. 148 Young and old together; Col. 3.12–17 The Word of Christ; Luke 2.41–52 The child Jesus in the Temple

> *'Let the word of Christ dwell in you richly; teach and admonish one another in all wisdom; and with gratitude in your hearts sing psalms, hymns, and spiritual songs to God.' Colossians 3.16*

I love carols

I love singing Christmas carols. I can never have too many of them. I expect most people are the same. Somebody told me that 'Carols are to the atheist what bacon is to a vegetarian.' Too delicious to say no, even though completely against their principles! It is quite interesting to look at the background to some of the carols, and find out how old they are.

Dance

Actually a carol was a form of dance long before it was associated with Christmas. The chorus in a Greek theatre were dancers, not singers, and if they danced to the accompaniment of the *aulos* or flute, they were the *chor-aules* – it is not hard to see how that could be shortened to 'carol'. The dances became popular songs of celebration. When the Christian Church decided to take over the pagan winter festival of Yule to celebrate the birth of Jesus, many of these entertainments came with it. 'The Holly and the Ivy' was a pagan fertility song long before it was given Christian words.

England

Carols came to England in the thirteenth century, when they were sung not only at Christmas but at Easter and other festivals. There were serious ones written for religious use; those written by famous composers for professional choirs; and the cheerful 'pop songs' which were sung in the inns. The first printed carol book was published in 1525, and Henry VIII wrote at least one himself, called

'Green Groweth the Holly'. Carols were banned by the Puritans and returned under Charles II, but they were rarely heard in church. In the eighteenth century the only carol allowed in the parish churches was 'While shepherds watched', because they considered this a New Testament equivalent of the metrical psalms. But 'O come, all ye faithful' was written for Roman Catholics, and Charles Wesley's 'Hark! The herald angels sing' for the Methodists – though the original words were 'Hark, how all the welkin rings'. In Queen Victoria's reign most houses except those of the extremely poor had a piano in the parlour with a printed book of carol music, and all the family would gather round and sing. At this period too they began to be sung in church again. Serious musicians like Cecil Sharpe and Ralph Vaughan Williams went round the country villages collecting folk songs which had never before been written down.

Choir carols

Many of these folk carols, in modern arrangements, were included in *The Oxford Book of Carols* in 1928. More recently the volumes of *Carols for Choirs* have followed; they are now up to Book Five, and they contain carols from France – 'Angels from the realms of glory' – Germany – 'Silent night' – Poland – 'Infant holy, infant lowly' – and many other countries, as well as some showing the influence of the American spirituals. Original compositions by modern composers are included, and the Service of Nine Lessons and Carols, broadcast by the BBC from King's College Chapel in Cambridge every Christmas since 1928 has led to churches of many denominations holding carol services, which have become very popular.

History

So the history of the carol has led us from the original dances, through songs used in the medieval Mystery Plays such as the Coventry Carol 'Lully, lullay'. Then beggars would sing them in the streets – 'Past three o'clock' – and when they were admitted to the homes of the rich: 'Masters of this Hall', and 'We wish you a merry Christmas'. Next came the Victorian art songs like 'Good King Wenceslas' and 'See, amid the winter's snow', and the twentieth-century carol 'This Christmas night all Christians sing', with the Caribbean-style 'The Virgin Mary had a baby boy', and secular songs like 'Jingle Bells' thrown in for good measure.

33

Inspiration

But all the carols draw their inspiration from the story of the birth of baby Jesus at Bethlehem. This story is one that we can see modelled in the figures of the Christmas crib and many a stained-glass window, and it is set in the most memorable and moving poetic language. So, because this is a story of God's care for each one of us, even the poor and the helpless infants, and his love coming into the world, the carols we sing at Christmastime have inspired great joy and happiness. Even for the atheists who hate them and love them at the same time.

All-age worship

Play at Victorian carol singers knocking on doors and singing carols in return for 'figgy pudding'.

Suggested carols

Any of the above.

St John, Apostle and Evangelist 27 December
Sons of Thunder

Ex. 33.7–11a The tent of meeting; Ps. 117 Praise God, all nations; 1 John 1 The word of life; John 21.19b–25 The Beloved Disciple

> *'Peter turned and saw the disciple whom Jesus loved following them; he was the one who had reclined next to Jesus at the supper and had said, "Lord, who is it that is going to betray you?" . . . This is the disciple who is testifying to these things and has written them, and we know that his testimony is true.'*
> *John 21.20, 24*

Who was the author?

We celebrate today 'St John, Apostle and Evangelist'. The verses I have just read imply that one of those who were at the Last Supper with Jesus, wrote down an account of the events, which formed the basis of the Fourth Gospel. He didn't actually write the Gospel in the version we now have it; that was done by others, calling themselves 'we', who recognize that his evidence to the life of Jesus is true. Some of those who have studied the Gospel in detail think that the original author wrote everything up to chapter 20, then some of his followers, the scholars suggest, added an epilogue, telling the story of the resurrection appearance of Jesus near Lake Galilee. But assuming that these words are literally true, we still don't know the name of the author. All we know is that it was the one whom Jesus loved in a very special way, and who reclined on the couch next to him at the Last Supper.

Beloved Disciple

This 'Beloved Disciple' is only described in this way in the Fourth Gospel. He was also commanded to care for the mother of Jesus at the crucifixion; and was the first to enter the empty tomb. Jesus loved all his disciples, but there must have been a very special friendship between this one and the Master, yet nowhere are we told his name. The word 'disciples', meaning 'pupils', is used of all the followers of Jesus, and there is no reason to assume that only 'the Twelve' were at the Last Supper. Roman Catholics believe that the Virgin Mary was also present, and there must have been other women, as at any other Passover meal, serving the food. From an early date it was assumed that the Beloved Disciple was John, son of Zebedee, but Lazarus and Bartholomew have also been suggested. Yet John was a very common name, and it is a big assumption to believe that the author of the Gospel, the three Letters of John, and the book of Revelation were all the same person.

Sons of Thunder

Assuming, then, that the author whose writings were edited to form the Gospel was John the son of Zebedee, what do we know about him? John and his brother James occur in all the lists of the Twelve. As fishermen, they were mending their nets when Jesus called them; immediately, they left the boat and their father and followed him. John tried to stop a man who was not 'one of them' from casting out demons using the name of Jesus. He and his brother asked Jesus to grant them places of honour in his kingdom. Only Peter, James and John were present when Jesus was transfigured on the mountain top. The same three were close to Jesus in the Garden of Gethsemane. After the resurrection of Jesus Christ, John and Peter healed a lame man outside the Temple, and successfully evangelized the non-Jewish

Samaritans. Peter, James and John are described by St Paul as 'pillars of the Church' in Jerusalem. But the most revealing thing about the brothers is that Jesus nicknamed them 'Sons of Thunder', or *Boanerges* in Greek, suggesting that they had a very fiery temper. So he was a strange choice to be Jesus's best friend. But then Jesus can choose anyone to be his friend, whether they deserve it or not. I mean, look at me! And dare I say it, look at you! None of us deserve to be called friends of Jesus. But according to the Fourth Gospel, Jesus said,

> You are my friends if you do what I command you. I do not call you servants any longer, because the servant does not know what the master is doing; but I have called you friends, because I have made known to you everything that I have heard from my Father. You did not choose me but I chose you. And I appointed you to go and bear fruit, fruit that will last, so that the Father will give you whatever you ask him in my name.

Thundery young John rose to that challenge, and the fruit that he bore was the sublime writing of the Gospel. Jesus loves us too; I wonder whether our friendship with Jesus will bear any fruit like that?

Suggested hymns

Peter and John went to pray; Rise and hear! The Lord is speaking; Word of God, come down from heaven; Word supreme, before creation.

Second Sunday of Christmas   3 January 2016
(The Epiphany may be transferred to this date, see page 291.)
Principal Service   **Imagination**
Jer. 31.7–14 God will send salvation; Ps. 147.13–21 God's Word brings peace, *or* Ecclus. (Ben Sira) 24.1–12 God's Wisdom comes to earth; *Canticle*: Wisd. 10.15–21 Salvation; Eph. 1.3–14 God's plan to gather everything in Christ; John 1.[1–9] 10–18 God gave grace through Jesus

*'Blessed be the God and Father of our Lord Jesus Christ, who . . .
chose us in Christ before the foundation of the world to be holy
and blameless before him in love. He destined us for adoption as
his children . . . With all wisdom and insight he has made known
to us the mystery of his will . . . as a plan for the fullness of time, to
gather up all things in him, things in heaven and things on earth.'
Ephesians 1.3–5, 8–10*

God's plan

Those words are astonishing! Put simply, St Paul writes to the
Ephesians that [even before God created the universe, God was
thinking about you. Yes, you, Joseph or Josephine Bloggs. God was
thinking, long before you were born, 'I've got a plan for you, Jo
Bloggs. I've selected you, and I'm going to forgive you all you've
done wrong; then I shall adopt you as my beloved child. Next,
when my plan is nearly complete, I shall gather you up, with the
souls of all the men and women who have ever lived, all the ideas
they've had and all the songs they've sung, and weave you together
into one great happy party in heaven. That's my personal plan for
you.'] Listen, I'll read it again; use your imagination and see if you
can hear God talking to you . . . (Repeat words in [. . .].)

Imagination

Did you begin to grasp how wonderful God's plan for you must be?
That's what happens when you use your imagination. Today I shall
take some ideas from a book by Bishop John Pritchard, called *How
to Pray.* He points out that people today don't come to Church,
because they think it's boring. They live in a world where new information is pumped at them every second, and the last thing they
want is somewhere where nothing ever changes. So it is vital that
Christians should use their imaginations to find new ways of looking
at things, saying things and doing things. This applies to what we do
in church, and the way in which we pray. Imagination, imagination!
The right side of the brain is where imagination, stories, art, poetry,
drama, play and humour take place. The left side is for cold logic and
rational thinking. We need to use both sides of our brains when we
pray. For, the creative side of us may give us our last chance to communicate with people who have forgotten the Christian story.

37

Try this

So the Bishop suggests various ways of developing our imaginative skills:

- Use water to remind you of God's love bubbling up and cleansing you.
- Take a stone as a sign of the rough, angular side of our nature and leave it at the foot of a cross.
- Picture Jesus looking at us lovingly and humbly.
- Light a candle and think of Christ the Light of the world, explaining things, guiding you, cheering you up.
- Use a mirror to remember that you are made in God's image, yet completely unique.
- Put up sticky notelets to remind you whom you should pray for.
- Or a map and compass, to think about the direction you should be travelling.
- And bread and wine to remind you of the presence of Christ.

Story

Bishop Pritchard finished this section of his book with a true story. A vicar was called to visit an old man who was dying. They talked about how difficult it is, sometimes, to pray. The vicar recommended talking to Jesus just as you would if he was sitting beside you. A few days later the man's daughter phoned the vicar to say that he had died. 'It's strange,' she said. 'There was a chair drawn up beside the bed, and Dad's head was just resting on the seat, as if he was resting in someone's lap.'

Conclusion

So a vivid imagination can be useful to you from the beginning to the end of your life. Imagine what God's plan is for you, as St Paul did in that passage I read. Then you'll never worry about anything.

All-age worship

Imagine Jesus and God his Father talking about you. What things would they like to change in your character? What wonderful experiences would they like to give you?

Suggested hymns

Be thou my vision; God is working his purpose out; See, amid the winter's snow; Who would think that what is needed?

Second Sunday of Christmas   3 January 2016
Second Service   **Loving the Delinquent**

Ps. 135 Greater than the idols; 1 Sam. 1.20–28 Hannah gives Samuel; 1 John 4.7–16 Love is from God; *Gospel at Holy Communion*: Matt. 2.13–23 Escape to Egypt

> *'God is love, and those who abide in love abide in God, and God abides in them . . . There is no fear in love, but perfect love casts out fear; for fear has to do with punishment, and whoever fears has not reached perfection in love. We love because he first loved us.' 1 John 4.16, 18–19*

Dream School

A few years ago, Jamie Oliver presented a series on Channel 4 called *Jamie's Dream School*. He brought together a group of kids who had dropped out of school, together with some experts and enthusiasts in different areas, who hoped to convey their enthusiasm to their pupils. Almost all the dropouts had been in a large class at a comprehensive school, where they were bored, so like most children they tested the boundaries of permitted behaviour. Their teachers hadn't had time to give them personal attention, so they bawled at them, telling them they were failures, and then punished them. If the delinquents were a minority, the rest of the class would sort them out. But if most of the kids were naughty, they encouraged each other into a downward spiral. If school bored them, they played truant. When they came to Jamie's experimental school, it was their last chance.

Discipline

At first the visiting experts tried strict discipline. As you might have guessed, it didn't work. But neither did sympathetic indulgence. What did work with most of the delinquents was praise. If a teacher noticed something that the child had done well, and told them so, they suddenly began to have hope. If the teacher found time to get them on their own and give them some individual tuition, they began to establish a relationship. So the child began to gain confidence in their own potential. In short, they discovered themselves as people. And then their talents blossomed.

The system

Would this method work all through the educational system? Frankly, it is unlikely. Teachers will point out that parents' income determines the catchment area in which they live, and the children of richer parents are taken into private education, so you are left with large classes almost all of whom are delinquents. The teacher has no time to give them individual attention. At home, long working hours and broken marriages make it unlikely that the children will feel that they are loved. One town in America passed a law that no school could have more than 40 per cent of the children on free meals or 25 per cent who were a year or more behind at reading or mathematics. This spread the problem children around better, and that town achieved better results than any other in the USA.

Love

But the significant discovery in all this is that delinquent children respond to love. If just one teacher, or a parent, will spend time with them and praise them, they stand a chance. There is a scientific reason for this. If a baby feels loved, the child opens up new neuronal pathways in its brain, and learns more quickly. Gradually the frontal lobes, which anticipate problems and allow rational thought, grow physically stronger. Whereas in children who do not feel loved, these areas grow weaker, and the older they are, the harder it is to make them change. As the Beatles sang, 'Love is all you need.'

God's love

But God knew this all along. In the first Letter of St John in the New Testament, it says that 'God *is* love'. He is constantly trying to convince each of us that he loves us, and values our unique talents. Then he sets up an intense one-to-one relationship with us through prayer: we live in God and God lives in us. God doesn't try to scare us into obedience, as some overworked teachers do: 'There is no fear in love, but perfect love casts out fear; for fear has to do with punishment, and whoever fears has not reached perfection in love.' Then, when we realize that we are worth loving, and that we *are* loved by God, the need to draw attention to ourselves by bad behaviour vanishes. God came down to earth at Christmas, to show us how much he loves us. When we realize that, we begin to love God in return, and to love other people as he loves them. 'We love because he first loved us.' If only teachers, parents, parsons and policemen would realize that you can't *frighten* selfish people into becoming unselfish – only by *loving* them can you change them – then there might be fewer dropouts, violent criminals, alcoholics and drug addicts, and more people who are willing to call themselves Christians because they have realized that God loves every single one of his children.

Suggested hymns

God whose love is everywhere; Love came down at Christmas; Of the Father's love begotten; While shepherds watched their flocks by night.

Baptism of Christ (First Sunday of Epiphany)
10 January
Principal Service   **Baptism and the Holy Spirit**
Isa. 43.1–7 When you pass through the waters; Ps. 29 The voice of the Lord is over the waters; Acts 8.14–17 Baptism and the Holy Spirit; Luke 3.15–17, 21–22 The baptism of Jesus

> *'Now when the apostles at Jerusalem heard that Samaria had accepted the word of God, they sent Peter and John to them . . . Then Peter and John laid their hands on them, and they received the Holy Spirit.' Acts 8.14, 17*

Christ's mission

Twelve days after Christmas we celebrate the coming of the wise men on the feast of Epiphany, on January the sixth. They were foreigners, non-Jews, and their coming shows that the Jewish God was to be no longer Jewish private property, but shared with every nation in the world. Jesus showed this in his preaching, teaching and healing ministry, beginning at his baptism, and after his resurrection spreading out

41

by the work of the Holy Spirit in the lives of the first Christians. So we call the first Sunday after the feast of the Epiphany, 'The Baptism of Christ', and think in the next few Sundays about how the good news of Christ is spread around the world, by professional missionaries and by the personal witness of other Christians – that means you and me.

The Spirit

Baptism was the ceremony when non-Jews were admitted to the Chosen People by washing away their sins. John the Baptist said that even those who were born and bred Jewish had to be baptized, to show their personal commitment to doing the work for which God had chosen them. This was to spread the belief in only one God for *all* the world, who wants us to love each other for his sake. The most striking thing that happened to Jesus at his baptism was that he received the Holy Spirit. Even though he was the Son of God, he was completely human, and he had a challenging task ahead of him. So his heavenly Father gave to Jesus the strength he needed to begin his mission, in the form of the Holy Spirit. The Spirit is offered to each of us at our own baptism, too, though we may not take up the offer until later. In the case of Jesus, the Spirit was seen in bodily form as a dove. The power of God is invisible, but people needed a symbol to remind them of the Spirit of God which hovered over the waters at the creation of the world, and the dove which Noah sent out, which returned with an olive branch. For Noah, this showed that peace had come, and those who had entrusted themselves to God's care in the ark had been saved.

Acts

The Acts of the Apostles tells how all those who had become Christians received the gift of the Holy Spirit at Pentecost. But in today's reading from Acts, we heard about some Samaritans – whom the Jews regarded as foreigners – who were baptized, but didn't immediately receive the Spirit. So St Peter and St John went to Samaria, prayed for them, and laid their hands on the heads of the new converts, and then they received the promised gift. Churches that baptize babies use this passage as the reason for teaching that when these children grow old enough to decide for themselves, they need to confirm their membership in the family of God, when a bishop lays his or her hands on their heads in confirmation. Other churches will invite their members to make a deeply emotional act of personal commitment, after which they receive the more dramatic gifts of the Spirit such as 'speaking in tongues'.

Commitment

Both approaches need to learn from each other. The magician called Simon, who wanted to pay for the gifts of the Spirit, is a warning to us against the temptation to seek our own advantage by demonstrating dramatic gifts. But the partial conversion of the Samaritan Christians reminds us that the formal ceremonies of the Church need to be accompanied by an acknowledgement that Jesus is our personal Saviour and Lord, inviting him to take charge of our lives. If you have not yet made that commitment, it is never too late to do so now – if you wish, you can ask me or somebody else to pray with you and lay hands on you. We are all involved in this task of spreading the good news of God's love. None of us can do it in our own strength; like Jesus, we need to pray for the Holy Spirit, empowering us to serve.

All-age worship

Show how an electric fan needs to be plugged in, then switched on. Baptism is when we are plugged into God's family; when we promise to serve God all our lives, we are switched on to God's power.

Suggested hymns

O happy day that fixed my choice; O Jesus, I have promised; Spirit of the living God, fall afresh on me; When we walk with the Lord (Trust and obey).

Baptism of Christ (First Sunday of Epiphany)
10 January
Second Service   Baptized into Christ
Ps. 46 There is a river, 47 Clap your hands; Isa. 55.1–11 Come to the waters; Rom. 6.1–11 Baptized into Christ; *Gospel at Holy Communion*: Mark 1.4–11 The baptism of Jesus

> 'Do you not know that all of us who have been baptized into Christ Jesus were baptized into his death?' Romans 6.3

Baptism

We all know that 'baptism' is the correct name for what is popularly called 'christening'. And we also know that christening is when we bring a little baby to the font in church and sprinkle water over its head. But when St Paul wrote to the Romans, baptism wasn't anything like that. Baptism in St Paul's day was almost always given to adults; it was a life-changing moment of decision; and it was done by total immersion in a river. This explains why Paul could write, 'all of us who have been baptized into Christ Jesus were baptized into his death', and be sure that he would be understood.

Sin

The purpose of Paul's letter was to help the Jewish Christians in Rome and the non-Jewish converts to understand each other, and then work together as one Church. He wanted to persuade the Jews that even those who knew nothing of the Ten Commandments could be forgiven by God, and welcomed into God's Chosen People. But Jewish Christians protested that if they promised that all sins could be forgiven, there would be no reason to stop sinning. They imagined a non-Jewish convert saying, 'God's grace is big enough to forgive any sin. So the bigger the sin, the greater will be God's grace. If grace is a good thing, then let's sin as much as we can, so as to produce more and more of this wonderful gift!' St *Paul* was 'ap*pall*ed' at this suggestion. In return, he imagined a conversation he would have with such an objector. And it all turned on the meaning of baptism.

Adult baptism

First, adult baptism was always the decision of one person to join the Church. Later on, whole families might be baptized at once, and baptized parents might have more children, and ask for them to join the rest of the family in the Family of God. But at the beginning, an individual had to make their own choice, which often meant leaving their family behind.

Life-changing

Second, in baptism a convert from paganism was cutting their life in two. The newly baptized Christian person had to be quite unlike the unreformed pagan person their friends had known before. A decision was made which meant literally beginning one's life all over again.

Immersion

Third, when a candidate was baptized by immersion, and the water closed over their head, it looked as though they were being drowned; when they climbed up out of the water they seemed to have risen from the dead. So Christians spoke of baptism as like dying to the old life of sin, and rising again to the new life of grace – or 'birth by drowning!'

Jews and Gentiles

These were words which could be easily understood by Jews and non-Jews alike. The Jewish ceremony of baptizing non-Jewish converts to make them part of the Chosen People was spoken of as rebirth, a fresh start, a public proclamation of repentance and faith. The Greek mystery religions typically acted out the absorption of the believer into the life of a god who died and came back to life, like the plants in winter and springtime. So St Paul drew out of this debate three principles of Christian living:

1 We must not trade on God's mercy as an excuse for sinning. It would be like a son considering himself free to disobey his father, just because he was sure his dad would always let him off lightly.
2 Living as a Christian means a completely new way of life. The old sinner has died; a new person has been born. One reason many people call themselves agnostics these days is because they know that being a Christian would involve giving up some of their favourite vices, and they are not yet ready to take that step.
3 When we accept Jesus into our lives, we become a different person. For physical life, we have to be in the atmosphere, and the air has to be in us. For spiritual life, we are in Christ, and Christ is in us. And we cannot involve Jesus in a life of sin.

So, as St Paul wrote: 'Do you not know that all of us who have been baptized into Christ Jesus were baptized into his death?'

Suggested hymns

A man there lived in Galilee; Amazing grace! How sweet the sound; I want to walk with Jesus Christ; When Jesus came to Jordan to be baptized by John.

Second Sunday of Epiphany   17 January
Principal Service   **Bad Evangelism**

Isa. 62.1–5 Nations shall see your salvation; Ps. 36.5–10 All peoples; 1 Cor. 12.1–11 Many gifts, one Spirit; John 2.1–11 The wedding at Cana

> *'How precious is your steadfast love, O God! All people may take refuge in the shadow of your wings.' Psalm 36.7*

Epiphany

At Christmas we celebrated the coming of Jesus into the world. Among the first to see him were some shepherds; the Bible tells us that 'When they saw this, they made known what had been told them about this child.' Then came the wise men, who were not Jews. They came from Persia, and laid their gifts at the feet of the Christ-child; then they returned home to tell other non-Jews what they had seen, and how important Jesus was for people of every nation. We commemorated the wise men on the feast of the Epiphany; Epiphany is another word for revelation. In the following Sundays we have a series of readings about times when God revealed publicly who Jesus was. The first occasion was at his baptism, when God was heard saying, 'This is my Son!' Today's reading tells of the wedding when Jesus turned water into wine, ending with the words, 'Jesus did this, the first of his signs, in Cana of Galilee, and revealed his glory; and his disciples believed in him.' So the theme of this season is mission: the mission of the Church, following on from the mission of Jesus, to reveal to everyone on earth who Jesus is. This has two parts, which are inseparable:

1   Living out a Christ-like life, imitating Jesus in social action and love for our neighbours, building the kingdom of God on earth.

2 Spreading the good news of who Jesus was, and what he said, until all the people in the world know him and what he did for us. In other words, we are thinking about the task which faces every Christian: that of evangelism.

Evangelism

'Evangelism', meaning 'spreading good news', is usually thought of as winning converts and getting people into church. Many Christians feel uncomfortable with the word. It is often associated with Evangelicalism. Evangelicals are a party or a wing within the Church, opposed to the Catholic wing. And many of us have no wish to split the one Church into two or more factions. Evangelicalism makes us think of American politics, where Evangelicals and the politicians they support are opposed to abortion and divorce; they are supporters of Israel against the Palestinians, and in favour of capitalism and wealth. Evangelicalism is often linked with fundamentalism, which stresses a literal interpretation of the Bible, and opposition to science and especially evolution. Believing in an imminent Second Coming of Jesus, fundamentalists see no point in building a more just society. They seem to use manipulative methods to brainwash potential converts into an emotional conversion experience. Is this what we are signing up to when the Bible calls us to do the work of an evangelist?

Bad evangelism

Of course not! What I have just described is best called 'bad evangelism'. Some Christians try to make converts from those of other religions or none, because they believe that only people who have gone through the same sort of emotional conversion experience as they have will be saved, and all the rest of us will be condemned to hell for eternity. You will have gathered by now that that is not what I believe. Jesus promised that those who are baptized and believe will be saved, but that does not prevent him from giving eternal life to those who do not fit into tidy pigeonholes. He said to old Nicodemus, 'You must be born again', but that meant making a fresh start, dependent on God's love, not our own virtues.

Good evangelism

But our suspicion of 'bad evangelism' doesn't absolve us from our duty to tell everyone about the love of Jesus. We must choose our moment. We must express it in words and images that will be understood to people of a different culture from the Bible – and that includes modern scientific thought. We must help them to take Jesus into their own culture, without rushing them into a change of religion which would cut them off from their families and friends. We should welcome what they have to teach us about God from their own experience. But despite our abhorrence of bad evangelism, we must put all our efforts into helping people of the same or different backgrounds to us to learn that they are God's beloved children, and that Jesus will pour his love into their heart if they pray, until they love all their neighbours as God loves them, for Christ's sake.

All-age worship

Find pictures of Jesus dressed as a Chinese, a black African, someone from the Middle East, etc. What can we learn from these images?

Suggested hymns

As with gladness men of old; God is working his purpose out; Hills of the North, rejoice; Jesus shall reign, where'er the sun.

Second Sunday of Epiphany 17 January
Second Service **Billy Graham**

Ps. 96 Tell of his salvation; 1 Sam. 3.1–20 The boy Samuel; Eph. 4.1–16 Unity in the Body of Christ; *Gospel at Holy Communion*: John 1.29–42 The first disciples

> *'Declare [God's] glory among the nations, his marvellous works among all the peoples.' Psalm 96.3*

Church growth

On the feast of the Epiphany ten days ago we celebrated the coming of the Persian wise men to Bethlehem. They were the first non-Jews to believe in Jesus. Later, Jesus invited his Jewish neighbours to follow him. Andrew accepted the offer, inviting his brother Peter to join him. Philip followed, and invited Nathanael. So the Christian Church began to grow, and the good news of God's love began to spread across the world. Sharing the good news is called 'evangelism'; 'epiphany' is another word for revelation; and 'mission' means being sent. So in the Sundays after Epiphany we think of God's call to every Christian to tell their neighbours the good news that God loves each one of us. The task of evangelism has to be repeated in every generation.

Billy Graham

In 1984, the American evangelist Billy Graham came to the UK for his second mission campaign here. He called it 'Mission England'. Different churches reacted in different ways; some people gladly accepted the offer of God's grace which he made, and decided to become committed followers of Christ. Some were profoundly changed, but didn't reach the point of commitment at that time. Others ignored it, and some were deeply offended. The gospel of Jesus Christ always creates a mixed reaction. But church growth reached a peak in the 1980s; some churches, of all denominations, were full again for the first time in years. Hardly any churches were unaffected, and many adopted an entirely new approach to evangelism. Those who hadn't sung any new hymns for a generation learnt lively modern songs from the specially compiled *Mission Praise*. The growth of the Church in the 1980s was caused by many factors, but Billy Graham's evangelistic campaign left a lasting impression.

Criticism

Many people criticized his approach. Christians should respond with love to persecution. But those who criticize Christian evangelists should think about the effect their words may have on those who are wavering on the edge of faith. Some who were uncertain when they discovered the campaign was controversial lost their nerve and never went to the meetings, thereby missing an opportunity to welcome joy and happiness into their lives. There are many ways of expressing the one gospel. Only closed minds are unwilling to learn from other traditions.

Unwelcome change

Some people refused to go to the meetings, from fear that they would be challenged to change. Religious prejudices go deep, and some were afraid that they would have to renounce their unchristian prejudices against those who are different from them. Many of us continue doing things which we know deep down to be wrong, and are afraid that we shall be challenged to give up these bad habits. But even painful change is better than persistence in wrongdoing.

Emotions

Society has changed a lot since the 1980s. Yet in every church which calls itself Christian, there must be a strong challenge from the pulpit for every individual to make a moment of commitment, when they surrender their lives and their futures to Jesus Christ. And from everyone who believes, there must be a concern to pray for each of our neighbours and friends, and help them to realize that they are precious in God's eyes. The word 'conversion' may be unpopular, but it simply means turning around, depending not on our own achievements but only on God's proffered forgiveness to bring us to eternal life. This fresh beginning is what Jesus meant when he said that everyone must be 'born again'. It may be a very emotional experience, but it may not; personal feelings are no barometer of God's love. It is not the fluttering of the heart but the determination of the will to follow Jesus that counts.

Billy Graham's success

Billy Graham never tried to stir up emotions. He gave a very simple account of God's love, and then invited his audiences to 'get up out of your seats', and come to the experienced Christians at the front, to surrender their lives to their Saviour. Tens of thousands came forward, and began at those meetings a truly Christian life, which, with the usual ups and downs, has lasted till this day. So what about you? Did you decide for Christ years ago, but need to renew your commitment? Or have you been sitting on the fence? Maybe today you will realize that you have to take sides, and decide for or against the way of universal love. Talk to somebody about it; if you wish, come and talk to me. Let's have a time of silence to think about what I've said.

God forgave my sin in Jesus' name; O happy day; One shall tell another; Sing to God new songs of worship.

Third Sunday of Epiphany   24 January

See also 'Week of Prayer for Christian Unity', page 294.
Principal Service   **Go Tell Everyone**
Neh. 8.1–3, 5–6, 8–10 Joy in the Commandments; Ps. 19 The heavens declare God's glory; 1 Cor. 12.12–31a The unity of Christ's body the Church; Luke 4.14–21 Jesus reads the Scriptures at Nazareth

> 'The Spirit of the Lord is upon me,
> because he has anointed me to bring good news to the poor.
> He has sent me to proclaim release to the captives
> and recovery of sight to the blind,
> to let the oppressed go free,
> to proclaim the year of the Lord's favour'
>
> *Luke 4.18–19, quoting Isaiah 61.1–2*

Shyness

When the subject of religion comes up in conversation, do you try to hide underneath the table? Many people do, you know. You hope that nobody will know that you are a Christian, and, worse than that, a church-goer. And please, God, don't let those who do know laugh out loud at my stupidity in believing in you. The trouble is, we know that we should be able to defend our beliefs, show how reasonable they are, and what a different quality it gives to our lives when we know that God loves us. But we are scared that we aren't clever enough; afraid that as soon as we open our mouths we shall confirm the mockers in their belief that we are simple-minded. We know that Jesus told us to spread the gospel, the good news about God's love. Yet we are too terrified to begin.

Spirit

Don't imagine that you are alone in this. Many Christians, perhaps most of us, are too modest to feel confident in our powers of reasoning, and our ability to put our thoughts into persuasive words. But don't worry: even if we *are* all too stupid to defend the faith against its opponents, we don't have to do so in our own strength – God has provided the answer, by giving us the Holy Spirit. That doesn't mean you have to be bubbling over with emotion, and daily experiencing what is called 'speaking in tongues'. What it means is that when you open your mouth to speak up for God, you may think you are talking utter rubbish, but God will make sure that the folk you are speaking to will hear what he wants them to hear; they will hear, not you, but God speaking to them.

Inspired

Jesus himself went back to the village where he had been brought up. That is the most terrifying place of all, because all the people there know all about your childish silliness, and will write you off before they have even heard you. But Jesus opened the Scripture at the book of Isaiah, and read words which he applied to himself, but which actually apply to each one of us:

> The spirit of the Lord GOD is upon me, because the LORD has anointed me; he has sent me to bring good news to the oppressed, to bind up the brokenhearted, to proclaim liberty to the captives, and release to the prisoners; to proclaim the year of the LORD's favour.

You too have been chosen and inspired to tell people the good news. When people know that God loves them, they forget their selfishness and anger, and a new world begins, starting with the Christians but spreading to include everyone on earth. It will be a world of justice, equality, peace and love, where everybody is obedient to God. That will be paradise; we call it the kingdom of God; it is already here now, in your heart, but it will spread and spread if you will only talk about it.

Apologetics

When we say that somebody is apologetic, these days, we mean they are always saying 'Sorry'. But originally it meant defending your beliefs by reasoned arguments. Alister McGrath, in his book *Mere Theology*, distinguishes between apologetics and evangelism. He writes that apologetics is an attempt to provide reasonable answers to the big questions in life, whereas evangelism is inviting other people to share the joy you find in believing. 'Apologetics is conversational,' he writes, 'evangelism is invitational.' *You* can do both of those through the power of the Spirit within you.

Go tell

All this is summed up in one of the jolliest of the modern hymns, by Alan Dale, 'God's Spirit is in my heart'. We can sing that God has called us, so we need not worry what we say, because the Holy Spirit of God will speak in our hearts. The task for which we have been chosen is to tell everybody the good news that God's kingdom has already arrived. So go out and do it, politely, trusting God to give you the right words to speak on his behalf.

All-age worship

Learn the song, and write a letter or a card to a friend telling them what fun you had in church today.

Suggested hymns

God is working his purpose out; God's Spirit is in my heart; Jesus shall reign, where'er the sun; We have a gospel to proclaim.

Third Sunday of Epiphany 24 January
(Eve of the Conversion of St Paul, see page 296.)
Second Service **Christianity in Greece**
Ps. 33 The greatness and goodness of God; Num. 9.15–23
The cloud of God's presence; 1 Cor. 7.17–24 The life that the
Lord has assigned; *Gospel at Holy Communion*: Mark 1.21–28
Authority over an unclean spirit

> 'Let each of you lead the life that the Lord has assigned, to which God called you. This is my rule in all the churches.' 1 Corinthians 7.17

St Paul

During the Epiphany season, thinking of the wise men coming from the East to worship the Christ-child, we reflect on the gospel spreading throughout the world, and think what part we can play in evangelism. But we mustn't be arrogant, as though Christianity started in Western Europe and America: the origins of the Christian Church were in the Middle East. St Paul began his missionary work in what we now call Syria, then Cyprus, then across the Greek-speaking cities, such as Ephesus, in what is now known as Turkey. Then he crossed over to Philippi, Thessalonica, Corinth and Athens, all in present-day Greece. All his letters, and the four Gospels, were written in Greek, and although he wrote to Rome, it was in Greek that he wrote. So Greece has a good claim to be the original centre of worldwide Christianity.

Ancient Greece

Ancient Greece was the cradle of Mediterranean civilization. It was Greeks who taught the western world to think philosophically, and it was to explain Christianity to philosophically educated Greeks that the faith was first translated into non-Jewish concepts. Homer's *Iliad* was the origin of European poetry. Alexander the Great was the first to have a vision of the whole known world becoming a single nation. And it was in Athens that democracy was born. After the collapse of Alexander's empire, the Roman Empire took its place, and in Rome the laws and administration were drawn up in Latin; but outside Italy, Greek was the *lingua franca* of the Roman Empire.

Patriarchs

Under attack from pagan tribes, the Roman Empire eventually split into two, and the Emperor Constantine made his capital in Byzantium, later called Constantinople, now known as Istanbul. As the Christian Church grew larger, it needed to be organized. Originally this was under four patriarchs, which means 'ruling fathers'. The Patriarch of Constantinople was called the Ecumenical Patriarch, meaning the father of the whole world. The other patriarchs were Antioch, which ruled over the Church in the East; Alexandria, supervising Christians in Africa; and the Patriarch of Jerusalem, chief of the Christians in the Holy Land and the Arab world. There were many fragmentations in the early Church, and, to distinguish themselves, the original Greek-speaking churches called themselves 'catholic', meaning 'for the whole world', or 'orthodox', which means 'worshipping correctly'; the two words were considered synonymous. The Celtic church in Britain learnt a lot from the Greek church.

Schism

In the sixth century, the Emperor appointed the Bishop of Rome to be the Patriarch of the West. In the Great Schism of 1054, Eastern Orthodox and Roman Catholics excommunicated each other. Although relations are now more friendly, the Eastern Churches regard Western Catholics and Protestants alike as a schism from the true Church. There is a list of differences which may seem trivial to us, but are important to them; including

- our insertion into the Creed, without consulting the Eastern Churches, after the words about the Spirit 'proceeding from the Father', the unauthorized words, 'and the Son';
- making the sign of the cross from left to right instead of the Orthodox way; and
- 'worshipping' statues of the saints, instead of honouring the icons as a sacramental sign of the presence of the departed and 'windows into heaven', as they do.

Now

Visitors to Greece now are struck by the worship: its beauty, music, mysticism – and length! All Greeks go to church at Easter, and share a feast of roast lamb afterwards. Each church has its own patron saint, often someone recently died who was sanctified by popular acclaim; and the relics will be carried through the streets on the patronal festival. Monasteries thrive, and insist on celibacy for the monks; on the other hand parish priests – known as Papas so-and-so – *have* to be married before they are ordained. So the bishops, who also have to be unmarried, are all drawn from the monks. Many Greeks, even though they may dislike the power of the bishops and monks, are loyal to the traditions of their Christian country, pray before the icon in their home, and show a profound holiness in their worship and their lives, from which we of the West could learn a lesson.

Suggested hymns

Father, we thank thee who hast planted (The Didache); From glory to glory advancing (Liturgy of St James); Let all mortal flesh keep silence (Liturgy of St James); Stars of the morning, so gloriously bright (St Joseph the Hymnographer).

Fourth Sunday of Epiphany   31 January

(or Candlemas; see page 298)

Principal Service   **The Languages of Love**

Ezek. 43.27—44.4 The glory of the Lord filled the Temple; Ps. 48
The greatness of God; 1 Cor. 13.1–13 Love; Luke 2.22–40
The presentation of Christ in the Temple

> *'Love is patient; love is kind.'* *1 Corinthians 13.4*

How to learn and grow in relationships

One of our basic human needs is to feel loved by another person
or persons. Therefore we need to hear the other one tell us they
love us. But this, as St Paul says, may be expressed in several different ways. Perhaps it would help to describe these as the many
'languages of love'. The first thought that comes to mind is the
love between spouses, or partners if you prefer that term. However,
the languages of love apply to all relationships, starting within the
family and extending to every relationship between individuals or
groups you can think of. The languages of love are what allow a
person to feel loved. The way someone behaves, who claims to love
them, should make them feel valued and 'special'.

Families

If you want the relationships within your family to grow strong, it
is very important to learn which 'languages of love' the different
members of the family are hearing. Not until you have thought
about this can you adapt your behaviour to each individual's unique
needs. This provides an environment where healthy relationships
can grow.

Languages of love

Each person's unique 'language of love' – the ways of expressing
love which they will immediately recognize – contains five basic
elements:

1   **Words of affirmation.** These are words that you should repeat
     often, which assure the loved one that they are valuable, and

that they matter to you as an individual. If you can find the sort of words that 'ring the right bell', they will be very powerful. Ring the changes, of course, but learn from experience which words have the right effect. People feel loved when they are given encouragement, receive kindness and hear well-thought-out compliments on their way of life and their goals. You should always show kindness in your words and your reactions; this includes not only what you say, but the tone in which you say it, and your use of silences.

2 **Use of time.** You express your love for someone by the way you plan your days. Of course we all have too much to do, and too little time to do it in. But if you can't find enough time to spend alone with the person you love, giving them your undivided attention, they won't believe you when you tell them you love them. Think in terms of togetherness, quality time and quality conversations. More listening and less saying is an essential ingredient in this language. This sort of individual attention is a universal need in children.

3 **Gifts.** Giving the loved one little gifts, not only on birthdays and Christmas but unexpectedly at other times, speaks volumes. They need not be expensive, it is the thought that counts. You can take time to be with them when they are doing something that matters to them, and then give them a token of your admiration when they succeed.

4 **Service.** There are always chores which need doing around the house. Some families get in the habit of saying, 'Oh, so-and-so always does that!' Well, give them a surprise by doing it yourself, unprompted – only be sure to do it well! Never nag if some job is not completed on time; suggest ways in which responsibilities could be better apportioned. Lastly:

5 **Physical touch.** Touching is an expression of love. We all need frequent hugs. Physical contact is a sign of recognition, and can be especially significant at moments of crisis or emotional distress.

Learning to love

Think about these five aspects of the language of love in your own family, and ask yourself where you could do better. Don't be ashamed to apologize where you think you have failed. You imagine that you know all about love when you marry, or bear a child, but in fact you never stop learning. Jesus told us to love our neighbours like ourselves, and the lessons we learn about love in the family are invaluable in showing us ways for expressing our love for others. Then Jesus told us to love God with all our heart, soul, mind and strength – because that is how God loves us. Think about ways in which you can show your love for God, through the language of love: words of affirmation; use of time; service; giving; and physical touch – and here's a clue for the use of touch: think of 'sacraments'.

All-age worship

List five things you can do today to show parents and siblings that you love them. Then list five things you can do for God.

Suggested hymns

Come, let us sing of a wonderful love; Gracious Spirit, Holy Ghost; Immortal love, for ever full; Such love, pure as the whitest snow.

Fourth Sunday of Epiphany   31 January
Second Service   **Of Your Own Have We Given You**
Ps. 34 O taste and see; 1 Chron. 29.6–19 Giving to the Lord; Acts 7.44–50 God does not dwell in temples; *Gospel at Holy Communion*: John 4.19–29a True worship

> '[King David prayed,] "All things come from you, and of your own have we given you."' 1 Chronicles 29.14

Loving your local church

Many people absolutely adore their local church. It may be a centuries-old gem, or a rusty tin tabernacle, but we all want to make it as beautiful as we can. We feel that by giving something to God, to beautify his house, we are making some return for all the blessings that God has given to us. God deserves the very best of everything, and we ought to be at least as concerned to make his house look fine as we are with our own. Very often the most trouble is taken over the churches in the poorest areas, as though by filling them with beautiful ornaments we can bring some colour into otherwise drab lives. This sort of thinking lies behind many passages in the Old Testament about the Temple in Jerusalem.

The Chronicler

One writer who was devoted to the Temple and its worship was the editor of the first and second books of Chronicles, and probably of the books of Ezra and Nehemiah too. We don't know his name, so we call him the Chronicler. After the Jews returned from exile in Babylon, the Chronicler wanted to unite the remaining tribes around the Temple in Jerusalem. So he tried to show that the destruction of the Temple by King Nebuchadnezzar when he deported the Jews to Babylon was a punishment for their sins. Thus the story of Israel and Judah must be retold, to show that it was their failure to be holy which had angered God so.

Offerings for the Temple

With this agenda, it's hardly surprising that the books of Chronicles vastly expand the accounts in Samuel and Kings of the collection of gifts, the building and the dedication of the Temple. In today's reading from First Chronicles 29, we have a detailed account of the precious goods which were donated for the building of the Temple – you can tell it was written after the exile because it mentions 'darics', a gold coin named after Darius the king of Babylon. Then King David speaks a great prayer, offering all these gifts to God.

All things come from you

But although King David is pleased with the generosity of his people which has prompted all these gifts, he is not proud. It is very easy for the wealthy to think that they have become rich because they are cleverer than anyone else; that they deserve their wealth because they are better people. King David knew that was not so. It was because God had been kind to them that he and his people had amassed their fortunes. David knew himself to be a sinner – adultery with Bathsheba and the murder of her husband Uriah were still on his conscience – and he knew that he didn't deserve God's kindness. Yet God had given him, or perhaps we should say lent him, many wonderful things. So David uttered the famous words:

Yours, O LORD, are the greatness, the power, the glory, the victory, and the majesty; for all that is in the heavens and on the earth is yours; yours is the kingdom, O LORD, and you are exalted as head above all. Riches and honour come from you, and you rule over all . . . For all things come from you, and of your own have we given you.

Planned giving

The media persist in their allegations that the Church is fantastically rich. Yet, apart from buildings which can never be sold, that is not true. If the local church that we love is to survive at all, even for our own lifetime, we have to plan to give a proportion of our income for its upkeep and beautification. It may be only the widow's mite, or it may be a rich man's tithe to rival King David's in its splendour; in either case, if our money is given to God's Church gladly from a grateful heart, God will accept it, and will love us for our generosity. But God cannot abide pride. Don't claim any merit because of what you have given; you can never, never *deserve* God's love. You are only giving back to God the things that belong to God – the money that, for a while, God has lent to you. Every time we put a penny in the collection or write out a cheque for a thousand pounds, we should repeat the words of King David: 'All things come from you, O LORD, and of your own have we given you!'

Suggested hymns

Angel voices ever singing; Great is thy faithfulness, O God my Father; O Lord of heaven and earth and sea; 'Lift up your hearts!' We lift them Lord to thee.

Sunday next before Lent   7 February
Principal Service   **Progressive Revelation**
Ex. 34.29–35 Moses' face is shining; Ps. 99 God spoke in the cloud; 2 Cor. 3.12—4.2 The Spirit unveils God's truth; Luke 9.28–36 The transfiguration [37–43a The epileptic boy]

> *'All of us, with unveiled faces, seeing the glory of the Lord as though reflected in a mirror, are being transformed into the same*

60

image from one degree of glory to another; for this comes from the Lord, the Spirit.' 2 Corinthians 3.18

Teaching children

When children go to school, we want them to learn. Nothing must stand in their way; there are no secrets. If they ask us a question, we have no wish to withhold anything from them. Is that correct? So when they start at infant school, would you give them a lesson on quantum physics? Well, according to what I just said, I ought to answer yes to that question. But obviously no teacher would agree – they would call me mad for suggesting it. What I omitted to say was that children have to learn progressively, step by step. When they have learnt one skill, they can then go on to practise another, but not before the first is completely assimilated – when children have learnt a few facts, then they can learn the conclusions which we draw from those facts.

God

Now I want you to put yourself in the place of God; in your imaginations, of course. Imagine you have just created human beings – or more likely you have caused them to emerge by the guidance of your unseen hand over the whole evolutionary process. They have come down from the trees, and have started to live in extended families, as hunter-gatherers. You, God, want them to learn that you love them, that you want them to love you and to love other people for your sake. Where would you start? Would you reveal to them, to begin with, the dangers of global warming, and the principles of international cooperation? No, of course not; as with the children, it would be madness to expect them to run before they can walk. So God taught those first hominids to obey the head of the family at all times, and to respect the forces of nature, because disaster would follow if they didn't. So the headman laid down rules for their life, and they offered sacrifices to the god of the trees and the storm and the harvest. Next they learnt to live in bigger tribes, with a single code of laws applying to every family, which even the heads of the families had to adhere to. Somewhere on the road between Ur of the Chaldees and Jerusalem, God revealed to a tribal leader, named Abraham, that the tribe would only be united if they had a single God, instead of a host of squabbling deities. A descendant of Abraham's, called Moses, replaced the first tentative legal codes with ten simple Commandments, showing that God cares about the way people treat each other. So God led them to the fundamental truth of ethical monotheism.

Jesus

Over the centuries the people of Israel learnt to put this into practice, though they still thought of God as their national possession, who would fight for them against their enemies. Another descendant of Abraham called Jesus of Nazareth showed them that what God requires of us is love, and that the nature of love is willing self-sacrifice for the sake of others. God revealed to the disciples at the transfiguration that Christ had the nature of God in human form. By his death on the cross, Jesus showed that self-sacrificing love is the nature of God himself, who loves *everyone* as his children. One of his followers, called Paul of Tarsus, revealed through the Holy Spirit that monotheism doesn't mean each nation having its own god, but that there is only one God, who loves every nation on earth. And I don't think we have fully learnt that lesson yet.

Progressive revelation

So we see a process called 'progressive revelation' at work all through history. The Bible was Key Stage 1 in that process of education, and we must never fall back below that level. But revelation didn't stop there; it is still going on in every nation, and in every human life. St Paul wrote:

> All of us, with unveiled faces, seeing the glory of the Lord as though reflected in a mirror, are being transformed into the same image from one degree of glory to another; for this comes from the Lord, the Spirit.

Are you aware of the process of progressive revelation taking place in your own life, leading you on to higher things and deeper faith; and are you open to keep on learning more about God, day by day?

All-age worship

What is a syllabus? Could you design a syllabus for teaching children that God loves them?

Suggested hymns

Lord, enthroned in heavenly splendour; Lord, the light of your love is shining; 'Tis good, Lord, to be here; We hail thy presence glorious.

Sunday next before Lent   7 February
Second Service   **From Tension to Triumph**
Ps. 89.1–18 The wonders of God; Ex. 3.1–6 The burning bush;
John 12.27–36a Glorify your name

> *'[Jesus said,] "Now my soul is troubled. And what should I say – 'Father, save me from this hour'? No, it is for this reason that I have come to this hour. Father, glorify your name." Then a voice came from heaven, "I have glorified it, and I will glorify it again."'*
> *John 12.27–28*

Tension

When the disciples first met Jesus, their life together was a paradise. He walked through the fields with them, admiring the lilies, healing the sick, preaching about the beautiful kingdom of God, and talking about love. But after a couple of years of this, things took a turn for the worse. Jesus had incurred the wrath of the scribes and Pharisees, and some said the authorities in Jerusalem were out for his blood. Yet Jesus insisted on heading towards Jerusalem once again, no matter what the leaders of the people threatened. When Simon Peter tried to point out, tactfully, that this folly could be fatal, Jesus called him a Satanic tempter. So their lovely life together had reached a point of tension. Would Jesus persist in putting his head in the noose? Would the disciples desert him? Would Jesus survive? Would *they*? Nobody knew.

Transfiguration

Then Jesus led the disciples up a mountain to pray. He was transfigured, shining with the light which the Old Testament calls 'glory'. Moses and Elijah were with him, to show that Jesus was fulfilling everything predicted in the Law and the prophets. The voice of God spoke from a cloud, as he had sometimes spoken to Moses, saying, 'This is my Son, my Chosen; listen to him!' So the disciples realized that the suffering of Jesus, which they had been so worried about, was actually his triumph, and everything was going to be all right.

John

St John's Gospel doesn't actually describe the transfiguration, though John himself says, 'The Word became flesh and lived among us, and *we have seen his glory*, the glory as of a father's only son, full of grace and truth.' But in place of the story of what happened on the mountain, St John recounts the prayer which Jesus offered to his Father when even non-Jews began to follow him. He said: 'The hour has come for the Son of Man to be glorified.' But he, also, had a moment of tension as he realized what this glory would cost him, and he prayed,

'Now my soul is troubled. And what should I say – "Father, save me from this hour"? No, it is for this reason that I have come to this hour. Father, glorify your name.' Then a voice came from heaven, 'I *have* glorified it, and I *will* glorify it again.'

So Jesus had to come through tension to transfiguration and triumph.

Triumph

So what about you and me? When we became Christians, we imagined everything in the garden would be lovely. We shall be walking with Jesus, we thought, who loves us, and tells us that God loves us. So with God on our side, giving us what we ask him for, what could possibly go wrong? And then things begin to go pear-shaped, and God doesn't always heal people when we ask him to, and we start getting tense again. Then we ourselves are in pain, and somebody we love dies, and we lose our job, and suddenly life becomes horrible, and we wonder why we wasted all those years praying to Jesus if this is what happens to us. But even as we say that, we know that we have got it all wrong. Suffering, or rather the courage which carries us through suffering, *is* our glory, our moment of triumph. Maybe we shall be healed, or maybe we shall die and go to heaven and share in the love of God and of all our friends who have died – either way, God's name is glorified. Because, as we responded to the suffering, our ideas of God were changing. He is no longer an indulgent sugar daddy, but somebody who has a tough lesson to teach the world, that only through the brave bearing of the cross can we come to glory. And he calls us to follow Jesus in showing in our lives that this is true. You see, while your ideas of God are changing, you are changing too. Though you would fiercely deny it, you are becoming one of God's suffering saints, who, together, will be the salvation of the world. Through tension, to transfiguration, to triumph – sorry, but it's the only way God has to make you into a Christian.

Suggested hymns

Christ, whose glory fills the skies; God of mercy, God of grace; Immortal, invisible, God only wise; 'Lift up your hearts!'

LENT

In the secular twenty-first century, sin is not a word that is generally understood. To many people, it only applies to sexual misdemeanours. This is not helped when Christians talk of the virgin birth of Jesus, and the immaculate conception, as being 'sinless', equating sin with sex, as though even intercourse between happy and devoted partners was against the will of God! Which is why, in my draft of 'How to Become a Christian', I have used the word selfishness instead of the word sin. Originally sin meant disobedience to God's commandments, and God commanded us to be unselfish, so 'selfishness' is a better translation than that which occurs to the minds of the secularists when you mention sin. Many people are utterly selfish who have never broken one of the commandments. To rid your heart of selfishness, you must be self-sacrificing, so Lent is a good preparation for Holy Week, when we ponder on the mystery of the self-sacrifice of Jesus on the cross. Our little tokens of giving up chocolate for Lent, then, are a training in sacrificial living; the absence of flowers in church, omitting the 'Gloria', and the solemn purple or sackcloth hangings, symbolize the penitential season, when we confess and repent for our selfish deeds, whether minor or major.

Ash Wednesday 10 February
Penance

Joel 2.1–2, 12–17 Rend your hearts, or Isa. 58.1–12 Care for the needy; Ps. 51.1–18 Cleanse me from my sin; 2 Cor. 5.20b—6.10 Suffering of an apostle; Matt. 6.1–6, 16–21 Secret fasting, or John 8.1–11 Adultery and forgiveness

> '[Jesus said,] "When you fast, put oil on your head and wash your face, so that your fasting may be seen not by others but by your Father who is in secret; and your Father who sees in secret will reward you."' Matthew 6.17–18

Ashes

In Australia and the UK, 'the Ashes' means a series of cricket matches. The author George Bernard Shaw joked that 'Unlike the Scots and the Welsh, the English are not naturally religious. So God created cricket to give them a sense of eternity.' But in the Jewish religion, dressing in coarse and tickly sackcloth, and sprinkling the ashes from the cold fireplace over your hair, while cutting back on what you eat, was a sign of penance. Our Muslim neighbours have a month of fasting during Ramadan, when they eat and drink nothing from sunrise to sunset. This is hard but not impossible, and during the feast of Eid, at the end of Ramadan, they feel a justifiable sense of pride that they kept the tradition without yielding to temptation. But some Jews, in the time of Jesus, went much further. They showed off that they could wear more uncomfortable clothing than anyone else, spread more ashes on their head, and go without food and drink for longer. Jesus condemned this proud boasting about one's humility; though he still thought there was a place for penitence in everyone's life. He told his disciples to continue to dress smartly when they were fasting, saying, 'When you fast, put oil on your head and wash your face, so that your fasting may be seen not by others but by your Father who is in secret; and your Father who sees in secret will reward you.'

Ash Wednesday

In modern Christianity, we are rather half-hearted about fasting. In some churches, a cross is made on the head of each worshipper, made out of ashes left after last year's Palm Sunday palm crosses have been burned, mixed in a little olive oil. Whether or not you wipe that off when you leave the church, or keep it on until you get home in order to witness to your faith, the warning of Jesus against boasting of our humility still needs to be heard. And our modern Lenten fast may be limited to giving up things like chocolates, smoking and alcohol – which are things that we should avoid consuming in excess all the year round, for the sake of our health.

Penance

But by our half-hearted fasting we miss the whole point of it, which is to demonstrate to ourselves and to God our deep penitence for things we have done wrong. You probably know from your own experience that, if you do something to upset somebody, your relationship will be strained until you have said sorry, and they have said, 'I forgive you.' They can't forgive you until you have apologized, and saying you are sorry is meaningless unless you genuinely feel it. You have to accept some of the blame for what has happened. So repentance is followed by apology, which is followed by forgiveness. But even after that, your conscience still troubles you, unless you can do something for those you hurt – give them a present, for instance – to make your repentance visible. It is not a punishment; the one you have sinned against will assure you that there is no need for that. But you need to do something to set your conscience at rest. Like a sacrament, this action is an outward and visible sign of an inward and spiritual feeling – in this case, remorse. We call it a penance.

Wounding God

Now if that is true when a relationship has been temporarily broken between two human beings, it is even more so when we wound our loving heavenly Father. God commanded us to love one another; whenever we mistreat somebody whom God loves, God is wounded by our heartlessness. So we need to apologize sincerely to God also. Our offence is forgotten the moment we have confessed it, by God. But we cannot quite believe that, and need to do something to show that we really meant it. God doesn't demand payment for our sins, but we need some sort of penance. And that is why we symbolically punish ourselves in Lent by going without something we really enjoy. It is not as violent as self-flagellation, nor as trivial as saying six 'Hail Marys'. But the Lenten fast is a genuine expression of our grief at the hurt we have caused to God's loving heart. It is just between God and me, so our fasting should be invisible to all except me and God.

Suggested hymns

Come, my soul, thy suit prepare; Forty days and forty nights; Lord, teach us how to pray aright; O for a heart to praise my God.

First Sunday of Lent   14 February
Principal Service   **You'd Better Believe It!**
Deut. 26.1–11 First fruits; Ps. 91.1–2, 9–16 God's providence; Rom. 10.8b–13 Faith, salvation and unity; Luke 4.1–13 The temptation of Jesus

> *'There is no distinction between Jew and Greek; the same Lord is Lord of all and is generous to all who call on him. For, "Everyone who calls on the name of the Lord shall be saved."' Romans 10.12–13*

Faith, not works

The cry of the Christian Reformation, in the sixteenth century, was 'justification by faith alone'. This was in reaction against the medieval Roman Catholic Church, which appeared to be saying that the priests had power over who should go to heaven, and if you paid them to say Masses for the dead, you could be let off the punishment due to you in purgatory, and go straight to heaven. Martin Luther said no; it is only by the grace of God, appropriated by the faith of the Christian, that we receive the free gift of forgiveness. He was, of course, quoting from St Paul, who faced a powerful Jewish group among the Christians in Rome, who insisted that non-Jews could not be saved, because they were not members of God's Chosen People and did not obey the Jewish Law. Paul and Luther both realized that nobody can earn a place in heaven by doing good works; salvation is freely given by God's loving grace, and appropriated by those who have faith.

68

Jesus

What Luther learnt from Paul, Paul learnt from Jesus, who also developed his teaching when confronted with a power-hungry elite. It was the priests of the Jerusalem Temple, in his day, who claimed the power to make animal sacrifices which could atone for the people's sins; and this had to be appropriated by the people obeying, to the letter, all the detailed laws in the Old Testament. Even the great Jewish scholar Claude Montefiore, at the beginning of the twentieth century, admitted that Jesus was right to criticize the legalistic Pharisees with their emphasis on God's punishment. He wrote:

> The tilt against exaggerations and perversions of the doctrine of tit for tat is a prominent and characteristic feature of the teaching of Jesus. What we receive from God is grace and goodness, and not reward . . . The *excessive* emphasis and elaboration of the doctrine of retribution was one of the weak spots of Rabbinic Judaism.

Though a learned Jew, Montefiore insisted that Jesus brought, to the downtrodden and outcast, who had been told by the Pharisees that they hadn't earned a place in the kingdom of God, 'a new message; he gave them a new hope; he brought to them a compassion and a love to which they had been unused before'.

Two meanings

But the word 'faith' has two meanings:

1   faith means what words you can give your assent to; and
2   faith means putting your trust in somebody reliable.

Jesus, Paul and Luther were using the second meaning: we are saved by God's grace because we trust in Jesus. But people who want power still use the first definition – 'We alone know what the Bible means, and anyone who disagrees with the words we use to explain it has rejected the one true faith, and cannot be saved,' they say. So they make 'assenting to a set of words' the new form of works, through which, they imagine, people can earn their own salvation.

69

Trust

No, I say! Scholarship can take us behind the King James Authorized Version of the Bible of 1611 to find what the original writers in Hebrew and Greek intended their words to mean to the people who first read them. But words change their meanings over the centuries, and the words they used then may not mean the same to people of today. The Bible and the Nicene Creed are the foundation of what Christians believe. But if you demand assent to a set of words you will have to keep retranslating them to fit a new context. Because of this misunderstanding of what faith means, I want to abolish faith. No, it's all right, I haven't become an infidel. It is just that I want to call for a temporary halt on the use of that word in either context. When we mean assenting to a set of words, I suggest we talk about 'beliefs'. When we mean trust, let's say 'trust'. For if you put your trust in God's unchanging love – after all, it is St Valentine's Day today – then you can say with the poet Robert Browning, 'God's in his heaven, all's right with the world!' And that trust will enable God to save you, which neither works nor words can do. God loves you, and in the American expression, 'you'd better believe it!'

All-age worship

Have a small child stand on a low table, blindfolded, and jump into the arms of somebody he or she trusts. This is the meaning of 'faith'.

Suggested hymns

Dear Lord and Father of mankind; Jesu, lover of my soul; O happy band of pilgrims; Through the night of doubt and sorrow.

First Sunday of Lent   14 February
Second Service   Choosing Your Own Religion
Ps. 119.73–88 Let those who fear you turn to me; Jonah 3 Nineveh converted; Luke 18.9–14 Pharisee and publican

> '[Jesus said,] "This [tax-collector] went down to his home justified rather than the [Pharisee]."' Luke 18.14

Decline

People say that religion is in decline these days, or even that it has gone away, apart from a few old fuddy-duddies. But now religion is making a comeback, yet in a very different form. Maybe it never went away, and was always there, but we didn't recognize it. Certainly there was a time when shiny new ideologies like communism and humanism were supposed to have taken the place of religion. Then those theories failed to produce the wonderful future that they had promised; and people turned away from them. In Western Europe they didn't return to the traditional churches, where attendance figures fell off catastrophically. But elsewhere, church attendance is booming.

Rebirth

Yet repeated surveys show that many non-churchgoers in this country still answer that they are Christians; though they usually say, 'I'm a Christian, but in my own way.' But we encourage people to think for themselves these days; they are better educated, and accustomed to making up their own minds on other matters, so why not on religion? Mind you, they know little about what religious people actually believe, so you can hardly call it an informed decision. But there is a growing interest in spiritual things. 'I'm not religious,' they say, 'but I do believe that there is a spiritual dimension to life, and it matters.' They will follow a royal wedding or a celebrity funeral on TV, and leave flowers at the place where an accident happened. Many bereaved people pay regular visits to the grave where their loved one's body lies, or reverence their ashes. About half the bereaved spouses in the UK say they experience the continuing presence of their partner, as a voice, a vision, or a feeling that they are not alone. They may not go to church much; but many people are still very religious in their own way.

Tradition

Although these people say they despise old-fashioned religion, underneath they are nostalgic for the old traditions. What they will not put up with, however, is being told what they *ought* to believe and how they *ought* to behave. Actually that is a form of progress. In the past, nobody paid much attention to what they were told to do, anyway, and now if they are thinking for themselves, they may begin to act on the beliefs they have themselves discovered.

Parable

Jesus told a story about two men who went to the Temple to pray: one was very religious, a Pharisee, who ensured that God was aware of all the religious things he did in his life. The other was a tax-collector, employed by the hated Roman occupying army, a traitor to his own people, and probably a fraudster as well. He wasn't at all religious, and he knew his life was far from perfect; but he simply prayed for God to have mercy. Jesus said, 'I tell you, this man – the irreligious tax-collector – went home as a friend of God, rather than the other – the religious Pharisee.'

Changing church

So we church-people need to change, too. We can tell others about the joy we get from the fellowship and love we receive from our worship. But we must not speak as though that earns us a place in heaven, nor appear to despise non-churchgoers. We must make our worship welcoming to all, and tolerant of the differences between individuals.

Flow chart

Finally, there is a flow chart going around on the internet, on 'Choosing your Religion'. It is facetious, but there is enough truth in it to make you think. The first question is, how many gods do you want to worship: a ton of them, only one, or none? If you opt for a ton, ask, do you want to be reincarnated? If no, follow the Mayan religion; if yes, do you own a black cat? If yes, be a Wiccan; if not, which sort of takeaway food do you prefer? If Indian, be a Hindu; if Chinese, be a Buddhist. If you want only one god, the next question is, how do you feel about bacon? If the answer is 'Yugh', how do you feel about hummus? If Yugh again, be a Jew; if you LOVE hummus, be a Muslim. If you LOVE bacon, ask are you a naturally annoying person; if yes, do you think underwear can be magical? If no, be a Jehovah's Witness; if yes, be a Mormon. If you want no god at all, ask, are you rich and insane? If so, be a Scientologist; if not, be an atheist. Oh, I nearly forgot. If you love bacon and are not annoying, 'Be a boring, generic Christian'!

Suggested hymns

And can it be that I should gain; God forgave my sin in Jesus' name; Just as I am, without one plea; O for a closer walk with God.

Search Google images for 'a flow chart for choosing your religion'.

Second Sunday of Lent 21 February
Principal Service **Asylum and Immigration**
Gen. 15.1–12, 17–18 God's promise to Abraham; Ps. 27 Faith and providence; Phil. 3.17—4.1 Citizens of heaven; Luke 13.31–35 Jesus' lament over the city

'Our citizenship is in heaven.' Philippians 3.20

Empire

St Paul was a Jew, but born and raised in Tarsus, in what is now called Turkey. When the tiny number who were born in Rome, and spoke Latin, captured a new country, they had to recruit people from all over the Roman Empire to administer, defend and supervise the trade in and out, so the majority of the important people in the Empire were Greek-speakers, like St Paul. St Paul was a Roman Citizen, and many people like the centurion who arrested him envied him this valuable privilege. One guess is that his father was a Jewish money-lender in Tarsus, and got the city out of trouble when it was going bankrupt. He and his family will have been rewarded with the gift of citizenship. Many citizens had never been to Rome, but dreamt of going there one day. Non-citizens also went there to work and to trade. In most places, the citizens were much less than 10 per cent of the population. But Philippi was a 'colony', which meant that most of the people were descended from soldiers who had been rewarded with citizenship after fighting in the battle of Philippi in 42 BC. But Paul turned their nationalistic pride on its head when he wrote to the Philippians that '*Our* citizenship is in heaven'!

73

Nationalism

He had a lot of trouble with nationalists, whether Jewish patriots who despised all the other nations or Roman aristocrats who did not want to share their privileges with the wretches from the ends of the Empire, who flooded into Rome hoping to find work. St Paul tells them that our principal loyalty should not be to Rome, but to the heavenly city, of which God has graciously granted us citizenship, and to which we hope to go one day to retire. Paul was probably accused of being unpatriotic because he wrote that.

British

We also are patriotic in the UK today. Which is strange since we are all descended from immigrants. The Celts moved in from France, interbred with Roman soldiers. and then with Anglo-Saxons from Germany. Around the coast there were Vikings from Scandinavia. Then came the Norman invasion, then Huguenot refugees fleeing from persecution in France, then Jews and black slaves. Each of us has a few genes inherited from each of those races; there is no such thing as a pure-blooded Brit. The whole situation is quite like the Roman Empire.

Melting pot

More recently we have become even more of a melting pot. We learn so much from people brought up in a different culture, with different traditions; they teach us tolerance, and contribute skills which we lack. Thirty-seven per cent of the doctors in the UK were trained abroad; without them the NHS would collapse. Immigrants do low-paid work in agriculture and factories, which residents turn their noses up at, boosting the economy and thus creating more jobs for local people.

Immigrants

International and national law distinguishes between refugees, asylum seekers, legal and illegal economic migrants, minority citizens, and others, though the media mostly ignore these distinctions. Refugees and asylum seekers flee from violent wars in their own countries, in which many of them have suffered indescribable torture. Few immigrants come seeking benefits; they mostly know little

74

about this country before they arrive except that they may be able to find work, which is totally unavailable to them in the lands they come from. Many are smuggled in by people-traffickers who submit them to slavery when they arrive. Under international law, anybody has the right to apply for asylum in any country, and to remain there until their case is heard, and no nation has ever withdrawn from this arrangement. The only way to prevent immigrants coming from the EU would be for the UK to withdraw from it, which would cause considerable hardship to the 845,000 British people who have settled there.

Our duty

Immigrants are about 3 million out of the total population of 61 million. God commanded the Israelites in the Old Testament to remember that their ancestors were immigrants in Egypt, and to care for the 'strangers within their gates'. We have a similar duty today, to correct misleading stories in the media, to protect immigrants against those who would take advantage of them, and learn to live together in love and mutual tolerance. Ultimately we are all of one race, the human race, and our citizenship is in heaven. The only way to reduce immigration is to raise the standard of living in the poor countries, so that people there will have no need to come here to find work and food.

All-age worship

Find out about an immigrant family living near you. What can you do to make friends with them?

Suggested hymns

Be thou my guardian and my guide; Fight the good fight; In Christ there is no East or West; Light's abode, celestial Salem.

Second Sunday of Lent 21 February
Second Service **Put Your Money Where Your Mouth Is**
Ps. 135 Praise for God's goodness; Jer. 22.1–9, 13–17 Sin in Jerusalem; Luke 14.27–33 Counting the cost

'[Jesus said,] "Which of you, intending to build a tower, does not first sit down and estimate the cost, to see whether he has enough to complete it?"' Luke 14.28

The cost of discipleship

Jesus asked us to imagine the situation we would find ourselves in if we started to build an extension, and found we hadn't enough money to complete it. Then everybody would laugh at us, because we forgot to count the cost before committing ourselves. His primary meaning was obviously to count the cost of discipleship, in terms of time and effort. During Lent, we give up a few small things, for 40 days, just to convince ourselves we could give them up completely if we had to. Before calling yourself a Christian, though, you should consider how much time you want to give to caring for others, helping the needy, and voluntary work to support the building where you worship. But we should also take Jesus literally, and think about how we spend our money.

Riches

Suppose somebody from a poor country came into this church now, and looked at how even the poorest among us is dressed, how well fed we look, how many expensive gadgets, like watches, we carry with us. They would think we are millionaires, compared to them, and wonder why we are not more generous in sharing our wealth with the poor. But it isn't simple. Jesus told a man whose whole life was devoted to building up great wealth to give it all away to the poor, but that would not be practical for most of us. First, we are too flabby to work as much and eat as little as poor folks do, and after a week or two we should collapse, and be no further use to anyone. Second, our sacrifice in giving everything away would not benefit the poor in other countries, as there are so many of them that each would only receive a few pennies.

On loan

Jesus taught us against trusting in money. When he said it is harder for a rich man to enter the kingdom than for a camel to pass through the eye of a needle, he was agreeing with the sentiment of the Beatles' song, 'Money can't buy me love'. St Paul, in his first letter to his friend Timothy, said that 'the *love* of money is the root of all evil'. But Jesus suggests that there is a right way to spend money. The widow who cast her mite into the Temple treasury, and the good Samaritan who spent his two pence to relieve the sick, had the right idea; the prodigal son who squandered his inheritance had not. Jesus wants us to regard our money as lent to us by God, to use as he approves, not how we choose. A town child once had the right idea when, on her first visit to the country, she asked, 'Would God mind if I picked one of his flowers?'

Where your mouth is

There is an expression used about people who talk about being generous without doing anything about it; we say, 'Why don't you put your money where your mouth is?' So we should each learn to use our income in proportion, as a means to an end, not an end in itself. We should spend it economically on necessary food, clothing, shelter, recreation and providing for our dependants. It must be possible to live in a way which does not absolutely flaunt our wealth, which is what most of us do now. Second, we must give a due proportion of our income back to God in the form of charity. The Jews used to tithe, that is, give back one-tenth of their income to God, and I think this is quite possible for everyone in this church today, if they would budget to make this their priority. I am not suggesting that you should give the whole tenth to the church, but that what you put in the collection plus other charities should equal a tenth of what you earn. But your giving must be proportionate and courteous. Select the charities you will support, as the church does, so that they will ensure that your gift will go to those who are most genuinely needy. And learn to give in such a way as does not cause the recipient to lose face, but encourages them to become self-supporting. It is difficult to give away a tenth of your income, and to do it well. But that is no excuse for giving nothing, or a mere pittance. Put your money where your mouth is.

Suggested hymns

O Lord of heaven and earth and sea; 'Lift up your hearts!' We lift them Lord to thee; Take my life, and let it be; Take up thy cross, the Saviour said.

77

Third Sunday of Lent   28 February
Principal Service   **Birds Nesting in Your Hair**

Isa. 55.1–9 A call to conversion; Ps. 63.1–9 Faith and providence; 1 Cor. 10.1–13 Temptation; Luke 13.1–9 The parable of the fig tree

'No testing has overtaken you that is not common to everyone. God is faithful, and he will not let you be tested beyond your strength, but with the testing he will also provide the way out so that you may be able to endure it.' 1 Corinthians 10.13

Luther

Martin Luther, who began the Protestant Reformation, said that there is nothing sinful about being tempted. It happens to everybody, and there is nothing you can do to prevent it. But you can avoid putting yourself in situations where you know that the temptations to misbehave will be very strong – sometimes called 'occasions of sin'. Luther said, 'You can't stop birds from flying over you, but you needn't allow them to nest in your hair!'

Jesus

Even Jesus was tempted in the wilderness, for 40 days, which is why we observe Lent for 40 days before Easter. He described this experience in terms of a dialogue with Satan. It was almost as if Jesus needed to look at the delights of living his life in the *wrong* way – with pride, self-indulgence, and miracles on demand – before he could make the conscious decision to live it the *right* way, the way of self-sacrifice, the way of the cross.

Job

That reminds us of the book of Job. Job is a good man who lives comfortably with his family. God calls his heavenly advisers, and proudly points out Job, on earth. One of them, called 'the Satan', says: 'Ah, it is easy for Job *now*, it is easy to be good, and to pray to God, when everything is going all right. But Job will soon turn into a good-for-nothing when he starts to suffer a little.' 'All right,' said God, 'I give you permission to cause him grief and distress, and we will see whether he remains faithful to me.' So the Satan destroys Job's health, his home and his family, and Job nearly gives in to his

78

wife's advice to 'curse God and die'. But he holds on by the skin of his teeth, until he is given a vision of God the creator, when he admits that he was being presumptuous. Thus his relationship with God became stronger because he overcame temptation.

Satan

In this story, the Satan seems to be doing God's will, and is not particularly evil. So it raises the familiar question: 'Did God create Satan, and if so, why?' Or, to put it another way, does God allow us to suffer in this life, knowing that we shall find it hard to keep our faith in God when we are in pain; and if so, why? But even Jesus accuses his best friend, Simon Peter, of tempting him, saying, 'Get behind me, Satan.' Perhaps Jesus did not think that the Satan was a person, but a personification of the tempting situations in which we find ourselves. God seems to have given us temptation, because it is good for us to practise resisting it.

Strength of character

Does this answer the question, why does God allow us to suffer? Perhaps the answer is, because it strengthens our character. Until we have felt how strong the desire is in us to do things which are selfish and wicked – or in other words, sinful – we shan't know just how hard it is to resist, unless we throw ourselves entirely on God's mercy and grace. St Paul, in his first letter to the Corinthians, describes how the Israelites in the desert were tempted to do wrong. They passed through the waters of the Red Sea, which Paul compares to Christian baptism; they ate manna, which Paul compares to the Holy Communion. There was even an old legend that the rock which flowed with water when Moses struck it followed them through the wilderness, and Paul compares Jesus to the rock. Yet still they were tempted to gluttony, sexual immorality, idolatry and grumbling against God. But temptation is necessary to our spiritual growth, and Paul reassures them that

> No testing – [the same word is translated as 'temptation' in other places] – has overtaken you that is not common to everyone. God is faithful, and he will not let you be tested beyond your strength, but with the testing he will also provide the way out so that you may be able to endure it.

So avoid situations where you might be tempted; remember, 'You can't stop birds from flying over you, but you needn't allow them to nest in your hair!'

All-age worship

List things that you sometimes want to do, although you know they are naughty. Make up a prayer asking Jesus to help you to say 'No'.

Suggested hymns

Be thou my guardian and my guide; Jesu, grant me this, I pray; Lift up your hearts! We lift them, Lord, to thee; Lord Jesus, think on me.

Third Sunday of Lent   28 February
Second Service   **No Deceit**
Ps. 12 No longer any godly, 13 How long?; Gen. 28.10–19a Jacob's ladder; John 1.35–51 The call of Nathanael

> *'Here is truly an Israelite in whom there is no deceit!' John 1.47*

Israel

Jesus said that Nathanael was 'an Israelite in whom there is no deceit'. Deceit, or 'guile' in the old translations of the Bible, means untruthfulness, telling lies, with intention to deceive. So someone in whom there is no guile is a person who is transparently honest and truthful. We would all like to be like that, but unless we have deceived ourselves, also, we all know that we are far from that description. We would all like to think that our own nation is the most truthful nation on earth, but we know that we are no better than most, and more deceitful than some. The Jews would have liked to believe that as a race, they are a people in whom is no deceit; but they were honest enough to know that this was not true. So, was Jesus, himself an Israelite, being sarcastic? To answer that, we must remember that the word Israelite means a descendant of the man called Israel in the Old Testament. Israel was not his original name; that was Jacob, and Jacob was an inveterate liar.

Jacob

Jacob was the twin brother of Esau, and even coming out of the womb he grabbed his twin by the heel to trick him into sharing the honour of being the firstborn. Jacob later described his brother Esau as an uncivilized, hairy man, and himself as 'a smooth man'. He was, indeed, a real slippery customer. He steals his elder brother's 'birthright', namely his entitlement to a double share of his father's estate, by persuading Esau to exchange it for a bowl of stew, or in the old translation, 'a mess of pottage'. Jacob tricks his father Isaac into supporting this injustice by putting an animal skin over his own hand, pretending to the blind old man that it is the hand of Esau, and therefore Isaac gives his final blessing to Jacob instead of his brother. Nobody would describe Jacob as 'an honest man in whom is no deceit'.

Conversion

But after that, Jacob had not one but two conversion experiences, and became a reformed character. The first was when he saw angels carrying our prayers up to heaven and bringing the answers down, on 'Jacob's ladder'; he called that place 'Bethel', the 'house of God'. His second experience was when he wrestled with God all night; Jacob called that place 'Peniel', meaning 'I have seen God's face'. There God gave Jacob a new name, 'Israel', meaning 'the man who struggles with God'. Isn't Jacob's pilgrimage through life much like that of each of us? Some children are brought up with a childish faith in a God who could easily be mistaken for Santa Claus; others are taught to think that any religious belief is old-fashioned and out-moded. But we learnt to struggle and fight, with our siblings, our parents, our teachers and those who sought to civilize us and make us unselfish. Yet there came a bad patch or a crisis in our lives. 'OMG,' we say, 'why is life so unfair? If only someone would give me justice!' Then we look again at the kindly God which we have rejected, and rather wish it was true. We struggle and grapple with these ideas, and begin to pray, having no idea how to set about it. Then eventually we realize that someone has been carrying our prayers up to God, and it is Jesus. And the mystery we have been wrestling with is in fact God himself, and we have seen the face of God while we were resisting the whole idea of there being any such character. Actually, God doesn't make life easy for us, but he gives us a title of honour if we persist: 'Israel' – 'The one who wrestles with God'!

Israelites

The fact that these stories are told in the Jewish Scriptures must reflect that they recognize something of selfish, cheating Jacob in their national character, but believe that if they struggle with the idea of God, they will be forgiven and accepted. If only we could all be as honest with ourselves! Jesus says to us what he said to Nathanael: 'John or Jane, you are a true wrestler with God, because you have rid yourself of your natural deceitfulness. I watch you as you seek for truth, each under their own vine and their own fig tree. So you have learnt to call me "Teacher, Son of God, King of all us strugglers". Yet you will see greater things than these. Very truly, I tell you, one day *you*, *too*, will see heaven opened and the angels of God ascending and descending upon the Son of Man.'

Suggested hymns

As Jacob with travel was weary one day; Come, O thou traveller unknown; Nearer, my God, to thee; O God of Bethel/Jacob, by whose hand.

Fourth Sunday of Lent   6 March
(For Mothering Sunday, see the Second Service.)
Principal Service   **Dear Mass-Murderer**
Joshua 5.9–12 Eating the Passover in Canaan; Ps. 32
Repentance; 2 Cor. 5.16–21 Forgiveness and reconciliation;
Luke 15.1–3, 11b–32 The prodigal son

> 'In Christ God was reconciling the world to himself.'
> 2 Corinthians 5.19

What would you say?

Dear Mass-murderer . . . No, as far as I know there is no murderer in this church, and certainly not anyone who has caused the death of numbers of innocent people. But I have been thinking: if ever I met such a terrible person, what would I say to them? So, to compose my thoughts, I have written down an imaginary letter which I would send to an imaginary mass-killer – anyone from Adolf Hitler to the Yorkshire Ripper. You are free to disagree . . .

82

you might write something totally different. But the attempt has made me think. Maybe listening to my floundering will help you to make up your mind, too, on what the Bible really means by forgiveness.

Dear Monster

So here goes: Dear Monster. Yes, I really believe you are a monster, and you have set me a real dilemma. You see, the Bible tells me to forgive you, and I shall never, never be able to do that. Because forgiveness means saying I no longer blame you, doesn't it? How can I say that to someone who consciously massacred so many people? I should feel implicated myself if I did. If it was a minor crime like stealing my purse I might get round to it eventually. But perhaps your killings weren't deliberate. Maybe you were so deranged that you no longer knew what you were doing. But forgiving you sounds like saying it doesn't matter. And what you did matters one . . . '*dickens*' of a lot.

Bible teaching

Yet Jesus taught us to pray that God would forgive us, as we forgive others. 'For,' he said, 'if you forgive others their trespasses, your heavenly Father will also forgive you; but if you do not forgive others, neither will your Father forgive your trespasses.' Which means that until I can find it in me to forgive you, God will still treat me as a guilty sinner. Help! I've done a few naughty things in my time, but nothing like what you did. But God regards every act of disobedience and lovelessness as a mortal sin, unless we repent. And Jesus told a parable about a prodigal son, who wasted his father's savings on drink and women. You may think that is not a serious sin, but demanding what he would have had in his father's will when he died was tantamount to saying, 'I wish you were dead already.' Yet the father came out to meet him and threw a party when he returned home. Then he told the naughty son's big brother off for not forgiving him! So I don't stand a chance of getting into heaven unless I forgive you, you swine. St Paul summed it up when he wrote, 'In Christ God was reconciling the world to himself, not counting their trespasses against them, and entrusting the message of reconciliation to us. So we are ambassadors for Christ, since God is making his appeal through us; we entreat you on behalf of Christ, be reconciled to God.'

Reconciliation

Perhaps that is where I'm getting it all wrong. God is not interested in forgiveness so much as reconciliation. Maybe 'Dear Mass-murderer, I forgive you' means not 'What you did doesn't matter', but rather 'It matters; however, our relationships matter more.' So, although it nearly chokes me, I now feel I can offer you my forgiveness for your terrible crimes, so that we can become friends. Yes, I said 'friends'! It won't happen, of course, until you can accept my forgiveness, and that won't be until you genuinely repent for what you have done.

Punishment

And it doesn't mean you shouldn't be punished. You need to show your repentance, and the rest of us require protection against your doing the same thing again. But the point is, I don't want to waste the rest of my life consumed with hatred, you miserable wretch. After all, Jesus said 'Father forgive them' when he was actually being killed by the people he was praying for. Jesus has forgiven me, and if you ask him to, I expect he will forgive you, however bad you have been. And then you and I might finish up in heaven, sharing a bunk-space for all eternity. So perhaps we had better become friends while we have the chance.

Yours absolutely sincerely (I think), [Your Name]

All-age worship

Write a letter to the school bully inviting him/her to your home, because you would rather be friends than enemies. Can you imagine God writing a letter like that to you?

Suggested hymns

Amazing grace; God forgave my sins in Jesus' name; 'Forgive our sins as we forgive'; I cannot tell why he, whom angels worshipped.

Mothering Sunday   6 March
(This is the second set of readings for Mothering Sunday from *Common Worship*.)

Family Relationships

1 Sam. 1.20–28 His mother offers Samuel to the Lord;
Ps. 127.1–4 Children a gift from the Lord; Col. 3.12–17 Love
and care; John 19.25b–27 Mary is your mother

> 'As God's chosen ones, holy and beloved, clothe yourselves with
> compassion, kindness, humility, meekness, and patience. Bear
> with one another and, if anyone has a complaint against another,
> forgive each other; just as the Lord has forgiven you, so you also
> must forgive. Above all, clothe yourselves with love, which binds
> everything together in perfect harmony. And let the peace of
> Christ rule in your hearts, to which indeed you were called in the
> one body. And be thankful.' Colossians 3.12–15

Mother–child

There are no one-way streets in the way people treat each other. By
which I mean, if you say, 'A mother should care for her children', then
you should also say, 'Children should care for their mother.' It is what
we call a 'mutual relationship'. A mother should love her children, and
show her love with kisses and cuddles; so children should love their
mummy and show it in the same way. Oh what fun! So much kissing
and cuddling! If she comforts them when they are feeling sorry for
themselves, then they should try to cheer her up when she is sad. Of
course it is not an *equal* relationship. For a start, Mummy is usually
taller than the children, and stronger, to begin with anyway. She has
learnt so many wise things in the years before the children were born,
that they haven't learnt yet, that she can give them good advice based
on her experience; all the children can do is to tell her things they have
learnt in school which she may have forgotten about.

Other relationships

The same applies to other relationships in the family: between father
and children, brothers and sisters, children and their grandparents.
Though, because this is Mothering Sunday, we shall concentrate today
on our mums, God bless 'em. These relationships are all two-way
streets. The older person in the relationship may be able to warn
the younger one when they are in danger; in return the younger one
should follow the older one's advice at once, and ask questions afterwards. Sometimes it is quite difficult to get these responses right, but

it comes with practice. And that is what families are for: so that we can learn how to treat each other lovingly at all times. Then we shall be ready, as we move out into the big wide world, to treat our teachers with respect and to support children younger than us with things they find it hard to do. Our families are God's cleverest invention: they are academies, where we learn to love.

Love

There are many references to love in the Bible. Jesus tells us to love our neighbours, and to love our enemies. We are to obey those in authority over us, but if we are in a leadership position, to behave as though we are servants of those we lead. So after we have learnt the simple lessons about love in the family, we need the fellowship of a church community to teach us the next stage. The Church is God's family, and here we learn also that God loves us, like the most loving parents love their children. So, if God tells us to love our enemies, we had better try to do it, difficult as it is, and do what God tells us, because he is like a shepherd to us.

Paul's advice

So when I read to you now what St Paul's advice was to the Christians in the city of Colossae, I advise you to think of each phrase in at least three ways: be grateful to your mother because this is how she has treated you; make up your mind to treat her in the same way; thank God that he has shown such love towards you, and decide to love God in return; and love all his children for his sake. Listen carefully while I read very slowly:

> As God's chosen ones, holy and beloved, clothe yourselves with compassion, kindness, humility, meekness, and patience. Bear with one another and, if anyone has a complaint against another, forgive each other – just as the Lord has forgiven you, so you also must forgive. Above all, clothe yourselves with love, which binds everything together in perfect harmony. And let the peace of Christ rule in your hearts, to which indeed you were called in the one body. And be thankful.

There you are. It's a two-way street. If you want to be loved like that, you should love your mother, and God, and everyone else you meet, exactly in that way. God bless you.

Suggested hymns

All things bright and beautiful; For the beauty of the earth; Jesus, good above all other; Jesus' hands were kind hands.

Fifth Sunday of Lent 13 March
Principal Service **The Evolution of Love**
Isa. 43.16–21 Salvation; Ps. 126 Salvation and joy; Phil. 3.4b–14 Perseverance; John 12.1–8 Mary and Martha

> *'Jesus came to Bethany, the home of Lazarus . . . There they gave a dinner for him. Martha served . . . Mary took a pound of costly perfume made of pure nard, anointed Jesus' feet, and wiped them with her hair.' John 12.1–3*

Sisters

The human race has evolved wonderfully. Have you ever wondered what the next step in our evolution will be? Let me remind you of the story in today's Gospel. Martha was behaving morally. She was obeying the law, which said you must always be hospitable to visitors. She was also obeying an age-old tradition, which said that women should get on with cooking and leave talking about serious matters to men. Her sister Mary, on the other hand, disobeyed both law and tradition, following the leading of her heart. She performed a very loving action: sacrificing the most precious thing she owned, a jar of perfume. A famous theologian, Paul Tillich, said: 'The law of love is the ultimate law, because it rejects the whole idea of law.' So Jesus saved the human race from having to follow a written code, and told us to show compassion instead.

Morality

Isaiah reminds us about how God saved the Israelites out of Egypt, but, he warns us, 'Do not remember the former things, or consider the things of old. I am about to do a new thing.' In other words, don't look backwards. God is always moving the goalposts, guiding an evolution in human society, which will leave nothing the same as it was. And the basis of human progress is 'love'. A few years ago our government set up the Jubilee Centre for Character and Values. They were concerned by widespread bad behaviour, in everybody from rioters to bankers, and wanted to get to the roots of this decline in society's morals. But telling people how to behave doesn't work; you have to change their motives. In the story of the good Samaritan, Jesus said the virtuous foreigner was 'moved to pity'; in other words, he was motivated by compassion. When St Paul listed the seven cardinal virtues of love, joy, peace and so on, he didn't say they came from training people's character; they are the fruit growing out of God's Spirit of love within us.

Evolution

So the evolution, or revolution, that God is working on is to make us more loving. Yet the human race doesn't see that, seeking to confine behaviour in a straitjacket of law and morality. Truly, laws were the essential first step in God's plan, but we mustn't get stuck there. When Jesus taught us to pray that God's will be done, and his kingdom come, he was looking forward to a new age on earth, when everybody would behave compassionately, because God wants us to. It is a long-term strategy; it doesn't happen overnight. Every time an individual behaves selfishly, it sets God's promised paradise on earth back. How dare we humans complain that this is not a perfect world, when it is we who are spoiling it? Is it a surprise that people are so badly behaved, when we try to control them by dozens of new laws, instead of setting them an example of love? There *has* been progress, from the slavery at the base of Roman society, and the brutality of the Middle Ages. But kingdoms still go to war with each other out of a lust for power, and the rich get richer with no concern for those at the bottom of the heap. If only we would step back, and survey God's long-term strategy for this world, we might cooperate with him a bit better in bringing the compassionate society a little nearer.

Eternity

Maybe paradise on earth will never come. Jesus promised the penitent thief that he would enter paradise on the day he died, in the next life. But God tries to prepare us for eternity, by teaching us to love in this life. Building good character in those around us may be a good idea, but it is hard to make it work. 'The Christian approach is more radical and demanding', as the

Reverend Dr Hugh Rayment-Pickard wrote in the *Church Times* a few years ago. 'It is', he said, 'the expression of love and forgiveness in the face of hatred and hopelessness, coupled with the critique of human power in all its forms'. The loving Marys of this world are much further in that evolutionary process than the busy Marthas.

All-age worship

Use scales and a tape measure to calculate volunteers' body-mass-index: weight-in-kilograms divided by ('height-in-metres')-squared. Those whose index is under about 35 live on average longer and are healthier than those above. Suppose there was a love/age index (kind-deeds-done-each-year divided by age-times-ten), is yours increasing to give you a happier life?

Suggested hymns

And now, O Father, mindful of the love; Immortal love, forever full; Let there be love shared among us; My song is love unknown.

Fifth Sunday of Lent   13 March
Second Service   **Josiah's Reforms**
Ps. 35 You deliver the weak; 2 Chron. 35.1–6, 10–16 Josiah's Passover; Luke 22.1–13 Preparing for Passover

> *'Hilkiah said to the secretary Shaphan, "I have found the book of the law in the house of the LORD" . . . Shaphan brought the book to the king . . . When the king heard the words of the law he tore his clothes . . . The king . . . made a covenant before the LORD, to follow the LORD, keeping his commandments, his decrees, and his statutes, with all his heart and all his soul, to perform the words of the covenant that were written in this book.' 2 Chronicles 34.15–16, 19, 31*

Authority of Scripture

Every Christian holds the Bible in high regard, because of the teaching it gives us about spiritual things. We learn from the Scriptures that we are here because God loves us, and that God wants us to behave lovingly to other people. That he wants us to build a just society, and that he will take us to heaven when we die. This infallible message is brought to us by means of stories like the parables, which are fiction, and by an interpretation of historical events from which we can learn moral lessons. But our respect for the spiritual meaning of the Bible does not necessarily imply that we believe that every historical detail has been infallibly reported. Under God's providence – I am sure – many new ways of investigating the history of the ancient world have been discovered over the past 150 years or so. Archaeologists have excavated many cities in the Holy Land and the countries around about it, and found different periods of building, one above the other covering many centuries. They found writing carved into stones, and vast collections of documents on papyrus, and have discovered how to translate them. Recently, they have used aerial photography to ascertain which fields were farmed at different periods, and estimate how big a population they could have supported. None of these has diminished our respect for the spiritual message; in fact it has increased it. But the history of the patriarchs and the kings of Israel and Judah has been radically reinterpreted.

Finkelstein

Israel Finkelstein is an archaeologist in Tel Aviv who has thrown the cat among the pigeons, among his fellow Jews. He suggests that the absence of archaeological evidence should make us very dubious of the details in:

1   the stories of the wanderings of the patriarchs;
2   the Exodus from Egypt;
3   Joshua's conquest of Canaan; and
4   the vast empires of David and Solomon.

History, in the days when few people could read or write, was passed down by word of mouth, and although such people had astonishingly good memories, they saw nothing wrong in reinterpreting the stories in each generation to meet fresh needs, he says.

Josiah's reforms

From the Old Testament today we heard how Josiah, the King of Israel, re-established the Passover as a celebration of their shared ancestry for all the 12 tribes of Judah and Israel combined. The previous chapter recounted how he had repaired the Temple in Jerusalem, and found a scroll which told him that God required a stricter application of the ritual regulations, which is why he re-introduced the Passover. For a long time Christians assumed that it was the book of Deuteronomy that he found. We now know that the same author who wrote Deuteronomy wrote many of the stories of the subsequent kings of Israel and Judah. This points towards the conclusion that the earlier word-of-mouth stories were not written down and collected together until Josiah's time. Maybe, say some, the 12 tribes never had been united. Yet, because they were all being harassed by Assyria and Egypt, there was a desperate need for a common loyalty. So somebody in Josiah's time wove together the different legends of each tribe to give them a common ancestry. Finkelstein says this process continued right up until the return from exile, when the need for unity was greater still. Undoubtedly something similar to what the Bible describes probably happened to somebody, sometime, somewhere – we have all the right stories in the Bible, 'but not necessarily in the right order'.

Unity

Whether you believe Finkelstein's conclusions or not, I think there is a very important lesson to learn from these ideas, and we should be grateful to King Josiah for teaching us. No nation, or group of nations, can survive until they come to some sort of spiritual unity under one God. So we must be ready to share our patriotic legends with our neighbours, making them not an excuse for strife, but a source of inter-tribal cooperation. There is no room for tribal politics, in a family, a city, a denomination or church, a nation or a continent. That's the real message of the Old Testament.

Suggested hymns

Bind us together, Lord; Jesus, stand among us at the meeting of our lives; There's a quiet understanding; Thy hand, O God, has guided.

HOLY WEEK

'Passiontide' is the name we give to the solemn week from Palm Sunday to Easter. That name was helpful in the days when people learnt their Bible in Latin, and even in the early days of the Reformation, for everybody knew that 'passion' comes from the Latin word for 'suffer'. Nowadays it means a strong feeling of lust; or occasionally for music or some other hobby. Once again, we must ration ourselves in the use of unexplained ancient language – and the doctrine of the atonement is a minefield of unexploded theological terms. Palm Sunday is easier – especially if you can get hold of a real donkey to take part in your procession – for everyone knows that a traditional king would have ridden a warhorse, and Jesus was breaking the mould. Even those who have never seen a live palm tree can picture the children waving the palm branches and shouting 'Hosanna', which means 'save us now'. On Maundy Thursday we remember the Last Supper, a Passover meal which Jesus celebrated in the Upper Room with his disciples: the name comes from the 'new com-*mand*-ment' which Jesus gave us, to love one another as he has loved us – not many people know that! The Eucharist on this day may include the foot-washing and stripping of the altars, reminding us how Jesus was stripped of his clothes by the mocking soldiers. I wonder how many people who go shopping on Good Friday, in places where it is not a public holiday, ever think of Jesus dying on the cross on that day. If so, we must seize the opportunity to explain what was good about that, and Peter Abelard's emphasis on the cross as a demonstration of the love of God is the easiest of the many doctrines of the atonement to explain in modern terms.

Palm Sunday   20 March
Principal Service   **The Liturgy of the Palms**
Liturgy of the Palms: Luke 19.28–40 Triumphal entry; Ps. 118.1–2, 19–29 Blessed is he who comes; *Liturgy of the Passion*: Isa. 50.4–9a I gave my back to the smiters; Ps. 31.9–16 Assurance in suffering; Phil. 2.5–11 Jesus' obedience unto death; Luke 22.14—23.56 The Last Supper to the burial, *or* Luke 23.1–49 The trial before Pilate to the death on the cross

'[Jesus said,] "Go into the village ahead of you, and as you enter it you will find tied there a colt that has never been ridden. Untie it and bring it here."' Luke 19.30

Palm Sunday

The 'lectionary' is the list of passages from the Bible to be read each Sunday in the Church of England and several other denominations. In it, the main service on Palm Sunday is described as 'the Liturgy of the Passion'. The readings each year tell the story, from the various different Gospels, of the trial and death of Jesus, from the Last Supper to his burial. But if you only use that service, you will never hear the story of how, five days before he was crucified, the children shouted 'Hosanna' and waved tree branches in front of Jesus as he rode into Jerusalem on a donkey. This story gave Palm Sunday its name, and it would be a shame to miss it out altogether. But the lectionary allows us to precede the Liturgy of the Passion with what it calls 'the Liturgy of the Palms'. At the Liturgy of the Palms, the Gospel reading each year is from one of the Gospel accounts of the 'triumphal entry'. [That is how we began our service today/Would you like to use that next year?]

Liturgy of the Palms

The wording used in the Liturgy of the Palms, in the Church of England, is usually taken from a book called *Lent, Holy Week and Easter*, or from the online version on the Church of England website [http://oremus.org/liturgy/lhwe/ps.html]. It begins with the words 'Hosanna to the son of David', paraphrased from Psalm 118; together with 'Behold your king comes to you . . . meek and lowly, sitting upon an ass', from the prophet Zechariah; the exhortation to ride on for the cause of truth from the 'royal wedding' Psalm 45. Jesus must have known that he was fulfilling these prophecies when he chose a donkey on which to ride into the city. He was claiming to be a king, but an unusually humble sort of king. The people in the crowds must have realized it too, when they shouted to him the Old Testament words for greeting a king. The priest leading the service is called 'the president' – but don't imagine that the President of the USA is going to come to your church on this day! The president welcomes the people, explains that we are

93

re-enacting what happened when Jesus entered Jerusalem, and says a suitable prayer.

Blessing of the palms

Palm crosses are made by folding the fronds from the leaves of a palm tree into the shape of a cross. Each of the people in the church holds up a palm cross, and the president says this prayer:

> God our Saviour, whose Son Jesus Christ entered Jerusalem as Messiah to suffer and to die, let these palms be for us signs of his victory; and grant that we who bear them in his name may ever hail him as our King, and follow him in the way that leads to eternal life; who lives and reigns with you and the Holy Spirit, now and forever.

And all the people show their agreement with this prayer by saying a loud 'Amen'.

Procession

Then the story of the first Palm Sunday is read from Matthew, Mark or Luke's Gospel, in rotation year by year. Finally every adult or child in church, who wants to, processes around the church, holding up their crosses, and singing one of the well-known Palm Sunday hymns. After this they return to their places, and the president says together the special prayer, known as the COLlect of the day because it colLECTs together our thoughts onto the meaning of what we have been doing – the service continuing from that point as usual.

Meaning

The ritual gives you a vivid sense of having been present when Jesus entered Jerusalem. You welcome him as your king, promising to obey him, and to follow his example of humility. But you also remember that the same crowd that greeted Jesus on the Sunday was shouting on Good Friday for him to be crucified. It is amazing how quickly good resolutions can evaporate; so it is right that we should pray for God's grace to keep us loyal to Jesus, no matter what other people may say.

94

All-age worship

Make paper palm branches to wave when you leave the church.

Suggested hymns

All glory, laud and honour; Make way, make way, for Christ the King; Ride on, ride on in majesty; You are the King of glory.

Palm Sunday 20 March
Second Service **God's Unrequited Love**

Ps. 69.1–20 Zeal for your house consumes me; Isa. 5.1–7 The Song of the Vineyard; Luke 20.9–19 The parable of the wicked tenants

> 'The owner of the vineyard said, "What shall I do? I will send my beloved son; perhaps they will respect him."' Luke 20.13

Unrequited love

Unrequited love is when you love someone but they don't love you back. The passion and care is unreturned. It is a common occurrence in romantic literature and, sadly, in real life also. Abraham Cowley, a seventeenth-century English poet, wrote:

> A mighty pain to love it is,
> and 'tis a pain that pain to miss;
> but of all pains, the greatest pain
> it is to love, but love in vain.

His contemporary, Andrew Marvell, wrote:

> My love is of a birth as rare
> as 'tis for object strange and high:
> it was begotten by Despair
> upon Impossibility.

W. S. Gilbert, in one of his operas, has a character sing:

> Love, unrequited, robs me of my rest:
> love, hopeless love, my ardent soul encumbers:

love, nightmare-like, lies heavy on my chest,
and weaves itself into my midnight slumbers!

And to end on a frivolous note, the cartoon character Charlie Brown said 'Nothing takes the taste out of peanut butter quite like unrequited love.'

God's love

God wanted to woo the human race to love him, so he sent his Son, Jesus Christ, to woo us on his Father's behalf. Jesus rode into Jerusalem on a donkey to usher in a new kingdom, based not on force but on love. He told a parable about some wicked tenants who rejected all the messengers that the landlord sent. So the landlord asked himself, 'What shall I do? I will send my beloved son; perhaps they will respect him.' But they killed the son instead. And the same thing happened to Jesus: the crowd that welcomed him on Palm Sunday, shouted for him to be crucified on Good Friday.

A broken-hearted God

It is almost impossible to imagine Almighty God being broken-hearted. Yet it is true. God made us to be his children, and has put us in a beautiful universe, and showered us with blessings, to show us how much he loves us. God sent prophets to tell us that he loves us, and when they were rejected, he sent us his only Son. Jesus preached about God's love for us, as passionate as that of the father in the parable for his prodigal son. And those who heard him, responded by crucifying him. What hurt most must have been not the self-centred governing class, but the number of ordinary people who couldn't be bothered to stand up for what was right. It has always been the same: God loves all his children, and longs for us to love him in return. But most people never respond at all, and even the best of us respond with a love nothing like as passionate as God's love for us. And it breaks God's loving heart in two.

Good Friday

Perhaps that is the point of Good Friday. To talk of Jesus paying the price for my sins is something I can't understand. But tell me that the cross is a cross-section of God's loving broken heart, and I will break down in tears. Every day God loves me with all of his heart, and desperately yearns for me to love him in return. Half the time I ignore him totally. In the other half, my interest in God is half-hearted, to say the least. But if I were able to put myself in God's place, and think of the passionate lover in search of an equal response from the cold-hearted beloved, I would bitterly regret the casual way I have treated God. When Good Friday comes, think about God's unrequited love for you. Surely nobody is so inhuman that it wouldn't make them want to love God with all their heart and soul and mind and strength, from now on in. Can you believe in a broken-hearted God, wounded to the core by his unrequited love for you?

> *There's a wideness in God's mercy
> like the wideness of the sea;
> there's a kindness in his justice,
> which is more than liberty.
>
> There is no place where earth's sorrows
> are more felt than up in heaven;
> there is no place where earth's failings
> have such kindly judgement given.
>
> For the love of God is broader
> than the scope of human mind;
> and the heart of the Eternal
> is most wonderfully kind . . .
>
> If our love were but more faithful,
> we should take him at his word;
> and our life would be all gladness
> in the joy of Christ our Lord.

*Check that this is the version in your church's hymnal.

Suggested hymns

And can it be?; My song is love unknown; There's a wideness in God's mercy; Who can sound the depths of sorrow?

First three days in Holy Week   21–23 March
Suffering and Perseverance

(These are the readings for Wednesday in Holy Week but the sermon may be used on any day.)
Isa. 50.4–9a I gave my back to the smiters; Ps. 70 Those who say Aha! Aha!; Heb. 12.1–3 Suffering and perseverance on the cross; John 13.21–32 Judas betrays Jesus

> *'Let us run with perseverance the race that is set before us, looking to Jesus the pioneer and perfecter of our faith, who for the sake of the joy that was set before him endured the cross, disregarding its shame, and has taken his seat at the right hand of the throne of God.' Hebrews 12.1–2*

Suffering

We all suffer, but everybody suffers in their own way. Many of us try to hide it from everyone except our own close family, and sometimes even from them. Keeping it to ourselves is better than pouring our grief over everybody we meet, but it brings its dangers. If you bottle up your emotions, they often burst out in unexpected and inappropriate ways. We may even damage ourselves and bring on a nervous breakdown. Other people may not understand why we seem so remote and unsympathetic to *their* problems. And we lose the chance of learning how to cope with our suffering by hearing how other people cope with theirs. If you cannot go to a trained counsellor, speak in confidence to me or some other person whom you trust, to discuss what is bothering you.

Jesus suffered

We often complain that God doesn't understand our pain and grief. Yet we believe that, as St Paul said, 'God was in Christ.' Jesus certainly knew what it means to suffer, as he suffered an agony and grief on the cross which is beyond anything we have ever endured. But he does not shut himself off from us; on the contrary he shares our suffering and fully understands how hard it is for us. You may know the story of the bereaved father who complained bitterly to his pastor, 'Where was God when my son died?' The pastor said, 'I think he was in exactly the same place as he was when his own Son died.'

Coping

When we encounter suffering or grief in our own lives, I think most people feel, 'I shall never be able to cope with this.' Of course you won't, not on your own you won't! But we have just discovered that God is right there, suffering with you. And so God will give you the moral strength which you lack within your own heart, to cope with whatever comes. That is, provided that you ask him. God can't do much for people who ignore him, or rebel against him, when they suffer, because he is unable to get through to them. But if you tell him quietly that, in spite of everything, you will struggle to trust him, then he will see you through.

Death

It is hard to cope with the death of someone we love; harder still when we face the probability that we ourselves shall soon die. We should never give up, but join with the doctors in fighting the sickness. But when it becomes clear that there can be no future quality of life for a sick person, the family may have to quietly give them permission to die when God calls them. Most people ask how they can be sure there is life in heaven when we die. Of course we can't; God never forces us to believe. But the evidence of the brave way Jesus overcame his doubts and assured those around him that he would see them again, and the number of people since then who have prayed to the living Christ and found their prayers were answered, makes it a very strong possibility. The Greek philosopher Socrates said at his trial, when he was accused of atheism:

> If you suppose that there is no consciousness, but a sleep like the sleep of him who is undisturbed even by dreams, death will be an unspeakable gain . . . But if death is the journey to another place, and there, as men say, all the dead abide, what good . . . can be greater than this?

Perseverance

So never give up. Seeing how bravely Jesus coped with his crucifixion – despite his pain, doubts and fears – we must resist the temptation to do what Job's wife told him to do: 'Curse God and die.' Times of suffering may be our greatest opportunity to witness to those around us that we believe that God's plan for us is more important than our own wishes. Another Greek philosopher, Aristotle, said, 'I count him braver who overcomes his desires than he who conquers his enemies; for the hardest victory is the victory over self.' That is what Jesus did when he was crucified; we must follow his example and be an inspiration to others.

Suggested hymns

Lead, kindly light; O love, that wilt not let me go; The day thou gavest, Lord, is ended; There's a wideness in God's mercy.

Maundy Thursday   24 March
Pass Over to Freedom

Ex. 12.1–4 [5–10] 11–14 The Passover; Ps. 116.1, 10–17 The cup of salvation; 1 Cor. 11.23–26 The Last Supper; John 13.1–17, 31b–35 Foot-washing

> *'Tell the whole congregation of Israel that . . . they are to take . . . a lamb for each household . . . then the . . . congregation of Israel shall slaughter it at twilight. They shall take some of the blood and put it on the two doorposts and the lintel of the houses in which they eat it . . . It is the passover of the LORD . . . when I see the blood, I will pass over you, and no plague shall destroy you . . . This day shall be a day of remembrance for you.' Exodus 12.3, 6–7, 11, 13–14*

Exodus

The Israelites were slaves in Egypt: living in poverty and quite without rights. Pharaoh had instructed the midwives to kill all their boy babies so that the number of immigrants should not swamp the local population. They dreamt that someone would lead them away from this tyranny, into freedom. When God called Moses to do just that, he told the Israelites to celebrate an annual festival to commemorate their liberation. When the angel of death flew over the houses in Egypt, to do to the Egyptians what they had done to the Israelite babies, it would see the blood of the Passover lamb, painted in a cross-shape, on the doorposts of the Israelite houses.

Then death would 'pass over' them without harming those who lived there. It took a sacrifice to give them their freedom, and they were saved from slavery by the blood of the lamb. Every year since then, our Jewish friends have celebrated Passover, and an important part of the God-ordained ritual is that a child, or the youngest person present, asks what the meaning of the celebration is, and the elders have to explain it. Thus the search for freedom can be passed down from generation to generation.

Eucharist

When Jesus came to celebrate the Passover supper with his disciples, in the last week of his life, all these ideas must have resonated in their minds. Jesus had told them that they were slaves to sin, and captives to their selfish habits. But God would send a Saviour to set them free. They had marked the cross in lamb's blood on their doorposts; then Jesus passed round the cup of red wine saying, 'This is my blood of the covenant between you and God.' So he told them to repeat this ceremony regularly to remember not the liberty which Moses brought to their ancestors, but in remembrance of him, Jesus. They were now no longer enslaved under the law, but free men and women in the new kingdom of love. The Eucharist is the Christian Passover.

Liberty

The liberty that Jesus brought was not just for individuals, but a charter of freedom for the whole nation and the whole world. Yet, hard as it is to escape from tyranny, it is harder still to create and sustain a free society. The freedom you create by overthrowing a tyrannical ruler or oppressive regime is only temporary. Jesus warned us that when we expel a demon we must quickly put something in its place, or seven other devils will rush in to fill the vacuum. Many revolutions merely replace the old guard with a new regime which is even worse. We need to put in its place a society which knows the value of freedom, and its cost. Democracy only thrives when every citizen understands that they may have to sacrifice their own cherished ideals to form a compromise with those who have different priorities. Justice is only possible when we put our own interests last, and dedicate ourselves to serving those who are worse off than we are.

Individuals

Now let's look again at individual freedom. Jesus emphasized the priority of love. Love, in this case, is not a slushy emotion, but a deliberate choice and intention to sacrifice your own interests in the service of others, doing for your neighbours what you would like them to do for you. That is a tough call, and only possible if we are strengthened by knowing that God loves each one of us. When the devil of selfish self-interest is cast out of our souls, we must fill the vacuum quickly with God's Holy Spirit. Then we can love others, with the power of God's love flowing through us.

Education

So it is all down to education. The purpose of the Passover meal was so that the meaning of liberation could be explained to the children, and passed down. The message of Maundy Thursday is that freedom will only come when every child has been educated to see this: that freedom for all is only possible when each individual is ready to sacrifice their personal interest for the sake of others.

Suggested hymns

An Upper Room did our Lord prepare; Dearest Jesu, we are here; Draw nigh and take the body; The heavenly Word, proceeding forth.

Good Friday   25 March
'Good' Friday?

Isa. 52.13—53.12 The suffering servant; Ps. 22 Why have you forsaken me?; Heb. 10.16–25, *or* Heb. 4.14–16; 5.7–9 Jesus the priest; John 18.1—19.42 The blood of the covenant

> 'My God, my God, why have you forsaken me,
> and are so far from my salvation,
> from the words of my distress?'
>
> Psalm 22.1 (Common Worship)

'Good' Friday?

Here is a poem I found in a book:

Say, how can they call this 'Good' Friday?
This day when it all went so wrong?
For this day is no holiday high-day,
no reason for parties and song!
So it ought to be called The 'Bad' Friday,
the Friday we wished we'd not seen,
or the 'Anything-but-Happy' Friday,
the worst day there ever has been.
For the Lord sent a Saviour in Jesus;
he came down from heaven above;
and he promised his coming here frees us,
and brings in the Kingdom of Love.
Yet some bad people cruelly arrested him;
aiming to put him to shame,
for they deeply despised and detested him,
called down a curse on his name.
Though the crowds in the streets listened eagerly,
calling him 'king' with each breath,
wicked priests fixed a trial illegally;
wishing to put him to death.

Suffering

Then the High Priests and lawyers insisted
'He said he was equal with God;
a most blasphemous claim,' they persisted –
their verdict was passed on the nod.
'For such wickedness we must inhibit,
and he must be punished,' they said;
'and he needs to be hanged from a gibbet,
and left there until he is dead.'
Yet his pain when his enemies hurt him
was nothing as great in its way
as when watching his best friend desert him
and run like a coward away.
All his closest disciples forsook him
and cowered in secret at home.
The next morning to Pilate they took him,
the Governor, sent there from Rome.
So when Jesus stood there, Pilate jested,

'They tell me you claim you're a king!
So then that's why they had you arrested –
I don't believe any such thing.'
Then he offered to free Jesus quickly;
'See him,' he said; 'there he stands.'
'No, not him,' cried the crowd gathered thickly.
The Governor just washed his hands.
Of his clothing the soldiers then stripped him
and pressed a thorn crown on his head;
then they mocked him and beat him and whipped him,
and wrapped a robe round him instead.
To King Herod next Jesus was taken.
'Just hang the imposter, today,'
said the king, who with laughter was shaken,
and then sent him back straight away.

Crucifixion

On '*Good*' Friday, then, cruel Roman soldiers,
with crowds round them shouting their hate,
put a great heavy cross on his shoulders,
and forced him to carry its weight.
Weeping women were there, wives and mothers –
'Not me should you weep for,' he said;
'for yourselves; for one day when these others
attack, then you'll wish you were dead.'
Next, 'To Golgotha!' orders were given:
they laid him down there in the heat;
then two nails through his wrist bones were driven,
and one more great nail through his feet.
Nearby, weeping, there stood Jesus' mother.
the cross slowly rose up on high;
with her grief now exceeding all other,
she watched her son hang there to die.
The distress of his breathing was horrid –
each word that he spoke filled with pain –
as the red blood ran down from his forehead
he groaned there again and again.
'Oh, forgive them,' he cried as they nailed him;
'In paradise,' said to the thief;
'How I thirst,' as fresh torments assailed him,

'Don't leave me!' he pleaded in grief.
Three long hours till it seemed he was sleeping;
and then, his last word, Jesus cried,
with a strange note of joy in his weeping,
'At last, my job's done.' Then he died.

But

But . . . then why say, 'My task is now over'?
What plan, then, had Jesus fulfilled?
For he certainly was not in clover . . .
unless he had done what God willed.
How can God then demand such an ending
from any mere man whom he sent . . .
but then, was it not *man* he was sending,
was God, then, the Being who went?
'For our God was in Christ,' says the apostle,
'who drew to himself all the world.'
So was this the amazing, colossal
design that the cross has unfurled?
And could God have felt love for his creatures
so much that he came down to earth
for himself – with a man's human features –
to show what our poor souls are worth?
And was this how God showed how strongly
our God suffers when we ignore
quite how deeply he cares, and then wrongly
decide we're not loved anymore?
Oh, then, thank you, my Father, for sharing
our pain in your home up above;
so I want to claim part of your caring
and you shall have all of my love.

Epilogue

So then, that's why they call this 'Good' Friday,
this day which is joyful and bright.
Surely this *is* a holiday high-day –
the day when it all went so right!

*© Michael Counsell 2015

105

Suggested hymns

Beneath the cross of Jesus; God with humanity made one; Morning glory, starlit sky; Nature with open volume stands.

*see Author Index

EASTER

They say that 'No man is an atheist when his car is heading at 60 miles an hour towards a tree.' Similarly, many people who have spent their lives insisting that there is no life after death begin to question their beliefs – or lack of belief – when the doctor tells them that there is only a low probability of their surviving more than another six months. They don't know how to talk about death, particularly their own death; but if a Christian minister comes by and tells them the Easter story, it gives them a great opportunity to mention the unmentionable, which often brings a visible relaxation of fear. The story of how Jesus died and came alive again, particularly if a Christian can link with it their own experience of coming through a time of grief with a strengthened faith, may win many converts who are unable to put their new-found faith into words. The white or gold hangings, and the sung 'hallelujahs', with the return of the *'Gloria in excelsis'* to its proper place, together with the Easter candle and the Easter garden, all emphasize the joy of this season.

Easter Vigil   26–27 March
The Life-giving God

(*A minimum of three Old Testament readings should be chosen. The reading from Exodus 14 should always be used.*)
Gen. 1.1—2.4a Creation, Ps. 136.1–9, 23–26; Gen. 7.1–5, 11–18; 8.6–18; 9.8–13 Noah, Ps. 46 Our refuge and strength; Gen. 22.1–18 Sacrifice of Isaac, Ps. 16 The path of life; Ex. 14.10–31, 15.20–21 The Exodus, *Canticle*: Ex. 15.1b–13, 17–18 The song of Moses; Isa. 55.1–11 Come to the waters, *Canticle*: Isa. 12.2–6 Great in your midst; Bar. 3.9–15, 32—4.4 God gives

the light of wisdom, *or* Prov. 8.1–8, 19–21; 9.4b–6 Wisdom, Ps. 19 The heavens declare God's glory; Ezek. 36.24–28 I will sprinkle clean water on you, Ps. 42 and 43 Faith and hope; Ezek. 37.1–14 The valley of dry bones, Ps. 143 A prayer for deliverance; Zeph. 3.14–20 I will bring you home, Ps. 98 Salvation and Justice; Rom. 6.3–11 Baptism, death and resurrection, Ps. 114 The Exodus; Luke 24.1–12 The empty tomb

> *'My soul is athirst for God, even for the living God;*
> *when shall I come before the presence of God?'*
>   *Psalm 42.2 (Common Worship)*

Vigil

'Vigil' means staying awake, especially on the night before a great Christian festival. The Easter Vigil forms a link between the sadness of Holy Week and the joy of the resurrection. In the early Church it lasted all night, and was a time for adult baptisms; nowadays some churches hold the Vigil on Saturday evening, and others celebrate very early on Sunday morning. Eleven readings are suggested, with alternatives for some of them. Most churches only choose a selection of these – as all of them, except the Gospel reading, are the same every year, choosing different ones each year makes for an interesting variety. But all the readings, as is appropriate, have the theme of new life coming out of death. Also, because of the possibility of baptisms, many of them refer to water.

Psalm 42

Both of these themes are mentioned in Psalms 42 and 43, which were originally joined up as a single Psalm, and which I have chosen for my text today [I think this is allowed, even if they haven't been chosen to be said or sung in today's service in this church].

> My soul is athirst for God, even for the living God;
> When shall I come before the presence of God?

We thirst for God like we thirst for water, and we hope to appear in the presence of God when we are given new life after we have died; and there are my two themes, water and new life. In the

Bible, 'the living God' and 'the God of life' both mean 'the life-giving God'. In fact the writer claims to be in 'the land of Jordan and . . . [Mount] Hermon'. Dr Michael Goulder suggested that Psalms 42 to 49 were sung at an autumn festival at the city of Dan, which was one of the sources of the River Jordan, which flowed from there to give new life to the crops all the way down its fertile valley. So when the Bible refers to 'living waters' it means flowing, life-giving waters, just as 'the living God' means 'the life-giving God'.

The gift of life

God is the source of all life. When molecules first combined into cells which could divide and multiply, it is truly incredible to suggest that this happened purely by accident. God gave us human life, then our ancestors evolved into beings able to think, choose and love. Jesus said to the Samaritan woman at the well, 'If you knew . . . who it is that is saying to you, "Give me a drink", you would have asked him, and he would have given you living water.' The woman thought he meant fresh-flowing water, which you cannot get from a stagnant well, but Jesus meant 'life-giving water'. Later he cried out in the Temple, 'Let anyone who is thirsty come to me. And let the one who believes in me drink. As the Scripture has said, "Out of the believer's heart shall flow rivers of living water."' Just as physical water gives life to our bodies, and we cannot survive without it, so the love of Jesus gives life to our souls, and without him we are spiritually dead. God gives to us, through Jesus, a life in this world which is more satisfying and exciting than the dull boring existence we had before we knew him.

Life after death

But when God raised Jesus that first Easter, he showed us that 'eternal life' is not limited to this world, but carries on into the world to come. Jesus was the first to experience life after death, and he offers to give it to all who believe in him: 'I am the resurrection and the life,' he said. 'Those who believe in me, even though they die, will live, and everyone who lives and believes in me shall never die.' Then he proved it by raising dead Lazarus out of his tomb.

Easter

So Easter is a celebration of the life-giving God. God gave life to inanimate matter; he gave to the first humans the power to think about life and make life-choices. Then God gave to you and me a deeper quality of life because we believe in Jesus. And finally, God will give us eternal life after we have died. 'Dear Lord Jesus Christ, Son of the Life-giving God, have mercy on us, now and in the hour of our death. **Amen.**'

Suggested hymns

As pants the hart; I am the bread of life; Sing choirs of heaven! Let saints and angels sing!; This joyful Eastertide.

Easter Day   27 March
Principal Service   **Another Dimension**
Acts 10.34–43 Peter and other witnesses to the resurrection, *or* Isa. 65.17–25 New heavens and a new earth; Ps. 118.1–2, 14–24 I shall not die but live; 1 Cor. 15.19–26 The last enemy destroyed is death, *or* Acts 10.34–43; John 20.1–18 Magdalene at the tomb, *or* Luke 24.1–12 The women see Jesus

> *'God raised [Jesus] on the third day and allowed him to appear. . . to us who were chosen by God as witnesses . . . he commanded us to preach to the people.' Acts 10.40–42*

Gospel

The good news of the Easter message is that God created us because he loves us, and wants us to live with him eternally. And that's the gospel truth. But this unchanging truth can be expressed in many different ways. People whom Jesus preached to thought of the kingdom of God as a new era in which Jews would rule the world. Jesus translated that into the vision of a just society. Following his resurrection, 'eternal life' was retranslated as 'endless life after death'. St Peter preached that even non-Jews can go to heaven, and it is the duty of Christians to attract people of all cultures to believe in Jesus. St Paul translated the unchanging gospel into terms of Greek philosophy, because few people in the Roman Empire could understand the Jewish way of speaking. But when Christianity spread to Western Europe it had to be translated again, this time into Latin, with its emphasis on Roman law. When the gospel came to England, our ancestors believed in God's kingdom, but there was a lot of Anglo-Saxon feudalism in the way they thought of it. Then British missionaries travelled to different lands to preach the gospel of God's love. The unimaginative ones tried to turn their converts into imitation English people, but the wiser missionaries learnt the language and the culture of the people they were preaching to, and some were successful in translating the gospel again into terms that their hearers would understand and be attracted by.

Science

Why then are so few people in Europe and America becoming Christians nowadays? Could it be because we ignore God's call to retranslate the Easter gospel into the language people speak today? Have we even asked ourselves what that language is? For most young people, it is the language of science. If we speak of heaven as a place above the clouds, where angels have wings and play harps, they will laugh us to scorn, saying: 'Passengers on jumbo-jets have travelled high above the clouds and seen no angels. Your God's just an outdated superstition.' And if they reject God's offer of eternal life, it is *our* fault for being too lazy to translate our message into their language.

Another dimension

So how do we set about reinterpreting heaven for today? I suggest that we use the concept of dimensions. A dot on the blackboard is one-dimensional; a line on the blackboard is two-dimensional. A box has three dimensions, width, depth and height; but if it is moving it has a fourth dimension, the dimension of time. Every schoolchild can understand Einstein's concept of a four-dimensional space–time continuum. But quantum science and string theory, [which I don't yet fully understand,] have made the idea that there is an infinite number of dimensions and multiple universes quite respectable. Some even suggest that the Big Bang was caused when two other universes collided. Of course we can neither prove nor disprove that, because by definition you cannot observe something which exists in other dimensions from ours. So, what if heaven were another universe, in another dimension, where God and the spirits of those who have died are not subject to the tyranny of time, but where they can observe us at any time, though we can't see them?

Heaven

So when we rise again, it will not be on this earth, as the Jews thought it would be, nor to a fantasy world of harps and haloes. It would be to another world, painless and happy, very close to ours, but unobservable to us because they inhabit a dimension we have little knowledge of. I don't say we are quite unaware, because many people say that they have a very strong feeling that their departed loved ones are still very near to them. You may think that is superstitious, too, but it is the language that people of today understand. So those you love have not gone to a place far away; they are very close, willing you to love the people around you with every particle of your being, so that we can all live happily together in eternity.

All-age worship

Look at a model railway. From above, you can see if two trains are about to crash, but the imaginary drivers could not. If God sees we are about to do something stupid, what can he do to stop us?

Suggested hymns

Alleluia, alleluia, hearts to heaven and voices raise; All heaven declares the glory of the risen Lord; I serve a risen Saviour (He lives); Jesus Christ is risen today.

Easter Day   27 March
Second Service   Witnesses of the Resurrection

Morning Ps. 114 The Exodus, 117 Praise the Lord; Evening Ps. 105 The Exodus, *or* 66.1–11 God holds our souls in life; Isa. 43.1–21 You are my witnesses; 1 Cor. 15.1–11 Witnesses of the resurrection, *or* John 20.19–23 Sunday evening appearance

'You are my witnesses, says the Lord.' *Isaiah 43.10*

The policeman

I may have told you this true story before, but it is worth repeating. A big burly policeman sang bass in a church choir, and the choir-boys were terrified of him. The first time he was invited to read the 'lesson', they sat trembling to hear what he would say. The reading was from Isaiah, and he boomed out the opening words: 'You are my witnesses, says the LORD.' The choirboys all wanted to plead guilty straight away!

Witnesses

The Easter story is true, because the Gospels record the testimony of eye-witnesses. St Paul, too, when writing to the Corinthians, says that 'he was raised on the third day in accordance with the scriptures, and . . . he appeared to [Peter], then to the twelve. Then he appeared to more than five hundred brothers and sisters at one time, most of whom are still alive, though some have died. Then he appeared to James, then to all the apostles. Last of all . . . he appeared also to me.' That's an awful lot of witnesses, and it is impossible to believe that they were all lying. All of them claimed to have been instructed by Jesus to tell other people what they had seen. Jesus said to them, 'You are my witnesses', or similar words.

Doubters

But non-Christians and doubters object that the witnesses must have been lying – you can prove it, they say, because of all the contradictions and inconsistencies in the Bible account. Now, if we want them to believe what we say, we must at least take their objections seriously. There are four Gospels, they point out, and there are slight variations between them. How many angels were there, one or two? How many women went to the tomb? Who went into the tomb first, one of the Marys or John the Beloved Disciple? Who was the first to see Jesus: Peter, James, Cleopas, John the Beloved Disciple, Mary Magdalene, or all 12 apostles at once? The doubters are right for once: all these so-called 'facts' are described in at least one of the Gospel accounts.

Variations

Actually, in any dramatic event, you would expect the accounts of different witnesses to stress different aspects of what they had seen, without any intention to deceive. You hear it in law courts and read it in the papers, how genuinely truthful witnesses give different versions of what they have seen. There is no doubt that they all saw the same event, but from different angles, and different aspects impressed themselves on their memories. The law courts know that you cannot shake the core value of a witness's testimony by casting doubt on a few of the peripheral details, because memory plays funny tricks on all of us. In fact, if you wanted to fabricate a false account of something that never happened, you would make sure to brief all the witnesses in advance, so that they should all give the same evidence. The discrepancies in the different accounts of the resurrection story actually prove that it really happened!

What sort?

But one question remains unanswered: that is, 'What *sort* of resurrection are they describing?' All but one of the testimonies describes seeing the risen Christ within 40 days after he was crucified; after that he ascended into heaven, and although billions of Christians have been fully aware of Christ's living presence among us, and many have had visions, nobody actually claims to have seen him except St Paul. Which is odd, because Paul was in no doubt that Jesus had died on the cross, and in his early writings he seems to believe that when we die we shall sleep somewhere, and then return to earth at a general, physical, resurrection. Later, however, as we see in his First Letter to the Corinthians, he seems to have matured in his thinking. 'Flesh and blood cannot inherit the kingdom of God,' he writes. He says that when each of us goes to heaven, we shall have what he calls a 'spiritual body'; a means of being recognized, communicating and influencing events, which is not in the least material. Perhaps all the witnesses were seeing a spiritual body, but at that stage of their maturing they didn't understand the difference. Perhaps we shall never know. But the basic fact remains: Jesus is alive; over 500 eye-witnesses bear evidence to that fact, and we prove it ourselves when he answers our prayers. Also, he has promised to give us eternal life with him when we die; and he wants us to witness to everyone on earth about it.

Suggested hymns

Alleluia, alleluia, give thanks to the risen Lord; Christ the Lord is risen again; Good Joseph had a garden; The day of resurrection.

Second Sunday of Easter   3 April
Principal Service   **Negative Theology**

Ex. 14.10–31; 15.20–21 The Exodus (*if used, the reading from Acts must be used as the second reading*), *or* Acts 5.27–32 Peter witnesses to the resurrection; Ps. 118.14–29 I shall not die but live, *or* Ps. 150 Praise in Heaven; Rev. 1.4–8 The firstborn from the dead; John 20.19–31 Thomas' doubt and faith

> *'Jesus said to [Thomas], "Have you believed because you have seen me? Blessed are those who have not seen and yet have come to believe."' John 20.29*

What is God?

In an all-age group of what is called 'messy church', the participants were invited to draw what they thought Jesus looks like. But one woman objected: 'I've no idea what Jesus looks like, I just feel him as an invisible presence.' A priest who was present was reminded of when he studied theology before he was ordained, and attended a lecture on the various heresies in the early Church, when Christians excommunicated each other because they disagreed over details of what God is like. He clearly remembered writing in his notes, and passing to his neighbour, 'This is what makes me think theology is rubbish.' Yet neither of them had any doubts that God exists, and reveals himself to us in many different ways.

Language

The trouble is, none of our human languages are adequate to describe God, who is beyond words. Any statement we make about God is bound to be misleading. That is why Jesus startled everybody by the ridiculous comparisons he made in his parables:

- God is like a silly shepherd, who leaves his flock to look after themselves while he searches for the one lost sheep.
- God is like an unjust judge, who won't give the persistent widow justice because she is right, but only to stop her pestering him.
- God is like a father, who, when his son has frittered away half the family fortunes, welcomes him back with open arms. And so on.

It was not what people expected to hear – it shattered their preconceptions and made them think. The disciples must have been quite bewildered. Then Jesus died, and came back to life. And Doubting Thomas was the first to grasp what it meant: 'Then God must be like Jesus,' he thought, 'all-loving and all-powerful at the same time.' Then he said aloud, 'So, if God is like you, Jesus, then you must be my Lord and my God!'

Negative theology

The name for the learning curve the disciples had experienced is 'negative theology'. God is too big for us to say what God *is*; all we can do is say what God *is not*. For instance:

- 'God is not ignorant' is more true than saying 'God is wise', because we don't know what wisdom is.
- It is better to say that 'God is not evil', because we cannot imagine supernatural goodness.
- God is not created.
- God is not located at any one point in space, or at any one moment of time.
- God does not *exist*, in the way we exist; he is too big for that, and we exist only because God exists; and
- God is transcendent, indescribable.

Steps on the way

Now this may sound depressing, as though God was unknowable. We must be humble enough to admit that God is beyond the grasp of our understanding. But this is not the end of the journey towards knowing God; it is a step along the way, necessary to cleanse our minds of misconceptions and false mind-pictures of God.

Revelation

The next step is to realize that, although we could never understand God by our own efforts, God wants us to know him, and to have something like a human relationship with him. So God reveals himself through the prophets, then comes down to earth, and reveals himself through Jesus. Jesus said to Philip, 'Have I been with you all this time, Philip, and you still do not know me? Whoever has seen me has seen the Father.' He proved God's love by dying for us, and he revealed God's power by rising from the dead. All we can say is, like Thomas, 'My Lord and my God'.

Story

To end with, here is an enigmatic story. The followers of a holy man were full of questions about God. The holy man said, 'God is the Unknown and the Unknowable. Every statement about him, every answer to your questions, is a distortion of the truth.' His bewildered followers asked him, 'Then why do you speak about him at all?' To which he simply replied, 'Why does the bird sing?'

All-age worship

Draw pictures of what you think Jesus looked like. Does it matter whether they are true, so long as they are helpful?

Suggested hymns

Alleluia! O sons and daughters; Blessed Thomas, doubt no longer; Good Christians all, rejoice and sing; Light's glittering morn.

Second Sunday of Easter   3 April
Second Service   Abide with Me
Ps. 16 The path of life; Isa. 52.13—53.12, *or* 53.1–6, 9–12 The Suffering Servant; Luke 24.13–35 The road to Emmaus

> *'As [the two disciples] came near the village to which they were going, [Jesus] walked ahead as if he were going on. But they urged him strongly, saying, "Stay with us, because it is almost evening and the day is now nearly over." So he went in to stay with them.' Luke 24.28–29*

Popular hymns

Lamentably, fewer families arranging a funeral ask for a Christian hymn to be sung. If they do, 'Abide with me' is one of the favourites. It was sung regularly at evening services in church; but in the television age fewer churches hold evening services. However, the last time the BBC published its list of the nation's top 20 favourite hymns, 'Abide with me' came fourteenth. It was in 1927 that the custom of singing this hymn at the Football Association Cup Final at Wembley stadium began. It is still a favourite at the Royal British Legion Festival of Remembrance at the Royal Albert Hall, and was played by a Salvation Army band at Ground Zero, soon after the terrorist attack on the Twin Towers of the World Trade Centre in New York, on 11 September 2001.

Henry Lyte

The words to this hymn were written by Henry Francis Lyte, who also wrote 'God of mercy, God of grace' and 'Praise, my soul, the king of heaven'. He was born in Scotland in 1793, and educated at Trinity College, Dublin, where he won the poetry prize three years running. He was then ordained, and served as a curate at several churches in Ireland and the West of England. In 1823 he became the incumbent, called by the curious name of 'the Perpetual Curate', of the fishing village of Lower Brixham in South Devon. There he remained, in gradually declining health, until he preached his farewell sermon on 4 September 1847, after which he sailed to Italy and died of consumption just over two months later.

'Abide with me'

It used to be thought that Henry Lyte wrote 'Abide with me' on the evening after his farewell sermon, and if he knew he was dying, that would have been very appropriate. But now, most people believe that he wrote it in 1820 when he was 27 and in good health. He had just visited an old friend, Augustus le Hunte, who was in his last illness, and kept saying the words 'Abide with me' as he lapsed into unconsciousness. That so moved young Lyte that he wrote the hymn around them. It was not published in his lifetime, but when he himself was dying he remembered these lines and gave them to a relative, who had them published.

Monk

Lyte himself wrote a tune for the hymn. But when the first edition of *Hymns Ancient and Modern* was compiled in 1861, the committee met in the home of William Henry Monk, the organist at St Matthias' Church, Stoke Newington, and they asked him to write a new tune for Lyte's words. After the meeting, he went out with his wife to watch the sunset together, and when they came back in again, he quickly wrote the tune 'Eventide', which has been inseparable from this hymn ever since.

Emmaus

As many people know, this hymn is based on the incident in St Luke's Gospel which we have just heard. On the day Jesus rose from the dead, two of his disciples, one called Cleopas and the other possibly his wife Mary, had not heard the news, and were making their way sadly towards their home in Emmaus. They were joined by the risen Christ, but did not recognize him as he spoke to them of how the Messiah was bound to suffer and then enter into glory. It was getting late, so they invited Jesus to spend the night at their home; in the King James Version of the Bible, 'Abide with us, for it is towards evening.' But when he broke the bread at their evening meal, they recognized him, and then he vanished. They realized at once that Jesus, who had died on the cross, was now far more intensely alive even than they were.

Resurrection

So 'Abide with me' is an appropriate hymn to sing in the evening, and at Eastertide. But with its clear invitation to Jesus to be close to us all through our lives, and especially to raise us to new life when we die, it is a good one to use when we are approaching death. As we are all going to die someday, the hymn helps us to accept that inescapable fact calmly, by reconciling ourselves to our Maker through reading again the words of Lyte's hymn.

Suggested hymns

Abide with me; Be known to us in breaking bread; Come, risen Lord, and deign to be our guest; Sun of my soul, thou Saviour dear.

Third Sunday of Easter   10 April
Principal Service   Stranger on the Shore

Zeph. 3.14–20 The Lord is in your midst (*if used, the reading from Acts must be used as the second reading*), or Acts 9.1–6 [7–20] Paul's conversion; Ps. 30 God brought me up from death; Rev. 5.11–14 Worshipping the Lamb; John 21.1–19 The lakeshore

> *'Just after daybreak, Jesus stood on the beach; but the disciples did not know that it was Jesus.' John 21.4*

Acker Bilk

Acker Bilk, a popular jazz clarinettist, when his daughter was born in 1960, wrote a piece of music which he named after her, 'Jenny'. It was then used as the signature tune of a BBC serial for young people, and the producer asked him if he would change the name of the piece to the title of the drama: 'Stranger on the Shore'. It rose to number 2 on the UK chart and then number 1 in the USA. In 1969, the crew of the moon-rocket Apollo 10 included this wonderful tune on a music cassette which they took with them on their journey to the moon. I expect if we ever do find any aliens from space, they will be humming 'Stranger on the Shore': dee-DAH, dee-DAH, dah-dee-dah-dee-DAH'!

Lake Galilee

When Jesus died and came alive again, he appeared to a group of his disciples on the shore of Lake Galilee. The end of chapter 20 sounds as though it was meant to be the end of St John's Gospel: 'these [things] are written so that . . . through believing you may have life in his name.' Then, as a footnote, John tells how Jesus later appeared to seven disciples who had gone on an unsuccessful fishing trip on the Lake. But they didn't recognize him. Jesus truly was, to them, the 'stranger on the shore'!

Instructions

Although they had caught no fish all night, Jesus called out to them to throw out their casting-nets on the right side of the boat, and they hauled in a huge number of fish. There was nothing miraculous in this; it is a well-known fact that due to the refraction and reflection of light, an observer on the shore can see much more clearly what is in the water than a fisherman in a boat. But why didn't they recognize Jesus at first? Possibly they were dazzled by the light of the sunrise; or maybe his resurrection body was subtly different from the body he had inhabited before; after all, the disciples on the road to Emmaus hadn't identified Jesus on the first Easter Day, until they spotted something distinctive in the way he broke the bread. At the lakeside, when John the Beloved Disciple recognized Jesus, he invited them to eat some of the fish they had caught, when they were cooked over the charcoal fire he had lit. There is something about a shared meal, in which the presence of Jesus is recognized. When Peter later counted them, there were 153 fish in the net, which some people say was the number of nations in the so-far discovered world. The disciples remembered that Jesus had called them to be not 'fishers-for-fish' but 'fishers-for-folk'. They realized that this was an acted parable, or 'sign', showing that they and their followers must be missionaries, making converts from every nation on earth.

Recognition

We very often fail to recognize the presence of Jesus, the 'stranger on the shore'. He is no longer limited by the restrictions of an earthly body, but he is always invisibly with us. On rare occasions, Jesus chooses to make his presence visible to us, but in unexpected ways. One instance is when St Martin was a soldier, he saw a poor man shivering on a cold day, and cut his heavy army cloak in two and wrapped the poor man in a half of it. That night he had a vision of Jesus wearing half a cloak, and realized that Christ was in the poor man – 'inasmuch as you do it to one of these, you do it to me,' said the Saviour. We are often tempted to doubt that those who have died are still invisibly with us, and long for a sign. Much more commonly, however, we recognize Christ's presence in a shared meal. It may be the hospitality of strangers, a parish supper, a quiet communion or a grand Mass, when we suddenly realize that the dead Christ is alive again, and very close to us. And if he is not far away, neither are those we love who have died.

All-age worship

The initials of the Greek words for 'Jesus Christ, Son of God, Saviour', make 'Ichthus', the word for fish. Make paper fish, and Blu-Tack® one to your bedroom door.

Suggested hymns

At the Lamb's high feast we sing; Come, living God, when least expected; Come, risen Lord, and deign to be our guest; Jesus, these eyes have never seen.

Third Sunday of Easter 10 April
Second Service Going Home
Ps. 86 You have delivered me from death; Isa. 38.9–20 The living thank you; John 11.[17–26] 27–44 The raising of Lazarus

> *'[Jesus] cried with a loud voice, "Lazarus, come out!" The dead man came out, his hands and feet bound with strips of cloth, and his face wrapped in a cloth. Jesus said to them, "Unbind him, and let him go."' John 11.43–44*

Lazarus

Jesus Christ's friend Lazarus had been dead for four days. Jesus called him to come out from the tomb, and brought him back to life. But nobody asked Lazarus whether he *wanted* to be resurrected!

A better place

Put yourself in Lazarus's place. Many people who have had a 'near-death experience' have described what it is like to die. They mostly agree that you feel yourself to be in a tunnel approaching a bright light. There is a sense of deep peace and happiness; sometimes you become aware of the presence of Jesus, or those you love who have died. Then, if the doctors cure you, even in some instances after you have been clinically dead for a short while, you feel that you are being called to return to earth. And though you are happy at the prospect of seeing your earthly friends again, there is also a deep regret and reluctance. All this, Lazarus must have felt intensely.

Questions

I wonder whether poor Lazarus ever got the chance to question Jesus about what had happened? 'Why me?' he would have asked. 'Why did you have to bring me back, just when I was beginning to enjoy myself? Our parents were there, I feel sure – I was looking forward so much to seeing them again. I thought when you talked about the kingdom of God, Jesus, you were talking about a new age on earth. Then those who had died would come back to an earthly paradise. But now I realize heaven is something we become part of the minute we die. I felt so at home there. Why did you drag me back to earth when the party was just beginning?'

Poor Jesus

Poor Lazarus, indeed. But poor Jesus, also! Any merely human healer would expect gratitude, and here was the man he had saved giving him a telling off! So he tried to explain, I think, something like this: 'I'm so sorry, dear friend. But it had to be done. Think first of your two kind sisters, Martha and Mary. The prospects for a woman without a man in these days are pretty grim. With nobody to give them an income, they have a choice between starvation or prostitution. I have a strong feeling that I shan't be around myself much longer to care for them. So I had to call you back, to save them from all that.'

Witness

'But more importantly,' Jesus would have continued, 'I needed you to come back to life to be a witness. I have the Sadducees to contend with, who don't believe there will be any resurrection. That's because they think of a purely material resuscitation to life on earth. I need somebody to tell them that the afterlife is quite different, and much better than this life. You remember the rich man in the story, when your namesake died on his doorstep? He said to Abraham, "If someone goes to [my brothers] from the dead, they will repent [of their wicked ways]." I very much doubt if they will, but I need you to tell people that death is not the end, and we have to repent for our sins. And finally, the day you long for *will* come to you eventually: the day of your second death, when you are repatriated to your homeland in heaven.'

Going home

Now that is all imagination; but it changes our attitude to death. Do you know the slow movement to Dvořák's 'Symphony from the New World'? Some rather banal words were written to that tune beginning, 'Going Home'. Here is another attempt to do the same thing, which tries to go deeper:

Christ the Way, ev'ry day,
we will walk with you.
No more fear, you are near,
loving us anew.
Friend of all, when we call,
bring us, as we roam,
all our days filled with praise,
nightly nearer home.

Those we love, now above,
live in rapture there;
happy they, night and day
in your love they share.
When they leave, while we grieve,
they are free from cares;
we rejoice in your choice
that your home is theirs.

All we do is for you,
Jesus, Lord most high;
so must we, therefore, be
unafraid to die.
Till that day, come what may,
when no more we roam,
let each breath sing till death
'We are going home.'

Then on high, when we die,
we shall be at home . . .
in our Father's home.

Suggested hymns

Christ is alive! Let Christians sing; Going home (above); Jesus lives! Thy terrors now; Now is eternal life.

*see Author Index

Fourth Sunday of Easter   17 April
Principal Service   **Apocalypse Later**
Gen. 7.1–5, 11–18; 8.6–18; 9.8–13 Noah's flood (*if used, the reading from Acts must be used as the second reading*), *or* Acts 9.36–43 Peter raises Tabitha; Ps. 23 The Lord is my shepherd; Rev. 7.9–17 The Lamb their shepherd; John 10.22–30 My sheep hear my voice

'God will wipe away every tear from their eyes.' Revelation 7.17

Apocalypse later

In 2013 a huge meteorite entered the earth's atmosphere near Chelyabinsk in Russia. Many observers captured on video the sight of this bright burning light shooting across the sky, seemingly not far above their heads. They must have felt that the end of the world had come. The book of Revelation, also called The Apocalypse, gives many descriptions of the suffering which will precede the end of the world. So when a movie was made describing the terrible suffering which was supposed to have followed in the track of an imaginary American general who had hidden himself in the hills and was fighting his own war, the film was called *Apocalypse Now*. Though, it cost so much and took so long to make that those involved in the filming nicknamed it *Apocalypse Later*!

Meteors

I think those who saw the meteorite in Russia must have felt that they had narrowly escaped the end of the world. The good news is that meteorites like that only strike the earth on average every hundred years. There are millions of rocky fragments left over from the creation of the solar system circling the sun in the asteroid belt.

But if something happens to knock one out of its trajectory, it could stray into the earth's orbit. Nowadays the position of every asteroid over a kilometre wide is carefully observed, so at least we should get some warning. Usually, if one such rock enters the earth's atmosphere it burns up, and is called a meteor. If small fragments fall to the ground they are called meteorites, and cause very little harm. But 65 million years ago, a 15-kilometre-wide meteor struck Mexico, leaving a crater, still visible, measuring 177 kilometres across, killing most living things on earth, and making the dinosaurs finally extinct. So the end of the world through a meteor probably won't happen in our lifetime. But it just might.

Ready for a tragedy

There are many other 'apocalyptic' events which could cause the extinction of the species Homo sapiens. Destruction of the environment, overpopulation, climate change, nuclear calamity, epidemics, to name but a few. How should we react to this news? The simple answer is 'Don't panic!' The people of Pompeii probably died within seconds of the ash cloud from Vesuvius striking them. Jesus spoke of a great tragedy impending, but even he didn't know on what date it would happen; probably he was referring to the destruction of Jerusalem by the Romans in AD 70, which caused much suffering, but wasn't the end of the world. John who wrote the book of Revelation spoke about 'the great Ordeal' and probably thought it would happen in his lifetime; it didn't, but that does not lessen the value of what he wrote. He emphasized the value of facing our suffering with courage and compassion. We should do what we can to prevent environmental disaster, but get our priorities right: 'Set your minds on things that are above, not on things that are on earth,' as St Paul said.

Martyrs

Christians are persecuted in many countries today, for daring to believe in Jesus. But 'the blood of the martyrs is the seed of the Church'. If we bear our suffering bravely, thousands will become Christians through our example. Friends and family may mock us as raving mad because we believe in God, but if we respond politely and humorously we may start them looking for what gives us hope.

Hope

But the final answer to our fear of death is to read the many poetic images in the book of Revelation. Comfort has come to millions of people who are suffering or bereaved, by the hope that the afterlife is so much better than this life, that we have nothing to fear from apocalyptic events, now or later:

> These are they who have come out of the great ordeal . . . For this reason they are before the throne of God . . . and the one who is seated on the throne will shelter them. They will hunger no more, and thirst no more; the sun will not strike them, nor any scorching heat; for the Lamb at the centre of the throne will be their shepherd, and he will guide them to springs of the water of life, and God will wipe away every tear from their eyes.

All-age worship

Choose short phrases from the above quotation about hope. Make a cardboard 'gravestone' and paint the best of these phrases as an 'epitaph'.

Suggested hymns

A brighter dawn is breaking; Give us the wings of faith to rise; The Lord is risen indeed; The strife is o'er, the battle done.

Fourth Sunday of Easter   17 April
Second Service   **The Promised Land**
Ps. 113 God raises the poor from the dust, 114 The Exodus; Isa. 63.7–14 God led them through the depths; Luke 24.36–49 Words of the risen Christ

> *'In all their affliction he was afflicted, and the angel of his presence saved them: in his love and in his pity he redeemed them; and he bare them, and carried them all the days of old.' Isaiah 63.9 (King James Version)*

Mother's tender care

Imagine a mother taking her little daughter to be vaccinated. When the child discovers the doctor is going to stick a needle into her, she is terrified. Mother tries to comfort her, and lets her child cry on Mummy's shoulder. 'It will hurt you, my darling,' says the mother – 'but not for very long. If you don't have this, you might become very ill, and that would be a much worse pain than the injection. I'll be right beside you, holding your hand. It'll hurt me when I see how it hurts you. So be a brave girl – if you are, I'll buy you an ice cream afterwards as a reward, to show you how much I love you.' Little daughter goes into the surgery, screams when the needle goes into her, sobs on her mother's shoulder, and Mummy cries a bit, too. Then daughter tries to be a good girl and stop crying, because she really, really wants that ice cream. Now here's a surprise: that little girl is you. And God is the mummy.

Moses

Some people would think that's rather shocking. God is indescribably higher than we are; how can you compare him to a very human mother? The answer is, 'Because God told us to.' In Isaiah 66, God says, 'As a mother comforts her child, so I will comfort you.' And in chapter 63, Isaiah makes the audacious suggestion that 'In all their affliction he was afflicted'. How can you talk about God suffering? Now to make my point, I have had to use the old Authorized Version. Those words appear in the NRSV translation, but only as a footnote. Originally this passage referred to Moses, suffering with the Israelites in Egypt, then, as God's messenger, leading them through the Red Sea into the Promised Land. But some well-meaning scribe tried to improve the text – and then they were in a right muddle!

Jesus

Nevertheless, this verse clarifies our thinking about Jesus. Like the child in the story we are scared to bear pain on our own, and we imagine nobody understands. But God understands, and when we suffer, God suffers with us. But how can God convince us of that? Just as God sent Moses as a messenger to the Israelites in Egypt, to suffer with them and bring them to the Promised Land, so God has sent Jesus to us. We see that Jesus on the cross shares our suffering and our pain; and he promises a reward, if we trust him, in the Promised Land of heaven. So we try to be brave, because we really, really want that painless existence. Yet many of the Israelites rejected Moses, because he was only a messenger; they wanted the real thing, God himself. And many of us feel ambivalent about

Jesus – after all, he was only human. How can his suffering on the cross be any concern of ours? That is why Jesus spent three years gently convincing his followers that 'I and the Father are one'.

Affliction

So it's true, little girl – or boy. Your parent loves you, and really does weep when you cry. It wasn't just Jesus suffering on the cross: it was the Word of God, who is like God, and who *is* God, and reveals God's love for you as he dies for you on the cross. Just as Jesus had power to rise from the dead, so he has the power to raise you up and carry you to the Promised Land. Paraphrasing Isaiah slightly:

> In all [your] affliction [God] was afflicted, and he [was present in Jesus his messenger and] saved [you]: in his love and in his pity he redeemed [you]; and he bare [you], and carried [you] all the days of [your life].

Promised land

You really, really want your reward, don't you? It's much better than ice cream! But the comparison with Moses is why so many hymns and spirituals refer to heaven as our 'promised land'. So be brave, little girl, or boy. Life often hurts us, but our parent is right here with us, sharing our pain. And as our reward, if we trust him, God will raise us up after we die and carry us to the promised land of heaven.

Suggested hymns

And can it be?; Come, ye faithful, raise the strain; Thine be the glory; When I behold the wondrous cross.

Fifth Sunday of Easter   24 April
Principal Service   The Long Goodbye
Bar. 3.9–15, 32—4.4 Wisdom, *or* Gen. 22.1–18 Abraham willing to sacrifice Isaac (*if used, the reading from Acts must be used as the second reading*), *or* Acts 11.1–18 Baptism of the Gentiles; Ps. 148 Nature praising God; Rev. 21.1–6 Death will be no more; John 13.31–35 The commandment to love

Goodbyes

The Long Goodbye is the title of a novel by Raymond Chandler, featuring the detective Philip Marlowe. As is typical in such books, the plot is very complicated; it is also quite different in many ways from that of the film which was based upon it. There are many murders, and apparent suicides that turn out to be murders, and even one case where the one, who was thought to have died, later turns up alive. So it is hard to discover where the title comes from – until you discover that Chandler's own wife was terminally ill while he was writing it, and he was reflecting on the difficulty of saying goodbye to someone who has not long to live. Sometimes people travel for miles to be with their parents at their deathbed, and when they meet, neither of them can think of anything to say.

Jesus' farewell

The best example we could follow is that of Jesus Christ. In John's Gospel chapters 13 to 17, Jesus wanted to share with his friends the lessons he had learnt during the past 30 years, and warns them how they should live when he has gone. Jesus is also sharing some precious insights into the character of God the Father. This final discourse takes place at the Last Supper, after the meal, when Judas Iscariot has already gone out to tell the High Priests where Jesus was going, so that his enemies can arrest him. First, Jesus stresses the importance of love. Then he tells his disciples that he is 'the Way, the Truth and the Life'. Then he explains what he means by the Holy Spirit. He says, 'I am the True Vine', and teaches them about suffering. He promises that those who follow him will know a very special joy and peace. Finally, he prays for the disciples, and for us who follow in their steps. Extracts from this long goodbye are read at this service and for the next four Sundays.

A journey

Jesus makes it clear that this is his final farewell. Life is a journey; he has reached the end of Stage One, but he is ready to start on the next phase. His friends will not see him again, to speak to, in this life. But he pours balm on their troubled minds, by gently suggesting that there *is* an afterlife: 'Little children, I am with you only a little longer . . . Where I am going, you cannot follow me now; but you will follow afterwards.' Poor bumbling Peter was baffled by this. Like modern sceptics, he wouldn't believe in anything until it was proved beyond a shadow of doubt: 'Where? . . . Where are you going? Why can't we see it?' If it was somewhere dangerous, Peter was willing to follow – even if it cost him his life, he boasted. Jesus knew human nature better, and recognized how few of our boasts of the good things we shall do in the future are ever fulfilled: 'Very truly, I tell you, before the cock crows, you will have denied me three times,' he warned.

Love

In the meantime, they must live good lives, following his example. Their Jewish teachers had told them that God cares about how we behave, but they couched it in the form of laws, listing the things we must not do. The teaching of Jesus, in contrast, was utterly revolutionary: 'I give you a new commandment, that you love one another. Just as I have loved you, you also should love one another.'

Last words

As you grow older, you couldn't teach those you love any better lesson than that. They may be frightened of death, but assure them that although none of us is perfect, still God loves us. Death is the start of a journey towards an 'undiscovered country'. Yet though we know little about heaven, we trust that God made us to live with him in eternity. Tell them you don't want an expensive funeral or monument; simply that, in memory of you, they should forget their squabbles and learn to love one another for your sake. That's what Jesus said, and your last farewell should be full of hope and love, as was his.

All-age worship

Imagine you are going on a journey, and write a 'see you again soon' letter to your family. Compare it with what Jesus said in today's Gospel.

Suggested hymns

Come, my way, my truth, my life; How sweet the name of Jesus sounds; Thou art the way – by thee alone; Ye choirs of new Jerusalem.

Fifth Sunday of Easter   24 April
Second Service   **The Den of Lions**
Ps. 98 God has done marvellous things; Dan. 6.[1–5] 6–23 The lions' den; Mark 15.46—16.8 The resurrection

> *'My God sent his angel and shut the lions' mouths so that they would not hurt me, because I was found blameless before him; and also before you, O king, I have done no wrong.' Daniel 6.22*

Novel

The book of Daniel, in the Old Testament, is a great favourite in Sunday schools and children's picture books. Most of these don't question whether this book is history or not; if they say it is, they get round the miraculous element by saying that God is all-powerful and God can do what God wants. But there are problems, because parts of the book are written in ancient Hebrew, like the rest of the Old Testament, and other parts are in Aramaic, which was a later dialect that Jesus spoke. Furthermore, it predicts accurately the events of Jewish history from the time of the exile in Babylon up until the reign of Antiochus Epiphanes, 400 years later; but then it stops short, after getting the date and place of his death completely wrong. The obvious solution is to say that it is a historical novel, written in the reign of Antiochus, describing events that are supposed to have happened several centuries previously. Nothing wrong with that: Shakespeare wrote historical plays about the kings of England, which are based on historical fact, but invented dialogue and events to make them dramatically interesting for the people of his own age. So there may have been someone called Daniel, but his story has been 'written up' to teach an important lesson to people in later ages. And if it was important to them, it probably has important lessons to teach us today – just like Shakespeare.

The lions' den

Today we read from this historical novel the story of Daniel in the lions' den. Daniel is a Jew, exiled in Babylon, who is promoted to a high position in the court of the Babylonian king. This makes the local princelings, called 'satraps', jealous, so they hatch a plot, and persuade the King to pass a law, sentencing to death anyone who prays to a foreign God. This does not stop Daniel, who continues to pray daily in his own room to the God of the Jews. When the satraps inform on Daniel, the King – who supports him – is obliged to sentence Daniel to be thrown into a pit full of hungry lions. But Daniel is found to be still alive the next morning, and reports that

> My God sent his angel and shut the lions' mouths so that they would not hurt me, because I was found blameless before him; and also before you, O king, I have done no wrong.

So the satraps who had informed against Daniel are thrown into the lions' den in his place, and are eaten alive by the lions as soon as their bodies hit the ground. Gruesome, or what?

Lessons

So why was this old story retold 400 years later? Obviously, because it had lessons to teach Jews who were suffering under a succession of Greek kings. The Greeks were trying to persuade the Jews to give up their own customs and adopt a Greek way of life. That included doing keep-fit naked in the gymnasium – which embarrassed circumcised Jewish men – and giving up their Sabbath customs; and many Jews were giving up their religion altogether. So the tale of Daniel was told to encourage Jews to remain faithful to the one God of all the earth, and be regular in their times of prayer. A message which is just as important to us today as it was then.

Christians

I wonder, then, why this passage was chosen for reading in Christian churches in the Easter season? Probably because the unrecognized 'angel' who shut the lions' mouths was identified with Jesus Christ. In the other famous story in Daniel, that of Shadrach, Meshach and Abednego in the fiery furnace, the unnamed fourth person who was with them and helped them to pass unharmed through the flames has often been regarded as our Saviour. Apart from Ezekiel, whose vision of the valley of dry bones was probably a promise of national renewal, Daniel was the first book in the Bible to speak of personal resurrection, in chapter 12 verses 1–3:

> At that time your people shall be delivered, everyone who is found written in the book. Many of those who sleep in the dust of the earth shall awake, some to everlasting life, and some to shame and everlasting contempt. Those who are wise shall shine like the brightness of the sky, and those who lead many to righteousness, like the stars forever and ever.

Suggested hymns

Come, my soul, thy suit prepare; Do not be afraid, for I have redeemed you; Through all the changing scenes of life; Who would true valour see.

Sixth Sunday of Easter (Rogation Sunday)   1 May
(*St Philip and St James Day should be transferred to Monday 2 May; if it is not, the sermon on page 316 may be used.*)
Principal Service   **Who Was John Writing To?**
Ezek. 37.1–14 The valley of dry bones (*if used, the reading from Acts must be used as the second reading*), or Acts 16.9–15 The baptism of Lydia; Ps. 67 Let the peoples praise you; Rev. 21.10, 22—22.5 The heavenly Jerusalem; John 14.23–29 Going to the Father, *or* John 5.1–9 The paralysed man at the pool

'In Jerusalem by the Sheep Gate there is a pool . . . which has five porticoes.' John 5.2

'[Jesus said,] "I am going away, and I am coming to you."' John 14.28

John's community

When you read the Bible, it is a basic rule that you must always try to understand the text in the same way as the first readers understood it. Only then can you go on to apply its message to our lives today. If you miss out this essential first step, and try to understand it as though it was originally directed at twenty-first-century people, you are very likely to get the wrong end of the stick. In the fifth chapter of St John's Gospel, he sets the scene of the miracle at a particular pool in Jerusalem, of which he gives us some interesting details, as though many of the readers have never been there, but it is important that they should be able to imagine it. Actually, until recently, nobody knew what he was talking about, until archaeologists found the remains of an oblong pool with a porch along all four sides, and another running across the middle, on which the people waited to be healed. It lay at the end of a water pipeline, which showed what is called a 'siphon effect', whereby only a little water trickles into the pool, and then a lot rushes in all at once. The sick people thought it was magic, but St John says healing comes from faith in Jesus. In the fourteenth chapter, Jesus says his words are to prepare his disciples for when he would leave the world on Ascension Day, and then return with the power of the Holy Spirit at Pentecost. So who were John's community?

Detective work

A lot of detective work has gone into finding an answer to this question. To summarize:

- The community who read St John's Gospel for the first time were Jews, because it is full of quotations from the Old Testament which John doesn't bother to explain because he knows they are familiar with it.
- But they live at some distance from Jerusalem, because John needs to explain the geography of the pool where the healing took place.
- Yet they speak Greek, because the Gospel is written in Greek. Jews who lived outside the immediate area of the capital city were more fluent in what was the common language of the Roman Empire than they were with Hebrew, which was only used in the synagogues.
- Next, the readers of St John either had been, or shortly would be, expelled from the synagogues. So they were Jews who had been accepted by their co-religionists for many years, but whose Christian teachings had diverged so far from traditional Judaism as to be no longer acceptable.

- Finally, they lived a generation or so after Christ died, because the Fourth Gospel, written so 'that they might believe', shows many signs of being rewritten and rearranged several times; the final chapter saying that the book is based on a first draft, written by 'the disciple who is testifying to these things and has written them' – *in the past tense* – 'and we know that his testimony is true'.

Lessons

Does this matter? Yes, in several ways:

- First, it teaches us *not* to look for simple answers to twenty-first-century questions; we *must* translate it into words which are familiar to young people today if we expect to attract them into becoming Christians.
- Second, we must not regard the derogatory references to 'the Jews' as being anti-Semitic; they translate 'Judaeans', which was the usual term among Greek-speaking Israelites of, for instance, Galilee, in speaking of the rigorously orthodox and anti-Christian Jews from the Jerusalem area.
- Finally, John's readers had had time to get used to the fact that, although Jesus was no longer visible to them since his ascension, he was still present with them in the Holy Spirit – which gave them power to think more deeply about his teaching than any of the other three Gospels, and to bear witness to him by the universal love they showed in their lives.

And now, having worked through that reasoning process, we can apply the Gospel to ourselves. Jesus *is* alive, and the power to think and to love, which is the Spirit's gift, is available to us, also, today.

All-age worship

Learn about Christians suffering for their faith today; e.g. from www.opendoorsuk.org/news/ *and* www.barnabasfund.org

Suggested hymns

Christ triumphant; Love's redeeming work is done; Now the green blade riseth; You shall go out with joy.

Sixth Sunday of Easter (Rogation Sunday)   1 May
Second Service   **Awe and the Presence of God**

Ps. 126 The Lord has done great things for us, 127 Unless the
Lord builds the house; Zeph. 3.14–20 God is in your midst;
Matt. 28.1–10, 16–20 The ascension command

*'The LORD has taken away the judgments against you, he has
turned away your enemies. The king of Israel, the LORD, is in your
midst; you shall fear disaster no more.' Zephaniah 3.15*

Awe

How often have you had that feeling which we call A W E 'awe'?
We feel it when we fall in love; when we see a sunset or a starry
night; when we hear beautiful music or see a wondrous work of art;
when we read a piece of great literature; when we see the view from
the top of a mountain. It is a strange mixture of terror and of joy,
of reverential wonder and dread; you can see nobody, but you have
a strong feeling that you are not alone. A writer called Rudolf Otto,
in a book called *The Idea of the Holy*, suggested that it was this
feeling in early humans which was the beginning of religion. Many
people, even those who do not intellectually believe in God, have
this sensation so strongly that they speak of a spiritual dimension to
life, which cannot be attributed to reason or logic. Poor things; life
is so much *simpler* when you admit to the possibility that you have
just had an experience of the presence of God!

Zephaniah

One of the minor prophets in the Old Testament, Zephaniah,
wrote of God's judgement, which would lead to the destruction
of Jerusalem. But after that, he said, the city would be rebuilt, and
foreigners would come to live there in peace and worship together
with the humble and lowly Jews who were left. He describes this
sense of God being there with them, which is quite true, he says:
God *is* there among them, even though they can't see him:

Sing aloud, O daughter Zion; shout, O Israel! Rejoice and exult
with all your heart, O daughter Jerusalem! . . . The king of Israel,
the LORD, is in your midst; you shall fear disaster no more . . .

136

The LORD, your God, is in your midst . . . he will rejoice over you with gladness, he will renew you in his love; he will exult over you with loud singing as on a day of festival.

Ascension

Also, when Jesus ascended into heaven, he promised his disciples that he would always be with them, even when they could not see him:

Go therefore and make disciples of all nations, [Jesus told them,] baptizing them in the name of the Father and of the Son and of the Holy Spirit, and teaching them to obey everything that I have commanded you. And remember, I am with you always, to the end of the age.

If we fully realized that, we would have a sense of reverence and awe night and day. Fortunately, we don't have that overwhelming emotion all the time, as it might prevent us getting on with our work and our family responsibilities. Console yourself by remembering that human emotions are not fully under our control. But once you have felt it, you will never again doubt the invisible presence of Jesus, whatever you are doing.

Footprints

I am sure you know a poem called 'Footprints in the Sand'. Many people get angry with God, because he is never there when you need him. The poem answers this by describing a dream about someone seeing their life story in the form of rows of footprints. Mostly there are two rows of footprints, but sometimes there is only one. This was in the times when she was feeling low and dispirited, and she complained that, although God had promised to be with her always, he deserted her in the time of her greatest need. God replied that there was only one set of footprints, because God was carrying her when she was distressed. The poem has become so familiar that it feels a little corny, but it conveys an important truth. Like Zephaniah and Jesus, the poet says that God is always with us, though we can't see him, whether or not we have that overwhelming sense of awe.

137

Copyright

You can buy copies of this poem in every souvenir shop, or download it from the internet. The internet version reads: 'Copyright © 1984 Mary Stevenson, from original 1936 text. All rights reserved.' So you would be wise not to print it; but remember the lesson it teaches: God is always with you, loving you, even though you cannot see him, whether or not you have that powerful sense of awe which so often catches us by surprise.

Suggested hymns

Be still, for the presence of the Lord; He is Lord, he is Lord; Jesus is Lord! Creation's voice proclaims it; This is the day, this is the day.

ASCENSION, PENTECOST AND TRINITY

Here are three festivals that are described by the Bible in terms that were very meaningful to the people of their times, but that mean practically nothing to the woman or man in the street nowadays. It was normal in the 'olden days' to speak of heaven as a place, up somewhere above the clouds. Now that many people have been in airliners high above the clouds and astronauts have been to the moon, it is no use taking such language literally. We have to explain, for the benefit of newcomers to the church, that this is a symbolic way of describing a 'higher level of existence', and that clouds are often used as a symbol in the Old Testament for the presence of God. Pentecost is a less well-known word than Whitsun; the former comes from the festival, 'fifty' days after Passover, when the Holy Spirit was given to the apostles, and 'Whitsun' from the white robes that were worn by candidates for baptism on that Sunday. But the symbols of a dove, tongues of fire and speaking in foreign languages means nothing to people today. What probably happened was an experience of *glossolalia* such as is often heard in Charismatic churches today, but St Paul emphasized that this was not helpful when strangers were present. Whereas if we speak to enquirers about moments when you feel inspired by a power from outside of you, many can relate that to events in their own experience. The word 'Trinity' is never used in the Bible, but the experiences that lie behind

---

the doctrine do. Jesus is described as the Son of God, and God is called the Father; Jesus said 'I and the Father are one', and St Paul wrote, 'God was in Christ reconciling the world to himself.' The Holy Spirit is described as the Spirit of God and the Spirit of Jesus. Yet the doctrine was formulated in the days when the philosophy of Aristotle was all the rage, with its distinction between the inner 'substance' of a thing and its temporary properties or 'accidents'. A clergyman who was trying to persuade churches in other parts of the Anglican Communion to break away from the Church of England recently suggested that a staggeringly high percentage of Church of England clergy do not believe in the doctrine of the Trinity. I have met many clergy, none of whom said they denied the essence of the doctrine, but most of whom found it very difficult to talk about. Perhaps we should admit that from the pulpit.

Ascension Day 5 May
A Two-Part Tale

Acts 1.1–11 The ascension (*must be used as either the first or second reading*), *or* Dan. 7.9–14 The Son of Man; Ps. 47 God has gone up, *or* Ps. 93 The Lord is king; Eph. 1.15–23 Christ is seated beside God; Luke 24.44–53 The ascension

> *'In the first book, Theophilus, I wrote about all that Jesus did and taught from the beginning until the day when he was taken up to heaven, after giving instructions through the Holy Spirit to the apostles whom he had chosen.' Acts 1.1–2*

Acts

St Luke wrote two books: the first we call *the Gospel according to Luke*, and the second is *the Acts of the Apostles*. At the beginning of Acts, Luke writes that he had written his Gospel to describe everything that Jesus did, up until the day he ascended into heaven. He writes as if he is communicating with somebody called 'Your Excellency Theophilus', presumably the governor of a province. Acts is the second chapter of a continuous story. In the Gospel, Luke tells us what Jesus did in his earthly life; in the Acts he goes on to tell the story of the Christian Church. But this is a story which has no ending: the Gospel was the *beginning* of what Jesus started to do and to teach; the Acts tells us about what God continued to teach us through St Paul, and what he is still doing to make the world a better place through your life and mine.

Hindu

A Hindu man approached an Indian bishop, enquiring about becoming a Christian. Nobody had approached the Hindu about this, but he had somehow acquired a copy of the New Testament translated into his own language, and without anyone to help him had read through Luke–Acts. The story of Jesus fascinated him, and laid its spell on him. Then he read on, and felt he had entered into a new world. 'In the Acts, what the disciples did and thought and taught had taken the place that Christ had occupied,' wrote the Bishop. 'The Church continued where Jesus had left off at his death. "Therefore," said this man to me, "I must belong to *the Church that carried on the life of Christ*."'

Chinese

A Chinese Christian, who was training candidates for the ministry in the 'Open Church' in China, spoke to an English visitor recently. 'Many people who support the "Underground Churches" in China,' he said, 'accuse the Open Church of being under the thumb of the Communist Government. My family and I suffered greatly under the "Red Guards", so nobody could accuse me of being pro-Communist. But I joined the Open Church because it provides me with a pulpit from which I can carry the message of Christ to large numbers of Chinese people. Yet I also spend a lot of time persuading the party cadres not to persecute the Underground Church, allowing them to carry on with one-to-one evangelization in their own way.'

Here

In this country, the institutional Church is widely criticized, and sometimes those criticisms are justified. But any voluntary movement which grows needs leaders and rules to hold it together. If the Christian Church did disappear from this land, a few scattered Christians might remain, but they would be nothing like as effective in providing care for the needy, education for the young, evangelism for those who have never heard the message of Jesus, and the encouragement of a community which isolated Christians so much need. So, with all its faults, we need the Christian Church to carry on the work of Christ; Christ has no other plan.

Ascension

You may feel that the astronauts have proved that there is no heaven 'up there'. If that is so, Jesus may still have wanted to provide a visual aid for his disciples, to convince them that he was no longer going to do God's loving work on earth; from now on it was up to them. St Luke realized this, and proclaimed it in the two-part tale we call Luke–Acts. You are not in this church because you like the music and liturgy, and enjoy the fellowship of like-minded people. You are here because Christ has called you to carry on the work on earth which he began.

Witness

That task is to witness on behalf of God that he loves all his children and wants all of us to live with him in eternity. When the American journalist Henry Morton Stanley had met the explorer David Livingstone, he uttered the famous words, 'Dr Livingstone, I presume'. Then he stayed with him for a while before returning to tell his story. 'If I had been with him any longer,' Stanley wrote, 'I would have been compelled to be a Christian – and he never spoke to me about it at all.' There was no need for words; the witness of Livingstone's life proved irresistible.

Suggested hymns

Christ triumphant, ever reigning; Crown him with many crowns; Hail the day that sees him rise; How lovely on the mountains.

Seventh Sunday of Easter   8 May
(Sunday after Ascension Day)
Principal Service   To Go Where Jesus Is
Ezek. 36.24–28 I will put my Spirit in you; (*if used, the reading from Acts must be used as either the first or second reading*),

Acts 16.16–34 Baptism of a jailer; Ps. 97 The Lord is king; Rev. 22.12–14, 16–17, 20–21 Come!; John 17.20–26 Church unity and love

'Blessed are those who wash their robes, so that they will have the right to the tree of life and may enter the city by the gates.' Revelation 22.14

Holidays

Where would you like to spend your holiday? If you have been working hard, at your job, at school, in the garden or in the kitchen, you would want to go somewhere really relaxing. You would like somewhere with a good view, interesting things to do, and fine food. Although getting away from your family might be pleasant for a short break, before long you would long to have them with you. Sounds like the ideal paradise, doesn't it? Well, paradise is just what I have described. And Jesus said to the villain who was being hanged on the other cross next to him, 'Today you will be with me in paradise.'

Paradise

Admittedly I have been too materialistic in describing the place to which Jesus was inviting the penitent thief, which must be a non-material experience, because we have never found heaven anywhere in this universe. But the holiday brochure I began with is intended to set your imagination whirling. If we describe it as a purely spiritual existence, that sounds too airy-fairy, wishy-washy and quite unattractive, and I want you to long for paradise with a passionate intensity, as far better than anywhere you have ever been on this earth. Because Jesus said,

In my Father's house there are many dwelling places. If it were not so, would I have told you that I go to prepare a place for you? And if I go and prepare a place for you, I will come again and will take you to myself, so that where I am, there you may be also.

Purpose

That is why God created you. Of course, he wanted you to have a good time on this earth, if possible; but he never created a pain- and worry-free paradise in this life, because that really would make you materialistic. No, this earth is a training ground, to make you long for something better, and help you to develop the qualities and character which will enable you really to enjoy the next life. For the next life will be a *community* experience. There will be a lot of people there: your family, your friends, those whom you admired from a distance, and those whom you read about in history books. So you need to learn how to get along with other people, including those who are quite different from those you have been used to. There will even be some who counted themselves your enemies, so you need to practise in this life how to forgive your enemies, and to accept the forgiveness of people you can't stand. It sounds a steep learning curve, doesn't it? But once you start learning how to love other people it gets easier as you go on. The trouble is, some folk never even start.

Incarnation

So how does God get you started in the kindergarten of love? It's no use giving people orders; God tried that, in the Ten Commandments, and nobody paid a blind bit of notice! As every parent knows, the only way to get people to love is to love them. Now God does love us, he always has. How can God get us to understand that? The only way was for God to come to earth and live as one of us, the Son of God but completely human. To show us love in the life of an ideal human being, and hope that it is catching. Then, in case we are in any doubt that God loves us, he has to sacrifice his life for our sake.

Ascension

After that, Jesus had to come to life again to show us that death is not the end. Then he has to return to the paradise he came from, to lead us there. Words are insufficient to describe how much better that life is than this, so we just say it is a higher state of existence, and Jesus 'ascended' to paradise, in inverted commas. Meanwhile, he gave us his Holy Spirit; but more of that next week. All of which is summed up in a memorable saying:

> Jesus came to where we are and became like us, so that we might become like him and go where he is.

143

All-age worship

Draw a strip cartoon of someone falling down a well and another climbing down with a rope to pull the first one out. Label it with the saying above.

Suggested hymns

Hail, thou once despised Jesus; Jesus is Lord! Creation's voice proclaims it; Jesus shall reign; Lord, enthroned in heavenly splendour.

Seventh Sunday of Easter   8 May
(Sunday after Ascension Day)
Second Service   Enthronement Gifts
Ps. 68 Let God arise; Isa. 44.1–8 I will pour my Spirit;
Eph. 4.7–16 Gifts of the ascended Christ; *Gospel at Holy Communion*: Luke 24.44–53 I am sending upon you

> *'When he ascended on high he made captivity itself a captive; he gave gifts to his people.' Ephesians 4.8, citing Psalm 68.18*

Triumph

When a king had won a victory in battle, in ancient times, he would ride through his home town in a procession which was called 'a triumph'. All the enemy soldiers he had taken captive in the battle were chained together and forced to stagger along behind the king's chariot. This was to make everyone who saw it realize how powerful this king was, so that they would take care not to oppose him in the future. To show that they had taken this message on board, local people and representatives of the kingdoms around them would bring gifts of gold and other precious materials to give to the king. Psalm 68 is probably an account of one of these triumph processions, when King David rode into Jerusalem, passing up the small hill known as Mount Zion to the Temple at the top of it, to thank the Lord for helping David to win. That is the context in which you should read this psalm in the Old Testament. In the NRSV translation, it reads:

You ascended the high mount,
leading captives in your train

and receiving gifts from people,
even from those who rebel
against the Lord God's abiding there.

Ephesians

St Paul quoted this psalm in his letter to the Christians in the great city of Ephesus, in what we now call Turkey. In that great city there were Christians from all over the known world. They all believed slightly different things about Jesus, so there had been a lot of squabbling. Paul wrote to them about the importance of unity and love between different members of the Church, despite their different beliefs. Because every Christian, said Paul, has some good qualities, and deserves to be admired by other Christians. But, he emphasized, these good qualities are nothing to boast about, because we didn't achieve them by our own efforts – they are the gift of God. One of our lovely old hymns describes this very well:

Our blest Redeemer, ere he breathed
his tender last farewell
a guide, a Comforter bequeathed
with us to dwell . . .

And every virtue we possess,
and every conquest won,
and every thought of holiness,
are his alone.

Ascension

So Paul quoted the verse from Psalm 68, turning the description of David going up Mount Zion into a reference to Jesus ascending into heaven, when he wanted his disciples to realize they would have to do without seeing him from now on. Though when we think of Jesus ascending, perhaps we should think of a worker being promoted to a 'higher position', rather than of a rocket going up into space, which is not a very helpful image these days. And then Paul boldly changes the Old Testament words from a reference to King David climbing up Mount Zion, and receiving gifts *from* his admirers, into a description of King Jesus, who came down from heaven to save us, now ascending back to heaven and giving gifts *to* us:

When he ascended on high he made captivity itself a captive; he gave gifts to his people.

And that sums up the whole difference between the Old Testament and the New: in the old, a jealous God insists on tribute being paid; in the new, a loving God pours out his gifts on those who love him.

Gifts

So whatever task God calls you to do, he will always provide you with the talents and qualities you need. This may be in the church, where you are being encouraged to become a member of a church committee, or help in the Sunday school, or arrange the flowers, and you have turned it down because you say that you do not have the necessary talents. Or God may be calling you to take on a task in the community around, whether a paid post or a voluntary one, to care for the needy, or help the children, or make government or business work more fairly, and you are reluctant to put yourself forward, because you think it is not your scene, and you couldn't cope with the demands it would make upon you. You are wrong; if God wants you to do it, he will give you the skills you need, and strengthen you to cope with problems. At the ascension, Jesus did not abandon this world, but he continues working here today, through his Holy Spirit, who brings life-changing qualities to you and me, so that we can quietly get on with the job of changing the world for him.

Suggested hymns

All hail the power of Jesus' name; At the name of Jesus; Our blest Redeemer, ere he breathed; The head that once was crowned with thorns.

Day of Pentecost (Whit Sunday)   15 May
Principal Service   **That's the Spirit!**
Acts 2.1–21 The day of Pentecost (*must be used as either the first or second reading*), *or* Gen. 11.1–9 The tower of Babylon; Ps. 104.26–36, 37b The Spirit in creation; Rom. 8.14–17 Adoption,

or Acts 2.1–21 The day of Pentecost; John 14.8–17 [25–27] The Spirit of truth

> *'[Jesus said to his disciples,] "I will ask the Father, and he will give you another Advocate, to be with you forever . . . You know him, because he abides with you, and he will be in you."' John 14.16–17*

Factory scene

The boss of the factory has given his workers a difficult task to do. They are all grumbling, full of negative comments: 'I couldn't do that! Far too difficult! Nobody could do as tricky a thing as that! The job's far too hard!' And so on and so on. Then one young apprentice steps forward, saying 'I am sure *I* can do it!' So the boss pats the apprentice on the back, saying '*That's* the spirit!'

Motivation

It is perfectly obvious what the boss means, though it is not a phrase we hear very often, alas! He is welcoming his apprentice's enthusiasm, meaning 'That is the right attitude!' Or, to use language that is too posh, even for most bosses: 'What you have just said gives preferred evidence of your high motivation.' Or something like that. Yet that confidence hasn't come out of nowhere. If the lad had been a cocky, conceited boaster, the boss would have recognized it at once. No, someone must have urged him to have a go at anything. 'You never know what you're capable of till you try' is the sort of thing that confidence-builders say. And it's true. But that sort of confidence is not natural. It only comes if someone encourages you. And not many people do that, these days.

Comforter

Jesus warned his disciples that they had hard times ahead of them, and difficult decisions to make. But he promised them that they would not be alone. He would give them the Holy Spirit. The word used in St John's Gospel for the Holy Spirit literally means someone called to your side. The old translations of the Bible called the Spirit 'the Comforter', but that word is far too cosy these days; in former days it meant 'fortifier' or 'strengthener'. Modern translations sometimes use the word 'Advocate', someone who is called to your side to speak for you, or 'Helper', someone called to assist you. God's Spirit doesn't take away your free will; the decisions are all yours; but the Spirit encourages you to have a go, and then gives you the inner strength, enabling you to succeed, more often than not, at things you had previously thought were beyond your capability. Then your Heavenly Boss, as well as your earthly supervisor, will pat you on your back and say, 'That's the Spirit!'

Recognizing

So we should learn to recognize the presence of God's Holy Spirit in our own lives, and in the lives of others. Whenever you decide to have a go at something difficult for the sake of other people, knowing in your heart of hearts that it is really too hard for you – and then to your surprise, and possibly to everyone else's, you pull it off – then you must say to yourself, 'Honest, that weren't me what done it; *that's the Spirit.*' Frequently I write a sermon which looks like a disaster on the page. 'The congregation's going to hate this,' I tell myself; 'it'll bore them to tears.' But I can't see how to improve it, so I say a quick prayer to the Holy Spirit, and put all I've got into delivering it in a meaningful way. Then someone comes up to me afterwards and says it was the best sermon they have heard for weeks, just what they needed to hear. Then to stop me being proud, they tell me what they heard, and it turns out they haven't heard what I intended to say at all, but something else that God wanted them to hear. So all I can say is, 'That wasn't me. That's the Spirit!' Ask yourself, hasn't that happened to you sometimes, in the different things you decide to have a shot at? Someone praises you for the encouraging remarks you uttered, or the beautiful thing you crafted, or the lovely letter you wrote. And you know full well you could not have done it on your own. So we must learn to recognize the presence of the Spirit when our third-rate efforts produce glorious results. But don't forget to pray for God's help, and to thank him when he has given it. That's right. That's the Spirit!

All-age worship

Draw some of the difficult things you have done this week, and write, 'Thank you, God, for helping me'.

Suggested hymns

Breathe on me, breath of God; Come down O Love Divine; Our blest Redeemer, ere he breathed; Spirit of holiness.

Day of Pentecost (Whit Sunday)   15 May
Second Service   The Presence of God

Morning Ps. 36.5–10 In your light we see light, 150 Everything that breathes; Evening Ps. 33.1–12 The breath of his mouth; Ex. 33.7–20 My presence will go with you; 2 Cor. 3.4–18 Letter and Spirit; *Gospel at Holy Communion*: John 16.4b–15 The Spirit of truth

> *'[God said to Moses,] "My presence will go with you, and I will give you rest."' Exodus 33.14*

Exodus

When Moses led the Israelites out of Egypt, they felt very alone. So God went before them in the form of a pillar of cloud by day and a pillar of fire by night. That was reassuring, but not very comforting. You can't have a personal relationship with a column of smoke! So Moses put up a tent, and told the people that God was inside it. He called it 'the Tabernacle of the Presence'. Every morning when the people broke camp, Moses would take down the tent, which they carried with them when they set off on the day's march, and then he would pitch it again where they stopped, some distance outside the camp. 'If you want to talk to God,' Moses told them, 'all you have to do is walk to the empty tent outside the camp, and you will know that God is there, and you can talk to him.' But that was hardly any better. The Lord used to 'speak to Moses face to face, as one speaks to a friend'. But for the rest of them, it was scarcely any easier to have a conversation with an empty tent than with a fiery pillar. They put the stone tablets with the Ten Commandments written on them in a box, called the 'Ark of the Covenant', to remind them that God had made a promise, or a covenant, to be with them always if they kept the Commandments. They carried the tent with them during their wanderings until they reached Jerusalem, where the tent was replaced by the Temple which Solomon built. But only the High Priest was able to enter the Holy of Holies where the Ark of the Covenant stood, and that only once a year.

Jesus

When Jesus was born, St John's Gospel says that the Word of God became flesh and dwelt among us. The word translated as 'dwelt' literally means God 'pitched his tent' among us. *Now* people could talk to God 'face to face, as one speaks to a friend'. But they hanged him on a cross outside the city walls, or, like the Tent of the Presence, 'outside the camp'.

The Holy Spirit

It was wonderful that Jesus brought the presence of God down to earth. But by becoming human, he was limited to one time and place, so that the crowds would be impossible if everybody wanted to speak to him at once. And he also became mortal; like the rest of us, he was bound to die one day. So Jesus promised us another Comforter: the Holy Spirit of God, present with us, and dwelling in us. If you trust Jesus, and call him your friend, his Spirit is with you always, everywhere, and you can talk to him whenever you want to. You can't see the Holy Spirit, admittedly; but you can be sure he is there in your heart, by the effect the Spirit has on your life. All those kind deeds which you couldn't or wouldn't do before, but are now eager to do, out of gratitude for what Jesus has done for you. All the things you wanted to say to encourage people, which you couldn't say before because you were scared, you now manage to find words for – haltingly, admittedly, but that makes them more effective, because people can see you are inspired to speak sincerely out of your own experience, not from a prepared script.

In your heart

So the place of meeting, the place where the Lord speaks with you face to face, as one speaks to a friend, is not in a pillar of cloud, or in a tent 'outside the camp', nor in a temple. It's right there, in your heart. God said, 'My presence will go with you, and I will give you rest.' And Jesus said the Holy Spirit is like the wind: you can't see the wind, but you can see and hear its effects. That makes you certain of its presence. Similarly, you can see the effects of the Spirit in people's lives. You don't need a great emotional conversion, or speaking with tongues, to know that God's Spirit is in your heart; just look to see if you are slowly becoming a kinder person. That's all the proof you need that God is present with you, Father, Son and Holy Spirit, in the trials of the day and the loneliness of the night. May the Spirit bless you.

Suggested hymns

Come, Holy Ghost, our souls inspire; Gracious Spirit, Holy Ghost; O thou who camest from above; Wind, wind, blow on me.

Trinity Sunday   22 May
Principal Service   **Lead Us Into All Truth**

Prov. 8.1–4, 22–31 Wisdom in creation; Ps. 8 Stewardship of nature; Rom. 5.1–5 God's love and Spirit; John 16.12–15 Spirit, Father and Jesus

> *'Does not wisdom call, and does not understanding raise her voice? . . . [saying,] '"The Lord created me at the beginning of his work, the first of his acts of long ago . . . then I was beside him, like a master worker; and I was daily his delight, rejoicing before him always, rejoicing in his inhabited world and delighting in the human race."' Proverbs 8.1, 22, 30–31*

Wisdom

In the book of Proverbs, in the Holy Bible, God's wisdom speaks, telling how she has assisted God in the creation, and been a teacher of the human race. Even the best pupils cannot learn everything at once; education has to be a slow, gradual process. Christians have always regarded the biblical picture of God's wisdom as a symbol of the Holy Spirit, a part of God, yet able to separate herself off from God the Father, and enter human hearts to teach us more. God is infinite, so the truth about God is vast. We can never know the whole of it, but we can always learn more than we know now. Jesus, the other partner in the Holy Trinity, himself said,

When the Spirit of truth comes, he will guide you into all the truth; for he will not speak on his own, but will speak whatever he hears, and he will declare to you the things that are to come.

So if we open ourselves to the Spirit, we shall never stop learning more and more about the character of the triune God.

Culture

Not only must we learn new truths about God, but the same old unchanging truths which we learnt long ago need to be re-expressed in new words. Every age has a different culture, with its own vocabulary, metaphors and images for expressing the old truths. If this age has turned its back on religion, it is largely our fault, because we are still trying to feed them the faith in the language of an old culture. Jesus conveyed his teaching about the kingdom of God and the Son of Man in terms of the Jewish culture of the Old Testament; St Paul translated it into the Greek culture of the Roman Empire, with words like justification and redemption. The doctrine of the Trinity was an attempt to express the truths of the Bible in a way that would be attractive to those educated in Aristotle's philosophy, in the language of substance and persons. Augustine developed the language of original sin. The first English Bibles had to invent new words like 'atonement'. But none of these terms mean anything to the man and woman in the street today.

Today

Today, most people talk the language of the soap operas, text messages and modern science. Unless we can translate the Christian gospel into a language that they can understand, they will think we are talking obscure old-fashioned nonsense. So, as the Holy Spirit teaches us new ideas about God, we may very well find that they are the old ideas, only in modern words. We must not cling nostalgically to the old way of talking, or we shall kill religion stone dead for the people of this generation. So we need to be bold in writing contemporary words to our hymns and songs, because the old ones are incomprehensible to most people. You should also expect some sermons that use quite bizarre language, because it is the only way to shake people out of their prejudices. Yes, occasionally the words of the sermon may verge on the edge of heresy, but that is no bad thing. God loves to make people sit up and think. The exiled Jews in Babylon thought God was dead because his Temple in Jerusalem had been destroyed, until Ezekiel startled them by suggesting that dry bones can live again. Then St Peter was so hidebound by the Jewish food laws that he wouldn't talk to the Roman centurion, until God gave him a startling dream of unclean animals for him to eat. If the Holy Spirit leads us into new ways of thinking about God, these may not be any truer than the older myths; but if they speak to scientifically educated folk they are worth the risk. The only real heresy is to imagine that your little brain contains the whole truth about God, and anyone who expresses it differently must be wrong.

All-age worship

Find verses in the Gospels where Jesus says God is like a mother hen, a woman searching for a coin, a priceless pearl, a slave-owner, a sower of seed, an over-generous father, a reckless shepherd. What do you think God is like?

Suggested hymns

Bright the vision that delighted; Father of heaven, whose love profound; Holy, holy, holy! Lord God Almighty!; Immortal, invisible, God only wise.

Trinity Sunday   22 May

(For Corpus Christi, the Thursday after Trinity Sunday, see page 320.)

Second Service   The Practice of the Presence of God

Morning Ps. 29 The Lord enthroned; Evening Ps. 73.1–3, 16–28 Hard to understand; Ex. 3.1–15 I AM; John 3.1–17 God so loved

> '[Nicodemus] came to Jesus by night and said to him, "Rabbi, we know that you are a teacher who has come from God; for no one can do these signs that you do apart from the presence of God."'
> John 3.2

Nicodemus

Nicodemus was a Pharisee with an influential government position. It was too dangerous for him to be seen talking to the heretic Jesus of Nazareth, so he visited him secretly in the dark. He was prepared to admit that the healings that Jesus was performing proved 'the presence of God'. Jesus replied, 'No one can see the kingdom of God without being born . . .' either 'again' or 'from above' depending on which translation you use, but both mean making a fresh start in life, totally dependent on God. Jesus spoke of the Father, the Son and the Spirit, which is why this passage is read on Trinity Sunday. Then he spoke words which sum up the whole gospel message: 'God so loved the world that he gave his only Son, so that everyone who believes in him may not perish but may have eternal life.'

Presence

But at least Nicodemus had recognized the *presence of God* when Jesus spoke. The Pharisee must have known that God is always and everywhere present with us, but we forget all about God most of the time. So we often behave as though God cannot see us, and feel as though God is far away. Yet the Pharisee recognized that Jesus was not like that, and that he always spoke and behaved as though he knew that God was invisibly present, beside him. We can all see that, so why shouldn't *we* behave as though God was beside us, too? In my own case, it is because I can't see God. My head tells me he must be here, but I don't *feel* his presence. To which Jesus would reply – with a smile, I am sure – 'If your brain tells you that God is probably present, why don't you put your doubts aside and try *behaving* as though God is present, whatever your treacherous and unreliable feelings tell you?'

Brother Lawrence

And that reminds me of the famous book by Brother Lawrence entitled *The Practice of the Presence of God*. This is a collection, assembled by Father Joseph de Beaufort, of the teachings of a seventeenth-century Carmelite monk known as Brother Lawrence, though his name before he entered the monastery was Nicholas Herman. It contains letters he wrote, together with memories of his conversations written down by his friends. It is a very practical, simple book, recommending that we always behave as though we were sure that God is with us, no matter how feeble our faith and unpredictable our feelings. At the age of 18 he was converted, when he realized that through God's providence, the trees whose leaves had died in winter would return to new life each spring. He became a monk when he reached 24, and stayed at the monastery in Paris till he died in 1691, aged about 86. Let me read you an extract, so that you can see how doing as he suggests would transform your life.

Quotation

The time of action does not differ from that of prayer. I possess God as peacefully in the bustle of my kitchen, where sometimes several people are asking me for different things at the same time, as I do upon my knees before the Blessed Sacrament. This *practice of the presence of God* must stem from the heart, from love. Love does everything, and it is not necessary to have great things to do. I turn my little omelette in the pan for the love of God. When it is finished, if I have nothing to do, I prostrate myself on the ground and worship my God, who gave me this grace to make it, after which I arise happier than a king. When I can do nothing else, it is enough to have picked up a straw for the love of God. People look for ways of learning how to love God. They hope to attain it by I know not how many different practices. They take much trouble to abide in his presence by varied means. Is it not a shorter and a more direct way *to do everything for the love of God*, to make use of all the tasks one's lot in life demands, to show him that love, and to maintain his presence within by the communion of our hearts with his? There is nothing complicated about it. One only has to turn to it honestly and simply.

Suggested hymns

Father, we love you; Firmly I believe and truly; Teach me, my God and king; Thank you, O my Father.

ORDINARY TIME

The Sundays after Trinity Sunday are not related to specific events in the life of Christ, as those from Advent to Pentecost are; so they are called 'Ordinary Time', and the readings are chosen according to the date, unlike the Collect, which is defined by the number of Sundays after Trinity Sunday. This is just a season of steady growth, which is why the church hangings and vestments are green, the colour of growing things. Nevertheless, the Gospel readings work through the four Gospels in a fairly systematic way, and this year is the Year of Luke. The Epistle has a similar theme to that of the Gospel; but there is a choice between two series of Old Testament readings and psalms. The first series of Old Testament readings and psalms given from Proper 4 to Proper 25 is the 'Continuous' sequence, which works through a particular book in the Old Testament for a while, and then follows a different one; the second one is the 'Related' Sequence, where the Old Testament reading and the psalm both have a similar theme to that of the Epistle and Gospel readings. Some churches do not have an Old Testament reading, which is a shame, so it is unwise to plan a sermon on the Old Testament reading or psalm in Ordinary Time unless you are sure which sequence that church is following this year. Preachers are allowed to choose readings which are not from the lectionary, especially if you plan to give a series of sermons on a particular theme, but you should be sure that the organist and those who read the Scriptures and who lead the intercessions are told well in advance of any changes, so that they can plan accordingly. You can list next Sunday's readings on the weekly service sheet if you have one, to give people fair warning. And to welcome newcomers to the church, say a few words of introduction to each reading – perhaps expanded from those given to each reading in this book – explaining why it is relevant to us.

First Sunday after Trinity (Proper 4)   29 May
Principal Service   **A Letter TO Paul FROM the Galatians**
(*Continuous*): 1 Kings 18.20–21 [22–29] 30–39 Elijah and Baal, Ps. 96 Praise God all nations; *or* (*Related*): 1 Kings 8.22–23, 41–43 Solomon's Prayer, Ps. 96.1–9 God's greatness; Gal. 1.1–12 No other gospel; Luke 7.1–10 Healing a centurion's boy

'Paul an apostle . . . To the churches of Galatia . . . I am astonished that you are so quickly deserting the one who called you in the grace of Christ and are turning to a different gospel.' Galatians 1.1–2, 6

Each of the Letters of St Paul to particular churches in the New Testament was written for a reason. He must have been answering questions which that church had asked in a letter to him. We now know that the Governor of Cyprus, who converted to Christianity because of Paul's preaching, had relations in Pisidian Antioch, in Galatia. Here's an imaginary letter which one of them might have written to St Paul:

From Lucius Sergius Paulus the younger, Governor of the Southern Galatia Province, to Paul the missionary. Greetings.

I have a problem, sir. It was very good of you to visit this out-of-the-way provincial capital. But we need your guidance. Please tell us, how should non-Jewish Christians behave?

I reckon it was because of my dad, the Governor of Cyprus, that you came here. He writes in his letters that you completely changed his life! Perhaps that's why you decided to adopt our family name. I bet he chatted to you about the Empire. How far it reaches, how a messenger, supplied with fast horses at each stage, can travel the Roman roads from end to end of the Empire in just over a month. Just think what an influence the Christian religion could have if a little cell of Christians was planted in each of the provincial capitals, to spread out from there. So my guess is that Dad gave you a vision: visit each provincial capital in turn. So you started here in Antioch-in-the-sticks!

Now, please can you solve the problem that's cropped up? We are being torn apart over the issue. Before long there will be two separate groups of Christians in Galatia, not speaking to each other.

The first place you went when you got here was the synagogue. Poky little place, isn't it? We non-Jews, gathered outside the windows, only heard half of what you said. We understood that this Jesus you preached about had died and come alive again. If that's true, you will have the whole Empire grovelling at your feet, begging to be saved. Coming back to life when you have died is a better bet, any day, than Charon's ferry-boat to Hades. But the Jews saw their position as a privileged minority vanishing into thin air if everybody became Jewish. So they drove you out of town when my back was turned.

157

When you came back, you turned to us Gentiles. Taught us to worship the one true God. Well you had my vote there, at least your God's got some dignity, not like the randy lot on Mount Olympus. So I was happy to be baptized and join this new 'Christian' religion, because it seems quite tolerant.

But a few months after you left, some Jewish Christians came all the way up here from Jerusalem, trying to undo all the good that you'd done. It's not enough to be sympathetic to Jesus, like I am, they said. God's covenant is with the Jewish people, by circumcision. Salvation and resurrection are only for those who have been circumcised. I ask you, at my age? Out of action for a month after an operation on the most sensitive part of . . . Not on your life! And then 'You've got to keep all the commandments,' they whined, 'you've got to keep all the commandments!' How did they think I was going to do that? And never eat pork? Most of the social functions of the town are held in one or other of the temples. I'd be ruling myself out of civic life and cutting myself off from my friends if I kept the Jewish law. We Gentiles couldn't do it. Then Christianity would become a branch of Judaism, and under persecution it would soon die out. What chance of uniting the Roman Empire then?

If your Jesus was the teacher of love you say he was, then there's a place even for me among those who have faith in him. But if your god's only interested in those who keep strictly to the Jewish law, then there's no hope of resurrection for any of us. Please, Paul, write to us and give us your advice.

Yours,

Lucius Sergius Paulus (the younger)

All-age worship

Search Google images for Pisidian Antioch. Notice especially the remains of the aqueduct, the stone inscribed with the name of Sergius Paulus, and the reconstruction of the temple gateway, which can be printed and coloured in.

Suggested hymns

God is working his purpose out; In Christ there is no east or west; We have a gospel to proclaim.

First Sunday after Trinity (Proper 4)   29 May
Second Service   **Disciples**
Ps. 39 Let me know my end; Gen. 4.1–16 Cain and Abel; Mark 3.7–19 The Twelve

> *'Jesus departed with his disciples to the sea, and a great multitude from Galilee followed him . . . And he appointed twelve, whom he also named apostles, to be with him, and to be sent out to proclaim the message.'* Mark 3.7, 14

The Twelve

Jesus appointed 12 men to follow him and be particularly close to him. Some people call them 'the twelve disciples', and others 'the twelve apostles'. Both titles are misleading, because both terms were applied by the Bible to other people who were not members of 'the Twelve'. There were many disciples; the word means a 'learner', and applies to all the followers of Jesus, male and female. There were other apostles, who were not members of the Twelve – St Paul, and his friend St Barnabas, were known as 'apostles'; and in his Letter to the Romans, St Paul sends greetings to several other apostles, of whom at least one, Junia, was a woman. 'Apostle' means someone who is *sent out* as a witness of the resurrection; in other words a missionary. Today's reading tells us that Jesus appointed 12 men, 'to be with him, and to be sent out to proclaim the message'. The significance of the number 12 was that, in the Old Testament, Jacob had 12 sons, who became the ancestors of the 12 tribes of Israel. Just as Jacob's sons became the foundation of the nation of Israel, so these 12 men were the foundation of the Christian Church. Jesus says he had chosen them to bring others, who were seeking to learn more about Jesus, or 'make disciples from every nation'.

Disciples

As I said, the word disciple means a 'learner'. You are a disciple; at least, I hope so, if you are committed to learning more and more about Jesus as time goes on. So you should acknowledge that you don't know everything about him yet, but you are filled with a burning curiosity to know more. By their commitment to learning, the disciples were distinguished from the crowd – those who follow Jesus from interest, but never make up their mind. Jesus fed the crowd, but was sad for them, because their non-committal attitude contributed nothing to the growth of his kingdom. So that is why I hope and pray that all of you have decided, or will decide today, to follow Jesus and share in the happiness and contentment which that brings.

The cost of discipleship

But make no mistake, the cost of discipleship keeps rising year by year. Jesus said, 'Take up your cross and follow me.' This seldom means you will be physically crucified; but you are likely to be opposed and ridiculed because you are a disciple of Jesus. And you will have to 'deny yourself', as Jesus put it; that means you must not be self-centred, but make what Jesus wants you to do the centre of your life. Being a *disciple* means being self-*disciplined*:

1 Learning from Jesus by reading the Bible regularly.
2 Setting aside time to talk to him in prayer.
3 Making time to meet with other disciples to learn together and to worship him.
4 Giving your time to serving other people.
5 Doing whatever it takes to attract other people to want to learn from Jesus.

This is a demanding lifestyle. But it is much more fun than being selfish. His disciples often failed Jesus at moments of crisis. If we can learn from our failures as disciples, they can actually become growth points, in which we learn that our worth to Jesus lies not in what we can achieve on our own, but in how we allow him to work through us.

Decision and commitment

But you never drift into being a disciple of Jesus. At some point you have to make a positive decision to stick with him, at all costs. Maybe you did that years ago, but the fizz has gone out of your discipleship. Maybe you doubt some of the things that Jesus taught; but that is no obstacle to putting your trust in him, believing that Jesus will make everything clear in the end. Maybe you are still hovering on the brink of decision, thereby denying yourself the unspeakable joy of knowing that Jesus loves you and has a plan for the rest of your life that will bring you job-satisfaction as a disciple that you never knew while you dithered. Commit yourself, or recommit yourself to Jesus, now, and promise to go on learning from him as long as you live. Or come and talk to me afterwards. Don't be afraid, Jesus said, 'My yoke is easy, and my burden is light.' He will give you all the strength of character that you need, to become a fine disciple that he can be proud of.

Suggested hymns

Dear Lord and Father of mankind; Disposer supreme and judge of the earth; Father, hear the prayer we offer; Take up thy cross, the Saviour said.

Second Sunday after Trinity (Proper 5) 5 June
Principal Service **Closure**
(*Continuous*): 1 Kings 17.8–16 [17–24] The widow's jar, Ps. 146 God upholds the widows; *or* (*Related*): 1 Kings 17.17–24 Elijah heals the widow's child, Ps. 30 Resurrection from death; Gal. 1.11–24 Paul's conversion and authority; Luke 7.11–17 The widow's son at Nain

> *'I did not confer with any human being . . . but I went away at once into Arabia, and afterwards I returned to Damascus. Then after three years I did go up to Jerusalem to visit Cephas and . . . James . . . Then I went into the regions of Syria and Cilicia.'* Galatians 1.16–19, 21

Dealing with the past

St Paul was a brave man. First he persecuted the Christians; then he was converted. Next he visited each of the places where he was virulently hated. First he went to Arabia, to be alone, think and pray. He concluded that God had chosen him to spread Christianity, not to destroy it. But *his* job was to convert, not his own race, the Jews, but the pagan idol-worshipping inhabitants of the Roman Empire. That infuriated many Jews, including Jewish Christians, who thought God had contracted with Abraham to save the Jews, by destroying every other race. Then Paul returned to Damascus, where he went after seeing a vision of the risen Christ. On that occasion the Christians there thought he was coming to destroy them; he said he was a changed man, but could they believe him? So he went there a second time, after he was converted, to deal with his former enemies face to face. Next he went to Jerusalem, where his former supporters thought he had betrayed them, and the Christians blamed him for moving the goalposts. Paul stayed with St Peter, arguing all night with him and St James, leaders of the Jerusalem church, who feared that Paul was planning to undermine their authority. But Paul assured them that God had made them missionaries to the Jews, while he was a missionary to the other races. Then Paul travelled to Tarsus, where he was brought up. His boyhood friends would think he was mad, and dismiss his beliefs with mockery and anger. Surely Paul could have found safer places to go at the beginning of his work? But Paul knew that the past has to be faced up to and dealt with.

Conscience

If you have done bad things at some time – and who hasn't? – memories of them will haunt your conscience for the rest your life, if you don't deal with them. A folk song tells of an army captain who 'seduced a maid who hanged herself one Monday in her garters. His naughty conscience troubled him, he lost his stomach daily; he took to drinking ratafia and thought upon Miss Bailey: "Oh, Miss Bailey, unfortunate Miss Bailey."' The song is meant to be funny, but it is uncomfortably true to life. You may tell yourself you have forgotten all about your misdeeds, but on a sleepless night you realize you can never forget them until you face up to them.

Solutions

The first step is to stop kidding yourself, and admit to yourself that you have done, and maybe are still doing, wrong things. Then get down on your knees and tell God you are sorry, and ask him what you should do. The obvious thing is to go to the person you have hurt and apologize; it takes courage, but it's worth it. But in some circumstances that may not be possible or wise. Miss Bailey was dead, so it was too late. And if you have flirted with somebody, then jilted them, and they have kept it secret, they won't thank you for making it public now. Maybe a private letter will do, provided nobody else knows about it.

Closure

The purpose of all this is that the person you hurt, and you yourself, should be able to deal with your past and lay it to rest. This is something like what the psychiatrists call 'closure'. Closure may be sought by a bereaved person who needs to accept that their loved one has gone, and that they will meet again in heaven. Or by someone who has been offended, and wants the offender to confess and be punished; and the offender may also need closure before they can sleep at night. I think Paul's visits to people who mistrusted him showed a need for closure, on his part and theirs; and it is a need that we all have at some time in our lives. Confessing our wrongdoings to the all-forgiving God is always the first step.

All-age worship

Tell God, by whispering into an empty jam jar, about times you have been naughty. Then smash the jar and dispose of it safely. Nobody else will know, but you will feel happier.

Suggested hymns

And can it be that I should gain?; God forgave my sin in Jesus' name; There's a wideness in God's mercy; To God be the glory.

Second Sunday after Trinity (Proper 5)   5 June
Second Service   Parables
Ps. 44 Come to our help; Gen. 8.15—9.17 God's covenant with Noah; Mark 4.1–20 Parable of the sower

'[Jesus] began to teach them many things in parables.' Mark 4.2

Open-air

The ministry of Jesus began in the synagogue, but this tied him down, for he was not free to say what he was thinking. So, very soon, we find him preaching by the lakeside, in the open-air. John Wesley preached for many years in the Church of England, and was, as he put it, 'so tenacious of every point relating to decency and order, that I should have thought the saving of souls almost a sin if it had not been done in a church'. But his friend George Whitfield was preaching in the open to sometimes as many as 20,000 miners at a time, and Wesley soon realized this was the only way the Church would grow in the eighteenth century. I wonder what he would have said in the twenty-first? But if we wish to win the crowds for Christ, we must think of new ways of appealing to them. For Jesus, this was the parable.

Parables

The Greek word 'parable' means something thrown alongside something else; in other words a comparison. Parables are often called earthly stories with a heavenly meaning. Now that we have stopped binding our Bibles in black, we realize that many of the parables were funny stories. Jesus chose to use these tales in his preaching, because they aroused people's interest and held their attention. Nathan the prophet told a parable when he wanted King David to admit to stealing Uriah's wife Bathsheba. He described a poor man who had only one ewe lamb left in his flock, and a neighbour who took even that away. 'Such a man deserves to die,' exploded King David, and then realized he had been trapped into condemning himself. The virtue of fiction is that it enables people to think about abstract ideas in a concrete logical way, by a comparison with down-to-earth facts. But, most important of all, the parable forces people to think for themselves. If you lecture people, telling them what they ought to do, most of them will do the opposite. But if they have worked the moral of the story out for themselves, there is no getting away from it.

The sower

So Jesus told a story of a farmer sowing seed, which was done by hand in those days, dipping one hand into the seed-basket, which you carried on a strap round your neck, and scattering it beside you as you walk. This meant that it fell randomly on different types of soil. Some fell on well-trodden earth beside the road; some on shallow soil where the bedrock was only a few inches down. Some fell where thorns were growing up; but mercifully some did fall on good soil and produced many plump ears of wheat. Now comes the comparison: *it's like that when you tell people about God.* Some of your words enter minds that have already been hardened by thinking only about money, and never about feelings; so the ideas never take root. Other ideas will grow for a while in your listeners' hearts, but they are shallow people, and so busy that they forget about them, and the good feelings shrivel up and die. Some ideas start growing well, but their lust – for sex, wealth and power – grows even faster than their good intentions and chokes them to death. But some of the ideas about God, which you shared, fell into receptive hearts, where they grow healthily, producing love for God and their neighbours, because you told them that God loves them.

The crunch

Now comes the crunch! Many ideas about how to live a good life have been sown, through the Bible, teachers and preachers, in *your* heart. *What sort of soil are you?* Are you a well-trodden materialist? Or a shallow, busy soul? Or does the desire for sex, money or power choke all your good resolutions before they come to fruition? OK, let's hope all of you are good soil, and the words of Jesus are growing healthily in your soul. *But is that every day, or only sometimes?* Each of us needs to be on guard against insidious worldly standards of work, work; money, money. By a form of osmosis, these standards can easily seep into our own soul, too. So you must make your minds receptive to the message of love, and put it into practice. There, you wouldn't have thought of that if I had read you a lecture. But instead, I told you a story, and you worked it out for yourself, didn't you? Then, in the words of the Master Storyteller, 'Go, and do thou likewise.'

Suggested hymns

Break thou the bread of life; God has spoken to his people, alleluia; Tell me the old, old story; Tell me the stories of Jesus.

Third Sunday after Trinity (Proper 6) 12 June
Principal Service **The Jackpot**
(*Continuous*): 1 Kings 21.1–10 [11–14] 15–21a Naboth's vineyard, Ps. 5.1–8 God's justice; *or* (*Related*): 2 Sam. 11.26—12.10,

13–15 David's repentance, Ps. 32 Forgiveness; Gal. 2.15–21
Law, faith and grace; Luke 7.36—8.3 A woman's repentance

> *'We have come to believe in Christ Jesus, so that we might be justified by faith in Christ, and not by doing the works of the law, because no one will be justified by the works of the law.'*
> *Galatians 2.16*

The jackpot

A man died and reached the pearly gates of heaven, where St Peter met him. 'Tell me all the good things you have done,' said St Peter, 'and I'll give you points for each item, according to how good it was.' 'Well,' began the man proudly, 'I went to church almost every Sunday all my life, and supported the church's ministry with my money and my time.' 'That's splendid,' said St Peter. 'That's certainly worth one point.' 'Only one point?' asked the man, who had expected 50 points at least. 'Well then, I started a food centre for poor people in my town, and worked in a shelter for homeless people.' 'Terrific!' said St Peter, 'I'll give you two points for that.' 'Only TWO POINTS!' exploded the man. 'At this rate the only way I shall get into heaven will be by the grace of God!' 'Wonderful!' beamed the Saint. 'You've hit the jackpot! Come on in!'

Achievements

The point of the story is that God's goodness and overflowing love for each one of us counts far more than what we have achieved. Of course, it's good to aim high, and try to succeed in doing good deeds for God and for other people. But if we become proud of our achievements, they are having the contrary effect from what we are aiming for. Jesus said that only two things are necessary: sacrificial love for God and unselfish love for our neighbours. Yet if our achievements make us proud and complacent, we become self-centred, and that is the very opposite of what Jesus asks of us.

Love

Love means forgetting ourselves, trampling on our pride and conceitedness, and putting other people and their needs at the focus-point of our lives. Love is giving up our own wishes and our own vanity; not making other people feel inferior, but giving ourselves selflessly to praising other people and building up their self-respect. When you do good things for other people, said Jesus in memorable words, 'don't let your left hand know what your right hand is doing! That way, your kindnesses may be done in secret; and your Father who sees what you do in secret will reward you.'

Happiness

Of course, some of the people you help will know who it is who gives their time to caring for them, and will praise you for it, never mind how often you ask them not to. They may have learnt, as you have, that the greatest thing you can do for somebody is to build up their self-respect. And that will make you happy; there's nothing wrong in that. But you mustn't let it make you conceited and proud. You should be able to look back at your life and say, 'What wonderful things God has helped me to do', and give all the praise to him.

Grace

The word the Bible uses for God giving you the power to do things *with his help* that you couldn't have done without him is 'grace'. We use another version of the same word when we say that God's love and forgiveness is given to us 'free, gratis and for nothing'. Secondly, grace also means the power to love our neighbours. God gives us this power, when we allow his Holy Spirit to dwell within us and work through us. God, in his grace, loves us and lets his love flow through us onto other people. It's as though God uses us as his tools to do the loving for him, not in our own strength but as a consequence of knowing that God loves *us*. And there is no room for conceitedness or pride in knowing that.

Justified

The phrase St Paul repeats over and over in his letters is that 'we are justified by God's grace, through our faith in God, not through the good works that we achieve'. 'Justified' is an almost untranslatable word; but the simplest way of putting it is to say that it is when God in his kindness declares us 'not guilty' when we really are guilty. As soon as we acknowledge that that is so, that is the end of complacency and pride – and bingo! We hit the jackpot, and gain our free entry ticket into heaven.

All-age worship

Learn, 'Patience is a virtue, virtue is a grace; Both put together make a very pretty face'.

Suggested hymns

Amazing grace, how sweet the sound; God moves in a mysterious way; God of mercy, God of grace; Rock of ages, cleft for me

Third Sunday after Trinity (Proper 6)   12 June
Second Service   Light under a Bushel
Ps. 52 A tree in God's house [53 Fools say]; Gen. 13 Abram and Lot; Mark 4.21–41 Parables and a storm

> *'[Jesus] said to them, "Is a lamp brought in to be put under the bushel basket, or under the bed, and not on the lampstand? For there is nothing hidden, except to be disclosed; nor is anything secret, except to come to light."' Mark 4.21–22*

Bushels

Most people are familiar with the phrase 'hiding your light under a bushel'. Far fewer know exactly what a bushel is. Some still think it is another word for a small bush, though hiding an electric torch under a holly bush would be a prickly operation, and doing the same with a candle might present a fire hazard. Older people remember that schoolchildren used to learn tables of weights and measures:

    2 pints = 1 quart
    4 quarts = 1 gallon
    2 gallons = 1 peck
    4 pecks = 1 bushel

These of course were the units of dry measure, measuring the volume of a load of seeds, such as wheat grains. They are not to be confused with the liquid measure, which sold you a pipkin of ale, or a firkin, or a hogshead, a tun, or a butt; or with measuring wood by the cord. And these are imperial measures, which are different from the metric or American measures.

Lights

It was Jesus who coined the phrase about hiding lights under bushels. What were the lights he was referring to? In his day, electric light was more than 1,800 years in the future, and even beeswax or tallow candles were still unheard of, so all the lamps were oil lamps. The lamp in the Roman Empire and most other parts of the ancient world was usually made of orange-coloured clay, formed into a shape rather like a small teapot, partially flattened and with no lid. The olive oil was poured in where the lid should be, and a string of cotton soaked up the oil inside the lamp and passed it up through the 'spout' to where the string, now called the wick, was set alight, giving out a fairly bright flame and a lot of smoke.

Hiding

The bushel measure was made of close basketwork, through which neither the corn nor any light could escape. Most agricultural families would keep a bushel basket in their house, to measure the produce of their fields when they sold it, and maybe the seeds they bought from other suppliers to make bread with, in which case the measure you give will be the measure you get. If you turned a bushel basket upside down and put your oil lamp under it, no light would escape, and soon the lamp would go out because of lack of oxygen. So who would do such a silly thing? Nobody but a stupid idiot, that's the joke. The purpose of the lamp is to give light to the whole house. And the purpose of the teaching which Jesus gave is to give understanding to the whole world. Anyone who keeps that teaching to themselves, without sharing it, would be a stupid idiot, missing the point altogether. A lamp is for illuminating, and the knowledge of God is for spreading – so don't be daft: use them for what they were intended for, instead of keeping them to yourself.

169

Lampstands

In a rich household the lampstand might have been a wooden table or a metal bracket; in most homes it was a simple recess in the clay wall, with a ledge to put the oil lamp on. The lampstand for the teaching of Jesus is your mouth, your loving words, your good deeds, the kindness of your personality. All around the ancient world there were so-called mystery religions – secret societies, which would only tell you their secret revelation of the truth about the world, the universe and everything, if you went through a long and unpleasant purification ceremony, and paid a hefty fee to the priests. Some Christians tried to imitate this, pretending that they had a secret knowledge that could only be revealed to the initiates. They called themselves 'Gnostics', from the Greek word for knowledge; and they wrote some of the apocryphal Gospels which are discovered from time to time, with phony 'new truths' about Jesus. No, the true gospel should shine out like a lighthouse. Never miss a chance to talk about your experience of Jesus, whenever you sense that people are willing to listen. And otherwise, show his light to them by the way you live your life. Don't, whatever happens, try to keep that light hidden, under a bushel or anything else. That would be idiotic. Light is for shining, and the good news of Jesus is for sharing. Don't leave that task to others; the reason you were given those ideas is so that you should share them as widely as you can.

Suggested hymns

Give me oil in my lamp; Hail, gladdening light; Lead kindly light; Sometimes a light surprises.

Fourth Sunday after Trinity (Proper 7) 19 June
Principal Service Law
(*Continuous*): 1 Kings 19.1–4 [5–7] 8–15a The still small voice, Ps. 42 and 43 Faith and hope; *or* (*Related*): Isa. 65.1–9 God's judgement, Ps. 22.19–28 Salvation; Gal. 3.23–29 The law our tutor till faith comes; Luke 8.26–39 Demons sent into pigs

> *'The law was our disciplinarian until Christ came . . . But now that faith has come, we are no longer subject to a disciplinarian, for in Christ Jesus you are all children of God through faith.'* Galatians 3.24–26

Pedagogue

In the translation I have just read from, St Paul says that the law was our 'disciplinarian', but only until Christ came. That sounds like a fiercely strict schoolteacher, and the word Paul used corresponds to our word 'pedagogue'. But in the Roman Empire the pedagogue was the slave who escorted his master's children to school. He didn't teach them, but he led them to where they could learn, and showed them that it was wise to go there regularly, even when they didn't feel like it. Children then were much the same as they are today. You have to set boundaries to their behaviour, to teach them that if they step over the boundaries they will suffer for it. But, provided they are given a bit of discipline in the early years, they will soon learn to discipline themselves.

Temporary

But the disciplinarian's job was a temporary one. You cannot treat adolescents as if they were still children. You have to leave them free to make their own decisions. They will kick over the traces, cross the boundaries and make mistakes. But if you teach them self-respect, they will learn from their mistakes. So, says St Paul, the law of the Old Testament was a temporary measure. It teaches us that God cares about whether we treat each other kindly or unkindly. But when we meet Jesus, the law is no longer relevant. All that matters then is living in a way that pleases him, allowing his love to flow through us into others. And, as St Paul said, 'for such there is no law'.

The Shack

I don't know if you have read a book called *The Shack*, by William Paul Young. It was, and continues to be, a best-seller, because, in a heart-rending but humorous fiction, it tells a story of a man meeting God the Holy Trinity in a shack in the mountains. I haven't the time to unwrap all the symbolism, but there is a passage in which God says he dislikes law, and the man asks God why he gave us the Ten Commandments then. God answers, in effect, that it was in order to drive people to despair who thought they could earn their way into heaven by obeying a set of rules. But for those who live 'under Jesus' 'all things are lawful'. Astonished, the man asks whether that means he doesn't have to obey the rules, and the Holy Spirit replies that we are all free, so long as we allow God to live in us. The man, who is called 'Mack', thinks this freedom is dangerous, and he would prefer everything to be under control. He likes the law, because it gives us some control. But the Holy Spirit says no, you like law because it gives you the power to judge others and feel superior to them. Asked to explain this, she – and the Holy Spirit is feminine in this book – she talks about friendship. If two people are friends, there is an expectancy of being together and laughing and talking together. Expectancy is alive and dynamic. Yet if you change that 'expectancy' into an 'expectation', law enters into the relationship. Friends are then expected to perform in a way that will meet each other's expectations. The living friendship rapidly deteriorates into a dead thing. But if you have no expectations, you can never be disappointed in each other. That is why God is never disappointed in any of us. God prefers living and loving relationships, which he calls verbs, to static rules and regulations, which he calls nouns.

Equality

I can give no more than a summary of what the book called *The Shack* says about law and grace. If you find this hard to follow, buy the book and read it through several times. St Paul said that if we are empowered by God's love, not restricted by God's law, then everybody is equal:

> There is no longer Jew or Greek, there is no longer slave or free, there is no longer male and female; for all of you are one in Christ Jesus.

After 2,000 years, we still haven't fully worked out what that means in practice.

All-age worship

Draw a picture frame and write on it, 'In Jesus all are ='. Inside the frame write 'Women=Men', 'Foreigners=British', 'Workers=Bosses', etc.

Suggested hymns

And can it be?; Come, O thou traveller unknown; For the healing of the nations; In Christ there is no east or west.

Fourth Sunday after Trinity (Proper 7)   19 June
Second Service   **Isaac and Rebekah**

Ps. [50 A sacrifice of thanksgiving] 57 In the shadow of your wings;
Gen. 24.1–27 Isaac and Rebekah; Mark 5.21–43 Jairus' daughter

> *'"Drink, my lord", [Rebekah] said, and quickly lowered her jar upon*
> *her hand and gave [Abraham's servant] a drink. When she had*
> *finished giving him a drink, she said, "I will draw for your camels*
> *also, until they have finished drinking."' Genesis 24.18–19*

Relationships

Rebekah, like so many of us human beings, had many good points
to her character, and a few bad ones. She married Isaac, her first
cousin once removed. Their common ancestor, Terah, lived in Ur
of the Chaldees, at the southern end of Mesopotamia, where the
Tigris and Euphrates rivers join. Two of Terah's sons, Abraham
and Nahor, left home: Abraham, to settle in what was then called
Canaan, which we now call Israel and Palestine; and Nahor, who
made his home in northern Mesopotamia. Isaac was the son of
Abraham, and Rebekah was the daughter of Bethuel the son of
Nahor. In those days, marriages were always arranged by the parents of the couple, with bride and groom never having met until
their wedding day. Abraham felt it was his duty to find a wife for
his son Isaac, but he didn't want him to marry one of the local
Canaanite women. Jews today still try to discourage their children
from 'marrying out of the faith' – with mixed success. Abraham is
too old to travel, so he sends his servant, who is never named in the
Bible, to the city of his nephew Nahor in Mesopotamia.

Matchmaking

Abraham's servant stops by the well outside the city and prays to
the Lord to give him a sign, to indicate which girl would be a suitable wife for his master's son Isaac. Before he has finished praying,
a young girl called Rebekah, whom the Bible describes as 'fair to
look upon', comes out of the enclosure round the well with, on her
shoulder, a jar of water, which she has just drawn for her family
to drink from. When the servant asks Rebekah to give him a drink,
she gladly does so, and then offers to draw more water for this
stranger's camels to drink. He sees that as a sign that this is the

kind and generous girl that the Lord has chosen to be Isaac's wife. This shows that the Lord has very good taste. These days, both men and women tend to choose their partners for their good looks; but far more important is to find someone who is good-natured and kind, not only to their family but to all the people they meet, as this promises a long and happy marriage.

Love

Rebekah then introduced Abraham's servant to her father and brother, and he explained his errand; gifts were exchanged and he stayed the night. Then Rebekah rode back to Canaan with the servant. When they saw a man in the distance, and she learned that it was Isaac, her future husband, she drew a veil over her face, as was the custom, so that he should not see her features until they were wed. They married each other, and then, says the Bible, 'he loved her'. It sounds like a modern soppy romance, but actually it is quite surprising in ancient literature like the book of Genesis. This is the first time in the Bible that the word 'love' is used of the relationship between a man and a woman; the next is between Rebekah's son Jacob, and Rachel, when he worked for 14 years to gain the right to marry her. Otherwise, in Bible times, a man married a woman, and then he 'knew' her, which is a euphemism for having sex together, and then she produced lots of children, fulfilling her only purpose, which was to ensure the survival of the tribe. It sounds as though true love between husband and wife is not natural for human beings, but is something which only grows when they learn that God loves them.

Favouritism

The story of Rebekah continues with her difficulty in conceiving, a problem pregnancy, and the birth of twins who 'fought together in her womb'. But then, in a spectacular fall from grace, Rebekah showed appalling favouritism between her two sons. Her husband favoured Esau but Rebekah favoured Isaac, and advised him how to cheat his elder brother out of his birthright. It is quite unforgivable for parents to show partiality between their children; and in this case it led to war between their descendants for many generations. I am sure God found a way of forgiving Rebekah, but we must not presume on his love. Unlike Rebekah, who was loving to everyone in her young days, but not so loving later, we must continue to be kind to all and sundry throughout our whole lives.

Suggested hymns

Come, O thou traveller unknown; The God of Abraham praise; Thine for ever, God of love; When Jacob with travel was weary one day.

Fifth Sunday after Trinity (Proper 8) 26 June
Principal Service **Church-Going**
(*Continuous*): 2 Kings 2.1–2, 6–14 Elijah's spirit given to Elisha, Ps. 77.1–2, 11–20 Remembering God's saving acts; *or* (*Related*): 1 Kings 19.15–16, 19–21 Elijah calls Elisha, Ps. 16 The path of life; Gal. 5.1, 13–25 The fruit of the Spirit; Luke 9.51–62 Endurance in following Christ

> *'The whole law is summed up in a single commandment, "You shall love your neighbour as yourself."' Galatians 5.14*

St Paul

Some people accuse St Paul of inventing a new religion, which has nothing to do with the simple message of Jesus. But the evidence of St Paul's writings does not support this idea. Jesus himself said that at the heart of his teaching were the two commandments to love God and to love your neighbour. In the passage from St Paul's Letter to the Galatians which was read just now, he emphasizes love, just as Jesus did, and analyses what love means in practice. Somebody who is filled with the Spirit of Jesus, writes Paul, will find loving traits growing in their character, not through any efforts of their own, but naturally, like fruits on a fruit tree. The fruit of the Spirit, says Paul, is love, joy, peace, patience, kindness, goodness, faithfulness, gentleness and self-control.

Proof

Well, 'the proof of the pudding is in the eating'. Is there any evidence that people who call themselves Christians do show those loving characteristics more than other people? Actually there is – sort of – but it is not quite as simple as that. In the year 2000, a ground-breaking book entitled *Bowling Alone* was published by Robert D. Putnam, one of America's greatest sociologists, a political scientist and professor of public policy at the Harvard University School of Government. He is also visiting professor and director of the Manchester University Graduate Summer Programme in Social Change, in this country. The title of the book grew out of his observation that more and more people are going ten-pin bowling these days, but fewer and fewer are joining bowling teams and clubs. They mostly go 'bowling alone'. That, thinks Professor Putnam, is a symptom of the breaking down of social relationships today. Our 'bonds of belonging', which sociologists call our 'social capital', are wearing thin. Politicians have spoken about the 'Big Society', in which expensive government programmes of caring for the needy will be replaced by crowds of volunteers. But they forgot to ask where all these volunteers will come from in an increasingly fragmented society. Ten years later, Putnam published another book identifying signs of hope in those who attend churches, synagogues or similar places of communal worship.

Worshipping together

A survey in the United States between 2004 and 2006 showed that those who regularly worship alongside other people build up bonds with each other and form into a community. Such people are measurably more likely to show active evidence of love in their lives than those who don't. They are more likely to spend time helping a neighbour who is depressed, become leaders in youth organizations, join neighbourhood groups, sing together, participate in local elections and demonstrations. They get involved, turn up and lead. Statistically it is perfectly clear that regular church-goers give more to charities, and do voluntary work for charities, whether the charity is religious or secular. Not so easy to measure, but equally true, is the fact that they help those who are outcasts from society, assist neighbours with the housework, and drive considerately.

Walking the walk

I have drawn most of this information from an article in *The Times* by Jonathan Sacks, the former Chief Rabbi. He says it is not what you believe that makes the difference to your character, but the fact that you worship in fellowship with others. He reported Professor Putnam as speculating that an atheist whose spouse takes them reluctantly to church may be more likely to volunteer in a soup kitchen than a believer who prays alone. This is because there is something about the interpersonal relationships in a religious community, like a church or synagogue, that teaches us, by example, how to form bonds with other people and provide practical care for them. And that is what Jesus *and* Paul meant by loving our neighbour. It is not enough to talk the talk; you must also walk the walk. There will always be some who prefer to walk alone, and that is fine provided you don't become grumpy or bitter. But if you pray regularly with others, the Holy Spirit, flowing through your veins like sap in a tree, will cause the fruits of love to grow in your heart, almost without you noticing.

All-age worship

Make yourself a crown of paper leaves. Cut out paper fruit shapes, labelling them with the six fruits of the Spirit (above). Hold out your arms like branches and hang the fruit from them.

Suggested hymns

Come down, O love divine; For the fruits of his creation; Gracious Spirit, Holy Ghost; Spirit of holiness, wisdom and faithfulness.

Fifth Sunday after Trinity (Proper 8) 26 June
Second Service **Cheating**
Ps. [59.1–6, 18–20 You are my fortress] 60 Human help is worthless; Gen. 27.1–40 Jacob cheats Esau; Mark 6.1–6 Jesus rejected at Nazareth

> *'Esau said, "Is he not rightly named Jacob? For he has supplanted me these two times. He took away my birthright; and look, now he has taken away my blessing."' Genesis 27.36*

Inheritance

The Old Testament is a peculiar book. It is made up of ancient legends of the Middle Eastern tribes, and passed down by word of mouth for generations. The legends were then edited to emphasize that the 12 tribes known as Israel had a common ancestry, and inherited the promises that God made to their ancestor Abraham. This included the right to own land and dwell in it. Strangely enough, the people who called themselves the Israelites included in their Scriptures a story that their ancestor Jacob, who later changed his name to Israel, obtained his land by cheating!

Jacob

[As I have said before], Jacob was one of the twin sons which Rebekah bore to their father Isaac. His brother Esau was the first to be born, and so should have inherited everything, but Jacob, while still in the womb, grabbed hold of his brother's heel, ensuring that they were born together, and shared the inheritance. Later, when Isaac was dying, Jacob disguised himself as his twin brother – uttering the immortal words, 'My brother Esau is a hairy man, but I am a smoo-ooth man.' Their father was thus tricked into giving the younger son the right to inherit land, which should have gone to his older brother. Esau was the ancestor of the tribe of the Edomites; and possibly the Israelites invented this story to show that they were much more civilized and canny than the hairy nomadic tribes which lived nearby, and so were entitled to God's blessing of land to settle on. Or it may have been told as a story of God's mercy: no matter what cheats your ancestors were, God will forgive, and make you his chosen people, appointed to tell the story of his love to the whole world. There are more stories of deceit; then Jacob wrestled with God, and God gives him the name of Israel; he became the ancestor of the 12 tribes of Israel. The name 'Jacob' sounds like the word for 'cheat', but when he matured, he put that behind him and became a respected patriarch and prophet.

Cheating

But we must not use this story as an excuse for cheating. God does not approve of any form of fraud or dishonesty. There are laws in this country against obtaining money or property by false pretences, but it is still possible to stick to the letter of the law while denying to others what they should, in a just world, be entitled to. Jesus commanded us to love our neighbours, and if we treat them meanly, unfairly or unkindly, that is a sin. Overcharging for goods and services is cheating; denying your marriage partner their rights by sleeping around is cheating; paying yourself a high salary while giving those who work for you hardly enough to live on is cheating; keeping quiet when you have been undercharged is cheating. Enjoying a high standard of living by paying other countries too little for their raw materials and paying starvation wages to those who work long hours in the sweatshops is cheating; paying too little taxes in the country where you earn the money by using a tax haven is legal, but it is still cheating. If you live in a country which cheats in these ways, without campaigning and demonstrating for international justice, you are caught up in the cheating.

Banks

This is a true story. A customer went into a bank and saw that they had had a makeover: new colourful carpets and furniture, and bright pictures on the walls. Behind the counter was a screen with a continually changing slide show of relaxing photographs. In among the scenery and the sunsets, there was one picture of a stained-glass window. It was very colourful, but obviously nobody recognized what the picture was of. It portrayed Judas Iscariot kissing Jesus in the Garden of Gethsemane, and thereby betraying his master so that he could be recognized, arrested and crucified, in return for 30 pieces of silver! That, in a bank where the directors pay themselves millions while advising their customers how to avoid taxes, and charge high interest rates to those struggling to buy their first home! Jesus will forgive cheating Jacob, and all others who defraud their neighbours in large ways or small ones; but it cost him his life to do so, and we should think of that, when we are tempted to make an unfair profit at other people's expense.

Suggested hymns

Great is thy faithfulness, O God my Father; 'Lift up your hearts!' We lift them Lord to thee; O God of Bethel, by whose hand; O Lord of heaven and earth and sea.

Sixth Sunday after Trinity (Proper 9)   3 July
(St Thomas the Apostle)
Principal Service   **Satan**
(*Continuous*): 2 Kings 5.1–14 Naaman healed from leprosy, Ps. 30 Healing; or (*Related*): Isa. 66.10–14 The motherhood of God;

Ps. 66.1–8 God's grace; Gal. 6.[1–6] 7–16 Circumcision; Luke
10.1–11, 16–20 Sending out the 70 disciples

*'The seventy returned with joy, saying, "Lord, in your name even
the demons submit to us!" [Jesus] said to them, "I watched Satan
fall from heaven like a flash of lightning."' Luke 10.17–18*

Stan

Some children were reading the Bible unsupervised, and asked their
teacher, 'Who is this man Stan we read about in Luke's Gospel? He
seems rather unsuccessful.' 'Stan?' mused the teacher. 'I've never heard
of Stan.' One child pointed to a verse saying, 'Here, where Jesus says,
"I watched Stan fall from heaven."' The teacher realized that they had
misread the word Satan! After explaining that Satan is the leader of all
the devils, the teacher agreed, saying, 'Yes, Satan is a bit of a loser.'

Satan

Satan is a Hebrew word meaning 'the enemy'. When Jesus said to
Peter, 'Get behind me, Satan', 'the Satan' is a job-description – so Jesus
meant, 'Get out of my sight, until you stop tempting me.' In the book
of Job, the Satan is 'one of the sons of God', a heavenly civil servant
whose job is to test Job to see whether his faith is as strong as he says it
is; God allows it, knowing that Job will end with a stronger faith after
resisting the temptation to give up. Satan tempted Jesus to draw back
from the path of self-sacrifice; and when people accused Jesus of using
demonic powers to heal demon-possessed people, he replied that Satan
is heading for disaster if one group of demons fight against another.
There are some passages in St Paul's letters where a person is 'handed
over to Satan' to ensure that they are saved at the Day of Judgement.
But, in the book of Revelation, Satan becomes a dragon; he and his
army fight against St Michael and the angels: Satan is defeated and cast
down. Eventually, says the Bible, Satan and his forces will be destroyed
by fire – a far cry from the medieval paintings of devils forcing bad
people into the fire with pitchforks.

Confused

Overall, the Bible gives a confused picture of who or what Satan
is; nothing like the medieval paintings of horns, hooves and a tail.

C. S. Lewis, in *The Screwtape Letters*, took the power of evil and temptation very seriously; but instead of being frightened by the demons he made them figures of fun. That is probably a good idea; resist temptation with deadly seriousness; but laugh at evil because in the long run it has the seeds of its own destruction within it. Like a modern-day terrorist, if the devil makes you afraid of him he has won the battle.

Possession

Some people today believe they are possessed by evil spirits. That may be true, or maybe they have a psychological illness, and use Bible language to describe it because they know no other words. If they do, we should take what they say seriously, and pray for any evil spirits to come out of them. But before you get involved in exorcism, seek advice from someone with experience in this field. In 1974 a group of Christians from different denominations in Barnsley in Yorkshire thought they had successfully exorcized a confused man, who afterwards went on to murder his wife. It is better to be less dramatic, and for an authorized representative of the Church to say a simple prayer for healing, acknowledging that the power of Jesus is greater than any other power. Christians in Africa see evil in oppressive governments, and describing it as Satanic helps them deal with it. In Europe and America, we regard the crimes of mass murderers as inexpressibly evil, and life in prison seems the only way of dealing with them; but we must always hold out the possibility of genuine repentance, even if they have to spend the rest of their life behind bars. There is more than one way of interpreting the Bible, and Christians have always said that if the literal sense causes problems, God is probably telling us to interpret it symbolically. There is more than one way of describing what a patient is suffering from, and the psychological way is frequently successful. But whatever you personally believe, you must always speak in the same terminology as the patient uses, if you are to communicate with them.

Finally

Finally, always remember that evil is very powerful, but the power of Jesus is greater. But the one thing which utterly defeats Satan is laughing at him; so if you want to call him Stan, go ahead!

All-age worship

Make up prayers for sick and troubled people you know or have read about.

Suggested hymns

And did those feet in ancient time?; Be thou my guardian and my guide; Forty days and forty nights; Jesus, grant me this I pray.

St Thomas the Apostle   3 July
Doubt: No Reason for Staying Away
Hab. 2.1–4 The righteous live by faith; Ps. 31.1–6 I trust in the Lord; Eph. 2.19–22 The foundation of the apostles; John 20.24–29 Doubting Thomas is convinced

> '[The risen Christ] said to Thomas, "Put your finger here and see my hands. Reach out your hand and put it in my side. Do not doubt but believe." Thomas answered him, "My Lord and my God!"' John 20.27–28

Doubting Thomas

Thomas's faith was shattered when he suffered grief at the execution of Jesus, his best friend. How could the loving God whom Jesus spoke of allow it? So he stopped meeting with Jesus's friends, and was utterly miserable all on his own. A week later, one of them said to him, 'Come to supper with us tonight – it won't kill you.' Reluctantly, Thomas went along with him – and then he had an experience which turned 'Doubting Thomas' into the first person to call Jesus 'my Lord and my God'! What that experience was, Thomas could never put into words. Was it a dream? But no dream ever invited someone to touch him. Had Jesus returned to physical life? But he was able to pass through locked doors. Yet Thomas realized at once that he had been wrong. Inability to explain something is no reason for staying away. But still today, people present at least four reasons for not going to church.

Feelings

First, many people stay away from church nowadays because they have no feelings to indicate that God is present. Maybe they only came for formal occasions, hatch, match and despatch and so on, and found it cold and unwelcoming. But even those who had good experiences of church when they were younger find that the 'first fine, careless rapture' fades with time. There is nothing unusual about this. Our feelings are largely out of our control, and the fact that you have no feelings about something does not prove that it is not true. Even romantic passion fades with time. God is different from us, so we cannot normally feel his (or her) presence as we do for someone whom we can see and touch. Yet God mercifully grants us occasional inklings, which point us in the direction of belief. But these touches of the Divine hand are unpredictable; and they are unlikely if we give up on God and refuse to worship with others – the very place where he is most often experienced. Other indications that God exists are in logic, loveliness and laughter. Feelings are wayward children; we need to discipline them by habits of prayer.

Doubt

The second mistake which causes church absenteeism is not recognizing that doubt is an essential part of faith. The more strongly somebody believes the world was made by a loving Creator, the more clearly they see tragedies everywhere which apparently give the lie to that belief. Yet, by holding faith and doubt together, we come to the only place where such questions can be answered: the cross of Christ. The only possible explanation of how God allowed the death of the most loving person who ever lived is if it was not just a man who died, but that somehow God was there, suffering in and with Jesus, as he suffers in and with you and me whenever terrible things happen to us also.

Grief

The third problem which all of us doubters have to face is that of grief. If there really is a life after death, we ask, why should we feel so awful when those we love are taken from us? Surely we should rejoice that they have gone to a better place? Now that is ridiculous.

Our logical minds tell us that, as St Paul said, 'my desire is to depart and be with Christ, for that is far better'; yet, when the earthly life of those we love is cut short, it is *for ourselves in our temporary loneliness* that we grieve.

Church as institution

The fourth commonest reason why people stay away from church is because they are disillusioned by the institution. Yet so are many of those who attend church regularly. Some sort of institution is needed to carry the insights of one generation to people who are not yet born. If Christianity had remained a movement of emotional individuals, it would have died out long ago. The institutional church ought to be a movement of tolerance and compassion, but there are always some who are more interested in authority and power. But not in the local congregation; despite the universality of temptation and sin, something comes over people when we worship together, which turns us, slowly, into better people. And if you stay away, you deny yourself the influence that a community of believers – who are also, each of us, doubters – can have upon you. Neither feelings, nor doubt, nor grief, nor disillusionment should make us forego that.

Suggested hymns

If you believe and I believe; Lead kindly light, amid the encircling gloom; Light's glittering morn (Part 3); Thine be the glory.

Seventh Sunday after Trinity (Proper 10) 10 July
Principal Service **Eternal Life**
(*Continuous*): Amos 7.7–17 The plumbline: judgement on the city, Ps. 82 Justice; *or* (*Related*): Deut. 30.9–14 The word is near you, Ps. 25.1–10 Truth and guidance; Col. 1.1–14 Prayer, faith and works; Luke 10.25–37 The good Samaritan

> *'A lawyer stood up to test Jesus. "Teacher," he said, "what must I do to inherit eternal life?"' Luke 10.25*

Lawyer's question

An expert in 'the Law', which was what Jews call the Law of Moses, asked Jesus a question about 'eternal life'. He did not ask Jesus to define eternal life, nor did Jesus ask the lawyer what he meant by the phrase. Both took it for granted that they shared an understanding of what 'eternal life' is from their reading. Yet in fact the phrase only occurs once in the Old Testament, in the book of Daniel, where a supernatural but human-like figure says,

> Many of those who sleep in the dust of the earth shall awake, some to everlasting life, and some to shame and everlasting contempt.

Yet the idea of everlasting life keeps cropping up in Jewish literature outside the Bible, as though they were haunted by the idea that death was not the end of life, but the beginning of something better. But there are several different ways of interpreting those words; I want to highlight four:

1 Everlasting life.
2 The life of the new age.
3 Eternal life.
4 Really living.

Everlasting life

Everlasting life sounds like life which goes on for ever and ever with no end. If that sounds boring to you, think of the times you have said, 'Life is too short! There is so much to learn and do, and not enough time to do it in.' Well, God has a solution to that problem; he can give you, literally, 'all the time in the world' to enjoy those experiences you thought you had missed out on. Everlasting life is a blessing for the curious, and boring for those with closed minds. As the hymn puts it, 'eternity's too short to utter all [God's] praise'.

New age

But in fact 'everlasting life' is a mistranslation. The original means more like, 'the life of the new age'. This is not 'new age' in the sense that hippies use those words, though it is based on the same idea. Human history is divided into various different ages: the Stone Age, the Ice Age, the Middle Ages, the Age of Technology and so on. We dream that one day the culmination of all this will come in a new and perfect age. The hippies imagined this in terms of freedom and drugs; the Jews of Jesus's time thought it would be brought in by God, when Jews would rule the world. For a Christian, the ideal world would be one where selfishness and violence gives way to mutual compassion and love. But will that day ever come on this earth?

Eternal

I don't know. Which is why the translation 'eternal life' which we started with is probably best, because it has nothing to do with time. Scientists have taught us that time is a dimension, like the three dimensions of space. If we live on after we die, it must be in another world, independent of this world of time and space. That doesn't mean there is no time in eternity; you can access any time or place in this universe or any other, just as God can. Won't that be wonderful?

Really living

But the important thing about the life that God gives us is not its length, but its quality. To a really boring person we say, 'Get a life'. And when you are excited you say, 'This is what I call really living!' You don't have to die to experience this; for Jesus said, 'whoever believes has eternal life' . . . *has*, as a present experience, not 'will have' sometime in the future.

Inherit

The questioner used a good lawyer's word, asking: 'What must I do to *inherit* eternal life?' When somebody dies, their children inherit their property. You could say that when Jesus died, he bequeathed to us a more satisfying way of living. But we can do nothing to deserve it; eternal life is a free gift.

Neighbourliness

So Jesus never answered the lawyer's question; instead he told him a story about a despised foreigner, a Samaritan, who found a wounded Jew and paid for his care until he had recovered. You cannot earn a truly satisfying quality of life. But you can start to experience it here and now by showing neighbourliness and compassion to others. 'This is eternal life,' said Jesus: 'that they may know you, the only true God, and Jesus Christ whom you have sent.'

All-age worship

Role-play the good Samaritan in modern dress, as if a member of a despised race or class were the hero.

Suggested hymns

Brother, sister, let me serve you; Gracious Spirit, Holy Ghost; When all thy mercies, O my God; When I needed a neighbour.

Seventh Sunday after Trinity (Proper 10)   10 July
Second Service   **Tradition**
Ps. 77 Remembering the past; Gen. 32.9–30 Wrestling Jacob; Mark 7.1–23 Tradition

> *'[Jesus said to the Pharisees,] "You abandon the commandment of God and hold to human tradition."' Mark 7.8*

Old Testament

The teaching of Jesus was entirely founded on the traditions of the Old Testament. His words are all chosen from the vocabulary of the Scriptures, and are riddled with quotations from the ancient writers. He was a Jew, and believed that God his heavenly Father had chosen the Jews to learn about the one, true God and spread that knowledge to all the other nations in the world. Jesus believed that obedience to God, as taught in the Law of Moses, was central to the fulfilment of God's plan for the human race. It would not be too strong to say that you cannot understand the teaching of Jesus unless you have already studied the Old Testament, for that is the springboard from which Jesus springs. In one puzzling passage Jesus said, 'Truly I tell you, until heaven and earth pass away, not one letter, not one stroke of a letter, will pass from the law until all is accomplished.' You probably know the old translation, which referred to 'no jot or tittle'. Remember that he was speaking to Jews only, and referring principally to the Ten Commandments. But he came up against Pharisees who interpreted the Scripture in a very different way from how Jesus did. They emphasized the details of the Sabbath law, not doing a stroke of work, or even a kind deed, on a Saturday. They were bothered about only eating kosher food, and ensuring that their eating utensils were washed in an elaborate ritual. In fact the legally minded Pharisees even used some of their traditional laws to get out of obeying the Ten Commandments, as we heard today. 'You abandon the commandment of God,' said Jesus, 'and hold to human tradition.'

Tradition

In fact Jesus was torn in two by tradition. He wanted his hearers to learn from the past, and build their way of life on the experience of their ancestors; but he would not allow any trivial regulation to get in the way of the law of love. He commanded us to love God and love our neighbours: 'On these two commandments,' he said, 'hang all the law and the prophets.' Traditional laws and customs are an attempt to apply the law of love to particular situations at one moment of history; but they cannot be applied when the circumstances are totally different.

David Sheppard

When David Sheppard, the famous cricketer who went on to become Bishop of Liverpool, was invited to attend a joint Anglican–Methodist consultation on evangelism in 1968, he was apprehensive. At the time negotiations were going on between the Church of England and the Methodist Church over plans to reunite the two denominations. They were going badly, and eventually the proposal failed, to the deep disappointment of many people. So he was expecting there to be deep divides. 'However,' he writes in his autobiography, 'the divisions were not between Anglicans and Methodists. They were between "conservatives" and "radicals" in both churches . . . joining in the discussions, I realized that the arguments were going on within my own mind, [because] both sides appealed to me.' The dilemma he describes is felt my many in all denominations who want to maintain the strong traditions of their inheritance, without which they fear that the Church will fall apart, and who also want the Church to address new opportunities in new ways, without which they fear the Church will die.

Body of Christ

A calm look at the history of human religion will show that we progressed from worshipping the forces of nature, to worshipping our ancestors, to recognizing that there was only one God for me and the other members of my tribe, to one God for the whole world, to a God who loves all humans equally. In the light of this, we can see that atheists are talking nonsense when they say that the next step is to believe in no God at all; more logical is to suggest that the next rung on that ladder is to progress to a kingdom of universal love. But to achieve that, we must all learn to ignore the peripheral quarrels and concentrate on the important matters at the centre of our faith; be willing to renounce our beloved traditions which dismember the one Body of Christ, tolerate the customs which other Christians hold so dear, and welcome developments which help us to love God and our neighbour better in a constantly changing world.

Suggested hymns

Bind us together, Lord; Faith of our fathers; Come, O thou traveller unknown; Dear Lord and Father of mankind.

Eighth Sunday after Trinity (Proper 11)   17 July
Principal Service   Mary, Martha and the Invisible God
(*Continuous*): Amos 8.1–12 Justice for the needy, Ps. 52 Justice for the needy; *or* (*Related*): Gen. 18.1–10a Abraham welcomes three guests, Ps. 15 Justice; Col. 1.15–28 Christ the head of the Church; Luke 10.38–42 Martha and Mary, works and prayer

'[Jesus] is the image of the invisible God.' Colossians 1.15

Images of God

The Ten Commandments forbid us to worship graven images. A statue is relatively small, immovable and powerless, whereas the

God we worship is infinite. But that applies also to our *mental* images of God. J. B. Phillips wrote a challenging book with the title, *Your God is Too Small*, warning us that however we think of God, the verbal image is inadequate to convey God's infinite greatness to our minds. But the solution to this problem is found in what St Paul wrote in our reading today, '[Jesus] is the image of the invisible God.'

Talking to God

That is a great comfort to people who find the idea of God difficult. How do you begin to talk to an old man on a cloud? Who would want to talk to a punishing judge? How can you begin to think about a force which is bigger than the universe? Probably when you were a child, you were told to say your prayers by somebody who said, 'Now we are going to talk to God.' And being a young child, you didn't ask difficult questions, and just accepted that this was like when you talk to Daddy on the telephone. Then you simply asked God, out loud, to bless Mummy and Daddy, and give you the toys you wanted. But as you grew older, you realized that this didn't fit with your increasingly grown-up ideas of the world. If nobody helped you with this transition, you may have dismissed praying as childish nonsense, and given up on God altogether. But I think there is a way through this problem, and that is to think of Jesus when you talk to God.

Mary and Martha

Mary of Bethany, whom we heard about in the Gospel, found that out when Jesus came to call. When her parents were alive, their home had been full of friends and relations, but neither Mary nor her sister Martha nor their brother Lazarus were very good at small-talk and making friends, so now their house was quiet and lonely. She tried to talk to God in the silence, and found it even harder than talking to strangers. Then one day, Jesus came through the door with his disciples. That's at least 13 healthy young men filling their living room, and asking Jesus deep questions about 'Life, the Universe and Everything'. So while Martha got them all refreshments, Mary sat on the floor near the feet of Jesus, and listened to what he had to say.

What Jesus is like

Jesus seemed to Mary to be quite unlike any man she had ever seen before. And yet he also showed the qualities she admired, only to a far higher degree than in any man she had met. Jesus was kind, understanding, tolerant and non-judgemental. He was sympathetic to people who had been pushed to the margins of society, and busy healing the sick and trying to put broken relationships back together again. If only everybody was like that! Then she paused for a moment, and thought about her difficulties with prayer. She wondered wistfully, 'If only God in heaven was like that!'

Father and Son

Jesus was talking about God as being like a father who welcomes back his prodigal son, despite the way he had frittered away the family fortunes. Jesus kept referring to God as 'my father'. And Mary thought of the popular saying, 'Like father, like son'. Children often resemble their parents, not only in appearance, but in their behaviour and attitudes. And it was to Mary as if a door had suddenly opened and she had entered paradise. Because it dawned on her that God is like Jesus. *God is like Jesus.* And if Jesus is easy to talk to, because he is so understanding and kind, then God must be easy to talk to also. Nothing complicated or theological here, though. Just, when you close your eyes, and try to picture the invisible God standing a few feet away from you, imagine that Jesus is there, and talk to him, naturally and intimately. For Jesus is the *image* of the invisible God. Not in appearance, but in personality, character and lovingness. And who could fail to chat away 13 to the dozen with someone as attractive and sympathetic as that? For Jesus is the image of the invisible God.

All-age worship

Make a splashy painting of Jesus being kind to people. Write underneath, 'God is like this'.

Suggested hymns

A man there lived in Galilee; Be still, my soul; Hark, my soul, it is the Lord; What a friend we have in Jesus.

Eighth Sunday after Trinity (Proper 11)   17 July
Second Service   **Humility**

Ps. 81 I rescued you; Gen. 41.1–16, 25–37 Interpreting dreams;
1 Cor. 4.8–13 Fools for Christ; *Gospel at Holy Communion*:
John 4.31–35 Ripe for harvesting

> *'I think that God has exhibited us apostles as last of all, as though
> sentenced to death, because we have become a spectacle to the
> world, to angels and to mortals.' 1 Corinthians 4.9*

Proud

The Christians in the Greek city of Corinth were proud of their achievements. They had established a Christian presence in one of the busiest
and most corrupt ports in the ancient world. By joining the Christian
community, many of their members had taken a step upwards in social
respectability. The slaves found that in meetings of Christians, posh
people treated them as equals. Labourers were treated as though their
opinions counted for something. Women were respected as the equals
of men. They all met weekly in the dining rooms of quite wealthy
home-owners, in the smarter parts of town. And all this they had
achieved through their own efforts. Or so they thought. They despised
St Paul and the other travelling missionaries, who owned nothing. So
St Paul needed to bring them down a peg or two.

Procession

Therefore he used a very graphic image. [I have told you before, that]
When a powerful Roman Emperor returned from conquering a
rebellious tribe, he always organized a procession, called a triumph.
In front rode the triumphant ruler in his chariot, followed by his
courtiers and the legionary soldiers. At the tail end of the procession
came the members of the defeated tribe, who could be jeered at by
the crowds, because they had been condemned to death. They were
probably in chains, which they dragged jangling behind them as they
walked. They were widely despised as the lowest of the low. Well,
wrote St Paul, you Corinthian Christians are the proud emperors,
boasting of their achievements. And we poor missionaries are the
'tail-end Charlies', the dregs, mocked by everyone because we have
lost all in life's battle. 'I think that God has exhibited us apostles as

last of all, as though sentenced to death,' he wrote, 'because we have become a spectacle to the world, to angels and to mortals.'

Humble

Or that was how it appeared. Yet a couple of verses before the passage from St Paul's First Letter to the Corinthians chosen for today's reading, he asks the crucial question, which defeats anyone who is proud of what they have done: 'What do you have that you did not receive?' *'What do you have that you did not receive?'* The answer, of course, is 'Nothing at all.' All our possessions that we take such pride in were given us by God. All our skills and abilities, with our capacity to organize other people, are due to God's inspiration. The things that people admire us for are there because they are the gift of God's grace. So it is about time we started to show some humility and gratitude to God for all the undeserved gifts he has poured upon us. As William Barclay writes, 'To the Corinthians, the Christian life meant flaunting their privileges; to Paul, it meant humble service and a readiness to die for Christ.'

Grovelling

And yet humility is not grovelling. We can stand proud of what God has achieved through us. We can be grateful that he has chosen us to play a small part in his mighty plan of making the world a better place for people to live in. We can rejoice that God has poured his love upon us, thereby giving us the grace which enables us to love other people for God's sake. We can recover our sense of worth, not through our achievements, but because, despite our unloveliness, God has found us loveable, and chosen to forgive us our sins and pour his undeserved love into our hearts.

Boasting

So, like St Paul, we do have something to boast about. But we don't boast about how clever we are. Instead, we boast because of the ill-treatment and ridicule we have suffered at the hands of people who should know better. We can rejoice because when physical pain comes to us, we can bear it bravely through the spiritual strength God has given us, and offer it to God as a sacrifice, to show our gratitude for all the undeserved good things that have happened in our lives up until now. 'Thank God,' said the martyrs, rejoicing as they were led to the stake, chosen to suffer for Christ's sake. 'Thank God,' say we, humbly, if anyone thanks us for good things we have achieved through his grace.

Suggested hymns

Just as I am, without one plea; Lord, it belongs not to my care; My song is love unknown. There's a wideness in God's mercy.

Ninth Sunday after Trinity (Proper 12) 24 July
Principal Service **Doors Fly Open**
(*Continuous*): Hos. 1.2–10 Hosea's family, Ps. 85 Forgiveness; *or* (*Related*): Gen. 18.20–32 Abraham's prayer for Sodom, Ps. 138 Prayer for grace; Col. 2.6–15 [16–19] Resurrection with Christ; Luke 11.1–13 Ask, seek, knock

> '[Jesus said,] "Ask, and it will be given you; search, and you will find; knock, and the door will be opened for you. For everyone who asks receives, and everyone who searches finds, and for everyone who knocks, the door will be opened."' Luke 11.9–10

Giving

Once upon a time an immigrant approached the English chaplain in a foreign town. He described how he was stranded in that town, had no money and no papers to go anywhere else. Then he asked for money. The chaplain apologized that he made it a rule never to give money, however deserving the person who asked him. 'But,' said the other, 'the Bible says, "Everyone who asks, receives."' 'I know,' answered the chaplain; 'and I tried doing that, literally, and soon I found I was giving away more than I earned, leaving me with not enough to buy food for myself. If I starve to death I can't help anyone. If I give to one I have to give to all who ask me. So with deep regret, and embarrassment at failing to obey the instructions of Jesus, I had to decide never to give cash to anyone.'

Lord's Prayer

But those verses are not actually about money at all. They are about prayer. They follow straight on from the teaching of Jesus about the Lord's Prayer, the model for all our praying. First, it acknowledges that God is the loving father of me, and all the other people in the world. We pray that the earth may become a place of justice and compassion, just like heaven. Then comes the request for daily bread: enough food to eat simply, but only just enough, no luxuries. Next follows our request for unconditional forgiveness, with the promise that the forgiveness we offer our enemies will also be unconditional. Finally we ask God to lead us away from situations where we are tempted to do wrong, so that evil may be unable to harm us. We say the Lord's Prayer so often, we sometimes forget to look at what it really says.

Divine generosity

What I want you to notice is that in the Lord's Prayer we are not asking God to give us *things*, but to change our attitudes. Make us more obedient, loving, forgiving and understanding. If we say that prayer sincerely, we may still have difficult times in our lives. Naturally we ask God for a comfortable life. But you know what happens to children whose parents give them everything they ask for? They turn into spoilt brats. Yet if a child says, 'Dad, show me how you would cope with this problem', their parents will give them wise advice and help them become stronger people. It is the same with us who are the children of a loving God. He doesn't give us a smooth ride, but he gives us the strength of character to cope with the problems that come our way.

Open doors

If you pray in that spirit, then your prayers will always be answered. If you ask for perfect health and a life of luxury, God may answer 'No'. But as St Paul wrote,

> No testing has overtaken you that is not common to everyone. God is faithful, and he will not let you be tested beyond your strength, but with the testing he will also provide the way out so that you may be able to endure it.

So if you pray for strength of character, God always answers 'Yes'. With this sort of prayer, Jesus says, 'ask, search, knock'; 'for everyone who asks receives, and everyone who searches finds, and for everyone who knocks, the door will [fly open!]' God knows what we need, much better than we do. If God doesn't give us exactly what we ask for, it is usually because he has a plan to give us something better.

Development

That doesn't alter the fact that the poor people feel hungry and the chaplain feels guilty. Perhaps what God wants is for all of us to start working actively for peace and justice within nations and between nations, so that the poor everywhere may get a fairer share of the world's wealth, and have no need to emigrate. That is the meaning of praying for God's kingdom to come. If we really hammer on God's door to ask for that, and also on the doors of the world's leaders, then we shall really find, as somebody once said, that 'the one who knocks, opens locks'.

All-age worship

Find out what makes poor people leave their own countries. What can we do about it?

Suggested hymns

Father, hear the prayer we offer; Our Father, who is in heaven (Caribbean); The Lord will come and not be slow; Thy kingdom come, O God.

Ninth Sunday after Trinity (Proper 12)   24 July
Second Service   **Examples for Us**
Ps. 88 Let my prayer come before you; Gen. 42.1–25 Joseph tests his brothers; 1 Cor. 10.1–24 Examples for us; *Gospel at Holy Communion*: Matt. 13.24–30 [31–43] Weeds

> *'These things occurred as examples for us, so that we might not desire evil as they did.' 1 Corinthians 10.6*

196

History

When Oliver Cromwell was planning his son's education, he said, 'I would have him learn a little history.' The German philosopher Hegel said that the only thing we learn from history is that we learn nothing from history. But Cromwell was right: by studying honestly the mistakes that our ancestors made in years gone by, we can prepare ourselves to avoid making the same mistakes if ever we find ourselves in a similar situation. To admit their errors is not to deny that they also did much that was good. And guilt cannot be inherited. In the past, people of other nations did bad things too, but we cannot blame their descendants, any more than they can blame us. The study of history is the best cure for exaggerated national pride.

Exodus

St Paul was a Jew, and he was understandably proud of the history of his people. But he saw also their faults, and said that 'these things happened as examples to us' – not examples to imitate and copy, but ghastly warnings of the dangers of arrogant complacency. In particular, he quotes the history of the Exodus, when the Israelites passed through the Red Sea, and crossed the howling wilderness into the Promised Land. They were given the blessings of God's protection, and the privilege of escaping from slavery, he writes. But they began to take these things for granted, and gave way to temptation, which should be a warning to us all. The Israelites committed these sins:

1   When most of the spies came back with negative reports, they lost courage, and doubted whether God would be able to keep his promises.
2   When Moses was receiving the Commandments, they worshipped a golden calf.
3   They committed fornication, which translates a word derived from the same root as our word pornography, and which means a prostitute. When the Bible condemns fornication, it means paying for sex.
4   They grumbled about the appalling conditions of their journey.

They would have done none of these things, writes St Paul to the Corinthians, if they hadn't taken for granted the great blessings God had given them.

Idols

Paul thought the Christians in Corinth were at risk in a similar way. Just as the Israelites had passed through the waters of the Red Sea, so the Christians had passed through the waters of baptism and been united with Christ. Most of the meat they ate came from animals that had been sacrificed to an idol in a heathen temple. No harm in that. But when their pagan neighbours invited the Christians to a party in the temple, and then challenged them that Christians accept idols as equal to their own God, becoming one with the idol by eating the food that had been dedicated to it, they chickened out. 'Don't make a fuss, or we shall become unpopular with the neighbours', that sort of thing.

Today

We too, like the Corinthians, need to learn from history. We have had many blessings as a nation, including democracy, a justice system and a standard of living higher than many other nations, largely with wealth formed from trading with those nations and extracting their natural resources. Yet, like the Israelites, we have become complacent, assuming that we have deserved these things because we are better than other people. So, like them:

1   We lose courage, and doubt whether God will keep his promises to those who love him. Thus many people in our nation have stopped going to church, and we who do are frightened to point out to them what they are missing.
2   The worship which should be God's alone we have transferred to the golden idol of seeking to become wealthier and wealthier.
3   We have compromised over sex. Sex is good when it is an expression of mutual caring between two people who intend to remain in a lifelong relationship, but temptations are all around us to demean ourselves by using sex in other ways.
4   We grumble, even though we have received so many blessings, because our lives are not perfect.

These are the temptations which come with success, and any successful nation is vulnerable. We must learn from history what happens to nations which yield to these temptations, and get a grip on ourselves before it is too late.

Suggested hymns

And did those feet in ancient time?; Be thou my guardian and my guide; Forty days and forty nights; Jesus, grant me this I pray.

Tenth Sunday after Trinity (Proper 13)   31 July
Principal Service   **Made in the Image of a God of Love**
(*Continuous*): Hos. 11.1–11 Fatherhood of God, Ps. 107.1–9, 43 Guidance; *or* (*Related*): Eccles. 1.2, 12–14; 2.18–23 Vanity and wisdom, Ps. 49.1–12 Wisdom and death; Col. 3.1–11 Selfishness or unity; Luke 12.13–21 The rich fool

> *'Do not lie to one another, seeing that you have stripped off the old self with its practices and have clothed yourselves with the new self, which is being renewed in knowledge according to the image of its creator.' Colossians 3.9–10*

Model-making

When you were young, did you enjoy model-making? Anything from sandcastles on the beach to model trains and model aeroplanes? It's not only boys who like making things, either: girls like dressing a doll or decorating an iced bun, which are also creative things to do; and both genders enjoy playing with ®Lego. In many cases, the model-maker buys a kit, and then glues the parts together, following the instructions in a book. Usually the instruction book, or the recipe book, will have a picture showing what the finished product is supposed to look like. If not, maybe you have an image in your mind of what your creation will be when you have finished it. I know quite a few adults, too, who like being creative, and why not? There is something God-like about creating things according to a preconceived plan.

Images

The Bible says that God created human beings, male and female, in his own image. Nobody is stupid enough to think that means we look like God, because all of us know that God is invisible. It means that we have the same qualities, characteristics and character as God, which the other animals do not have. The first such quality must be that we, like God, can be creative. To do that we need to be able to think. Many animals, too, are creative and thoughtful, but not to the degree that human beings are. Similarly we can make choices, with much more freedom than animals have. And then we have the capacity to love. The picture in the front of God's mental instruction book, when he set out to make human beings, was the image of God himself.

Progress

Some people imagine that God created us perfect; but Genesis does not say that. Human beings were easily tempted by their desire to experience evil, as well as good, and soon gave way to that temptation. The skeletons of early human beings which have been dug up in recent years, with marks of fighting and even cannibalism, suggest that in those days, we were very far from god-like. But we have always had the *potential* to become wise, just and loving. The image in the mind of our creator was of a perfect human being; but God hasn't finished with us yet. The story of the world is the history of human progress towards the ideal; a progress which is still going on today.

St Paul

St Paul told the Colossians that one way in which we fall short of the model-maker's plan is that we are not truthful; he wrote:

> Do not lie to one another, seeing that you have stripped off the old self with its practices and have clothed yourselves with the new self, which is being renewed in knowledge according to the image of its creator.

When we became Christians, says Paul, there was such a radical change in us that it was as though we had stripped off our dirty old clothes and put on beautiful new clothing. But we didn't become perfect overnight; we are progressing towards the ideal human being, the image of which was in God the model-maker's plan.

Society

Christianity teaches us that God is not a lonely old man; God is a fellowship of Father, Son and Holy Ghost, bound together by love. Therefore God doesn't try to make us perfect as individuals; he is trying to give us better relationships, driving out bad things like lying, and helping us to progress towards a perfect, just community, full of mutual and unselfish love. That is why Christians are busy trying to build a 'model' society, in which we care for each other's human rights and freedoms, helping poor nations to have enough and encouraging rich nations to be more generous. God is love; and the image in the handbook from which he tried to build 'model' human beings was of loving individuals building a loving society together throughout the world. Are you ready to cooperate with God in that?

All-age worship

Dress up dolls in wedding clothes. Discuss what the 'model' (ideal) husband and wife would be like.

Suggested hymns

God is working his purpose out; New every morning is the love; One more step along the road I go; Thy hand, O God, has guided.

Tenth Sunday after Trinity (Proper 13)   31 July
Second Service   Tongues
Ps. 107.1–32 Thanksgiving for deliverance; Gen. 50.4–26 Deaths of Jacob and Joseph; 1 Cor. 14.1–19 Tongues and prophecy; *Gospel at Holy Communion*: Mark 6.45–52 Walking on water

'I thank God that I speak in tongues more than all of you; nevertheless, in church I would rather speak five words with my mind, in order to instruct others also, than ten thousand words in a tongue.' 1 Corinthians 14.18–19

Corinth

The church in Corinth was split down the middle. There was arguing, there was quarrelling, there was snubbing, there was ignoring
each other, there was gossip and slander. That sort of thing happens in every church from time to time, but never to that extent
or for so long. And what had caused this fragmentation of what
was supposed to be a united community? The Holy Spirit. No, I'm
wrong: God's Spirit of Love never causes bad things like that; it was
disagreements about the Holy Spirit that had upset the Corinthian
apple cart.

Everyone

Every Christian receives the Holy Spirit, whether they realize it or
not. Jesus said:

> If you love me, you will keep my commandments. And I will ask
> the Father, and he will give you another Advocate, to be with you
> forever. This is the Spirit of truth . . . You know him, because he
> abides with you, and he will be in you.

There is nothing complicated about this; it simply means that God
is inside us, helping us to talk convincingly and behave lovingly.
And we can all remember times when we have done things, and
then thought, 'I could never have done that without God's help.'
But when you think of it, that is quite an amazing thing to say, that
the Creator of the universe has made a home for himself in your
heart. If you really realize what you are saying, it can make you
quite emotional.

Emotion

Now, emotion is a good thing; the meaning of the word is, something which sets you in motion, keeps you going. The British have
been trying to keep a stiff upper lip for so long that some of them
have forgotten what an inspiring thing emotion can be. If someone
tells you they love you, it is not surprising if a few tears hover on
your eyelid. And the Holy Spirit is God's way of telling you that *he*
loves you. But there is a difference between feeling emotions and
being emotional. The Corinthian Christians were being emotional,
hyped up, spilling their emotions all over themselves and each other,

and whipping themselves up into a frenzy. There are good ways in every religion of getting in touch with your feelings. Jesus did it by fasting and spending nights in prayer. The Sufis do it when they become whirling dervishes. The smell of incense does it for some people. Some even use drugs. Some of these ways are harmless, and others are deeply dangerous. St Paul told the Corinthians that emotionalism is fine at home or in a small group, but it is meaningless when you whip it up in a community.

Tongues

The form it took in Corinth was called 'speaking with tongues'. If you sit alone and think how much God loves you, you will feel an emotion. If you let that emotion bubble up inside you, you will want to speak to God, but you probably won't be able to think of the right words. But if you then relax and open your mouth, sometimes the sounds will come babbling out faster than you can think. That babbling is called 'speaking with tongues'. Try it if you want to, but don't be disappointed if nothing happens; Paul said, 'I thank God that I speak in tongues more than all of you . . . but does everyone speaks in tongues?' It was those who said, 'If you don't speak in tongues you are not a real Christian', who were splitting the church. So Paul wrote to them saying, emotions are fine at home, but discourage the display of them in public.

Love

There is a lot more that we could say about the Spirit. Rejoice that God has given to you, just like every other Christian, the spiritual strength to overcome all life's problems and seize its opportunities. And remember, emotion is fine when it leads to love, joy and peace, which are the fruits of the Spirit. But whipping up emotionalism is bad when it leads to pride and division. Paul summed it up when he wrote: 'If I speak in [tongues:] the tongues of mortals and of angels, but do not have love, I am a noisy gong or a clanging cymbal.'

Suggested hymns

Dear Lord and Father of mankind; Gracious Spirit, Holy Ghost; Our blest Redeemer, ere he breathed; There's a quiet understanding.

Eleventh Sunday after Trinity (Proper 14) 7 August
Principal Service **Tricycles and Sports Cars**

(*Continuous*): Isa. 1.1, 10–20 Justice is better than sacrifice, Ps. 50.1–8, 23–24 Covenant; *or* (*Related*): Gen. 15.1–6 Promise to Abram and his faith, Ps. 33.12–22 Faith; Heb. 11.1–3, 8–16 Abraham's faith; Luke 12.32–40 Treasure in heaven

> '[Jesus said,] "Where your treasure is, there your heart will be also."' Luke 12.34

Toys

What was your favourite toy? Do you remember, as soon as you were given something that really excited you, you started asking for a bigger one? You were given a little blue tricycle, and you had a lot of fun with it. The next day, however, you went into your parents' bedroom, saying, 'I must have a bigger tricycle. And it must be red, not blue, like the one the boy down the road has got.' And your parents said, 'You're not big enough yet; if you had a bigger tricycle your feet wouldn't reach the pedals; you'd fall off and hurt yourself.' But children are stubborn, and you probably said, 'I could reach the pedals if I try. And I wouldn't fall off, honest.' 'Come to us when you're bigger,' said your parents, 'in a couple of years' time, and we'll think about it.' And you grumbled about how unfair parents are. And your parents grumbled too, because your grown-up brother was pestering them for a sports car, and they were afraid that if they gave him one, he would drive too fast and kill himself. Perhaps you never had a tricycle, nor an elder brother, but all children are much the same, so you can imagine the scenario I'm talking about.

Comparisons

So picture the next scene in this drama. Younger sibling goes to big brother, and asks why he wants a sports car. 'Because it would be so much fun,' says the older one. 'I have a friend who's got one, and he says the fun you can have with it is just . . . unimaginable!' 'I can't picture that,' says the kid. 'All I want is a bigger tricycle – or maybe one day a bicycle. Why should anyone want more than that?' 'That's your trouble,' says the senior wrangler;

'lack of imagination. Tell you what: think how much more fun a bicycle is than a tricycle – say, ten times as much? Then imagine that driving a car is ten times as much fun as riding a bicycle. Now can you picture it?' The younger one grudgingly admits that they can understand what the other means — but they can't imagine it, it's too big.

Proportion

Mathematicians say, 'car is to bicycle in the same proportion as bicycle is to tricycle', meaning that each is ten times as much as the other. Now comes the religious point of all this: heaven is to earth in the same proportion as sports car is to tricycle. In other words, the pleasures we receive by being in heaven are, compared to the greatest pleasures we have on earth, in proportion as the pleasures of driving a car are, compared with the pleasure of riding a tricycle.

Heaven

That was a complicated way of reaching that point. But just think how many times you have dismissed the idea of heaven because you just cannot imagine it. Jesus said, 'Make purses for yourselves that do not wear out, an unfailing treasure in heaven . . . For where your treasure is, there your heart will be also.' In other words, think of how much joy you had on the best day of your life, compared to the other ordinary, boring days. Was it a hundred times better? Well, the pleasures of being in heaven will be a hundred times better than that. In that case, you'll stop worrying about how much you have in your bank account (your treasure on earth), because it's nothing compared with the joy of being invited to live with Jesus, and all those you love, for all eternity. That is your 'treasure in heaven'.

Kind or rich?

If you make the effort to imagine that, all your priorities change. You stop dreaming of being richer; you will dream of being kinder. You will no longer think, 'How can I get money out of these people', and start thinking, 'How can I love these people more?' You will no longer fear death as the end of everything, but look forward to it as the beginning of true happiness. It is hard to imagine, but comparing the joy you get from driving a car to that you receive from riding a tricycle is as good a place to start as any other.

All-age worship

Imagine the pleasure you get from the most enjoyable experience you ever had. Then imagine a hundred times that pleasure. Next imagine the joy of heaven. Whom would you like to meet there?

Suggested hymns

Alleluia, alleluia, hearts to heaven and voices raise; Give us the wings of faith to rise; Jesus lives! Thy terrors now; Thine be the glory.

Eleventh Sunday after Trinity (Proper 14) 7 August
Second Service **Under Pressure**
Ps. 108 Love as high as heaven [116 The cup of salvation];
Isa. 11.10—12.6 Return from exile; 2 Cor. 1.1–22 God's 'Yes';
Gospel at Holy Communion: Mark 7.24–30 The foreign mother

> *'Blessed be the God and Father of our Lord Jesus Christ, the Father of mercies and the God of all consolation, who consoles us in all our affliction, so that we may be able to console those who are in any affliction with the consolation with which we ourselves are consoled by God.' 2 Corinthians 1.3–4*

Under pressure

Do you sometimes feel you are under a lot of pressure? Yes, who doesn't? Pressure from your employer to work long hours; pressure from your family to keep them entertained; pressure from the Government to pay taxes that you can ill afford; pressure from the advertisers to buy things you don't really need. Those above you pressure you to be strict, and those whom you have to control pressure you to be lenient. Then there are more serious pressures: the pressure of sickness and pain, when you know you should be brave but you feel like screaming at God. And for the Christian, there is pressure from your atheist friends to renounce what they call your irrational and outmoded faith. Well, cheer up, even the

206

best people feel under intolerable pressure at times. Even St Paul, though in today's reading from 2 Corinthians the word for pressure is translated 'affliction'. From Ephesus, he writes:

We do not want you to be unaware, brothers and sisters, of the affliction we experienced [here]; for we were so utterly, unbearably crushed that we despaired of life itself. Indeed, we felt that we had received the sentence of death so that we would rely not on ourselves but on God who raises the dead.

He may have meant that his opponents actually threatened to assassinate him. Yet he describes these threats as good for him, because they taught him to rely not on himself but on God.

Endurance

So Paul writes to the Christians in Corinth about the pressures they were under. He suggests, humbly, that these pressures might teach them to be brave and patient, and hold on without giving way. Endurance is the first lesson we learn from our sufferings. When a mixed alloy of silver and other metals is heated in a refiner's fire, the impurities are burnt off, and the silver emerges pure and beautiful. So it is with our character, if we learn to endure the pressure upon us bravely and patiently. A man had been sick for a long time, and one of his friends said, 'Suffering does *colour* life so.' To which he replied, 'Yes. But I intend to choose the colour.'

Strengthening

And just as exercise strengthens our muscles, so the pressures on us strengthen our character. The word which is misleadingly translated as 'consolation' in this passage really means 'fortifying' or making somebody brave. When Polycarp, the second-century Bishop of Smyrna, was about to be burnt at the stake, he prayed to God in these words: 'I thank you that you have judged me worthy of this hour.' Paul's sufferings had made him brave, too. So he wished to share the lessons he had learnt with the Christians of Corinth. J. M. Barrie, the author of *Peter Pan*, wrote that when one of his brothers died, 'That is where my mother got her soft eyes, and why other mothers ran to her when *they* had lost a child.'

Driving us back to God

But above all, writes St Paul, the chief blessing which suffering, or any other sort of pressure, brings to us, is that it drives us back to God. When things get really bad, God is the only one who can help us. Not by taking away the pain, but by sharing it with us, and accepting it as our self-sacrificing offering, in union with the sacrifice of Jesus on the cross. It is the brave bearing of suffering that redeems the world. A life without any pressures would be boring: there is an Arab proverb which goes, 'All sunshine makes a desert.' Abraham Lincoln said, 'I have often been driven to my knees in prayer, because I had nowhere else to go.' God doesn't want us to suffer, but if it does fall to us to share some portion of the weight of the world's woe, then the Lord wants us to make use of that, to grow in strength of character, and to drive us back into the arms of Jesus, who understands what suffering is all about. That applies to everything from the pains of death to the niggling frustrations of daily life; learn from them that God is the only sufficient source of strength to bring us triumphantly through the pressures which afflict us all.

Suggested hymns

All ye who seek for sure relief; Morning glory, starlit sky; My song is love unknown; Take up thy cross, the Saviour said.

Twelfth Sunday after Trinity (Proper 15)   14 August
Principal Service   Signs of the Times

(*Continuous*): Isa. 5.1–7 The song of the vineyard, Ps. 80.1–2, 9–20 The vine; *or* (*Related*): Jer. 23.23–29 The word of God, Ps. 82 Justice; Heb. 11.29—12.2 Faith and perseverance; Luke 12.49–56 Interpreting the time

> '[Jesus] said to the crowds, "You hypocrites! You know how to interpret the appearance of earth and sky, but why do you not know how to interpret the present time?"' Luke 12.56

Forecasting

Often I go without a raincoat because the radio says it will be fine, and then get drenched to the skin. Yet, with the aid of computers, weather forecasting is improving. The trouble is, we ask the wrong questions, wanting predictions for a whole nation or continent, or contrariwise for our own street, which may have its own microclimate.

Signs of the times

When Jesus lived on earth, people lacked the computer skills, but by observing the clouds and the winds, a farmer could come up with a reasonable prediction. If you were wise, you based your day's plans on what was forecast. Jesus said, 'You can do that with weather, why can't you do it with politics?' He meant, if you look at history, you see that if one lot of people have power over another, and use it unjustly, the oppressed eventually rise up. The oppressors lose everything, the rebels get very little of what they demanded, and many people suffer and die. But, said our Lord, if you would read 'the signs of the times' as carefully as you read the signs of the weather, you could predict this and prevent it.

Jewish revolt

Jesus wasn't talking about the end of the world; he seldom did. The Romans had built an empire round the Mediterranean, bringing a stable economy, good straight roads and a just set of laws. This was paid for by a tax-collecting system which was totally corrupt, and the taxpayers had no say in how their taxes were spent. Jesus spoke in AD 30, and said, 'This cannot go on.' In AD 70 the Jews rose in revolt, were cruelly crushed, and thrown out of the Promised Land. The decline and fall of the Roman Empire took a little longer. But any fool could have predicted this would happen, if the Romans remained oppressive and their colonies fomented revolutionary nationalism.

Today

The Bible is no more use than the weather forecast if you ask either of them the wrong questions. It contains no predictions for the twenty-first century – how could it, because they would mean nothing to the centuries in between? But it reveals basic principles which you can apply to any age. A blog on Facebook read: 'People were created to be loved. Things were created to be used. The reason the world is in chaos is because things are being loved and people are being used.'

Rich and poor

There is a widening gap between rich and poor individuals and nations. A few wealthy individuals feed off the poor, starving majority. Tax dodgers keep for themselves money which should be helping poor nations to develop. That means that the burden of all the other things which are going wrong falls unfairly on the shoulders of the poor and hungry. For instance, global warming, whether it is a natural cycle or whether it is aggravated by carbon emissions, means that food crops fail, prices go up, and the poor cannot afford to buy themselves anything to eat. HIV/AIDS is aggravated in poor nations, because the people there cannot afford the education that would teach them how to prevent it, or the medical treatment to cure it, nor the healthy food that would help them to recuperate. The population explosion is greatest where education is low; where people cannot afford birth control; and where large families are essential, because most children die before they are five, and you must have at least one child to support you in your old age. The burden of national debt, and unfair trading patterns, prevents poor nations getting out of poverty. If we go on like this, the poor will rise up and demand the right to live where food is available. Their revolt will be crushed, just like the Jewish revolt was, but the wealthy will be ruined and many people will suffer and die unnecessarily.

Political

So it is urgent that we correct the imbalance between rich and poor nations before it is too late. Is this too political to include in a sermon? Ask Jesus. I think his reply would be, 'Why are you so good at reading the weather signs, but so slow in reading "the signs of the times?"'

All-age worship

Find out how much food most people can afford in poor countries compared with rich nations. What can we do? Make up a prayer.

Suggested hymns

For the fruits of his creation; Inspired by love and anger; Jesus Christ is waiting, waiting in the streets; When I needed a neighbour.

Twelfth Sunday after Trinity (Proper 15)   14 August
Second Service   **Generosity**

Ps. 119.17–32 Your decrees are my delight; Isa. 28.9–22 A foundation stone; 2 Cor. 8.1–9 Generosity; *Gospel at Holy Communion*:
Matt. 20.1–16 Labourers in the vineyard

> *'Now as you excel in everything – in faith, in speech, in knowl-*
> *edge, in utmost eagerness, and in our love for you – so we want*
> *you to excel also in this generous undertaking.' 2 Corinthians 8.7*

Jerusalem

Christianity began as a sect within the Jewish religion. The first
Christians were all Jews, and they wanted to show that they were
loyal to the Jewish laws and traditions. Overseas Jews had adapted
to a greater or lesser extent to the foreign customs of the Roman
Empire, and, as so often happens with people from the colonies moving to the centre of an empire, they had prospered in the process.
Many of the overseas Jews had also become Christians, and then
they had converted non-Jews to the Christian faith, also. But, to the
alarm of the loyal Jewish Christians back home in Jerusalem, the
converts were allowed to keep many of their metropolitan customs,
and to ignore the Jewish law altogether. Once this was known in
Jerusalem, there was a risk that Christianity might become associated
with slackness in religious observance, and the Jerusalem Christians
could be expelled from the Jewish community. Hence, great tensions
arose between Jews in Jerusalem and the rest of the Roman Empire.
St Paul had a brilliant idea to overcome this: he organized a collection, through which the richer Christians throughout the Empire
might give money to meet the physical needs of the poor Christians in
Jerusalem. Then the homeland Christians would feel indebted to the
others, which would cure them of their prejudice. He hoped.

Generosity

One of the reasons why Paul wrote his second letter to the Christians
in Corinth was to encourage them to give generously to the collection for the Christians in Jerusalem. It was not a begging letter; it was an appeal for charity. That particular charitable cause
is now long forgotten. But some of the reasons the Apostle gives in
favour of generous giving still apply to us today. Generosity means

giving without expecting anything in return. We can give generously of our time, assets or talents, to aid someone in need. John Bunyan, author of *The Pilgrim's Progress*, wrote: 'You have not lived today until you have done something for someone who can never repay you.'

Five reasons

So St Paul used five arguments to persuade the Corinthians to be generous:

1   He describes to them some people he knows: Christians in Macedonia, at the opposite end of Greece to Corinth, who were poor and in trouble, but nonetheless had given generously to the appeal.
2   He reminds them of the generosity of Jesus, who gave up the glories of heaven in order to come to earth to save us, and then surrendered his life to show us how costly love is.
3   Paul reminds the Corinthians of their own generosity in the past, and encourages them to live up to their track record.
4   He praises them for their noble feelings, and encourages them to turn those feelings into action.
5   He reminds them that those who are generous often find others being generous to them. Although virtue is its own reward, it is gratifying when you have done something good to somebody else if a third party, for no particular reason, decides to be good to you.

Praise

Kindness goes round in circles. The best way to start it off is to praise somebody. The Apostle writes to the Corinthians:

> Now as you excel in everything – in faith, in speech, in knowledge, in utmost eagerness, and in our love for you – so we want you to excel also in this generous undertaking.

This was not flattery – Paul was being absolutely sincere. This was what he thought the Corinthians were like, and he had lived several years among them. He was not afraid to criticize them when they were squabbling. But underneath, he had a deep faith in their virtue.

He assured them of his love for them. If you want somebody to behave well, it's no use railing at them and being critical. You have to make them feel good about themselves, make them feel loved. Then they will want to live up to your high opinion of them. It worked with the Corinthians, for Paul. Perhaps it will work with you, when I assure you that I have the highest opinion of you, and so does God, and he loves you more than you can imagine. Then you can use sincere praise while trying to raise funds for charity yourself. It works.

Suggested hymns

From heaven you came; O Lord of heaven and earth and sea; 'Lift up your hearts!' We lift them Lord to thee; Take my life, and let it be.

Thirteenth Sunday after Trinity (Proper 16)
21 August
Principal Service   **Mental Health**
(*Continuous*): Jer. 1.4–10 Jeremiah's call, Ps. 71.1–6 Providence; or (*Related*): Isa. 58.9b–14 The needy, Ps. 103.1–8 Forgiveness and healing; Heb. 12.18–29 The mediator of a new covenant; Luke 13.10–17 Healing on the Sabbath

> *'There appeared a woman with a spirit that had crippled her for eighteen years. She was bent over and was quite unable to stand up straight. When Jesus saw her, he called her over and said, "Woman, you are set free from your ailment." When he laid his hands on her, immediately she stood up straight and began praising God.' Luke 13.11–13*

Mind over matter

Jesus was in a Jewish synagogue on a Saturday, the Jewish Sabbath when no work was allowed. He was there to teach, but his fame as a healer had gone before him, and a handicapped woman sort of popped up in front of him, obviously asking to be healed of her disability. The chairman of the synagogue committee kept nattering on to everybody present that healing was work, and therefore should only be done on weekdays. But Jesus was quite clear that the law of love overrules all other laws. Yet it was complicated by the fact that nobody was sure what was wrong with her, or even whether she was sick at all. She was bent double, and no massage, exercises or medicines helped her to stand upright. The experts stood all round, arguing over her, and came to the conclusion it was all in her mind, not a physical illness at all. Jesus asked the woman her opinion, which nobody had done before. She described how guilty and oppressed she felt, with no energy, no hope for things to get any better, and how she despised herself as a sinner and a weakling. She agreed that the problem was in her mind, yet she had no control over her mind. She had come to the conclusion that her mind had been taken over by some evil spirit, like a big black dog sitting on her shoulders and weighing her down. Well, actually I'm not sure that she used those actual words, but 'the Black Dog' was how Winston Churchill described *his* depression, and I'm guessing that was her problem, too. When Jesus lived, nobody thought there was any cure for depression, and many people today are under the same delusion. But Jesus said to her, 'You feel trapped, do you? I'm telling you that from now on you are free. And to prove it I want you to stand up straight.' And that, which she had not done for 18 years, is what she did, proving the power of mental healing to remove physical symptoms – in other words, mind over matter.

Mental health

Mental illness is as much a treatable condition as physical disease. We shouldn't normally expect to heal mental illness as quickly as Jesus did: he had an instinctive insight into the workings of the mind, which takes doctors today years of study. But in the UK a report showed that as many people are suffering from mental health problems as from all the physical illnesses added together. Six million people in the UK suffer from depression, and 700,000 children have behaviour problems or anxiety. And mental disorder causes physical problems – mind over matter, again. An unwell mind can make existing physical illness worse, adding at least £10 billion to the annual cost of the NHS.

Hope

Not all physical illness is caused by mental problems, but much of it is aggravated by wrong mental attitudes. What can we do about mental health, then? Taking our cue from Jesus, the first step is to give the patient hope. Tell them to gradually reduce their dependence on antidepressants, see a doctor as soon as possible, and get referred to a counsellor who can help them talk through their problems. Look at their diet and exercise programme. But above all, urge them to have faith. If you believe you can get better you probably will; and vice versa. So we, the patients' friends, can praise them, give them back their self-confidence, and reassure them that even if they have occasional lapses, real progress is possible.

Faith

I'm not suggesting you 'ram religion down their throats', whatever that means. But it will be a great blessing if you can help them towards a sincere faith. Surely it is good to pray with the patient to Jesus the healer, and reassure them that Jesus loves them and wants them to be well. We all have days when we feel a bit low, and we need to hear Jesus saying to us, as he said to the disabled lady in the Gospels, *you are set free* from your hysteria and depression.

All-age worship

Make badges reading 'Jesus turned my sadness into gladness'.

Suggested hymns

Colours of day; From thee all skill and science flow; Lead, kindly light, amid th'encircling gloom; Thine arm, O Lord, in days of old.

Thirteenth Sunday after Trinity (Proper 16)
21 August
Second Service **'This Is the Way; Walk in It'**
Ps. 119.49–72 I was humbled that I might learn; Isa. 30.8–21 This is the way; 2 Cor. 9 A collection; *Gospel at Holy Communion*: Matt. 21.28–32 The two sons

> 'When you turn to the right or when you turn to the left, your ears shall hear a word behind you, saying, "This is the way; walk in it."' Isaiah 30.21

Minced oaths

The Ten Commandments warn us, 'Thou shalt not take the name of the Lord thy God in vain.' Probably this was originally a warning against swearing in a court of law: 'I swear by the name of Jehovah that my evidence is true', to guarantee the truth of a statement which is in fact a lie. It soon became interpreted as forbidding ever pronouncing the syllables which lie behind the euphemism, 'Jehovah'. Then the other use of the word 'swearing' supplanted the law-court usage, namely using a taboo or naughty word to express one's anger. Why using God's name as a swear word should make you feel better I have never understood; perhaps it is simply that doing something forbidden diverts your feelings of guilt away from your anger. Soon a lot of euphemisms arose which everybody knew meant something else; these have been referred to as 'minced oaths' and they are manifold: for instance 'Lawks a-mercy' for 'Lord have mercy'; 'Bloody' for 'By our Lady'; 'Gosh' for 'God'; 'OMG' for 'Oh my God'; 'Crikey' for 'Christ', and so on. This is all quite unnecessary; I am sure God has far more important things to worry about than whether you use his name to vent your spleen. One which became widespread in the 1930s and '40s was 'Jiminy Cricket' for Jesus Christ.

Pinocchio

It had been used in many films before, but it became famous when Walt Disney made Jiminy Cricket a character in his 1940 film *Pinocchio*. This was based on a story published in 1883 in Italian by Carlo Collodi. Pinocchio was a puppet, carved by a woodcarver named Geppetto, which dreamed of becoming a real boy. The carving had a small nose, which grew longer if the puppet started to tell lies. A minor character in Collodi's story was 'Il Grillo Parlante' or 'The Talking Cricket' – a cricket being a type of grasshopper. In Disney's film he was transformed into Jiminy Cricket, a comical and wise partner who accompanies Pinocchio on his journeys, appointed by the Blue Fairy to serve as the puppet's official conscience. He rides on the puppet's shoulder, whispering warnings into his ear whenever he is tempted to tell a lie or commit any other misdemeanour. The implication, surely, is that for an inanimate object to become human, it must acquire a moral sense, enabling it to choose between right and wrong.

216

Isaiah

The idea of a voice whispering into one's ear probably comes from today's reading from Isaiah: 'When you turn to the right or when you turn to the left, your ears shall hear a word behind you, saying, "This is the way; walk in it."' Perhaps some people actually do hear the voice of God helping them choose between right and wrong – lucky things. For the rest of us, life isn't that simple. It is too easy, when you want to do something selfish, to assign your ideas to your conscience: 'I felt in all conscience that I owed that to myself. God knows, I deserve it.' And then you use the imagined voice of God to justify doing something which God finds totally abhorrent.

Educating the conscience

So Christians down the ages have taught that our consciences need to be educated. If you think about what is right and what is wrong, searching the Bible for guidance, ignoring your own preferences, and then pray about it, you will usually come to a conviction about what God wishes. You probably won't hear a voice – that was Isaiah's metaphor. But when you have made up your mind about 'what would Jesus do' in such and such a situation, then, if you start to take the wrong path, part of your mind will give you a very uncomfortable stabbing feeling; whereas if you make the right choice, you will be cosy in the knowledge that you are doing the will of God.

Prayer

So praying to Jesus is an important part of developing an educated conscience, and 'Jiminy Cricket', a euphemism for 'Jesus Christ', is a very good name for it. This is summed up a few verses later by Isaiah, when he writes, 'Thus said the Lord GOD, the Holy One of Israel: In returning and rest you shall be saved; in quietness and in trust shall be your strength.' Only if you allow enough time in your busy life for returning and rest, for quietness and trust, can you be sure that you are behaving conscientiously.

Suggested hymns

I heard the voice of Jesus say; Lord Jesus, think on me; Put thou thy trust in God; Thy hand, O God, has guided.

Fourteenth Sunday after Trinity (Proper 17)

28 August

Principal Service   **Hospitality**

(*Continuous*): Jer. 2.4–13 Living water, Ps. 81.1, 10–16 God's justice; *or* (*Related*): Ecclus. (Ben Sira) 10.12–18 Pride and judgement, *or* Prov. 25.6–7 Pride and humility, Ps. 112 Righteousness; Heb. 13.1–8, 15–16 Righteousness; Luke 14.1, 7–14 Pride and humility

> '*Let mutual love continue. Do not neglect to show hospitality to strangers, for by doing that some have entertained angels without knowing it.*' Hebrews 13.1–2

Parties

At a banquet, Jesus noticed how the most important people sat near the host, and mere nobodies were relegated to seats further away, where nobody would notice them. The pompous guests, full of their own importance, elbowed their way to a place in the limelight. So Jesus asked them to imagine a man who seized the number-one place at a party, next to the host. When someone more important than he arrived at the last minute, he had to give way to the real VIP, and the only seat he could find was among the hoi polloi, while everybody laughed at him. The people who were at dinner with Jesus quickly realized the joke was on them, and felt ashamed of their arrogance.

Hosts

Then Jesus turned to the host, speaking about rewards in this world, and being praised by God in the world to come. 'Don't invite rich people to dinner,' he said, 'because they'll invite you back, and nobody will praise anyone.' Instead, 'invite the poorest of the poor, because they can't repay you here and now, but God will repay you in the afterlife.' The value of hospitality, he said, is that you try to give pleasure to others, not to seek glory for yourself.

Raphael

People from prosperous countries, who visited those who lived in poverty, reported with astonishment that the starving people brought what little food they had and presented it to their guest. Moreover, they are deeply insulted if you refuse it. Hospitality, for them, is a way of showing that they are our equals in giving pleasure to their guests. It is the very opposite of being self-centred. The author of the Letter to the Hebrews in the Bible writes: 'Let mutual love continue. Do not neglect to show hospitality to strangers, for by doing that some have entertained angels without knowing it.' Remember that people who saw angels in the Old Testament never describe wings or white robes, but thought at first that the angels were ordinary human beings. In one of the books in the Apocrypha — which is in the Greek Bible but not in the Hebrew text – Tobias travels around 600 miles accompanied by the archangel Raphael, and nobody recognizes him – not even the dog! – until he tells them who he is, and that he has been acting unselfishly on behalf of the unselfish God whom he serves.

Hospitable God

So we see from the Bible that self-giving love is the character of God. We have a God who is hospitable, welcoming us to the world he created, pouring upon us the gifts of all the world's beauty and love, for which we can never repay him. The only way to show our gratitude for what God has done for us is to be hospitable to other people. We don't have to offer open-house to everyone like God does – our homes are not big enough nor our pockets deep enough for that – but we can do what we can to give pleasure to others. On the surface hospitality is a matter of etiquette and entertainment. But at a much deeper level, it involves showing respect for your guests, providing for their spiritual needs, as well as their need for food and comfort, and treating them with respect. Hospitality towards strangers means spending time with them, paying them your full attention, so that they can feel at home, and become a friend instead of an enemy. When we show hospitality to someone, we are not trying to change them, but to offer them freedom to think things over, and to change if they want to. At its best, it is not trying to bring other people to agree with us on everything, but to offer them freedom to make up their own minds, and show that we respect their opinions. If that sounds a difficult task, just remember that this is how God treats us in his gracious hospitality, not forcing us to obey him, but wooing us with his love. And at the end, inviting us to live with him in his heavenly home.

All-age worship

Make a list of people you would like to invite to your next birthday. Why did you include some and not others? Whom would you ask if your parents only had room for six? What would you do to make those who were crossed off feel better?

Suggested hymns

All my hope on God is founded; Beauty for brokenness; Brother, sister, let me serve you; Such love.

Fourteenth Sunday after Trinity (Proper 17)
28 August
Second Service   **To See the King in His Beauty**
Ps. 119.81–96 Like a wineskin in the smoke; Isa. 33.13–22 To see the king in his beauty; John 3.22–36 I must decrease

> *'Your eyes will see the king in his beauty.' Isaiah 33.17*

Invisible

Many people are frustrated, because they can't actually see the God to whom they pray. Which is hardly surprising because God has no body, is invisible, and the Bible says, 'No one has ever seen God.' To very rare individuals is given the privilege of a vision of Jesus, perhaps once in their lives; the rest of us have to accept that God's character is like that of Jesus whom we have read about, and make do with the logical certainty that our Creator is with us at all times, whether we can see him or not. Jesus remarked that 'The wind blows where it chooses, and you hear the sound of it, but you do not know where it comes from or where it goes.' So he said that you can't see the wind, but you *can* see the effects of it – the bending of the branches in the trees, the washing of the waves in the storm; and similarly you can't see God, but you can see what God is doing in your life.

Turning

But first you have to turn your eyes away from the things that are distracting them from looking at God. Today's reading from Isaiah tells us how we have to prepare ourselves if we want to see God at work:

> Those who walk righteously and speak uprightly, who despise the gain of oppression, who wave away a bribe instead of accepting it, who stop their ears from hearing of bloodshed and shut their eyes from looking on evil, they will live on the heights; their refuge will be the fortresses of rocks; their food will be supplied, their water assured. Your eyes will see the king in his beauty.

Ignatius

St Ignatius Loyola, the founder of the Jesuits, wrote some practical advice on how to see God our king in all his beauty, by means of a short meditation which he called a 'daily examen'. In five short steps it helps us to reflect on the events of the day, in order to recognize God's presence in our lives, and work out what God wants us to do for him.

The first step is to **become aware of God's presence.** Reflect on the truth that God is right beside you, loving you and wanting you to do well. Then look back over the events of the past day, and ask God to help you to see them clearly with understanding.

Second, **review the day with gratitude.** The foundation of our relationship with God is to thank him constantly for all the good things that have happened to us. Take a mental stroll through what happened in the past 24 hours, and thank God for its joys and delights. Focus on the work you did, and the people you met. Ask yourself, 'What did I receive from these people? What did I give to them?' Pay attention to small things – the food you ate, the sights you saw, and other small pleasures. God is in the details.

Third, **pay attention to your emotions.** St Ignatius taught that we can detect the presence of the Spirit of God in our changing feelings. Modern psychiatrists would agree on the importance of our feelings, but they were not the first to realize this. Reflect on the feelings you experienced during the day. Were you happy? Sad? Bored? Excited? Confident? Resentful? Angry? Sympathetic? Then ask yourself, what is God saying to you through these feelings? God will probably show you some ways in which you fell short of his wishes and your own ideals. Make a private note of these sins, and tell God you are sorry. If you are frustrated, does God want you to explore new directions? Are you worried about your friend? Maybe God wants you to reach out to them.

Number four: **choose one feature of the day and pray about it.** A feeling, someone you met, a moment of pleasure or of peace. Think about it. Pray – expressing intercession, praise, repentance or gratitude.

Fifth and last: **look forward to tomorrow.** Ask God to guide you through tomorrow's challenges. As you work out what you expect will happen, imagine what your feelings will be, and turn these feelings into prayer. Seek God's guidance. Pray for hope.

Five steps

Five steps, then:

1 Become aware of God's presence.
2 Review the day with gratitude.
3 Pay attention to your emotions.
4 Choose one feature of the day and pray about it.
5 Look forwards to tomorrow.

If you do something like that most days, you will truly see God the king, as he interacts with your life, in all his beauty.

Suggested hymns

Christ is surely coming; Fairest Lord Jesus; Judge eternal, throned in splendour; My God, how wonderful thou art.

Fifteenth Sunday after Trinity (Proper 18)
4 September
Principal Service   **Slavery Today**
(*Continuous*): Jer. 18.1–11 The potter, Ps. 139.1–5, 12–18
God knows us; *or* (*Related*): Deut. 30.15–20 Choose life,
Ps. 1 Righteousness; Philemon 1–21 The runaway slave;
Luke 14.25–33 The call to take up the cross

'[Welcome Onesimus] no longer as a slave but more than a slave, a beloved brother.' Philemon 16

Onesimus

Philemon was a rich man, who owned a slave called 'Onesimus' [Oh-NEE-simm-us]. Fed up with his brutal treatment, the slave ran away, and made his way to the house where Philemon's friend St Paul was staying. There he heard St Paul preach the astonishing doctrine of equality, suggesting that 'in Christ' slaves were of equal worth with their owners; so Onesimus became a Christian. Yet it was illegal to protect somebody else's slave, so Paul sent him back to Philemon, with a letter in which he made the revolutionary suggestion that he should welcome him back, not as a slave, but as a brother Christian: 'welcome him as you would welcome me,' wrote Paul.

Abolition

In his other letters, Paul instructed Christian slaves to obey their masters for the time being; Christianity could not risk becoming known as a revolutionary movement. Until the eighteenth century, people used these texts as an excuse to ignore what Paul had written to Philemon about equality. But eventually, Christians began to see how wicked it is to claim ownership of another human being, and just over 200 years ago the British Parliament passed the Act abolishing slavery within the British Empire. You might think that was the end of the matter, but today there are 21 million people enslaved worldwide, and there are more slaves in Britain now than there were in the 1760s. People-trafficking is a 32-million-dollar business.

Different types

There are many different types of slavery today. Most people think immediately of prostitution, but 40 per cent of the people considered to be in slavery today are men. Men, women and children work in factories, in the fields, on construction sites, in brothels and in people's homes, living in fear and appalling conditions. I will give you some examples in that order. I hope all of you committed Christians will become very angry about it.

Factories

Some Polish workers in a chicken-packing factory near Exeter lived in a house with no furniture, a dangerous electric cooker, and were threatened with eviction and loss of two weeks' wages if they spoke about it.

Fields

Fruit-picking and hop-picking is seasonal work which used to be done by poor families from London's East End during their summer holidays. Nowadays no British worker will touch it, as they would lose their benefits, so immigrants are paid a pittance, and are then helpless when the season ends. The Morecambe cockle-pickers who drowned in 2004 were in a similar plight.

Construction sites

Immigrants are also brought into the country to work on construction sites, because British men won't accept the low pay which is offered. They dare not leave or seek another job because they have no papers.

Brothels

Maria came from Eastern Europe. Her family was poor and she had little education. When she was 13 she was sold to a man who took her to Italy, sold her to another man who raped her, and then smuggled her into England, where she was beaten, cut with knives and forced into prostitution. She escaped and returned to her family, who promptly sold her again, and the process was repeated. She worked every day for five years, seeing up to 70 customers a day, too terrified of what her owners would do to run away. She is now covered in scars and suffers depression. Many British children in local authority care are tempted to run away, trapped into the sex industry, arrested, sent back into care, and escape again because that way of life is less unpleasant.

Homes

Samolatha was working as a maid for a family in Jordan, who brought her with them when they moved to the UK. Here she continued to work a 16–18-hour day for £200 a month, and was never allowed to leave the house. These examples are typical of hundreds of people in slavery in this country today.

Action?

What should we do about slavery today?

- First, get very angry.
- Phone Crimestoppers on 0800 555 111 if you become aware of cases of exploitation, or dial 999 in emergencies.
- Demand that the police and social services become more aware of the problem.
- Write to your MP suggesting the police must prioritize victim protection, not immigration charges.
- Demand laws which impose prison for anyone involved in trafficking, even lorry drivers; and for anyone caught paying for sex, from navvies to government ministers.
- Then pray, as St Paul did for poor Onesimus.

All-age worship

Make a short summary of 'Good King Wenceslas'. Look up hopeforjustice.org.uk to see what help can be offered to people who have been trafficked.

Suggested hymns

All my hope on God is founded; Brother, sister, let me serve you; Good King Wenceslas looked out; I heard the voice of Jesus say.

Fifteenth Sunday after Trinity (Proper 18)
4 September
Second Service   **Unto the Hills**
Ps. [120 Deliver me] 121 I lift my eyes; Isa. 43.14—44.5 A new thing; John 5.30–47 Search the Scriptures

> *'I lift up my eyes to the hills;*
> *from where is my help to come?'*
>
> *Psalm 121.1 (Common Worship)*

Question?

There are no question marks in the ancient Hebrew manuscripts. So for centuries those who translated the psalms thought that the first verse of Psalm 121 was a statement. Many people know by heart the version from the Book of Common Prayer:

I lift up my eyes unto the hills,
from whence cometh my help [full stop]
My help cometh even from the Lord,
who hath made heaven and earth.

That was a fine statement: just as the hills have endured unchanged for years, so God's loving care never alters. God sits above us looking down benevolently upon us, as benign as the everlasting hills. Except that this is not what the original poem said. Most modern translations put back the missing question mark, asking, in effect, 'The hills of the robbers frighten me when I look up to them, so I ask: where will the help come from that will save me from all the wickedness up there [question mark]'

Help

It doesn't really matter, however, because the answer in either case is that God is our protector, because he made the heaven and the earth, and is greater than anything else that may threaten us. And that is a good thing to remember when you feel frightened. You may be scared of bad people, or bad illnesses, or an economic crash, or losing your job, or the inevitability that we shall die one day. But worry not! God, who made the hills, will give you a helping hand – he may not prevent the misfortune from happening to you, but he will give you the strength of character to brave the threats. Trust God to bring good out of the evil circumstances in the long run, by making you a stronger person.

Hills

So let's look back at the old way of reading these verses. In England and Ireland we have many beautiful rolling hills, covered with bracken, or picturesque woodland, or fields of crops; but very few threatening mountains. Scotland and Wales have their striking mountain ranges, but no robbers have lived up there for a very long time. The uplands and highlands are usually very beautiful, and it is reassuring to think that they were made by a God who is an artist and a nature-lover. They look like a protective barrier that God has arranged around us, to protect us from invading armies. The psalm continues:

> He will not suffer thy foot to be moved:
> and he that keepeth thee will not sleep.
> Behold, he that keepeth Israel shall neither slumber nor sleep.
> The Lord himself is thy keeper:
> the Lord is thy defence upon thy right hand;
> so that the sun shall not burn thee by day:
> neither the moon by night.
> The Lord shall preserve thee from all evil:
> yea, it is even he that shall keep thy soul;
> the Lord shall preserve thy going out, and thy coming in,
> from this time forth for evermore.

When the weather is hot we need a barrier cream to protect us against sunburn and sunstroke; and God will fulfil that function, says the psalm. But the assurance against the moon sounds more like magic, when it was believed that the lunar rays of the moon's brightness could give you 'lunacy'. Yet whenever anyone informs you that there is an evil spirit in their house, or a ghost, or that someone has put a curse on them, then, whether you believe in that sort of thing or not, you can assure them that God's power is greater than any other power. God will drive away any lesser powers, if you ask him. And then recommend that they read through Psalm 121.

Sleepless

Verse 4 assures us that 'He that keepeth Israel shall neither slumber nor sleep.' When Elijah was having a competition with the prophets of Baal, no fire came down from heaven in answer to their prayers. So Elijah mocked them:

> Cry aloud! Surely he is a god; either he is meditating, or he has wandered away, or he is on a journey, or perhaps he is asleep and must be awakened!

Then Elijah called on the Lord his God, and fire fell from heaven onto his sacrifice, as he had requested. The one true God never slumbers nor sleeps; he is on duty 24/7 and will always answer your prayers, one way or another. So when you are feeling low, remember that God is always there, as constant as the everlasting hills, and he will always give you the power to overcome your difficulties.

Suggested hymns

All praise to God who reigns above; Fill thou my life, O Lord my God; I lift my eyes to the quiet hills; Saviour, again to thy dear name we raise.

Sixteenth Sunday after Trinity (Proper 19)
11 September
Principal Service   **The Ninety and Nine**
(*Continuous*): Jer. 4.11–12, 22–28 Judgement, Ps. 14 The fool has said; *or* (*Related*): Ex. 32.7–14 The golden calf and a prayer for forgiveness, Ps. 51.1–11 Prayer for forgiveness; 1 Tim. 1.12–17 Christ brings salvation; Luke 15.1–10 A lost sheep, a woman's lost coin

> '[Jesus asked the scribes and Pharisees,] "Which one of you, having a hundred sheep and losing one of them, does not leave the ninety-nine in the wilderness and go after the one that is lost until he finds it?"' Luke 15.4

Sankey

Ira D. Sankey was born in Pennsylvania in 1840, and was converted at a revival meeting in a nearby Methodist church when he was 16. At a YMCA convention in Indianapolis he met the evangelist Dwight L. Moody, who invited him to sing at his revival meetings, and was so impressed he invited Sankey to resign his job and work full time as a singer. They paid their first of many visit to the UK in 1872.

Singing

Moody pointed up the importance of Sankey's singing when he said, 'If we can only get people to have the words of the love of God coming from their mouths it's well on its way to residing in their hearts.' A collection of 1,200 hymns that were used at their meetings was published under the name of *Sacred Songs and Solos*, which was popularly known simply as 'Sankey and Moody'. The two evangelists were in a train on their way from Glasgow to Edinburgh in 1874 when Sankey was browsing through a weekly newspaper. He spotted a poem by Elizabeth Clephane, called 'The Ninety and Nine'. She had written it in 1868, and died in 1869, five years previously, quite unaware that her poem would become one of the nineteenth century's most famous hymns. Sankey cut out the quotation and slipped it in his pocket. That evening Moody preached on 'the Good Shepherd' and at the end of the meeting asked Sankey if he had a suitable song to end with. Even though nobody had written a tune to the words he had found in the newspaper, Sankey decided to improvise, and seated at the organ, half-singing, half-speaking, he developed the melody as he sang through the five verses. Moody walked over to him with tears in his eyes, asking him, 'Where did you get that hymn?'

Poetic language

We may find the poetic language old-fashioned, but this hymn still has power to make people weep:

There were ninety and nine that safely lay
in the shelter of the fold,
but one was out on the hills away,
far off from the gates of gold.
Away on the mountains wild and bare,
away from the tender shepherd's care.

Lost

Some people say aggressively, 'I'm not religious', to which I can only reply, 'I'm so sorry, you are missing the joy of knowing that you are loved':

'Lord, thou hast here thy ninety and nine;
are they not enough for thee?'
But the shepherd made answer: 'this of mine
has wandered away from me;
and although the road be rough and steep,
I go to the desert to find my sheep.'

Unworthy

Yet others may say wryly, 'If I went into church the building would fall down!' The reply to which is, 'I doubt it. We are all sinners there, and Jesus loved to forgive sinners':

> But none of the ransomed ever knew
> how deep were the waters crossed;
> nor how dark was the night the lord passed through
> ere he found his sheep that was lost.
> Out in the desert he heard its cry,
> sick and helpless and ready to die.

Costly

Think about it: it cost Jesus his life on the cross to call you back onto the path to heaven:

> 'Lord, whence are those blood drops all the way
> that mark out the mountain's track?'
> 'They were shed for one who had gone astray
> ere the shepherd could bring him back.'
> 'Lord, whence are thy hands so rent and torn?'
> 'They are pierced tonight by many a thorn.'

Music

The music, like the words, is dated, but it was the popular style of its day:

> And all through the mountains, thunder riven
> and up from the rocky steep,
> there arose a glad cry to the gate of heaven,
> 'Rejoice! I have found my sheep!'
> and the angels echoed around the throne,
> 'Rejoice, for the Lord brings back his own!'

Contemporary

So God bless those who are writing hymns in today's 'pop music' style. You may feel that it is unsuitable for singing in church. But we must find some way of touching the hearts of young people today, who feel lost and unloved just as much now as in Ira Sankey's day.

All-age worship

Bring or make toy sheep, and carry them around your shoulders home to the fold.

Suggested hymns

Loving shepherd of thy sheep; The king of love my shepherd is; The Lord's my shepherd; There were ninety and nine (see http://cyber-hymnal.org/htm/n/i/90_and_9.htm)

Sixteenth Sunday after Trinity (Proper 19)
11 September
Second Service   Enlightenment
Ps. 124 If the Lord were not on our side, 125 Those who trust in the Lord; Isa. 60 Arise, shine; John 6.51–69 I am the living bread

> *'Arise, shine; for your light has come, and the glory of the LORD has risen upon you.' Isaiah 60.1*

Enlightenment

During a dark night in the open air, you can see nothing. You stumble over things, and you cannot understand why things happen to you. Then the sun rises, light shines on everything around, and you can recognize and understand things that were previously a mystery. This experience has often been used as a metaphor for many forms of intellectual understanding. 'I suddenly saw the light,' we say. 'I had a light-bulb moment.' 'All at once, everything was as clear as daylight.' Or, in a single word, 'I became enlightened.' This then became applied to a period in the seventeenth and eighteenth centuries, called the Age of Reason, or the Enlightenment. Until then, few people could read Greek, but when they did, they rediscovered many of the ideas the Greek philosophers suggested about how the physical world works. This led to the scientific method, which starts when someone makes a hypothesis. That is another way of saying an inspired guess, about cause and effect. Next they suggest something that could be predicted if the hypothesis is right, and perform an experiment in controlled conditions, taking measurements to see whether the prediction has come true. This way of reasoning shone fresh light on many things that happen in the material world.

Philosophers

Alongside this went a revolution in philosophy. The Enlightenment wanted to reform society using reason, to challenge ideas based on tradition and religious revelation, and advance knowledge by means of the scientific method. It encouraged scepticism and opposed superstition and intolerance, especially in the Roman Catholic Church. Philosophers like Spinoza, John Locke, Voltaire, and the physicist Isaac Newton are associated with the age of the Enlightenment, but it took different forms in different countries. In Scotland, David Hume took a fresh look at political economy; in Germany, Goethe and Schiller were more concerned with cultural issues. In the USA, the Enlightenment influenced Benjamin Franklin and Thomas Jefferson, and played a major role in the American Revolution and the Bill of Rights. Only in France did it take an extreme form, with the publication of the great *Encyclopaedia*, with contributions from Voltaire, Rousseau and Montesquieu. But when this led into the violence of the French Revolution, the deficiencies of the Age of Reason became clear, and it was abandoned in favour of the emphasis on emotion in the Romantic Movement.

Religion

Meantime, the Enlightenment had a great influence on religious thinking. Appalled by the way religious tensions allied to extreme nationalism had led to conflict between Protestants and Catholics, culminating in the Thirty Years War, Enlightenment theologians sought to return to the non-confrontational roots of religion, while still maintaining a true faith in God. For most, this resulted in a return to the Bible. John Locke wanted belief in Christ the redeemer, avoiding more complex debate. Thomas Jefferson abandoned miracles, angels and physical resurrection, and tried to return to a simple moral code from the New Testament. Spinoza wanted to remove politics from religion and vice versa. Deism emerged as a

232

belief in a Creator who has little interest in his creation. But there was almost universal rejection of atheism, which thinkers of the Enlightenment believed could only result in immorality. And while the scientific method was useful in solving physical problems, most people rejected materialism, which was the idea that the material world is all that exists, and any spiritual ideas such as love, which cannot be weighed or measured, are complete nonsense.

Today

Some Christians from the Third World, encouraged by fundamentalists from the USA, have criticized liberal churches of Europe and America of 'selling out to the Enlightenment' by rejecting a literal interpretation of the Bible, and reinterpreting the miracles and resurrection in a way quite unlike the traditional understanding of those things. They have a point, and we must be cautious not to abandon 'the Rock from which we were hewn'. But Isaiah is describing a spiritual enlightenment when he calls his readers to turn away from darkness: 'Arise, shine; for your light has come, and the glory of the LORD has risen upon you.' The task of the churches, where many of the population are well educated in science, is to reinterpret traditional teaching so as to show that there is no conflict between materialistic science and spiritual religion. Unless we can demonstrate this, those who think scientifically will reject religion entirely. The decline of church attendance in the West is not because we have bought into the Enlightenment, but because those from a more traditional background refuse to re-express their faith in more flexible ways. Without that, evangelism is dead.

Suggested hymns

Above the moon earth rises; Every star shall sing a carol; Lord of the boundless curves of space; The spacious firmament on high.

Seventeenth Sunday after Trinity (Proper 20)
18 September
Principal Service   **Shrewd Stewardship**
(*Continuous*): Jer. 8.18—9.1 Balm in Gilead, healing the nation, Ps. 79.1–9 Suffering, prayer for forgiveness; or (*Related*): Amos 8.4–7

> *'[Jesus said,] "His master commended the dishonest manager because he had acted shrewdly; for the children of this age are more shrewd in dealing with their own generation than are the children of light."' Luke 16.8*

The Ladykillers

One of the funniest of the old Ealing comedy films was called *The Ladykillers*. In it a group of villains use a room in a sweet old lady's house, which one of them has rented as a lodging, as cover for planning a robbery. But the lady finds out, and the criminals decide they will have to murder her. Yet by a hilarious series of mishaps each of them dies, and the lady remains alive. The audience feels a degree of sympathy for the criminals, even admiration for their ingenuity, without ever forgetting that what they are planning is morally wrong. One critic wrote that to be frivolous about frivolous matters is boring, but to be frivolous about something deadly serious, like murder, is true black comedy.

Unjust steward

Perhaps that explains the story that Jesus told in today's reading about the dishonest steward – it was a joke. Our Lord may have had a well-developed sense of humour. He told a tall tale about a rich man who employed a manager, or steward, to run his business. But the manager was dishonest, and was skimming off some of the money he was entrusted with, for his own use. When his employer challenged him to present his accounts for auditing, the steward thought up an ingenious way of protecting his own interests. He told each of the tenants to falsify the records of how much rent they owed. By these crooked means, the steward ensured that any of the tenants would give him a roof over his head after he was sacked; and by making them complicit in his crime, he could bribe them to give false evidence if necessary. When the landowner found out, he gave out a great guffaw, and praised the wicked steward for his low cunning. There are no nice characters in this story, but we feel a sneaking admiration for the time and trouble they put into protecting their own interests.

Meaning

So why did Jesus joke about such wicked behaviour? Principally to ask why people take so much trouble about their short-term interests, but put so little effort into ensuring their eternal future.

Long-term

Teenagers are often criticized for seeking short-term pleasure and forgetting about their long-term needs. But we all do it. The present is real and tangible, whereas the future is vague and requires an effort of imagination. We run up a debt without thinking twice about it – not only as individuals, but as a nation – imagining that all we have to do is print more money, and borrow from Peter to pay Paul. We all live on virtual money. If we have a windfall, we spend it on an expensive holiday, rather than on paying off the mortgage. As for what happens to us when we die, that's a long way off, we imagine, and we don't want to think about it. Even the dishonest steward planned for the future, but we never give it a second thought.

Eternal life

But Jesus warns us that we shall all die sometime, and then we shall be asked for an audited account, not of our money, but of how much good we have done for other people with the material resources that God has lent us. When Jesus commented that 'the children of this age are more shrewd in dealing with their own generation than are the children of light', he meant that Christians are never so ingenious and eager in their attempts to become virtuous as worldly people are in seeking money and comfort. If only we would pay as much attention to what concerns our souls as we do to our business, we would be much better people. But we devote 20 times as much money and time to hobbies, sport or gardening as we do to our church, so it is no wonder that the church is making so little impression on this materialistic world. The parable of the shrewd steward uses humour to show up the folly of ignoring the future, as surely as the film about *The Ladykillers* warns us that selfishness is no laughing matter.

All-age worship

Draw up a pocket-money budget in three columns: To make me happy now; To make me happy in the future; Kind deeds to make me happy in heaven.

Suggested hymns

Great is thy faithfulness, O God my Father; Let us talents and tongues employ; O Lord of heaven and earth and sea; Take my life, and let it be.

Seventeenth Sunday after Trinity (Proper 20)
18 September
Second Service   **Sent by God**
Ps. [128 Domestic Bliss] 129 Cursing the persecutors; Ezra 1 Permission to rebuild; John 7.14–36 The one who sent me

> *'Jesus answered them, "My teaching is not mine but his who sent me." John 7.16*

Ambassadors

An ambassador is someone who is sent by the government of one country to speak on their behalf to the leaders and people of another nation. It is not their own opinions that they are voicing, but those of the government that sent them. In a democracy, that means they represent the views of the majority of voters. But because every nation has its own language and culture, ambassadors have to begin by learning the ways in which the people think and speak, to whom they have been sent, so as to be able to express the views of their home country in a way that will not be misunderstood. Sometimes if there has been a serious misunderstanding between the two nations, ambassadors seek to act as peacemakers, reconciling two peoples who have come to think of each other as enemies. Nowadays we have ambassadors of the United Nations, who represent not just one country but the whole world, which is concerned that the internal disputes in the nation to which they are sent may disturb the peace of everybody in the world. Perhaps Jesus had ambassadors in mind when he answered the people in the crowd in Jerusalem. They were divided between those who regarded him as a good man, and those who thought he was making up false teaching to deceive the crowd. His reply to this accusation was, 'My teaching is not mine, but his who sent me.' In other words he was an ambassador for God, his heavenly Father. He was not expressing an individual opinion, but bringing messages from God, and trying to translate them into the thought patterns of the Jewish people to whom he had been sent.

Sent

The word 'sent' occurs several times in these verses:

> My teaching is not mine but his who *sent* me . . . Those who speak on their own seek their own glory; but the one who seeks the glory of him who *sent* him is true, and there is nothing false in him . . . I have not come on my own. But the one who *sent* me is true, and you do not know him. I know him, because I am from him, and he *sent* me.

But the Jews were expecting not a teacher or ambassador, but a Messiah – an anointed king, who would lead them into battle, to drive out the occupying Roman army. Yet Jesus refused to fit their definition of a Messiah:

> Some of the people of Jerusalem were saying, 'Can it be that the authorities really know that this is the Messiah? Yet we know where this man is from; but when the Messiah comes, no one will know where he is from.' Then Jesus cried out as he was teaching in the temple, 'You know me, and you know where I am from . . . I will be with you a little while longer, and then I am going to him who sent me.'

He was not going to build an earthly kingdom. Christ was an ambassador from heaven; he was appealing on God's behalf for peace and reconciliation, between the peoples of the world, and between God's rebellious children and their Father in heaven. The kingdom he is building is in heaven, and he was going back there to lead the way for us all to dwell there through all eternity.

Ambassadors for Christ

Christ was an ambassador from God, speaking with full authority on his Father's behalf. St Paul, in his second letter to the Corinthians, says that you and I are ambassadors for Christ. We have been sent by Jesus to represent him in the kingdom of the world, to speak on Christ's behalf to the people we meet, telling them that God loves them and forgives them. We are to try and reconcile people to each other, and above all to make them friends with God. It is a responsible task, yet Jesus has promised to give us the strength and the wisdom we need to speak for him. But first we must be reconciled with those who count us their enemies, and say sorry to God for all the ways in which we have hurt him, so that we can re-establish the 'special relationship' with God that he wants. In this way the ambassadorial task of Jesus will be completed, on behalf of God who sent him.

Suggested hymns

Happy are they, they that love God; Jesus, stand among us at the meeting of our lives; There is a Redeemer; You, living Christ, our eyes behold.

Eighteenth Sunday after Trinity (Proper 21)
25 September
Principal Service **Temperature of Hell, Furniture of Heaven**
(*Continuous*): Jer. 32.1–3a, 6–15 Buying a field, Ps. 91.1–6, 14–16 Providence; *or* (*Related*): Amos 6.1a, 4–7 Possessions, Ps. 146 The needy; 1 Tim. 6.6–19 Possessions, the needy; Luke 16.19–31 A rich man and Lazarus

> '[Jesus said,] "It came to pass, that the beggar died, and was carried by the angels into Abraham's bosom: the rich man also died, and was buried . . ."' Luke 16.22 (King James Version)

Lazarus

In order to bring home forcibly the dangers of being mean with our money, Jesus told a story about an unnamed rich man, and a poor man called Lazarus, both of whom have died. The rich man is described as being in torment, but he can see in the distance Lazarus, as the King James Version puts it, 'in Abraham's bosom'. Between them there is a great uncrossable gulf or chasm. Is this a literal description of the afterlife, or is Jesus using poetic language to get his meaning across, to convey an idea which, in reality, is quite indescribable? The first thing to notice is that Lazarus, the name of the poor man, is an uncommon name, short for Eleazar, and was the name of Jesus's friend, whom he raised from the dead at Bethany. It seems odd to use the name of your best friend for a fictional character, unless Jesus was asking his hearers to imagine what had *already* happened, during the three days when Lazarus had been dead.

Abraham's bosom

Second, notice that the poor man is, literally, 'in Abraham's bosom'. The angels carried him there, but there is no mention of God. But the most flattering thing you can say about a Jew is that she or he is a descendant of Abraham. That defined that they were one of the Chosen People, and inheritors of the promises that God made to their ancestors. And when they gave a party, they were reclining on couches, leaning on their right elbow, with the host in the centre and the most important guest, the guest of honour, reclining on his right. So when he leant across to speak to the host, the guest was literally leaning on the chest of the host. In St John's Gospel, the disciple whom Jesus loved was reclining in Jesus's bosom, and in heaven, Jesus is in the Father's bosom. Even the New Revised Standard Version of the Bible gags at mentioning bosoms, because the word has shifted its meaning, but it is simply a metaphor for being highly honoured. The penniless beggar had become the most honoured of his race.

Grand Canyon

The rich man can see Abraham. If that is taken literally, either heaven and hell are both above the clouds, or both under the earth, or both on earth, on either side of the Grand Canyon. The rich man says he is 'in agony in these flames'. This image comes from Jesus's description of the wicked being destroyed, like garbage thrown onto the city rubbish tip. These are all thought-provoking images, but taken literally, and applied to the billions of humans who have died, they just don't fit together.

The absence of God

I cannot help thinking that, eventually, God in his mercy will allow those who rejected him to descend into nothingness. Hell has been described as 'the utter absence of God'. But I surely think it is more just that, before that, the wicked and the unbelievers should have a brief vision of what they have rejected, and suffer deep feelings of regret. Without that, there is nothing to deter the godless from living a devil-may-care life up until they die.

Niebuhr

The great German theologian Reinhold Niebuhr remarked that 'the Bible says little about the temperature of hell nor the furniture of heaven'. So I think the story of the rich man and Lazarus is a wonderful poem, designed to teach us that bad deeds have bad consequences, sooner or later, and we shall regret them. Like the rich man's brothers, we need to pay serious attention to the warnings against selfish behaviour that are in the Bible, however we choose to interpret it. But leave others to worry about the temperature and the furniture.

All-age worship

Make a big pair of scales standing on a card. On the card underneath one tray write 'Eternal Life' and under the other 'Eternal Death'. On the 'death' tray put a large weight labelled 'Selfish Deeds'; and on the other, a small weight, 'Good Deeds', and another labelled 'God's Grace'. Together they weigh more, and bring the scales down on 'Eternal Life'.

Suggested hymns

All my hope on God is founded; Amazing grace; Immortal love, for ever full; Rejoice, the Lord is King.

Eighteenth Sunday after Trinity (Proper 21)
25 September
Second Service   Slaves of Sin
Ps. 134 Night-time in the Temple, 135 The acts of God; Neh. 2 Surveying the walls; John 8.31–38, 48–59 Jesus and Abraham

'Jesus answered them, "Very truly, I tell you, everyone who commits sin is a slave to sin."' John 8.34

240

Freedom

Every free man and woman is inordinately proud of their freedom. At the last night of the Proms, patriotic promenaders proclaim, 'Britons never, never, never shall be slaves', and they really mean it. Sometimes, pirates might have captured a few Brits and sold them into slavery, perhaps in the harem of some Arab sultan. There they might be well looked after, even pampered, but nothing could make up for the fact that they could make no choices and come to no decisions for themselves. So the great fear of the British people was that they might be defeated by some aggressor, and the whole nation would be taken into slavery. But in the ancient world, slavery was so common that it was reckoned that in great cities like Ephesus there were eight slaves for every freeborn husband and wife. Their only hope was to save up enough in tips to one day buy their freedom, or find a generous donor who would become their redeemer by buying them from their slave owner and setting them free.

Addiction

But as Jesus pointed out, there is more than one sort of slavery. If you get into a bad habit, and cannot give it up, you may correctly be described as a slave to your desires. The most obvious example is slavery to alcohol. The alcoholics who say in a slurred voice, 'I musht have another drink', believe in their muddled minds that they could give up the demon drink if they wanted to; but in fact the addiction has such a grip on them that without some very unpleasant drying-out treatment, they will be slaves to the habit until it kills them. From that you can see how people become slaves to narcotics, or even to prescription tranquilizers and pain-killers, which actually kill more people every year than heroin and cocaine. Then there is obesity, which may have a medical cause, but is often due to slavery to fattening foods. These are the obvious enslavements. But there are many less noticeable addictions which victims cannot break free from. The playboy and the nymphomaniac are slaves to their sex habits; the gossip is slave to the habit of criticizing other people; the bully is addicted to violence; some people are addicted to lying, and the shoplifter to thievery. While all these people claim they could break free from their habit if they wanted to, they are no more free than was the black slave from the slave-driver.

241

Jesus

So Jesus said, 'Very truly, I tell you, everyone who commits sin is a slave to sin.' That sounds pretty far-reaching, because we mostly think of sin as being minor peccadilloes which harm nobody. But in fact the essence of sin is selfishness; what makes a deed sinful is that you have put your own wishes before the needs of others. It is the sinner who suffers most, as they grow a hard shell of self-centredness over their finer qualities. Not until they realize that is there any hope for a cure. We imagine that we are free to do what we like. But if we allow some pleasure or other to take hold of us so completely that we cannot do without it, we are slaves to our pleasures. The Greek philosopher Socrates demanded, 'How can you call someone free when their pleasures rule over them?'

Redemption

Yet every slave can be redeemed if they find a redeemer. The two disciples on the road to Emmaus said they had hoped Jesus was the one who would redeem Israel. In fact he is far greater than that, for he is the Redeemer of every sinner who calls to him for liberation. Jesus said to the Jews who had believed in him, 'If you continue in my word, you are truly my disciples; and you will know the truth, and the truth will make you free.' He set the agenda for his ministry, and that of the Church which continues his work, as bringing in the Jubilee year, when all slaves were to be given their freedom:

> The Spirit of the Lord is upon me, because he has anointed me to bring good news to the poor. He has sent me to proclaim release to the captives and recovery of sight to the blind, to let the oppressed go free, to proclaim the year of the Lord's favour.

Jesus invites us to exchange our bitter slavery to sin, for becoming free and voluntary servants of God. In the beautiful words of the Book of Common Prayer, God's 'service is perfect freedom'.

Suggested hymns

And can it be?; Guide me, O thou great Redeemer; Our blest Redeemer, ere he breathed; There's a wideness in God's mercy.

Nineteenth Sunday after Trinity (Proper 22)
2 October
(Alternatively the Dedication Festival)
Principal Service **Faith**

(Continuous): Lam. 1.1–6 The nation, suffering, *Canticle*: Lam. 3.19–26 New every morning, *or* Ps. 137 Suffering in Babylon; *or* *(Related)*: Hab. 1.1–4; 2.1–4 A watchman, Ps. 37.1–9 Faith and justice; 2 Tim. 1.1–14 Faith and justice; Luke 17.5–10 Faith and obedience

> *'The apostles said to the Lord, "Increase our faith!" The Lord replied, "If you had faith the size of a mustard seed, you could say to this mulberry tree, 'Be uprooted and planted in the sea,' and it would obey you."' Luke 17.5–6*

Gambling

Probably most of you would be offended if I said that you are gamblers. But in fact, when confronted with a choice between two courses of action, we often cannot be sure what the results of each of them will be. We have to weigh up the probabilities, and plump for the one that seems most likely to produce an auspicious result. In the absence of certainties, we have to gamble. Every time you leave your house, there is a chance that something harmful might happen to you. But you take a gamble that if anything goes wrong today, you will be able to cope with it. You have to have faith in yourself. If you never took any risks, you would never be able to go out at all.

Science

In science, too, you need faith. Some theories can be tested by experiment, but when you get down to the subatomic level and quantum theory, you can only say 'this calculation fits the observable facts best', and have faith that it is the right answer. On human or animal behaviour, you make a survey, observing that there is often a correlation between two sets of circumstances, and have faith that they are cause and effect. On the individual level, you must have faith that if you treat your beloved right, he or she will still love you when you become Darby and Joan; if you wait for concrete proof, you will never get past first base.

Tennyson

So the whole of life is one big gamble. Tennyson wrote it in his poem 'In Memoriam':

By faith and faith alone embrace,
believing where we cannot prove.

Being a Christian is a gamble. Nobody can prove that there is an afterlife, and nobody can prove that there isn't. But there are many indicators that there probably is. People feel the presence of their loved ones who have died. People have 'near-death' experiences of seeing a bright light. People in every age have described having visions of heaven.

Jesus

Above all, there is the evidence of Jesus, who was not someone who would mislead us. He predicted his own resurrection, and over 500 people saw him alive after he had died. Millions of prayers every day are addressed to Jesus, and are answered too often for it to be a coincidence. He promised that those who have faith in him would share in eternal life, and today's readings illustrate the power of faith.

The greatest gamble

None of these pieces of evidence individually amounts to a scientific proof. But together they can be explained better by belief in eternal life than by any other theory. So you are faced with a choice. Are you prepared to bet your life on the belief that Jesus was telling the truth? The probability of your being right is far more likely than not. If you have faith that there is a better world after this; then, as trillions of Christians bear witness, life is fun, satisfying, and we are given the strength to triumph over difficulties. If your gamble was right you will go on to a better world than you had ever imagined. But in the unlikely circumstance that you were wrong, then, when you die, that will be the end of it, but you will have enjoyed a satisfying and purposeful life while it lasted. Whereas if you bet that

244

there is no afterlife, there are again two possible outcomes: either you were right, and you will vanish into nothingness, without having ever known the joy of believing yourself to be loved by God; or, if you were mistaken, there is a heaven for those who believed, from which, unless God is very merciful, you may find yourself excluded.

Summary

Let me repeat: life's greatest gamble is to bet that eternal life is possible. If you have faith in that, life will be happy and purposeful, whether or not you were right, and death will be followed, possibly by eternal forgetfulness, but more likely by glory beyond our imagining. The only losers in this gamble are those who refuse to bet.

All-age worship

Make a poster reading 'I trust that Jesus is . . .' and then write words beginning with A, B, C, all the way to Z.

Suggested hymns

Dear Lord and Father of mankind; Give me the wings of faith to rise; O thou who camest from above; To God be the glory.

Nineteenth Sunday after Trinity (Proper 22)
2 October
Second Service   Siloam
Ps. 142 My portion in the land of the living; Neh. 5.1–13 Social justice; John 9 Spiritual blindness

> *'[Jesus said to the blind man,] "Go, wash in the pool of Siloam" (which means Sent). Then he went and washed and came back able to see.' John 9.7*

Imagine

I want you to close your eyes and imagine you have come with me on a pilgrimage to Jerusalem. Downhill, just south of the ancient walls of 'Jerusalem the Golden', we are going through the ornate gateway of a theme park, recently established, labelled 'The City of David – Ancient Jerusalem. Jerusalem Walls National Park.' Can you picture it? You wait inside the gateway while I buy your tickets, then we walk down a winding lane between the ruins of the walls which King David built, to the entrance building to Hezekiah's Tunnel. The only natural water source in Jerusalem was the Gihon spring, but it was outside the walls, so if Jerusalem was besieged it would be without water – unless they built a tunnel down which the water from Gihon could be sent to a pool inside the city. We go down some steps and walk along the low, narrow stone tunnel – I hope none of you suffer from claustrophobia! In the eighth century BC it was built by King Hezekiah to send water from the Gihon Spring for 533 meters. It is mentioned in the Old Testament. The workmen started from both ends, and met up having created a tunnel with a steady drop of merely 30 centimetres. They left a tablet describing their achievement at the point where they met, and it was discovered in 1880.

Three Valleys

With a sigh of relief we come up from the tunnel, and make our way to the Three Valleys lookout. Picture the Mount of Olives on your left, separated from Jerusalem by the Kidron Valley. On your right is the Valley of the Cheese-Makers, which ran through the centre of Jerusalem. In front of you is the Valley of Hinnom, formerly Jerusalem's municipal rubbish tip, where the worms never die, and the fire is never quenched. Jesus therefore used it as a symbol for telling people they were a load of rubbish. The Greek version is 'Gehenna', misleadingly translated as 'hell' in the New Testament.

Siloam

Now we walk down to what is now considered to be the remains of the Pool of Siloam. Remember, that was mentioned in today's reading, when Jesus said to the blind man,

> 'Go, wash in the pool of Siloam' (which means Sent). Then he went and washed and came back able to see.

It was only discovered in 2004. Steps lead down to the site of a large pool, which appears to have covered the whole area of the adjacent orchard. Screens at one side have been covered with life-sized paintings illustrating what it looked like when in use in Roman times. Jesus also referred to 18 men who were killed when the tower at Siloam fell on them, emphasizing that God does not send natural accidents to punish people – bad things happen to good people, too.

Stepped street

If you have now soaked up the atmosphere of this large, recently rediscovered pool which is mentioned so many times in the Gospels, come with me up a steep, stepped, stone street back towards the Temple Mount. Jewish pilgrims may have come to purify themselves in the waters of Siloam before going up these steps to worship in the Temple. We pass the sunken remains of the Byzantine Pool of Siloam, probably built by Empress Eudokia in the fifth century. Until 2004 pilgrims visited this, thinking wrongly that it was the pool that Jesus spoke about.

Conclusion

Now, if your eyes are still closed, please open them. Remember: the name 'Siloam' is Hebrew for 'sent'; the water is *sent* to the pool through the tunnel; Jesus *sent* the blind man to wash there. He didn't know why, but when he obeyed, he was healed. Then he was cross-questioned by the Pharisees, who thought Jesus was a sinner for healing on the Sabbath. The man who had been blind answered, 'I do not know whether he is a sinner. One thing I do know, that though I was blind, now I see.' The Greek for somebody who is sent is *apostolos*. So the apostles were sent to tell the world that Jesus loves us. The equivalent Latin word is *missio*. So God *sends* us all to be missionaries. If we go where we are sent, and to whomever we are sent, even if we don't understand, then, when we get there, we shall see what our mission is. It may be simply to describe our own experience of faith: once we were spiritually blind, but we did what Jesus told us, and then we saw the light.

Suggested hymns

Amazing grace; I heard the voice of Jesus say; Forth in thy name, O Lord, I go; We are marching in the light of God.

Twentieth Sunday after Trinity (Proper 23)
9 October
Principal Service Outcasts

(*Continuous*): Jer. 29.1, 4–7 Support the city, Ps. 66.1–11 What God has done; or (*Related*): 2 Kings 5.1–3, 7–15c Naaman healed from leprosy, Ps. 111 The works of the Lord; 2 Tim. 2.8–15 Suffering and perseverance; Luke 17.11–19 The healing of a leper and his thanks

> 'Ten lepers approached [Jesus]. Keeping their distance, they called out, saying, "Jesus, Master, have mercy on us!"' Luke 17.12–13

Leprosy

Leprosy is now known as 'Hansen's disease'; it is a bacterial infection of the nervous system, causing lesions on the skin, and numbness causing patients to injure themselves without realizing it. It can be cured with antibiotics, and is only contagious if there is a lack of personal hygiene. But in the past, anyone with a rash on their skin, from dermatitis to syphilis, was called a leper. Because of exaggerated fears of contagion, lepers were banished and outcast, forced to live outside the towns and villages, beg for food, and call out a warning so that nobody should accidentally touch them. The only way they could be readmitted to society was if the priests would give them a certificate to vouch that they were no longer contagious.

Jesus

So when Jesus met a group of lepers, they dared not ask him to cure them with his healing touch. So, in the pathetic phrase used by St Luke, '*keeping their distance*, they called out, saying, "Jesus, Master, have mercy on us!"' On other occasions, Jesus ignored the social stigma and embraced lepers. This time, he tested their faith. Although they were still showing the symptoms of leprosy, he sent them to the priests to demand a certificate that they had been cured. They trusted him and, *as they went*, they were cured. Only one returned to thank Jesus, and he was not a Jew, but one of the despised Samaritan foreigners.

Outcast

We see from this story how Jesus treated the outcast, by building up their self-respect. There are few lepers around these days, but many people feel outcast. They include people who don't belong in their main social area, pariahs, underdogs, for example 'beta-males' and 'slummy mummies'! We can all think of misfits we have met, people with few social skills, who for various reasons are despised by others and shunned by respectable society. This can be because they are gay, suffer from AIDS, come from another ethnic origin, are unemployed or homeless, illegal immigrants, drug addicts, alcoholics, have red hair, or speak with a local accent. Nowadays many people treat anyone who believes in God as old-fashioned, deluded and irrational. Some people speak of the physically handicapped as though they are not there, and we seem terrified of those with mental illness. These are just a few out of the many examples; but little has changed since the days of Jesus in the way we treat people who are different from us.

Treatment

There are no antibiotics to cure these outcasts with. But we can learn from Jesus ways to relate to them which can bring such people to feel accepted. It literally depends on the treatment they receive – not in the medical sense, but meaning the way we relate to them. First, Jesus encouraged the lepers to speak to him. If people sense that we are standing in judgement on them, they won't tell us what they are feeling, or how hard it is to be accepted. Yet unless we are willing to listen, without pigeonholing them, but treating them as human beings, they will never feel accepted. Second, Jesus built up the lepers' self-respect. We can always find something in people's characters that we can praise them for. Then, as they gain in self-confidence, they will begin to do things that will help them to turn the corner. Because, third, Jesus forced the lepers to believe that a cure was possible, we must give the untouchables hope that an end to their troubles is in sight. Fourth, Jesus told them to show themselves to the priests. Outcasts must be willing to meet those who have treated them as *persona non grata*, to claim, without denying their previous failings, that they are now entitled to be treated with respect.

Curing

If you feel yourself to be a social outcast, you have my sympathy and my prayers. Look at the way Jesus treated the lepers, and imagine him doing the same to you. But if you get a chance to speak to those whom society has sidelined, don't appear cold and forbidding, but remember to give them:

- a listening ear
- self-respect
- hope, and
- confidence.

It may sound daunting, but unless you can bring yourself to treat the social lepers in such a way, how can you call yourself a follower of Jesus of Nazareth?

All-age worship

List the ways in which you can help those who are unpopular at school.

Suggested hymns

Help us to help each other, Lord; Lead, kindly light; My song is love unknown; Rock of ages, cleft for me.

Twentieth Sunday after Trinity (Proper 23)
9 October
Second Service   **Altruism**
Ps. 144 Prayer for peace; Neh. 6.1–16 Rebuilding the Temple; John 15.12–27 Friends of Jesus

> *'[Jesus said to his disciples,] "This is my commandment, that you love one another as I have loved you."' John 15.12*

Comedian

Robert Newman is a comedian who in the past, with a show called *The Mary Whitehouse Experience*, poked gentle fun at narrowly religious people. But in 2013 he toured in a stand-up comedy show called 'A New Theory of Evolution'. In an interview in the *Metro* free newspaper he explained that this was a reply to the atheist Richard Dawkins' book *The Selfish Gene*, which argues that we are all born selfish. He argued that cooperation is as important in evolution as competition. Dawkins, he said, was very anti-Darwin in his ideas, and the show looked at the past 150 years of attempts to solve what Darwin called 'the greatest riddle' – how 'altruism' could have evolved. Darwin, Newman claimed, says that we have social instincts that have come from a million years of falling out with each other and making up again. Darwin thought communities flourished best the more empathetic they were. And a certain Prince Kropotkin wrote a book in 1882 called *Mutual Aid: A Factor of Evolution*, which tried to rescue Darwin's ideas from Herbert Spencer's 'survival of the fittest' idea. This, said Newman, had led politicians to make cuts in the welfare state because they thought that those on benefits could be made to work if their survival depended on it.

Christians

Leaving aside the comedian's conclusions, Christians will be interested to know that other scientists disagree with Dawkins because of the prevalence of self-sacrifice in the animal kingdom. Birds which have lost their fledglings to predators will spend the rest of the season helping to feed their neighbour's brood. Vampire bats share some of the animal blood they have collected with other bats who have none. Ants will sacrifice their lives by forming a bridge to enable the swarm to cross floodwater. So Christians who agree with Darwin are beginning to ask whether the progress of evolution is no longer merely physical, but has moved into an evolution of society. Something of the sort was suggested by the French priest-scientist Teilhard de Chardin, who in the 1920s suggested that evolution was progressing towards an 'omega point', which sounds like a totally unselfish society resembling what Jesus called the kingdom of God on earth.

Providence

The nature of science requires that it must not consider in its reasoning anything except measurable material forces. But that does not mean that other forces do not exist, and Christians would say that the most powerful force of all is God's providence. Without interfering with the processes of natural selection, a Creator Spirit could perfectly well have overseen the whole process in order to ensure that it progressed towards a desirable conclusion. In fact the emergence of thinking beings with the power of choice is inexplicable unless you believe that God was somehow involved. Contrary to what Richard Dawkins suggested, evolution appears to have moved in the direction of unselfishness.

Evolution

This would then give us an overall picture of a timeless Creator causing the Big Bang, ensuring that it did not collapse, but formed into galaxies. Then he would cause the sun and one of its planets to have just the right range of temperature and gravity so that life could emerge. Then, by a process of cell-division, he would bring vertebrate animals into being. These would evolve the power of thought and choice, and the humanoid would come down from the trees to form tribes of hunter-gatherers, in which a high degree of cooperation was essential. Then, as they evolved into stable agricultural societies, they formed nation states, where God taught them through Jesus that 'No one has greater love than this, to lay down one's life for one's friends.' So the teaching and example of Jesus led to the next stage of evolution, when he said, 'This is my commandment, that you love one another as I have loved you.' When we have enlarged our loyalty to the nation-state into an international society – where state does not fight against state, and where everybody lives a life of self-sacrificial unselfishness – then the earthly kingdom of God will have come. Each of us has a part to play in this; indeed God's kingdom cannot come, nor his will be done on earth, until you have learnt to love all your neighbours near and far. But even that is only a foretaste of the kingdom of heaven, for which our life on earth serves to prepare us. Science plays its part in showing us this. But it would be ironic if it took a stand-up comedian to reveal to us the whole picture of the evolution of love!

Suggested hymns

Above the moon earth rises; Come down O love divine; Love divine, all loves excelling; The spacious firmament on high.

Twenty-first Sunday after Trinity (Proper 24)
16 October
Principal Service   Corruption

(*Continuous*): Jer. 31.27–34 The new covenant, Ps. 119.97–104
Love for God's Law; or (*Related*): Gen. 32.22–31 Wrestling
Jacob, Ps. 121 Providence; 2 Tim. 3.14—4.5 The word of God;
Luke 18.1–8 Perseverance in prayer

> *'[Jesus said,] "In a certain city there was a judge who neither feared God nor had respect for people."' Luke 18.2*

Judge

Jesus told a funny story about a corrupt judge, who refused to give judgement in anyone's favour unless they gave him a hefty bribe. This meant that poor people, who couldn't afford the backhanders he expected, never received the justice they deserved. Until one day a poor widow – who perhaps claimed that she had been cheated by a neighbour, and wanted her money back – thought up a way to get the better of the dishonest magistrate. After her case was dismissed, the next day when his office opened she was first in the queue standing at the door, and before he could open his mouth, 'I want justice, please, your honour,' she said. He brushed her away, but when he came out for his lunch break, she was still standing in the doorway and would not move until he had made a vague promise to give her what she wanted tomorrow. Then she discovered where he lived, and when he tried to sleep, she was beneath his window pleading for a favourable verdict. After a few days of this, the wicked old man swore a mighty oath, and awarded her the amount she had claimed. Nobody else had got a favour out of the old rogue without a substantial bribe; but the poor widow had triumphed over his dishonest heart, simply by being an intolerable nuisance!

Persistence

Jesus told this story to encourage us to be persistent in prayer. He wasn't suggesting that God is in any way like the corrupt judge. On the contrary, Jesus had found a memorable way of impressing on us that we must put at least as much energy into spiritual things as we do into meeting our material needs.

Corruption

But the story is not a period piece. Corruption abounds all round us every day. In this country the judiciary are totally honest. But in industry and business, you don't get far without offering those with whom you deal a foreign holiday, or at least an expensive dinner. And in many other countries it is far worse. In some, you cannot even get a government doctor's appointment without offering a plain brown envelope stuffed with cash. In others, most of the services provided by the government, which everyone is entitled to for free, cost the poor a bribe which many of them cannot afford. Where a corrupt society has long been in place, businesses from this country who wish to do business with them have to agree to hefty handouts or they will never get a contract signed. The deaths of poor people from the collapse of badly built and poorly maintained buildings indicates that money seldom reaches the pockets for which it is intended.

Aid

Corruption is a continual problem in the area of overseas aid. Governments know that much of the aid they give to other governments, for the relief of poverty, in fact lines the pockets of government officials and even ministers. But the donors keep quiet because they want contracts to sell goods and arms to that country. Even aid charities find it hard to ensure that their donations go 100 per cent to the people for whom they are intended. Thank God, charities with a Christian basis are almost free from blame in this area, and everyone who cares about world poverty should give generously to Christian charities. But they will never eliminate poverty without inter-governmental aid to help them. So we must address urgently the universal problem of corruption. Like the poor widow in the story that Jesus told, we need to make such a nuisance of ourselves that the corrupt people in positions of authority have to give way.

Morality

Christians and Jews agree that taking a bribe is stealing, a breach of the eighth Commandment. Yet few pay any attention to our warnings, partly because religion has been so marginalized nowadays, but mainly because the unconverted are only willing to follow moral guidance when it is to their own advantage. We need a worldwide campaign against corruption, encouraging and empowering people in each country to point out that everyone suffers when the rich get richer at the expense of the poor. As Jesus suggested, we need to be persistent in prayer. And like the poor widow in his story, we need to make a terrible nuisance of ourselves, until somebody listens to our persistent protests against all forms of corruption, great and small.

All-age worship

Role-play the story of the poor widow and the corrupt judge. Wave banners protesting against bribery and corruption.

Suggested hymns

Father, hear the prayer we offer; For the healing of the nations; O God of earth and altar; The Kingdom of God is justice and joy.

Twenty-first Sunday after Trinity (Proper 24)
16 October
Second Service **Starving Beggars**
Ps. [146 Freedom] 149 Justice; Neh. 8.9–18 Rejoice in the law; John 16.1–11 Stumbling

> '[Jesus said to his disciples,] "I did not say these things to you from the beginning, because I was with you. But now I am going to him who sent me . . . for if I do not go away, the Advocate will not come to you; but if I go, I will send him to you."' John 16.5, 7

Indigestion

Imagine a starving man who finds the door of the food shop unlocked. He goes in and gobbles the food down until he can eat no more; then he has violent indigestion and brings it all back. Not a nice story to tell in church, but I want you to think about how alike our brains and our stomachs are. We can only absorb so much truth at one time; too much gives us mental indigestion. God knows that, and he only reveals his truth to us in bite-sized pieces, as much as we can take in at our present stage of spiritual growth. We call this, 'progressive revelation'. It describes how God reveals himself to an individual like you and me, but it also explains why the whole human race is only slowly learning to understand the truth about God.

Revelation

It is obvious when you put it like that. The God we worship wants to reveal herself or himself to us, so that we should pray to God, worship God and obey God's will. Yet the human mind is too small to accept all the truth about infinity at once. So God has to teach us one lesson at a time, usually by some life-changing experience; and then, when we have digested that, leading us on to another discovery. We shall then have to find words in which to express the new truth. No other way would work. So we shouldn't be surprised if some of the earlier revelations are only partial and incomplete. Christians have long puzzled over why the Old Testament reveals a God who, while admirable in many ways, is ignorant about scientific matters, fierce and judgemental, petty and wrathful, and encourages his followers to go to war in his name, killing their adversaries for his sake. This is particularly problematical if you believe that God, speaking the language that his followers at that time used, dictated the whole Bible to passive scribes, who took it down in shorthand and wrote it out word-for-word. But the problem disappears if you believe that the eternal God revealed some new aspect of his nature and his will to a particular individual, not in words but by some experience, which they then tried to express in a way that would be meaningful to other people of their own day. This then formed the launch pad for another revelation, which could be absorbed by another insightful individual in the next generation.

Jesus

Of course we believe that the life of Jesus was God's supreme revelation, in which we were shown what a god-like human life would consist in. But the disciples only gradually realized this, and, even after he rose again, they were slow to appreciate its full implications. But when he returned to heaven, he gave them his Holy Spirit, with the promise that the Spirit would lead us into all truth. That couldn't happen all at once, but, as before, step by step in an ongoing revelation. Jesus explained that he could not reveal the full truth to his disciples while he was with them and teaching them by his example. But he would send the Spirit, which, like an advocate explaining things to a jury, would explain what Jesus had done, gradually, as their simple minds were ready to receive it. And that process continues still today.

Tradition

This way of looking at the Bible will not be popular with funda-mentalists, strict biblicists or firm traditionalists. But progressive revelation does not deny the earlier revelations. Yet the way in which humans express the unchangeable truth varies from age to age. Unless we are willing to change the traditional words into terms that people speak today, we cannot expect anyone to be attracted by the good news of Jesus. That is not just a question of translating the Hebrew and Greek Bible into modern English. We must learn to draw on the metaphors and images that modern people think in today. Whatever traditional words we use in our private prayers, in public we must re-express the old truths in words that people in a scientifically educated society can grasp. This is no hobby. If we are to obey the command of Jesus to proclaim the good news to all peoples, it is essential that we transform our Christian way of speaking, under the guidance of the Holy Spirit's progressive revelation, to attract people who have dismissed us as old-fashioned and irrelevant.

Suggested hymns

Break thou the bread of life; Lord, thy word abideth; Tell me the old, old story; Thanks to God, whose word was spoken.

Bible Sunday   23 October
(Alternatively the Last Sunday after Trinity (Proper 25) or the Dedication Festival)
The Authorized Version

Readings for the Principal Service on Proper 25:
(*Continuous*): Joel 2.23–32 Harvest, Ps. 65 Harvest; *or (Related)*:
Ecclus. (Ben Sira) 35.12–17 Justice for the needy, or Jer. 14.7–10, 19–22 Repentance, Ps. 84.1–7 The Temple; 2 Tim. 4.6–8, 16–18

Fight the good fight; Luke 18.9–14 Pharisee's pride, taxman's humility

Readings for the Principal Service on Bible Sunday:
Isa. 45.22–25 A word that shall not return; Ps. 119.129–136 Your word gives understanding; Rom. 15.1–6 Written for our instruction; Luke 4.16–24 Jesus reads the Scripture

> *'Whatever was written in former days was written for our instruction, so that by steadfastness and by the encouragement of the scriptures we might have hope.' Romans 15.4*

Bible Sunday

The Last Sunday after Trinity, that is, the one before 30 October, is given a set of readings, in the Revised Common Lectionary, called 'Proper 25'. But it can alternatively be called Bible Sunday, or the Dedication Festival, and special readings are allotted for both of these. So, to make a change I decided to preach on Bible Sunday today; I hope I gave the readers sufficient notice of the change. The Bible is the very basis of our Christian faith, God's way of communicating to us and revealing his will for our lives. God declared his love to prophets and poets in the past, inspiring them to write it down and pass it on to future generations. It was written in Hebrew and Greek, and interpreters have translated it into thousands of different languages. Scholars have researched the vocabulary and grammar of the original languages, and the way of life and thought of people at the time the Bible was being written, by archaeology and in the literature of that time. Thus we come closer to what the original writers intended to say, and how those who first heard it will have understood it. There may be different attitudes to how it is to be interpreted, and what inspiration means, but all Christians agree that regular reading of the Scriptures, and discussing how to apply them, will bring us closer to the mind of God.

Authorized Version

I want to concentrate on the English translation of the Bible known as the Authorized Version, which influenced the development of the English language as much as William Shakespeare. Its correct name is the King James Version, because it was translated by a series of committees on the instructions of King James I in 1611. It was never actually authorized, though the publishers claimed that it was 'appointed to be read in churches'. English, which until then had been divided into regional dialects, became a unifying factor due to the Authorized Version, copies of which were placed in every parish church. Somebody has counted that 251 common idioms in modern English had their origin in the King James Version of the Bible, such as:

- a drop in the bucket
- a fly in the ointment
- a labour of love
- a leopard cannot change its spots
- a nest of vipers
- a thorn in the flesh
- a wolf in sheep's clothing
- all things to all men
- as old as the hills
- as white as snow
- at his wits' end

and so on!

Earlier translations

But things are never quite so simple. There were at least six English translations of the Bible before the Authorized Version:

- Wycliffe in the 1380s.
- Tyndale, who was actually the original source of some of those quotations.
- Coverdale, whose version of the Psalms in *The Great Bible* is better known than the AV because it is still used in the Book of Common Prayer.
- The Matthew Bible.
- The Geneva Bible, the favourite of the Puritans, who replaced the mistranslations 'bishop' and 'priest' with the more accurate 'overseer' and 'presbyter'.
- The Bishops' Bible in 1568.

I may talk about these another day. The 47 translators appointed by King James were all members of the Church of England, and put the words 'bishop' and 'priest' back because the King thought that was supportive of monarchical government. Otherwise it was an accurate translation for its time. Many recent discoveries have made modern translations more accurate, and it is unkind to ask someone to read the AV who is unfamiliar with seventeenth-century English. But even if it is rapidly becoming a museum piece, the AV has had an inestimable part to play in making the UK a Christian nation. If we lose our familiarity with the Scriptures, we risk reverting to paganism.

All-age worship

Young people should each read aloud a short passage from the AV Bible, asking a grown-up to explain unfamiliar words.

Suggested hymns

Break thou the bread of life; Lord, thy word abideth; Tell me the stories of Jesus; Thanks/Praise to God, whose word was spoken.

Bible Sunday   23 October
Bible Translation in the Seychelles
(Alternatively the Last Sunday after Trinity (Proper 25) or the Dedication Festival)
Readings for the Second Service on Proper 25:
Ps. 199.1–16 How can young people be pure?; Eccles. 11 and 12 Remember your Creator in your youth; 2 Tim. 2.1–7 Crowning an athlete; *Gospel at Holy Communion*: Matt. 22.34–46 Love God and love your neighbour

Readings for the Second Service on Proper 25:
Ps.119.1–16 Happy are those who walk in God's law; Jer. 36.9–32 Reactions to the scroll; Rom. 10.5–17 Faith comes from what is heard; *Gospel at Holy Communion*: Matt. 22.34–40 Love fulfils the law

> 'Faith comes from what is heard, and what is heard comes through the word of Christ.' Romans 10.17

Seychelles islands

In the Indian Ocean, between India and Africa, the Seychelles islands rise up out of the equatorial waters. They are now a favourite holiday destination, but 40 years ago, when an English Anglican priest arrived to work there as a missionary, they were still quite primitive. They were settled in the eighteenth century by the French, who bought slaves from India and Madagascar who spoke no French. Just as an Englishman abroad will simplify his language when speaking to foreigners – you know: 'Please you tell me where box where put letters', that kind of thing – so the French developed a pidgin French to speak to their slaves. The slaves' children grew up ignorant of their native tongue, and their only language was pidgin French. So they developed it until it could cope with all their daily needs. At that point, the language is no longer a pidgin – it is called French Creole.

Bible study

One year, the priest whom I mentioned found himself the only Protestant minister on the main island of Mahé, and was asked to lead the Bible study in Creole. There were no printed books in Creole then, so those who could, read from the French Bible, and explained it in Creole to the rest. 'In other words you are translating the Bible,' he said; 'why don't you write it down?' 'We can't,' they answered, 'nobody has invented a way of spelling Creole.' So the Minister of Education called a conference and a temporary way of writing the language was decided upon – a few years later a more phonetic spelling was developed. Various people, not all of them practising Christians, were invited to jot down how they thought a few verses of St Mark's Gospel would sound in Creole. Then the group discussed it: one would say, 'Nobody ever says that in our language', and the priest would say, 'That doesn't correspond to what the original Greek says.' Then he would type their suggestions for further discussion; he typed the whole of Mark's Gospel in Creole four times before they were satisfied. Then a retired missionary gave her life savings to pay for a few hundred copies to be printed at cost price by the government printer, and given away to any Creole speaker who could read. Since then the project has been taken over by the Bible societies, who have printed the whole New Testament in the new spelling.

Learning

Everybody found themselves on a learning curve. One elderly woman who could read English had thought for many years that when Jesus spoke of hiding your light under a bushel, he meant a small bush. They had never seen a leather wine bottle, but they thought that a *calbasse*, a type of gourd, was also brittle when old, but flexible enough when new to cope with the ferment of new ideas which Christianity brings. There were problems: the Creole word for 'sinner' is *pecheur*, but that is also the word for a fisherman, and since not all fishermen are sinners they had to say 'a man who sins' and 'a man who catches fish'! The version they produced had to be a 'common language' translation: neither too slangy for the surveyor nor too high-falutin' for the fisherman. But gradually both the Creole speakers and the English priest came to know Jesus as a human being just like themselves, and yet so challenging that he must have been more than human.

Reactions

After the Gospel of Mark was printed, a dramatized reading of it was broadcast on the local radio station. The priest watched an illiterate group of local people listening to it. They were soon all nodding approval or tut-tutting, not at the translation but at the actions of the people described. He realized that for the first time they were entering into the Bible stories as though the characters were people who lived in the same village as themselves, and then applying what they learnt to their own lives. If only we would all do that when we read the Bible in our own tongue.

Suggested hymns

God's Spirit is in my heart (Go tell everyone); Jesus shall reign, where'er the sun; Sing to God new songs of worship (Beethoven); We have a gospel to proclaim.

All Saints' Sunday   30 October
Principal Service   **Poverty**
(These readings are used on the Sunday, or, if this is not kept as All Saints' Sunday, on 1 November itself; see page 355 (All Saints' Day).)
Dan. 7.1–3, 15–18 The people of God will receive power; Ps. 149 The victory of God's people; Eph. 1.11–23 Christ rules with the saints; Luke 6.20–31 The sermon on the plain

'[Jesus] looked up at his disciples and said: "Blessed are you who are poor, for yours is the kingdom of God. Blessed are you who are hungry now, for you will be filled." Luke 6.20–21

Blessed

In St Matthew's Gospel, the passage we know as the Sermon on the Mount describes the character a Christian ought to have – the character of a saint. St Luke gives a list of qualities which is similar but not identical; we call Luke's version the Sermon on the Plain. Both are suitable for reading on the Sunday before All Saints' Day. Whereas Matthew gives a spiritual interpretation of what Jesus said – 'Blessed are the poor in spirit' – Luke, in the passage we heard today, chooses a down-to-earth understanding, in which Jesus congratulates those who are financially poor. They have no riches to distract them from their total dependence on God, so they gladly accept God as their king. Like Jesus, his followers should be compassionate towards the poor, in this and every land.

Always with you

But then, Jesus said, 'The poor are always with you.' Does that mean there is no point in the relief of poverty? No; he wanted us to see that we shall always have to readdress this problem in every generation. In his so-called 'Nazareth Manifesto', Jesus said that he had come to 'bring good news to the poor'.

At home

Poverty in this country is getting worse. The gap between rich and poor is getting wider. In trying to eliminate benefit fraud, we must remember that those with no other source of income, and those who slip through the system, can find life at certain times extremely hard. We must resist the temptation to judge others without fully under-standing their circumstances. A charity called 'Christians Against Poverty' was founded over thirty years ago, to bring relief in the worst cases, but also to persuade public opinion that something *can* and *must* be done to abolish the *causes* of poverty. Partly as a result of pressure from Christians, food banks and debt counselling centres have been established, both of them frequently on church premises. Credit unions are encouraged, shelters for the homeless are opened.

Dealing with the causes

But charitable efforts can distract us from pressing the government to work on the root causes of poverty, by ensuring that generous welfare goes to those who most need it, and, for instance, setting an interest rate cap for Pay-day loans. We must stop firms denying their workers the minimum wage, and make sure that the minimum wage is a living wage. Unemployment must be cut, by ensuring that education gives children the skills they need to find a job, and parents must accept responsibility for raising their kids to want to work. Community projects must be set up wherever there is poverty, and local residents encouraged to get involved. Individuals must have the freedom to grow rich, but realize that this brings with it a responsibility to take corporate action to address inequality. Let's face it, capitalism is good at creating wealth, but rotten at distributing it.

Abroad

But the war on poverty doesn't end in this country. All of us Brits are millionaires compared with those who live in the third world. Yet our extravagant way of life is doomed for disaster, unless we deal with global poverty. Better healthcare brought a population boom, which created starvation; better education is the only way to address it. Add to this the problem of international debt, and you will see that Christians are the only people who can deal with it. People grumble about immigration problems, but the only way to solve them is by equalizing everyone's standard of living.

Saints

Like God, every Christian must have a bias towards the poor. Many saints have been involved in the relief of poverty – St Martin who divided his cloak with a poor man; St Francis and many other monks and nuns who vowed to live in poverty; Mother Teresa giving the penniless a 'good death'; and lots of others. Many ordinary Christians are generous with what they have; others lobby on behalf of the poor. We must show the politicians that Christians judge a political party, not by what it does for me and mine, but for the poorest of the poor.

All-age worship

Make a display of what is being done for the poor in your neighbourhood.

Suggested hymns

Blest are the pure in heart; For all the saints, who from their labours rest; Give us the wings of faith to rise; Rejoice in God's saints, today and all days.

Fourth Sunday before Advent   30 October
Second Service   **Hallowe'en**
Ps. 145 Praising God; Lam. 3.22–33 New every morning; John 11.[1–31] 32–44 Lazarus raised

> *'The dead man came out, his hands and feet bound with strips of cloth, and his face wrapped in a cloth. Jesus said to them, "Unbind him, and let him go."' John 11.44*

Lazarus

When Mary and Martha saw the body of their brother Lazarus, who was undoubtedly dead, rising from the grave, they must have thought they were seeing a ghost. But Jesus said, 'Unbind him, and let him go.' It was as though death was a temporary restriction from which we can be released by the word of Christ. Ghosts get a lot of publicity these days, especially at Hallowe'en. Now I think it is very likely that God allows people who have died to appear in visions to their loved ones, to reassure them that everything is all right. Perhaps people who have never been taught about heaven get frightened by this. It is possible that those who have heard that an awful crime has been committed somewhere get a spooky feeling when they visit the place. The Bible has several accounts of dead people being brought back to life, but the only reference to ghosts is in the story of the witch of Endor, which makes it quite plain that seeking to make contact with the dead can be very dangerous indeed.

Hallowe'en

Older people will tell you that when they were children, Hallowe'en was almost unheard of. The celebration was brought here from the USA by toymakers, so that they could make a lot of money out of frightening children. It was probably brought to America by the immigrants from Ireland, where the old pre-Christian religions were still strong, and the countryside was believed to be thronged with fairies. Certainly Ireland was where the 'trick or treat' custom originated, as practised by criminals as a means of frightening money out of vulnerable strangers. Also, in Catholic countries, people prayed for the souls of the departed to become saints at Hallowmas, which was the old name for All Saints' Day and All Souls' Day; in Protestant countries this was banned, and Guy Fawkes' Day took its place. In Canada, the Scottish traditions described by Robert Burns in his poem *Hallowe'en* filled their imaginations with dancing witches.

Harmful?

Possibly there could be no danger in these customs today, being seen by many as a harmless game. It may be that, like the rash of horror films we see in the cinema and on the television, they are intended to make people laugh, and perhaps to teach children how to live with fear. But somehow I think there is more to it than that. In Celtic belief, evil spirits were particularly active at this time of year, and the souls of the dead returned home. So fires were lit to drive them away; witchcraft was practised to seek their advice; and prayers were offered to the devil. Is this what we want to teach our small children? Or is this a sinister plot by the secularists to ridicule all religions, including Christianity?

Children

Humans have always made jokes out of what they fear. But though Hallowe'en may be seen as ridiculous, children need to be warned of the dangers, and reassured at Hallowe'en that the power of Christ is stronger than any other power. How much better to come to worship on All Hallows – All Saints' Day – itself, 1 November, to commemorate those who have died, knowing that the love of Jesus has overcome the fear of death.

Alternatives

Some local councils issue a label for people to put in their window reading 'Trick or Treat – No Thanks'. J. John, of the charity the Philo Trust, has published a pamphlet on their website, philotrust.com, suggesting that Hallowe'en is not as harmless as people think. He writes that Hallowe'en is 'An event that glorifies the dark, creepy and scary side of life. Children and adults dress up as figures that are "evil" . . . This is hardly harmless.' On this one day, he says, we 'glorify everything that is evil and unpleasant'. York Diocese has set up a website to provide ideas for an alternative Hallowe'en event. The charity World Vision wants people to celebrate Hallowe'en as a Night of Hope, by carving a *heart* into their pumpkin instead of a grinning face. 'By doing this,' they say, 'we provide an alternative for hundreds of Christians', and also, 'create an opportunity to show how much we care about children living in fear every single day'.

Suggested hymns

And can it be that I should gain?; I danced in the morning when the world was begun; O when the saints go marching in; There is a land of pure delight.

See http://eepurl.com/GfFqr.

Third Sunday before Advent   6 November
Principal Service   **Sheol**
Job 19.23–27a My redeemer lives; Ps. 17.1–9 Prayer for salvation; 2 Thess. 2.1–5, 13–17 Perseverance; Luke 20.27–38 The wife of seven brothers

> *'Jesus said to [the Sadducees], ". . . Those who are considered worthy of a place in . . . the resurrection from the dead neither marry nor are given in marriage . . . because they are like angels and are children of God, being children of the resurrection."' Luke 20.34–36*

Marriage

Unlike the famous film called *Seven Brides for Seven Brothers*, the story told by the Sadducees in Luke's Gospel is of *one* bride who was married to all seven brothers, one after another. It was a fantasy, of course, but to understand it you must realize that attitudes to marriage were very different in those days. When infant mortality was high, it was essential that every young man in a tribe should beget a large number of children, so that at least one boy should survive to adulthood, to care for his parents in their old age and to ensure the continuance of the tribe. When a boy grew to puberty, his parents paid a lot of money to buy him a wife who looked capable of bearing dozens of healthy babies. But it cost a lot to bring up a daughter, so in return for their investment, the parents claimed a high bride-price in return for selling their daughter to the new husband. Marriage was a financial contract concerned with producing babies; love might or might not follow. In this story, the bride's first husband died before begetting any children with her. She would take his property out of the family if she remarried. So the law of the Old Testament demanded that one of his brothers should marry her, even if he already had one or more wives: bigamy was compulsory in those days.

Resurrection

The Sadducees were the arch-conservatives of the day, who protested that the old laws must be obeyed, even if they were no longer socially relevant. The Law was all that interested them; the resurrection of the dead is an idea that comes from the later prophets, so they did not accept it. Jesus did. So the Sadducees invented this fantastic story to prove him wrong. Yet the idea they rejected was of a purely physical resurrection, or resuscitation, when the dead bodies would rise from their tombs to live for 1,000 years in the earthly kingdom ruled over by the Messiah. In that case, whose husband would the unfortunate widow be? But Jesus would have nothing to do with this legalistic antiquarianism. The world had moved on, the old laws were irrelevant, and the resurrection would be into a spiritual world, where buying and selling brides was no longer necessary. For Jesus, the purpose of marriage is so that couples should learn the meaning of unselfish love, thus preparing themselves for the life of heaven, where all is imperishable love.

Sheol

What, then, did the Sadducees believe happens to us when we die? The Old Testament reveals that the Jews, up until the time of Christ, held that everyone, when they die, goes to a place underneath the earth called Sheol; a place of gloom and decay, better known by its Greek translation as Hades. The story of the witch of Endor, who calls Samuel back from the dead, shows him as a shadowy figure, looking much the same as he had done in his old age. Many English Bibles translate Sheol as 'hell', but this is quite wrong. There are, indeed, two references to the unrighteous being punished in Sheol, but for the righteous it was simply a place of sleep. The Jewish idea of the afterlife was rather like a railway terminus on a foggy day: great confusion, many people arriving and nobody going anywhere! So we can understand why the teaching of Jesus, that God welcomes to heaven all who repent, came as joyous good news to those who first heard it.

Bereavement

It is natural that when somebody dies, those they loved should feel left alone. Marriage, for us, is not just a financial arrangement, it is passion leading into mature devotion. You cannot tell a grieving widow to snap out of it; she will take time to work through her feelings. But you can share with her the message of Jesus that we shall rise again in heaven, which is a spiritual domain full of loving individuals who have been eternally reunited. There may be no material buying and selling of brides in heaven; but the experience of being in love, there, is even deeper than in the most romantic love affair on earth – because it is a purely spiritual love, lasting for ever.

All-age worship

Make invitations to a wedding in heaven, where loving couples who have been divided by death will be joined again in everlasting love.

Suggested hymns

Love's redeeming work is done; Now is eternal life; O God, our help in ages past; You, living Christ, our eyes behold.

Third Sunday before Advent   6 November
Second Service   **Anti-Christian Violence**

Ps. 40 I waited for the Lord; 1 Kings 3.1–15 Solomon's prayer
for wisdom; Rom. 8.31–39 The love of God in Christ; *Gospel at
Holy Communion*: Matt. 22.15–22 The tribute money

> *'In all these things we are more than conquerors through him
> who loved us.' Romans 8.37*

Clash

Many people say that what we see in the world today is a clash of
cultures, even a clash of religions. In the past, wars were caused by
the rivalry between nations and the lust to own more land. That was
true up to the cold war. But now the iron curtain has been replaced
by the velvet curtain of different religions, so they say. Some argued
against this idea, saying that secularism was taking over in many
countries, thus weakening the power of religions to cause strife. But
then the horrific events of 9/11 showed the awful bloodshed which
could be caused by one religion setting itself against another.

Religions

But to talk about a clash of religions is an oversimplification. For
Muslims to say that they are opposing 'western civilization' means
setting themselves against a vast area, covering several continents,
and including adherents of widely differing religions or even none.
Many of the recent bitter wars in the Middle East have been within
Islam, between Sunni and Shia Muslims. Islam itself has followers
in Arab, Malay and Turkish areas, with widely differing cultures,
but all eager to embrace the material benefits of westernization. It
seems that many people simply use religion as an excuse for killing their historic enemies, though the reasons why they hated them
have been long forgotten.

Christians

Christians have suffered particularly severely from this; not in the
powerful western nations, but in their historic homelands, where
they lived in large numbers before Islam was born, and are now

a persecuted minority. A non-religious research organization, the International Society for Human Rights, has worked out that 80 per cent of all recent religious conflicts have been aimed at Christians. By simple arithmetic, that means that, on average, 100,000 Christians have been killed each year in the last ten years. Let that soak in: 100,000 Christians slaughtered all over the world every year, simply for being Christians. Countless others raped, maimed, bereaved or driven into exile from their homeland. Yet this tragedy is almost totally ignored by the western media.

Examples

In Iraq, for example, two-thirds of the Christian population have been exiled or killed over the past 20 years. A survey has calculated that Christians in 139 nations have been widely discriminated against, either by unjust laws or by illegal attacks from non-Christians which the local police consistently ignore. Recent examples include Pakistan, Kenya, Nigeria, India, Burma and North Korea. In northern Nigeria, the Muslim jihadist group Boko Haram has bombed churches and killed around 1,000 people each year, mostly Christians, in pursuit of creating a state entirely subject to sharia law. But this is not just about Islam; Hindu radicals in the Indian State of Orissa caused the deaths of 500 Christians, and made 50,000 homeless. Our educated Indian friends in other parts of the subcontinent write that as the government is doing nothing about it, they fear for their own lives if the violence spreads. In North Korea, 300,000 Christians disappeared, and were probably killed, because they would not worship the nation's founder, Kim Il Sung.

Response

A few Christians have regrettably responded to violence with violence, and we must condemn this. Instead, we should concentrate on pressurizing our own government, and, through the United Nations, the governments of other nations, to institute a zero tolerance policy against the persecutors of our Christian sisters and brothers. We must send support, prayer and sympathy to their victims. But, at the same time, perhaps we should return to the tradition in the early Church of glorifying Christian martyrs who have suffered for their faith. St Paul wrote:

Who will separate us from the love of Christ? Will hardship, or distress, or persecution, or famine, or nakedness, or peril, or sword? As it is written, 'For your sake we are being killed all day long; we are accounted as sheep to be slaughtered.' No, in all these things we are more than conquerors through him who loved us.

This may encourage Christians on the point of death in many countries, and comfort the bereaved. And, remembering the old saying, 'the blood of the martyrs is the seed of the Church', we should warn the persecutors that their violence may have the opposite effect from what they intended, and result in millions of new Christians joining the Church, when they see how bravely we are willing to triumph over suffering and, if need be, to die for our faith.

Suggested hymns

How bright these glorious spirits shine!; Lo, round the throne, a glorious band; Lord, it belongs not to my care; Oft in danger, oft in woe.

See http://www.releaseinternational.org.

Second Sunday before Advent   13 November
(For Remembrance Sunday, see page 274.)
Principal Service   Warlike Hymns
Mal. 4.1–2a Judgement; Ps. 98 A new song; 2 Thess. 3.6–13 Perseverance in good works; Luke 21.5–19 Perseverance

'Brothers and sisters, do not be weary in doing what is right.'
2 Thessalonians 3.13

'By your endurance you will gain your souls.' Luke 21.19

Applying oneself

When we are employed to do a particular task, we work hard to succeed, because we know that, if we don't, we shall soon be out of work. When we have a favourite hobby, we apply ourselves to it diligently, both mentally and physically, whether it is vigorous sport or stamp-collecting, because we draw a deep satisfaction from completing our self-imposed task. But surely our faith is more important to us, both now and in our eternal future, than either our employment or our hobbies? Whereas many people treat religion as a spare-time occupation, to be taken up when we have nothing better to do.

Perseverance

Yet the Bible often urges us to persevere in matters of faith. St Paul, in today's New Testament reading, warns us: 'Brothers and sisters, do not be weary in doing what is right'; and Jesus in the Gospel exhorts us: 'By your endurance you will gain your souls.' They were living in the Roman Empire, when the Roman roads were thronged with Roman soldiers. St Paul, in fact, was in a Roman prison, chained to a Roman guard, when he wrote some of his letters. So he had plenty of opportunity to observe at first hand how diligently they persevered with their duties; and he used military metaphors to point to the importance of Christian perseverance. Paul wrote:

- 'The night is far gone, the day is near. Let us then lay aside the works of darkness and put on the armour of light . . .'
- 'Put on the whole armour of God, so that you may be able to stand against the wiles of the devil . . . Stand therefore, and fasten the belt of truth around your waist, and put on the breastplate of righteousness . . . take the shield of faith . . . the helmet of salvation, and the sword of the Spirit . . . and always persevere in supplication for all the saints.'
- 'I am giving you these instructions, Timothy . . . so that by following them you may fight the good fight' – 'Fight the good fight of the faith' – 'I have fought the good fight, I have finished the race, I have kept the faith.'

Victorian hymns

The nineteenth century, too, was a time of great military presence, with 'Tommies' in red coats praised for defending the Empire against those who wanted to make it their own. So it was hardly surprising that the Victorian poets took up these metaphors in some of their hugely popular hymns. Think of 'Fight the good fight with all thy might', 'Onward, Christian soldiers' and 'O valiant hearts', and 'I vow to thee, my country . . . the love that asks no questions . . .

that pays the final sacrifice'. While we can heartily endorse the message of perseverance these hymns proclaim, now, in the twenty-first century, we feel less happy with the warlike words. We have seen too many 'wars to end war', which did nothing of the sort, and military adventures which tried to win peace by killing people, and only strengthened the resolve of our enemies. So while we remember with pride those who have died because they were told it would bring freedom, we feel uncomfortable using apparently war-mongering words in our hymns to God. Too many people in the past have manipulated religion to justify unjust campaigns.

The answer

Some of these hymns have been rewritten in various hymnals to remove the offensive words. Churches that use a projector or print their own hymn sheets can search for a sanitized version. Some of the hymns that appear objectionable at first sight turn out to be pleas for peace, such as 'God of our Fathers, known of old' and 'Judge eternal, throned in splendour'. So unless you can write new words for them, you may have to drop the more militaristic hymns for a while, until people realize that they refer not to wars which kill people, but to perseverance in the struggle to overcome the evil in the world, and promote the peaceful virtues of tolerance, unselfishness and self-sacrificing love. For the kingdom of God will not come if we are idle; we have to struggle diligently, by peacemaking words and the example of our own lives of tolerance, to build it ourselves.

All-age worship

Write a hymn to a well-known tune, praying for world peace.

Suggested hymns

Judge eternal, throned in splendour; Lord, while for all mankind we pray; O God of earth and altar; When a knight won his spurs.

Remembrance Sunday   13 November
Balancing Act
(The readings of the day, or those for 'In Time of Trouble' can be used. These readings are for 'The Peace of the World'.)

Micah 4.1–5 Swords into ploughshares; Ps. 85.8–13 God will speak peace; James 3.13–18 The harvest of peace; John 15.9–17 No greater love

'[Jesus said,] "This is my commandment, that you love one another as I have loved you. No one has greater love than this, to lay down one's life for one's friends."' John 15.12–13

Remembrance Sunday

Remembrance Sunday does what it says on the tin: it helps us to remember those who died as a result of war. Jesus said, 'No one has greater love than this, to lay down one's life for one's friends.' Most of those who died in battle joined the armed forces because they wanted to defend their country, their families and loved ones. They would do whatever it costs to achieve this end. Letters written from the front reveal that after a few weeks in the trenches or on patrol, most of them had seen many of their friends killed, and realized that even today 'death's dark angel' might well pay a visit to any of them. Those who then committed acts of bravery made a bold decision to sacrifice their own lives so that they could save the lives of their mates. Yet even those who died, simply because they did not desert when things looked bleak, should be remembered with gratitude. The purpose of their deaths was often to preserve the freedom of the rest of us. Even if you do not choose to die, then willingly going where there is danger is a noble self-sacrifice.

Bereaved

Another reason for Remembrance Sunday is so that we can share the grief of the bereaved. They did not choose that their loved ones should die, but the results for them are often catastrophic. Their family may be left without the breadwinner, and with only one parent, and the stability which had come to their emotions through a happy marriage is destroyed at a stroke, leaving them floundering in uncertainty and misery. We must use this day to support them by our sympathy and prayers; to ensure that their practical needs are being met; and to listen sympathetically to their complaints. Then we should try to share with them the good news, brought by Jesus, that there is a better life beyond the grave, where there is no more pain and death, and where we shall meet again and spend all eternity together in loving joyfulness. If we say that, some people will accuse us of 'ramming religion down people's throats'. I have never actually heard anyone ramming religion down anybody's throat, and I don't think anyone can complain if we humbly share with others a belief that we ourselves have found helpful.

Peacemakers

But for the Church, Remembrance Sunday is a balancing act. There are some people who think that war is such a terribly wrong thing that we should not get dragged into celebrating it. Siegfried Sassoon wrote a poem about the devil praying at the Cenotaph that the people who march by should forget what the memorial means, and begin to believe again that war is somehow cleansing. Another modern poet has written how a veteran, having watched young men carrying the coffins of their comrades, would feel the weight of the medals on his chest too heavy to wear in a procession. There is no doubt that generals have sent their troops to unnecessary deaths because instructed to do so by politicians – who believe that the electorate would be more likely to re-elect them if they lead the country into a victorious war. Which means that we, the voters, are directly responsible for the deaths we commemorate this day. Maybe we were right, and that refusing to fight would have caused more deaths at the hands of dictators than resulted on both sides from the fighting. But we should not go into battle without weighing up carefully the costs, and we should not seek to shift the blame onto anyone else.

Balancing act

So you see what I mean about a balancing act. At one and the same time, today, we have to express our gratitude to all those who died as a result of war, and our sympathy with the bereaved. But we also have to express our determination that there should be no more wars unless they are absolutely necessary. We should calculate the probable casualties, and weigh them against the chance of life being better afterwards. These two things, honouring the dead and expressing our opposition to war, are not incompatible. But we need to be extremely careful what words we use to proclaim them.

All-age worship

During the service, children can be shown how to draw and colour poppies on pieces of card.

Suggested hymns

And did those feet?; For the healing of the nations; God of our Fathers, known of old (Melita); O God, our help in ages past.

Christ the King   20 November
Principal Service   **The Branch of David**

Jer. 23.1–6 Bad and good shepherds; Ps. 46 God is our refuge and strength; Col. 1.11–20 Forgiveness in the Son through the cross; Luke 23.33–43 The thief on the cross

> 'The days are surely coming, says the LORD, when I will raise up for David a righteous Branch, and he shall reign as king and deal wisely, and shall execute justice and righteousness in the land. In his days Judah will be saved and Israel will live in safety.' Jeremiah 23.5–6

Kings

The United Kingdom is a constitutional monarchy. The Queen is the symbolic head of state, but she has no actual power in herself, and since Britain became a democracy the actual power rests with the people. Yet in the feudal period, all power was held by an individual, called a king or an emperor. Some were good rulers, caring for their people; others were selfish, power-crazy, and only wanted to make themselves rich. This was true of Israel in the Old Testament; only, when the prophets protested against unjust government it was safer to write about good shepherds and bad shepherds than good kings and bad kings. The kings of Judah are described as 'the House of David', because they were all descended from King David. David, though a flawed individual, was a good king, as was his son Solomon. But after that there was a succession of real duds. So the prophets looked forward to the day when they would have a good king. Isaiah was the first to describe his hope in the image of a tree with sound roots, but rotten branches which needed to be cut down. But when that happens, often a strong healthy shoot springs up out of the stump of the original tree. So the longed-for good king was described by Isaiah as a shoot coming out of the stump of Jesse; a branch growing out of David's family tree.

Jeremiah

A century later, the prophet Jeremiah took up the same image. Judah was threatened by Assyrian invaders. There had been a succession of bad kings. But Jeremiah still had hope. He wrote:

> The days are surely coming, says the LORD, when I will raise up for David a righteous Branch, and he shall reign as king and deal wisely, and shall execute justice and righteousness in the land.

Alas, he was disappointed; the following kings were so bad that Israel was decimated and Judah exiled to Babylon.

Messiah

But the dream never died. One day, said the Jews, one day there will be a really good king, an ideal ruler. They called this dreamt-of ideal king 'the Anointed King', 'the Messiah' or 'the Christ'. But when Jesus came, they could not agree whether he was the king they were waiting for or not. He answered: 'I *am* the good shepherd. When you see the Son of Man coming in his glory . . .' When Peter said, 'You are the Messiah, the Son of the living God', Jesus praised him, saying, 'Flesh and blood has not revealed this to you, but my Father in heaven.' When a Samaritan woman said, 'I know that Messiah is coming . . .', Jesus said to her, 'I am he, the one who is speaking to you.'

Good Shepherd

So, after a long run of bad kings, Jesus was the good leader they had dreamt of, the branch from the family tree of David. But then he surprised them by refusing to lead them into battle against their enemies. He said to Pontius Pilate, 'My kingdom is not from this world. If it were, my followers would be fighting to keep me from being handed over to the Jews.' And using the shepherd as an image of leadership, Jesus said, 'I am the good shepherd. The good shepherd lays down his life for the sheep.' So the image of a leader Jesus wants to give us is of one who sacrifices their own interests for the sake of those whom they lead. And that goes for an MP or a president or a teacher or a parent or a team leader. Our gold standard for good leadership is Christ himself, the good king, the shepherd who lays down his life for the sheep. When a leader of industry or an MP turns out to be utterly selfish, it makes you weep. It was the thief on the next cross who recognized true majesty in the one who was being crucified, when he said to Jesus, 'Remember me when you come into your kingdom.' The only way to turn our society into the kingdom of God is if everyone who has authority over another tries to live as sacrificial a life as Christ the King.

All-age worship

Put paper crowns on your heads, then wash each other's feet.

Suggested hymns

Jesus, remember me (Taizé); Make way, make way for Christ the king; The kingdom of God is justice and joy; Thy kingdom come, O God.

Christ the King 20 November
Second Service **St Edmund, King and Martyr**
Morning Ps. 29 Enthroned, 110 The king at your right hand; Evening Ps. 72 An ideal king; 1 Sam. 8.4–20 The demand for a king; John 18.33–37 My kingdom is not of this world

> *'Jesus answered, "You say that I am a king. For this I was born, and for this I came into the world, to testify to the truth. Everyone who belongs to the truth listens to my voice."' John 18.37*

Or for St Edmund: Prov. 20.28; 21.1–4, 7 His throne upheld; Ps. 88 A vine; Rev. 12.10–12a The kingdom of our God; Matt. 10.34–39 Those who love this life (*Exciting Holiness*, p. 528)

'Those who find their life will lose it, and those who lose their life for my sake will find it.' Matthew 10.39

Black-letter saints

Most churches do not commemorate the minor saints' days. The important ones, commemorating the apostles and other significant people in the Bible, are called 'red-letter days', because when the prayer books and missals were printed in two colours, this was how they were distinguished in the calendar. So the rest, important as they are, were called black-letter saints' days. They were celebrated in churches dedicated to that saint, or in the area where they lived, but that was all. But this year, by a happy coincidence, the feast of Christ the King, which is today, happens to coincide with the commemoration of St Edmund, King and Martyr, on 20 November.

Edmund's life

St Edmund was King of East Anglia from about 855 until his death on 20 November 869. He was said to be the son of a king of 'Saxony', maybe meaning Kent, where the Saxons settled. Then he was adopted as their king by the people of East Anglia. He was a just and popular ruler, but in 869 his kingdom was invaded by a Danish army led by Inguar and Hubba. After they killed him, the Danes destroyed all the contemporary records of his reign, but his story lived on in his people's hearts. It was said that he was only 14 when he succeeded to the throne, so 28 when he died. The Danes are reputed to have captured him in battle, and offered to set him free if only he would share his reign with Inguar, but he replied that as a Christian he refused to be yoked with a pagan, and refused their demand that he renounce Christ. The Danish bowmen then used him as a target for archery practice, yet even when he was pierced by dozens of arrows he did not die, so they beheaded him.

After death

After his death, Edmund became a hero to the people of East Anglia. When East Anglia was absorbed into the kingdom of Wessex, coins were minted with the image of Edmund's head on them, and he became a cult figure. In the tenth century, his remains were transferred to a place which was then called St Edmundsbury, and is now called Bury St Edmunds. There had been a monastery on that site since 633, and after the saint's relics were buried there it became a great centre of pilgrimage. Now it is the see city of the Anglican diocese of St Edmundsbury and Ipswich. The saint's remains were temporarily moved from Bury St Edmunds to London for safekeeping in 1010. His shrine was visited by many kings, including Canute, who was responsible for rebuilding the Abbey of St Edmundsbury – it was rebuilt again in 1095. During the Middle Ages, Edmund was regarded as the patron saint of England, until the returning crusaders replaced him with St George. The magnificent abbey grew wealthy, but his shrine was destroyed at the Dissolution of the Monasteries.

Now

After the Reformation, a parish church was built in the grounds of the ruined abbey, on the site of one dating from the twelfth century dedicated to St James; it has a fine nineteenth-century hammer-beam roof, with carvings of angels. When it was made a cathedral in 1914, a rebuilding programme was begun. The tower was completed in 2005, making it the last English cathedral to reach completion. The thousand or so embroidered kneelers are an example of how ordinary Christians still like to involve their voluntary efforts in the decoration of their churches.

Lessons

So what lessons for how we live our own lives can we learn from the example of St Edmund, king and martyr?

- First, that when we are in an awkward spot, we should be willing to understand our opponents and negotiate with them, but never, never to compromise.
- Second, that we should take pride in the region where we live, and discover as much as we can of its history and traditions. This is one very practical way of obeying the command of Jesus to love our near neighbours.

- Third, to value the heritage of beautiful old buildings in the Church's care; and do all in our powers to conserve them.
- And finally, the message of the feast of Christ the King is that anyone in authority should be willing to make costly sacrifices of their own wishes, for the sake of public service, a concept that must never vanish from British public life.

Suggested hymns

Christ triumphant, ever reigning; Crown him with many crowns; The Lord's my shepherd; Thy kingdom come, O God.

Sermons for Saints' Days and Special Occasions

SAINTS' DAYS

People who visit your church for the first time when you are celebrating a saint's day may be quite puzzled. Either they will ask, 'Oh, is that the person your church is named after? What made her or him famous?' Or else, 'Never heard of them. Why are we bothering with somebody who lived so long ago?' In either case, they will be frightened away, never to come again, unless you explain something of the life story of the saint or saints in your sermon, and what lessons we can learn from their example. Every sermon we preach ought to be welcoming, understandable and challenging to anyone coming to the church without any experience of Christianity. If your regular congregation object that they know all that already, because you told them last year, explain that you speak for the benefit of any newcomers. Then sprinkle your sermons with phrases like, 'Of course, as most of you already know . . .'. Then you can explain that the hangings are red for the blood of a martyr, a white or gold for a saint who was a shining example but never called on to die for their faith. Many of the saints also have a symbol which you can explain. Finally, remember that the best preachers always preach to themselves, to arouse repentance in their own hearts for the selfish and thoughtless things they have said and done. If you admit that, nobody will think you are picking on them!

St Stephen, Deacon, First Martyr
26 December 2015
The Blood of the Martyrs

2 Chron. 24.20–22 The stoning of Zechariah, *or* Acts 7.51–60
The death of Stephen; Ps. 119.161–168 Persecuted without a
cause; (*if the Acts reading is used instead of the Old Testament
reading, the New Testament reading is* Gal. 2.16b–20 Crucified
with Christ) Matt. 10.17–22 Persecution

> '[Jesus said,] "You will be hated by all because of my name.
> But the one who endures to the end will be saved."' *Matthew
> 10.22*

Persecution

Whenever brave people stand up for those who are weak, and allege
wrongdoing by those who have power, they are immediately hated
by those they criticize. These may be what the psalm calls 'Princes
[who] persecuted me without a cause', or the mob who are benefit-
ing by the corruption which the righteous condemn. Persecution
may lead to martyrdom, which means killing somebody who stands
up to be counted, as a witness to the truth. The Jewish Revolt
against a combined government of corrupt priests and Greek conquerors, around 160 BC, resulted in many deaths, especially in the
family of Judas Maccabeus, who were honoured as martyrs and
declared to have a special place with God in heaven. These deaths
led to a wave of sympathy for the protesters, and the downfall of
the corrupt authorities.

Stephen

Today we honour St Stephen, the first of the Christian martyrs. One
of those who saw how bravely he died was Saul of Tarsus, who
was so impressed that, after an inner struggle, he was converted
on the road to Damascus, becoming St Paul, a leading missionary for the Christian cause which he had previously persecuted.
More Christians were persecuted in the following centuries, and the
people of the Roman Empire were so moved by their witness that

thousands were converted and the Church grew like wildfire. So the saying was passed around: 'The blood of the martyrs is the seed of the Church.' It was as though, everywhere a martyr's blood soaked into the ground, new converts sprang up like the green shoots of wheat leading to a bumper harvest. 'The blood of the martyrs is the seed of the Church.'

Persecution today

Still today the Church is being persecuted in many countries. We seldom hear about it in the media, but active persecution of Christians is now taking place in, among others,

> Afghanistan, Algeria, China, Egypt, India, Indonesia, Iran, Iraq, Kyrgyzstan, Nigeria, North Korea, Pakistan, the Philippines, Saudi Arabia, Somalia, Sudan, Syria, Tunisia, Turkey and Uzbekistan.

Ought we not to be publicizing these brave Christians, praying for them, and sending aid and relief? Ought we not to be celebrating their witness despite opposition? They are the successors of St Stephen, and should be honoured on this day and all the year round!

Non-violence

Of course, it is never simple. In some of these countries the persecuted Christians seek violent retaliation against those who attack them. That is their decision, and we have no right to interfere; but they should be warned that it muddies the waters and makes it hard for Christians in other countries to support them without interfering in local politics. And some Christians are so keen for the glory of martyrdom that they actively provoke their opponents, hoping to be killed. Seeking martyrdom, which was condemned by the early Church, is the same psychology that motivates the suicide bombers, and leaves us with no leg to stand on when we criticize terrorists. Moreover, if the blood of the martyrs is the seed of the Church, it works both ways. If we hope to eliminate terrorism by killing as many terrorists as we can, we are only helping their cause by raising the sympathy of the so-called 'moderate' population. Bombing London in the Blitz increased British hostility to the Nazis, and the same principle operates today.

Church growth

But St Stephen didn't retaliate. He suffered in silence and commended his soul, and his cause, to God. Hundreds, maybe thousands, of Christians are doing the same today. We should praise them loudly and clearly, proclaiming that their deaths are likely to lead to a rapid growth in church membership. We can see it in China, where the increase of Christians in the unregistered churches is one of the fastest rates of church growth in the world. If only the opponents of Christianity would realize this, they might be reluctant to help our cause by slaughtering innocent believers. Equally, it might deter persecuted Christians, and Christian governments, from using violent means to defend themselves, to know that violence always results in growth of sympathy and numbers for those who are attacked. Over the entrance to Westminster Abbey are the busts of twentieth-century Christian martyrs. We should also be celebrating twenty-first-century St Stephens who are dying for their faith today, shouldn't we?

Suggested hymns

For all thy saints, O Lord; Good King Wenceslas looked out; How bright these glorious spirits shine!; Stephen, first of Christian martyrs.

St John, Apostle and Evangelist   27 December
(See page 34.)

Holy Innocents   28 December
Bereaved parents
Jer. 31.15–17 Rachel weeping for her children; Ps. 124 When our enemies attacked us; 1 Cor. 1.26–29 God chose what is weak; Matt. 2.13–18 The massacre

> *'Herod . . . sent and killed all the children in and around Bethlehem who were two years old or under . . . Then was fulfilled what had been spoken through the prophet Jeremiah: "A voice was heard in Ramah, wailing and loud lamentation, Rachel weeping for her*

children; she refused to be consoled, because they are no more."'
Matthew 2.16–18

Holy Innocents

The grief of the parents of the Holy Innocents slain by Herod in Bethlehem is compared to that of Rachel, in the Old Testament, weeping for her children: 'she refused to be consoled, because they are no more'. Parents whose child has died know a depth of shock and horror greater than almost any other. We always expect to outlive our own children, and when they die before us the world seems turned upside down.

A true tragedy

Here is a true story, or rather a true tragedy. The mother and father of a child who had been killed sat on the Vicarage sofa and thanked the vicar for agreeing to take their daughter's funeral. They had moved away from his parish, but as he had married them and christened little Tina, he replied that he thought it was only natural that they should 'come home' for the funeral. 'No,' they said, 'it's not just because of that. It's because we wrote to you when your own child was killed crossing the road two years ago. We felt you would really understand what we're going through.'

Anyone can help

Other clergy could have helped them, though it would have been difficult. There is no death so sad as the death of a child, and mercifully it is not so common as it was in our grandparents' time. Nevertheless most Christians have to cling to their faith to see them through difficult times of some sort, if only the much more expected death of elderly parents. They should be ready to 'comfort others with the same comfort wherewith they themselves have been comforted'. However, in the particularly acute grief of seeing dead a child into whom you have poured so much love and hope, many bereaved parents *feel* that nobody else can know what they are suffering, and regard it as somewhat insincere if one who has never lost a child says, 'I know what you must feel.'

Don't shrink away

It is not only clergy – any Christian may be called on to say words of comfort to a relative or friend who has lost a child. Some feel so inadequate that they shrink away from it. No doubt there is proper humility in this, and a wish not to intrude upon the parents' grief. But the parents' reaction is more likely to be a feeling of rejection. One of the most hurtful things about bereavement is the way some friends cross the road to avoid meeting us. Yet often the greatest comfort is received from those who put their arms around us and say something like, 'I don't know what to say, but I wanted you to know that we're thinking about you.'

Listening

The vicar in this true story found that the most important thing his wife and he could do was listen to Tina's parents, who wanted to talk about their dead child, and how she had died, and for various reasons were unable to do so within their family. In fact, some parents find it hard to speak even to each other in their grief, and this can be a cause of great tension in a marriage, because they don't realize that the other parent is grieving just as deeply, but probably expressing it in quite a different way. So talking together to a sympathetic third party may be the only way they have of communicating with each other.

Answers

The vicar I have described and his wife answered the parents' questions in the simplest terms possible. Their answers were based, of course, on the gospel of the resurrection, but there was not too much direct quotation of the Scriptures. Instead they talked about how they had cried out to Jesus when their own child died, and Jesus, who suffered on the cross 2,000 years ago, heard their prayer and gave them a strength and a peace which they knew could not have come from within themselves. He *must* be alive, then, and so, therefore, are those we love who have died.

No explanations

What you should never do, however, is try to explain why innocent children die: Jesus didn't; instead he shared our suffering, and promised us that death is going home to our Father's house where there is room for all, and where, in God's good time, we shall all meet again.

Suggested hymns

Lully, lullay, thou little tiny child; Morning glory, starlit sky; Unto us a boy is born; When Christ was born in Bethlehem.

Naming and Circumcision of Christ   1 January 2016
The Future

Num. 6.22–27 Aaron's blessing; Ps. 8 From the mouths of babes; Gal. 4.4–7 Born under the law; Luke 2.15–21 Naming and circumcision

> 'The LORD bless you and keep you; the LORD make his face to shine upon you, and be gracious to you; the LORD lift up his countenance upon you, and give you peace.' Numbers 6.24–26

Blessing

Those words are from Aaron's blessing, which God told Moses that his brother the priest should use when assuring the Israelites of God's guidance in the future. Today is New Year's Day, which is a good time to be looking forward to what will happen during the coming year. On this day Mary and Joseph took the week-old baby Jesus to the local rabbi for naming and circumcision. It was like when Christians christen a baby, they formally adopt the name the parents have chosen for them. The angel had told the baby's parents that they should call him 'Jesus', the Greek form of 'Joshua', which means 'the Lord saves.' So, at his naming ceremony, his parents looked into the future and saw that Jesus was going to be a Saviour. But what sort of a Saviour, and what he would save us from, they didn't know – God gives us a general idea of our future, but we have to work out the details stage by stage as each challenge confronts us along the way. Then the ceremony of circumcision was when Jesus was formally made a member of the Jewish people: his future was to lead his own community forward in doing God's work. The task God had given to the Jews was to teach the rest of the world that there is one God for every nation, who loves us and wants us to love each other. Jesus went further in doing this than any Jew before him.

New Year

So what are you looking forward to in the coming year? We wish each other health, long life and happiness, and God also would like us to enjoy those things. But in an imperfect world, those things are not possible for everyone. So, instead, God gives us faith, hope and love, enough to carry us through the difficult times, provided we pray to him every day.

Layman's Ten Commandments

Where then shall we go for guidance during the coming year? Obviously, to the Bible, provided that it has been sensitively explained by somebody who knows the culture and language in which it was written. The Ten Commandments are vital guide-lines to the areas in which we should make moral choices; though as Jesus clearly taught, they can't be applied literally in every circumstance, but have to be made subject to the law of love. Yet someone has written these words, which sum up well how a Christian should behave, and sent them round as an email headed 'A Layman's Ten Commandments'. They are a bit 'corny', but they are quite memorable and give you something to think about in the coming year. If you do, your life will be changed for ever:

1 Prayer is not a 'spare wheel' that you pull out when in trouble, but it is a 'steering wheel' that directs us along the right path throughout the journey.
2 Why is a car's windscreen so large and the rear-view mirror so small? Because our past is not as important as our future. So, look ahead and move on.
3 Friendship is like a book. It takes a few minutes to burn, but it takes years to write.
4 All things in life are temporary. If life is going well, enjoy it – the good times won't last for ever. If it is going wrong, don't worry – the bad times can't last long either.
5 Old friends are gold! New friends are diamond! If you get a diamond, don't forget the gold; because to hold a diamond, you always need a base of gold.

6 Often when we lose hope and think this is the end, God smiles from above and says 'Relax, sweetheart, it's just a bend, not the end!'

7 When God solves your problems, you have faith in his abilities; when God doesn't solve your problems, he has faith in your abilities.

8 A blind person asked St Anthony: 'Can there be anything worse than losing your sight?' He replied, 'Yes, losing your vision!'

9 When you pray for others, God listens to you and blesses them. Sometimes, when you are safe and happy, remember that someone has prayed for you.

10 Worrying does not take away tomorrow's troubles, it takes away today's peace.

Like a copy?

Remember those in the coming year. Let me know if you would like me to print them on paper or circulate them as an email. May the Lord bless you and keep you, in the name of Jesus!

Suggested hymns

How sweet the name of Jesus sounds; Jesu, the very thought of thee; Lord, for the years; Thy hand, O God, has guided.

Search the internet for 'layman's ten commandments'; it is quoted on many sites.

Epiphany   6 January
(Or may be celebrated on Sunday 3 January, see page 36.)
What Shall I Give Him?
Isa. 60.1–6 Bringing gold and incense; Ps. 72.[1–9] 10–15 Kings will bow before him; Eph. 3.1–12 Preaching to Gentiles; Matt. 2.1–12 Visit of the Magi

> *'On entering the house, [the wise men] saw the child with Mary his mother; and they knelt down and paid him homage. Then, opening their treasure chests, they offered him gifts of gold, frankincense, and myrrh.' Matthew 2.11*

Christina Rossetti

The Christmas carol 'In the bleak midwinter' is one of the most popular carols in English. It was written by Christina Rossetti, who was born in London in 1830 and lived until 1894. Her father was a poet and a political exile from Italy; her brother Dante Gabriel Rossetti was also a poet and a leading painter in the Pre-Raphaelite movement; she several times served as his model for the Virgin Mary. Christina was the youngest of five children, and dictated her first fairy story to her mother before she could write. The family all became devout members of the Anglo-Catholic movement in the Church of England. She was engaged three times, but never married, probably for religious reasons: her first fiancé became a Roman Catholic. Her most famous poem was 'Goblin Market', published in 1862. 'In the Bleak Midwinter' was written before 1872 in response to a request from the magazine *Scribner's Monthly* for a Christmas poem.

Gustav Holst

The poem appeared in *The English Hymnal* in 1906 with a musical setting by Gustav Holst, who is most famous for composing *The Planets* Suite. He wrote his setting in about 1904 in response to a request from Ralph Vaughan Williams, one of the compilers of *The English Hymnal*. It was intended as a congregational hymn.

Harold Darke

By contrast, Harold Darke's setting of 1909 was intended as a choral anthem, in which the first and third verses were given to soloists. Underneath the haunting melody is a lilting organ part. It was this setting that was named the world's best Christmas carol in a poll of leading choir directors and choral experts in 2008. Harold Darke was born in London in 1888 and studied at the Royal College of Music. He was the organist of St Michael's Church, Cornhill, for 50 years, where he founded the St Michael's Singers and gave regular organ recitals up until his eighty-fifth birthday, when he played at the Royal Festival Hall.

The poem

It is often assumed that Bethlehem, being on the edge of the Judaean Wilderness, must have a hot desert climate all the year round. But those who have been there in winter know that there can be a cold wind and driving sleet which makes it very uncomfortable. Perhaps 'earth stood hard as iron, water like a stone, snow on snow', is an exaggeration, and the shepherds would never have let their sheep stay out in such conditions. But the second verse leads us to think of the unimaginable greatness of God, and of Jesus the Son of God: 'heaven cannot hold him'. This is then contrasted with the poverty and cramped stable to which he submitted at his incarnation, with only his mother worshipping him with a kiss.

What can I give him?

But my excuse for mentioning this carol in my sermon on the feast of the Epiphany is the mention of the wise men in the last verse. The angels were worshipping the Christ-child as they thronged the air above the stable; his mother was giving him a kiss. The shepherds gave him a lamb, and the wise men gave precious gifts of gold, frankincense and myrrh. The poet feels a desire to make a suitable present to Jesus, to mark her acknowledgement of his greatness, and her gratitude for his humility in coming to earth to be a human being just like us. But what can she give him that will compare with the generosity of the three kings?

Give my heart

The answer comes to her in the incredibly moving final line of the song. Nothing that any of us possesses is worthy of being made a present to King Jesus. But there is one thing that he wants from each one of us, and that is our heart. Often considered to be the core of our being, and the seat of the emotions, the heart represents a passionate and all-embracing love, the offering of our whole life to Christ. Jesus wants us to love him with all our heart and soul and mind and strength. Our love for Christ must be heartfelt and heart-warming. The sacrifices we make for him may have to be heart-rending, and we may have to be heartbroken for his sake. But:

> If I were a wise man,
> I would do my part;
> Yet what I can I give him–
> Give my heart!

Suggested hymns

Brightest and best of the sons of the morning; In the bleak mid-winter; O worship the Lord in the beauty of holiness; We three kings of orient are.

Week of Prayer for Christian Unity   18–25 January
Enemies of Christ

Zeph. 3.16–20 Bring you home; Ps. 133 Brothers at unity;
1 John 4.9–15 We ought to love one another; John 17.11b–23
That they may be one

> '[Jesus prayed,] "I ask not only on behalf of these, but also on behalf of those who will believe in me through their word, that they may all be one. As you, Father, are in me and I am in you, may they also be in us, so that the world may believe that you have sent me."' John 17.20–21

The prayer of Jesus

Are you an enemy of Christ? Obviously not, for when you declared yourself to be a Christian, you signed up to be on his side in every battle. But just occasionally, do you say and do things that actually work in the opposite direction to the changes Jesus prayed for? You see what I mean? Anyone whose actions undo the improvements that Jesus prayed for, is an enemy agent, working against Christ in the battle of good against evil. What's that you say? You've never ever worked against the cause of Christ? I do hope you are right. But before we can be sure, we need to see what Jesus prayed for. During the Last Supper, Jesus offered up a long prayer. First, Jesus asked the Father to bring glory to his Son, then to the Son's disciples, and then to those who would be converted by their preaching. He prays that we may be 'consecrated', pure and holy, and set aside for God's service.

In the world

Jesus prays for you and me, that we may be *in* the world, but not *of* the world. He wants us to be involved in the world, trying to change it for the better, without being corrupted by the wrong attitudes of those around us. The world hates good people, because we show up the world's wickedness. So he prays that we may be protected from the world's attacks on us, and from 'the evil one'. Satan attacks us, not by physical force, but by tempting us to conform to the world's standards.

Unity

Then Jesus prays for us that we might be one, so that the world may believe. Our task, for which Jesus has chosen and consecrated us, is to convince the world that God loves them. To do that, we need to radiate love in our own lives. The world will never believe in a God of love, if they see God's people forever squabbling among themselves. So the crucial verse in this passage is when Jesus prays that you and I may be one, so that the world may believe.

Missionary

A Christian missionary was learning Chinese from a polite, thoughtful teacher. The missionary said, 'You behave in a very Christian way. Why don't you get baptized and become a Christian?' To which the Chinese courteously replied, 'I will become a Christian when Roman Catholics, Protestants, Pentecostals and all the other sorts of Christians agree on what Christianity is.' There was no answer to this. How can we expect others to share our faith when we can't even produce a common explanation of what that faith is? So our disunity actively dissuades people, who are attracted by Jesus, from joining the Church. No wonder Jesus prayed that we might be united, so that the non-believers may put their faith in him. No prayer of his has been so hindered by the stubbornness of his followers. The world cannot be evangelized by competing churches.

Undesirable

Of course unity doesn't mean uniformity. It is hardly possible, and probably undesirable, that we should all be members of one rigid organization, worshipping in the same way, and believing in the same things. The Church is a family, in which each member has the freedom to express their own individuality. It is by our tolerance of difference that unbelievers will be led to see that there is room even for them in the pilgrimage towards the truth which we call Christ's Church. Jesus didn't pray for unity of organization, or even in the details of faith. It was a unity of personal relationships that he prayed for, and that will bring the world to believe. Every time you say unkind, intolerant things about other Christians, members of your own congregation or another denomination, you make it harder for others to believe that you are inspired by a God of love. Even if we go on our own sweet way, ignoring the other churches in our neighbourhood for 364 days of the year, people will ask, 'Where is the unity for which Christ prayed?' Unless you are actively promoting cooperation between Christians, you are actually fighting against that process for which Christ prayed. If we are not one, so that the world may believe, we are the enemies of Christ.

Suggested hymns

A new commandment I give unto you; Bind us together, Lord; Jesus, stand among us at the meeting of our lives; Thy hand, O God, has guided.

Conversion of St Paul   25 January
Did St Paul Invent Christianity?

Jer. 1.4–10 The call of a prophet; Ps. 67 Let all the peoples praise you; Acts 9.1–22 Saul's conversion (*if the Acts reading is used instead of the Old Testament reading, the New Testament reading is* Gal. 1.11–16a Called me through his grace); Matt. 19.27–30 The reward of eternal life

> *'Now the word of the LORD came to me saying, "Before I formed you in the womb I knew you, and before you were born I conse-crated you; I appointed you a prophet to the nations." . . . Then the LORD put out his hand and touched my mouth; and the LORD said to me, "Now I have put my words in your mouth."' Jeremiah 1.4–5, 9.*

Inventor?

Sometimes you will hear the opponents of Christianity sneering, 'No, Christianity has nothing to do with Jesus of Nazareth – it was all invented after his death by a man called Saul of Tarsus.' These critics are not entirely wrong – much of what we know as Christianity today was developed in Greek by St Paul, though based very closely on what Jesus had said in Aramaic, the contemporary dialect of Hebrew. But most of the civilized world in those days spoke Greek, and Paul realized that even if he made a word-for-word translation into Greek of what Jesus said, it would not attract any converts, because the thought patterns of those who spoke those languages were so different. Jews thought in terms of mysticism, Greeks in terms of magic; Jews spoke in poetry, and Greeks in philosophy; Jews believed in one God, who was a fierce judge of those who broke his laws, but Greeks worshipped a number of very fallible gods, who could be bribed by sacrifices to give us what we ask of them. Jewish Christians spoke of Jesus as the Son of Man, meaning the human figure in Daniel's prophecy who turned out to be divine; Greek Christians couldn't understand that, so Paul called him the Christ, which means 'the anointed King' in Greek.

Translator

Saul, brought up in a Jewish family living in a Greek university town, was the ideal man to translate the new Jewish religion into Greek ways of thought that would attract Greek-speakers to become followers of Jesus the Jew. So God called Saul, just as God had called Jeremiah centuries ago, to be a prophet to every nation, speaking the words that God had put into his mouth:

> 'Before I formed you in the womb I knew you, and before you were born I consecrated you; I appointed you a prophet to the nations' . . . Then the LORD put out his hand and touched my mouth; and the LORD said to me, 'Now I have put my words in your mouth.'

Now, in 'Galilee of the Gentiles', as they called it, people spoke a mixture of Aramaic and Greek. So Jesus used a few Greek ideas, especially when he crossed the lake to the Greek-speaking Decapolis on the eastern side. But the Lord's Prayer, for instance, is couched entirely in Hebrew terms. Paul tried valiantly to explain what these ideas meant to his Greek readers, and worked hard to achieve unity and harmony between the Greek and Jewish converts in the churches he wrote to. 'Salvation' translated easily – everyone knows what it is to be saved from danger. But he introduced new ideas into Christian thought, such as 'redemption' – which was the price you paid to set a slave free, and there were many slaves and ex-slaves in the new Christian congregations. There are many phrases which were almost new-minted on the lips of St Paul, like 'Christ emptied himself', 'a spiritual body', 'Christians', 'the Church, the body of Christ', 'mystery', 'knowledge', 'righteousness', 'justification', 'the Second Adam' and 'speaking in tongues'. Whereas whole new shades of meaning were taken on by familiar words in his writings, such as 'eternal' meaning timeless, and 'apostles' meaning missionaries.

Science

St Paul addressed the Greek philosophers in Athens, beginning,

> Athenians, I see how extremely religious you are in every way. For as I went through the city and looked carefully at the objects of your worship, I found among them an altar with the inscription, 'To an unknown god.' What therefore you worship as unknown, this I proclaim to you.

From this we see how far St Paul had gone in translating Hebrew terms into words that would be understood by Greeks. Today we have the task of reinterpreting it again, to a world that thinks in Greek scientific and philosophical ways. So much of what we now know as Christianity is based on Paul's reinterpretation of the teaching of Jesus. Without it, we should be quite unable to proclaim the one, unchanging gospel to the people of today.

Suggested hymns

A heavenly splendour from on high; Disposer supreme, and judge of the earth; Hail, thou source of every blessing; We sing the glorious conquest.

Presentation of Christ in the Temple (Candlemas)
2 February (*or may be celebrated on Sunday 31 January*)
Atonement
Mal. 3.1–5 The Lord shall come to his Temple; Ps. 24.[1–6] 7–10 Open the gates for the Lord; Heb. 2.14–18 Jesus became like

the descendants of Abraham; Luke 2.22–40 The presentation of
Christ in the Temple

> 'There was also a prophet, Anna the daughter of Phanuel . . . At
> that moment she came, and began to praise God and to speak
> about the child to all who were looking for the redemption of
> Jerusalem.' Luke 2.36, 38

Atonement

When Jesus, 40 days old, was presented in the Temple, Anna the
prophetess declared that he was the one who would bring redemption. That was a word used for buying a slave's freedom, and
Christians believe that Jesus bought our freedom from slavery to
sin by dying on the cross. We all believe that Jesus achieved something for us by his death, but it is not easy to explain what he did
and how. So a number of theories have grown up, linked under the
title of 'doctrines of the atonement'. Atonement is a made-up word
derived from 'at-one-ment', the theory of how Jesus made us *at
one* with God. It attempts to outline the reasons for believing that
Christ died to save us from our sins.

Justice

One approach is to think about justice. All groups have leaders,
whose task is to administer the group justly. Traditionally the UK
has a monarch, commercial companies have a managing director and
Boy Scouts have patrol leaders. Effective leaders need to deter those
in their charge from acting in a way that interferes with the leader's
aims. Traditionally there has been the idea that those who please
leaders should be rewarded, those who displease them should be punished. When captains of sailing vessels in the Royal Navy discovered
transgressions of discipline among their crew, they had the transgres-
sors flogged. More severe transgressions, like leading a mutiny, led
to execution. Punishments were meted out to show others what they
will bring on themselves if they transgress the leader's wishes.

Punishing the leader

But the ship's captain is under the authority of the admiral of the
fleet. If the ship goes down due to the captain's negligence, say in

not noticing that the helmsman has made an error, the captain is punished in the helmsman's place, and the helmsman goes free. The comparison is sometimes made with Jesus Christ, who bears the punishment we deserve for our sins. Of course it is not an exact parallel, because we are free to disobey Jesus, in a way that the helmsman is not free to disobey his captain. But this metaphor helps us to see how serious the consequences of our disobedience really are.

Sin

As Christians we are conscious we are not perfect and do sometimes sin. Even when we try not to, we still sin, and sinning interferes with what God wants of us. He exhorts us to behave lovingly, and our disobedience matters to him. As our ultimate leader, God must, in order to be effective, treat us justly, and that includes punishing us so that we shall try not to sin again. However, God also realizes that many people try to avoid sinning, but just cannot steer clear of sin altogether. So, rather than punishing us, God has punished his Son, our captain, in our place. This punishment, of being nailed to a cross, would have been cruel had not Jesus willingly taken it on himself. But it shows us how much our disobedience hurts our heavenly Father, and Jesus our friend. Seeing this, we try very hard not to sin again.

Poor analogy

It is not a perfect analogy, and there are lots of holes in the logic. But God always exceeds our powers of description, and if a word like 'redemption' helps us to catch a glimmer of the truth, then it is worth using it for lack of a better theory. This is what Anna the prophetess, with all her years of meditation and experience, knew well. Another old resident of Jerusalem, named Simeon, had just said to Mary, 'This child is destined for the falling and the rising of many in Israel, and to be a sign that will be opposed, so that the inner thoughts of many will be revealed – and a sword will pierce your own soul too.' In other words, we fall away from God through our secret sins, and rise again because he forgives us; but this is only possible through much pain – pain to Jesus, and therefore to his mother Mary too. We may not be able to explain how this happens, but we know through our feeling of at-one-ment with God that he has forgiven us, and that somehow the death of Jesus was necessary to bring that about.

Suggested hymns

Faithful vigil ended; Hail to the Lord who comes; Of the Father's love begotten; Virgin-born, we bow before thee.

St David, Bishop of Menevia, Patron of Wales
c. 601   1 March
Legends of St David

Ecclus. (Ben Sira) 15.1–6 Whoever holds to the law will obtain wisdom; Ps. 16.1–7 I have a goodly heritage; 1 Thess. 2.2–12 Entrusted with the gospel; Matt. 16.24–27 Take up your cross

> *'As you know and as God is our witness, we never came with words of flattery or with a pretext for greed; nor did we seek praise from mortals, whether from you or from others.' 1 Thessalonians 2.5–6*

Name

St David, to give him his English name, is the patron saint of Wales, and he is known as Dewi Sant in Wales. For those who can speak Welsh, his name can be transliterated as Dafydd. He is known as 'David the Water Man', either because the monks in the monasteries that he founded were completely teetotal, or because he used to submerse himself to meditate.

Fact and legend

Many stories are told about the life of St David, and it is difficult to be sure which are fact and which are imaginative fiction. He would probably have said he was not interested in the flattering portrait of him given in some of the legends, but I shall recount a few of them, and you can decide which sound factual to you. Many of the traditional tales about David are found in a book written in his honour in the late eleventh century by a monk called Rhygyfarch, who claimed it was based on documents found in the cathedral archives. Modern historians are sceptical about this, arguing that it was an attempt to claim that the Welsh church was independent of the Church in the rest of Britain, and that their archbishops were the equals of the Archbishops of Canterbury. The Welsh church did not use the Latin Mass of the

301

Roman Catholic Church until the eighth century. It was claimed that St David made a pilgrimage to the Holy Land, and was consecrated as an archbishop by the Patriarch of Jerusalem, who was not subject to the popes in Rome. It is also said that David was descended from the aristocracy, because his father belonged to a princely family named Sant. His mother, St Non, was also well connected, it is believed. His birth date is still uncertain, as suggestions range from 462 to 512, and it is said that he died in 569. He chose to become a monk, and went to study under a famous Welsh saint, named Paulinus, on a remote island, though nobody is quite sure where that was. It is said that the agèd St Paulinus was blind when St David first met him, allegedly from weeping over the sins of the world, and when St David prayed for him, God restored the old man's sight.

Pelagianism

St David was famous as a teacher and preacher, and founded monasteries and churches in Wales, Cornwall and Brittany. St David's Cathedral stands on the site of a monastery he founded on the coast at the south-west corner of Wales. He presided over two synods, at Brefi in about 560 and at Caerleon in around 569, which were called to deal with the Pelagian heresy. Pelagius was a Celtic Christian who lived from about 390 to 418. He laid a great emphasis on the doctrine of free will, to the extent that he was accused of claiming that human beings could go to heaven by their own efforts, without the need of God's grace – in effect that we can pull ourselves up by our own bootlaces. Pelagianism was strongly opposed by St Augustine, a famous Christian teacher from Hippo in North Africa. However, modern scholars have pointed out that Augustine's teaching that we have all inherited guilt from the original sin of Adam is influenced by his early membership of the Manichean religion, which taught that the material world is evil, and Pelagius may not have been as heretical as Augustine thought. Nevertheless, Pelagianism was attractive to the Christians in Britain, with their tradition of sturdy independence and self-help, and St David argued persuasively against it. He became well known in Rome for his teaching ability and his skill at public speaking.

Monasteries

David gathered a group of supporters, and settled with them in a remote corner of Wales to form a strict monastery; this was followed by many others. The monks had to earn their own living by hard work. Whatever our uncertainty about what Pelagius actually taught, let us learn from St David the lesson of not being too independent in our thinking, nor too confident in our ability to do good without praying for God to help us.

Suggested hymns

Faith of our fathers, taught of old; Father, hear the prayer we offer; Guide me, O thou great Redeemer (Cwm Rhondda); Love divine, all loves excelling (Blaenwern).

St Patrick, Bishop, Missionary, Patron of Ireland
c. 460   17 March
Celtic Prayer

Deut. 32.1–9 Let my teaching drop like rain, *or* Tob. 13.1b–7 In the land of my exile; Ps. 145.2–13 Make known to all peoples; 2 Cor. 4.1–12 This ministry; Matt. 10.16–23 Warnings for missionaries, *or* John 4.31–38 Ripe for harvest

> *'We have this treasure in clay jars, so that it may be made clear that this extraordinary power belongs to God and does not come from us.' 2 Corinthians 4.7*

Culture

To understand St Patrick, we must see him as part of the culture of the people he preached to. Although the heart of their preaching remains the unchanging gospel of the love of God, every missionary has always translated it into the local language, with the images and metaphors that will appeal to their hearers, and an appeal to their own experience. St Patrick was probably born in Cumbria, soon after the Roman Legions had withdrawn. He came from a Christian family, so his ancestors were probably locals who had learnt about Jesus from the legionaries, but spoke a Celtic language at home. Then he went to work in Ireland, which had never been part of the Roman Empire. He will have used this Celtic background to communicate with the people of Ireland when he went there as a missionary. Although the language borrowed a few words from Latin, it was a world away from the cultured Latin spoken in Rome. Celtic culture was much more down to earth. This is not to say that they were a separate church, or that they lacked respect for the Bishop of Rome; but when most people travelled on foot, the Celts were a long way from the heart of the Roman Empire.

Celtic prayer

Because of this, the Celts produced a very down-to-earth version of Christianity, rooted in the world of nature, and the rural life of the peasant tribes. They had different art forms – think of the illuminated manuscripts and the Celtic crosses – different liturgies, and even a different date for Easter. And they developed a strong tradition of Celtic prayer. They prayed about the events of daily life – they had prayers to use while building a cottage, setting out on a journey, and even to pray while milking a cow! – and they saw the activity of God and his angels all around them, in the beauty of the natural world, the rotation of the seasons, and the ebb and flow of the sea. Towards the end of the twentieth century, there was a great revival of interest in Celtic prayer, and many new prayers were written in approximately the same style, which has something important to teach us all about our own prayer life.

Down-to-earth prayer

There is a danger that our prayer becomes too posh. If we banish prayer to church, with its Sunday-best atmosphere of thees and thous, then we shall be scared to pray in the midst of our daily life. Some graffiti were written on a bridge recently, reading 'Prepare to meet thy God – evening dress optional'! But it is vital in our growth as Christians that we learn to pray, in our own stumbling ungrammatical words, when work is hell on Monday mornings, when we're watching the football at the weekends, on gloomy rainy days, when the car breaks down, when the bank statement arrives, when the children are naughty, and at all the little frustrations which crop up in our daily life. We shouldn't take the beauty of God's world for granted, but thank him for it whenever we see a mountain or a sunset.

Circling

The old Celts had a ritual they called 'circling'; try it when you are praying for someone or for a home. With your finger draw a circle round what you are praying for, or do it mentally in your mind. Then say out loud or silently words like 'Circle, O Lord, your servant Anne with your healing, as she goes to hospital for her chemotherapy treatment'; or, 'Circle, O Lord, your servant Peter as he sits his exam today.' Then give thanks for the tools you use daily, from the water which flows from the tap to the mobile phone which helps you keep in touch with those you love.

Patrick's Breastplate

Finally, learn some of the old Celtic prayers. The famous hymn called 'St Patrick's Breastplate' comes from a little later than the saint's lifetime; copy it from a hymn book or the internet, and learn it by heart for daily use:

> Christ be with me, Christ within me,
> Christ behind me, Christ before me,
> Christ beside me, Christ to win me,
> Christ to comfort and restore me.
> Christ beneath me, Christ above me,
> Christ in quiet, Christ in danger,
> Christ in hearts of all that love me,
> Christ in mouth of friend and stranger.

Suggested hymns

I bind unto myself today (St Patrick); I cannot tell why he whom angels worship (Londonderry); Lord, while for all mankind we pray; Inspired by love and anger (Salley Gardens).

St Joseph of Nazareth   19 March
Daddy

2 Sam. 7.4–16 Descendants of David; Ps. 89.26–36 David's line; Rom. 4.13–18 Abraham's descendants; Matt. 1.18–25 Joseph's dream

> *'When Joseph awoke from sleep, he did as the angel of the Lord commanded him; he took [Mary] as his wife, but had no marital relations with her until she had borne a son; and he named him Jesus.' Matthew 1.24–25*

Abba

When Jesus was talking to God, what name did he use to speak to him? Here's a clue: it begins the Lord's Prayer, but not in the version we use in church. Jesus seems to have taught that prayer in two forms: one for use when Christians pray together, which begins 'Our Father', and the other for individual use, recorded in St Luke's Gospel, which begins simply, 'Father'. In the particularly intimate moment when Jesus prays in the Garden of Gethsemane, St Mark reports the Jewish word: '[Jesus] said, "Abba, Father, for you all things are possible; remove this cup from me; yet, not what I want, but what you want."' St Paul tells us that even the Christians in Rome, few of whom spoke Hebrew, had picked up this word in their prayers: 'For you did not receive a spirit of slavery to fall back into fear, but you have received a spirit of adoption. When we cry, "Abba! Father!" it is that very Spirit bearing witness with our spirit that we are children of God.' It was the same among the Greek-speaking Gauls of Galatia: 'Because you are children, God has sent the Spirit of his Son into our hearts, crying, "Abba! Father!"' Abba was the second word a Jewish baby learnt. It corresponds to 'Dadda', the word our babies struggle with when they have just mastered 'Mamma'. So Jesus addressed the Creator of the universe, and taught his followers to, by the name 'Daddy'. And where did he learn that this word was used for a loving authority figure? Surely, from observing his own daddy, 'Daddy Joseph'!

Parenting

This is an amazing tribute to Joseph's qualities as a parent. Jesus was not, of course, Joseph's son, but Joseph generously adopted him when he married Mary, after her 'illegitimate' child, so to speak, had been born. Nevertheless, he cared for the child lovingly, taught him to be a carpenter, taught him to love and respect his mother Mary, and gave him an image of what fatherhood meant. If we really believe that Jesus laid down his godhead when he came to earth, that means that baby Jesus at first had no idea who he was, and who God is. He had to learn it all from Mary and Joseph. 'Day by day like us he grew, he was little, weak and helpless, tears and smiles like us he knew; and he feeleth for our sadness, and he shareth in our gladness.' Joseph probably worked on building the new town of Sepphoris, a few miles from Nazareth, so he could return home each evening and, like any good father, share in the care of the children. In the Old Testament there are three or four places where God is described as the father of the nation; and Job, Jeremiah and some of the psalms speak to God with surprising intimacy; but, before Jesus, nobody had addressed God as 'Dadda'. This remarkable new understanding can only have come from Jesus observing the combination of parental authority and devoted care shown him by Joseph. It is still regarded as blasphemous by Jews and Muslims.

Adoption

Because Joseph was his adoptive parent, Jesus came to see that anybody can claim God as their adopting Father. St Paul took up this idea when he wrote to the Ephesians, '[God] destined us for adoption as his children through Jesus Christ, according to the good pleasure of his will.' With a natural parent, a father can be told he has a duty to care for his children, 'otherwise he should not have fathered them'. But when a man adopts a fatherless child, it is out of the goodness of his heart that he devotes his time and resources to caring for them. So whenever we speak intimately to the Maker of the Universe, picturing him as our loving heavenly Father, it is Joseph we have to thank for giving Jesus a human model through which to explain to us that God is a God of love. Think of the old carol:

Carol

'Joseph dearest, Joseph mine,
help me cradle the child divine;
God reward thee and all that's thine
in paradise,'
so prays the mother Mary.

Chorus
He came among us at Christmastide,
at Christmastide, in Bethlehem;
men shall bring him from far and wide
love's diadem: Jesus, Jesus,
lo, he comes, and loves, and saves, and frees us!

'Gladly, dear one, lady mine,
help I cradle this child of thine;
God's own light on us both shall shine
in paradise,
as prays the mother Mary.'
Chorus

Suggested carols:

Hail to the Lord who comes; Joseph dearest, Joseph mine; Once in Royal David's city; The great God of heaven is come down to earth.

Annunciation of Our Lord to the Blessed Virgin Mary   4 April (transferred)
Seven Joys of Mary

Isa. 7.10–14 The sign of Immanuel; Ps. 40.5–11 I love to do your will; Heb. 10.4–10 I have come to do your will; Luke 1.26–38 The angel's message

> *'In the scroll of the book it is written of me
> that I should do your will, O my God;
> I delight to do it: your law is within my heart.'*
> *Psalm 40.9 (Common Worship)*

Joy and sorrow

Perhaps we are attracted to the Blessed Virgin Mary because her unique life-story was in one respect just like ours: a mixture of joy and sorrow. We need to keep a balance when we look at the sorrows and the joys of Mary, as we do when we look at our own lives. But at this service I want to concentrate on the joyful aspects of her life; maybe on another occasion we can look at the darker side of the picture.

Gawain and the rosary

One of the most popular poems in the Middle Ages was called *Sir Gawain and the Green Knight*. In this it is stated that the hero, Sir Gawain, drew his strength from meditating on the five joys of

Mary. This medieval list became the first section of the popular devotion to Mary using the beads of the rosary. This begins with the Five Joyful Mysteries, which the devout user meditates on while saying Hail Marys and the Lord's Prayer. They are:

1. the Annunciation, when the Archangel Gabriel announced to Mary that she would become the mother of Jesus;
2. the Visitation, when she visited her cousin Elizabeth;
3. the Nativity, when she gave birth to Jesus;
4. the Presentation, when she and Joseph offered their baby to God in the Temple; then bought him back for the price of two pigeons; and finally;
5. the Finding of Jesus in the Temple, when his parents had lost him.

There were slight variations in this list from time to time. But these were certainly moments in the early life of Our Lady which gave her great joy.

Number seven

But for some reason human beings are fascinated by the number seven: seven days in the week; lucky number seven; the seven deadly sins; and being in the seventh heaven. The Bible refers to the seven deacons, the seven churches of Asia, and the seven words from the cross. So it was small wonder that the number of the Joys of Mary soon got inflated to seven, which is how they are widely pictured in medieval art, and how most people remember them these days. The Seven Joys of Mary are spread throughout her life, and are:

1. the Annunciation by the Angel Gabriel;
2. the Birth of Jesus in Bethlehem;
3. the Adoration by the Magil;
4. the Resurrection of Christ;
5. his Ascension into heaven;
6. Pentecost, when the gifts of the Holy Spirit fell upon the 12 apostles, and probably the Virgin Mary and several other women;
7. an event that is not in the Bible, though Roman Catholics believe in it firmly – the Coronation of the Blessed Virgin Mary as the Queen of Heaven.

Carol

But once again there are variations in the list, particularly when it was turned into a Christmas carol, which exists in English and American versions. So this, for the time being, is the version of 'Joys Seven' which I grew up with; maybe some of you know other versions. Among all the tragedy, Mary could find much to rejoice in and thank God for. Let that be an example for us all to follow:

The first good joy that Mary had,
it was the joy of one;
to see the blessed Jesus Christ,
when he was first her Son.
When he was first her Son, Good Lord;
and happy may we be;
praise Father, Son, and Holy Ghost
to all eternity.

The next good joy that Mary had,
it was the joy of two;
to see her own Son Jesus Christ,
making the lame to go.

The next good joy that Mary had,
it was the joy of three;
to see her own Son Jesus Christ,
making the blind to see.

The next good joy that Mary had,
it was the joy of four;
to see her own Son Jesus Christ
reading the Bible o'er.

The next good joy that Mary had,
it was the joy of five;
to see her own Son Jesus Christ,
raising the dead to life.

The next good joy that Mary had,
it was the joy of six;
to see her own Son Jesus Christ
upon the Crucifix.

310

The next good joy that Mary had,
it was the joy of seven;
to see her own Son Jesus Christ
ascending into Heaven.
Ascending into Heaven, Good Lord;
and happy may we be;
praise Father, Son, and Holy Ghost
to all eternity.

Suggested hymns

Joys Seven; Her virgin eyes saw God incarnate born; Shall we not love thee, Mother dear?; Sing we of the blessèd Mother.

St George, Martyr, Patron of England c. 304
23 April
Patron Saint of Unity

1 Macc. 2.59–64 Be courageous, *or* Rev. 12.7–12 Michael fights the dragon; Ps. 126 Restore our fortunes; 2 Tim. 2.3–13 A soldier of Christ; John 15.18–21 They will persecute you

> *'War broke out in heaven; Michael and his angels fought against the dragon. The dragon and his angels fought back, but they were defeated, and there was no longer any place for them in heaven.'*
> *Revelation 12.7–8*

England's patron

We celebrate today England's patron saint, St George. St George's flag, the red cross on the white background, is England's national flag, and supporters of the England football team wrap themselves in the flag or paint it on their faces. It has become such a sign of quintessential Englishness that we sometimes assume that we have a monopoly on St George. But that isn't really true, and it may serve as a corrective to aggressive English nationalism to remember that other nations have an interest in St George also.

History

First of all, remember that George was a real person, not a myth, though mythical tales have gathered around him; and he was not an Englishman. There is a problem straight away, because there were two people called George, and they have become confused. Probably the original George suffered martyrdom near Lydda – now the site of Lod airport in Israel – sometime before the Emperor Constantine put an end to the persecution of Christians around AD 312. Little is known about him, but by about the sixth century his cult became popular in that region. The legend of George and the dragon first emerged at the end of the twelfth century, and was made popular in Europe by a thirteenth-century book in Latin called *The Golden Legend*. Nobody knows what race this George came from; he could have been Jewish, but if he was a Greek-speaking Roman soldier he could have come from anywhere in the Roman Empire, though it is very unlikely that he would have been recruited from among the troublesome Britons. He is often confused with George of Cappadocia – an area of what we now call Turkey – who was a bishop of Alexandria in Egypt. He was an unpleasant character, but he was murdered by the rabble on Christmas Eve in 361, so qualifying to be honoured as a martyr. It was Edmund Gibbon in *The Decline and Fall of the Roman Empire* who suggested that this was the historical St George, but few people believe that now.

Crusades

St George of Lydda became popular in Palestine, and perhaps because his name means farmer, he was worshipped as a source of fertility. Up until recently, many Muslim women could be found kneeling at the churches dedicated to St George, asking him to pray to God that they might conceive a child. So in fact it may have been from the Muslim Saracens that the crusaders learnt to honour St George. His story had been translated into Anglo-Saxon, and a church was dedicated to him in Doncaster as early as in 1061. The crusaders brought back with them St George's flag, and from the fourteenth century it became a kind of uniform for English soldiers and sailors. St Edward the Confessor was England's patron saint until King Edward the Third founded the Order of the Garter in St George's Chapel, Windsor, in about 1347.

Patron saint of unity

So perhaps, with this mixed background, St George ought to be regarded as the patron saint of international unity. The cross on his flag celebrates the murder of Jesus, a Palestinian Jew. His cult was introduced to this country by Norman-French kings and crusaders, ruling over a mixed population of German Anglo-Saxons, Celtic Welshmen and Scandinavian Norsemen; though all the kings called George were descended from a German family. We sing on St George's Day the hymn 'I vow to thee, my country', with words by Cecil Spring Rice, an American, and music by Gustav Holst, who came from a Swedish family who had lived in Russia and Latvia. St George is also the patron saint of Portugal. He gave his name to the Caucasian Republic of Georgia, which became independent of Russia in 1991, as well as the American State of Georgia; George Town, which was the original name of Penang in Malaysia; George Town, the capital of the Cayman Islands; and another Georgetown, the federal capital of Guyana. Certainly he can't be claimed in support of right-wing political prejudice against foreigners, since he was himself foreign. Instead we should ask him to carry to God's throne our prayers for a growth of international tolerance.

Suggested hymns

And did those feet?; I vow to thee, my country; Lord, while for all mankind we pray; When a knight won his spurs.

St Mark the Evangelist   25 April
Staying Power

Prov. 15.28–33 Good news, *or* Acts 15.35–41 Paul rejects Mark; Ps. 119.9–16 How can young people keep their way pure?; Eph. 4.7–16 The gift of an evangelist; Mark 13.5–13 Staying power

> '[Jesus said,] "The one who endures to the end will be saved."' Mark 13.13

Gospel-writer

Children used to be taught to pray when they went to bed:

Matthew, Mark, Luke and John,
Bless the bed that I lie on.

That taught them to remember the order in which the four Gospels are printed in our Bibles, but that was not necessarily the order in which they were written. St Mark's is the shortest of the four, and almost everything in his Gospel appears to be copied by Matthew and Luke, either verbatim or making small amendments in such a way that it is obvious that Mark was the original. So we can confidently describe him as the first to write the life-story of Jesus, and the first to call his biography a 'Gospel', which means 'good news'. Mark chapter 13 is a collection of the sayings of Jesus which refer to troubled times to come, so that it is often called 'the Little Apocalypse'. Many of these predictions were fulfilled when the Roman army destroyed the city of Jerusalem in AD 70, but they make no mention of the fire which destroyed the city, so most people think the Gospel was written either before or soon after that date. There is a very old tradition that Mark was St Peter's secretary, and may have based his Gospel on what he heard Peter say.

Coward

Mark's account of the arrest of Jesus in Gethsemane ends with the words, 'A certain young man was following him, wearing nothing but a linen cloth. They caught hold of him, but he left the linen cloth and ran off naked.' Neither Matthew nor Luke bothers to copy this incident, which they obviously regarded as quite unimportant. But it was clearly important to the young man, and many people think that he was Mark himself. In which case it was honest of him to report his own cowardice and shame.

Acts

The Acts of the Apostles tells us that, for the first few years, the Christians of Jerusalem met in 'John Mark's mother's house'; probably she was a widow. Together with his Uncle Barnabas, Mark accompanied St Paul on his first missionary journey to Cyprus, but when Paul suggested going into the wild regions on the edge of the Roman Empire, Mark panicked and deserted. However, he and Paul were later reconciled, and Mark was St Peter's assistant in Rome.

Staying power

Mark's lack of staying power when he deserted St Paul is reported in Acts, yet he later became a transformed man. He reported the words of Jesus in the apocalyptic thirteenth chapter of his Gospel, 'The one who endures to the end will be saved.' But now he had learnt from his early failures, and showed great persistence in his mature years. He travelled widely, and the people of Alexandria in Egypt have always claimed that he was their first bishop. One story is that he was dragged through the streets of the city by a rope tied around his neck, and this was the cause of his death.

Endurance

As Jesus had predicted, the first Christians were cruelly persecuted, by their rulers and their neighbours, in the years leading up to the destruction of Jerusalem. It is easy to become dispirited if even members of your own family betray you, to curry favour with the authorities. Romans called Christianity a new and evil superstition; some Jews accused the Christians, who ate bread calling it the body of Christ, of cannibalism. It was easy in those circumstances to give up and renounce your faith. Dr G. J. Jeffrey, a minister in Glasgow, refused to have his biography written in his lifetime, because, he said, 'I have seen too many men fall out on the last lap of the race.' Christianity is not a short sprint, it is a very demanding marathon. A book by Peter Fryer on the history of black people in Britain, beginning with the Roman Empire and up until now, is titled *Staying Power*. Another book, about Shackleton's incredible voyage, is called *Endurance*. There are many countries in the world today where Christians are suffering and dying for their faith, by comparison with whom our sufferings in life seem quite small. But God could easily say, in the words of the Canadian hip-hop artist Shadrach Kabango or 'Shad',

> I beg your pardon,
> I never promised you a rose-garden.

St Mark the Evangelist had learnt from his own life that we are in it for the long haul; and he recorded for us the words of Jesus, so beautifully set to music in Mendelssohn's *Elijah*, 'He that shall endure to the end shall be saved.'

315

'The kingdom is upon you'; The kingdom of God is justice and joy; The saint who first found grace to pen; We have a gospel to proclaim.

SS Philip and James, Apostles 2 May (transferred)
Dogma
Isa. 30.15–21 This is the way; Ps. 119.1–8 The way of the Lord; Eph. 1.3–10 The mystery of forgiveness; John 14.1–14 I am the way

> 'Jesus said . . . "I am the way, and the truth, and the life. No one comes to the Father except through me."' John 14.6

Truth

Truth is elusive. Materialists are those who say that nothing is true except the material world, where everything can be demonstrated by scientific experiment. Yet even in science there are many things which can only be expressed as a statistical probability – for instance, the exact position of an electron at any moment of time. Any scientist who has ever fallen in love knows for certain that there is a spiritual world of the heart which science can say nothing about. But with deep spiritual truths, it is very difficult to find the right words to express them in. Language can describe the things which we see, hear, feel, smell or taste. Everything else has to be expressed by comparisons or metaphors, and although metaphors can point you in the right direction, you have to use your imagination to interpret them, and you can never be sure that *I* am imagining the same thing as *you* are imagining. Words are a very clumsy way of expressing truth.

Philip

Jesus said that the truth about God can never be expressed in words, but only through a person.

Thomas said to him, 'Lord, we do not know where you are going. How can we know the way?' Jesus said to him, 'I am the way, and the truth, and the life. No one comes to the Father except through me. If you know me, you will know my Father also. From now on you do know him and have seen him.' Philip – [whose day it is today] – said to him, 'Lord, show us the Father, and we will be satisfied.' Jesus said to him, 'Have I been with you all this time, Philip, and you still do not know me? Whoever has seen me has seen the Father. How can you say, "Show us the Father"? Do you not believe that I am in the Father and the Father is in me? The words that I say to you I do not speak on my own; but the Father who dwells in me does his works.'

Teaching

So his first disciples had only to look at Jesus, and say, 'God is like that.' The truth was standing before them. But when they came to explain their new ideas about God to people who had never seen Jesus, the disciples had to use words. Words that you use for teaching are called 'doctrine'. But not all teaching about God is true; there is such a thing as false doctrine. Suppose someone says, 'Jesus was not really human, he only seemed to be, so God does not care about the material world, and you can do what you like.' That is a heresy, known as the Docetic heresy. If your friend says that in their living room, you can reason with them. If they preach it from the pulpit, saying 'This is the official teaching of the Church – anyone who disagrees with me is not a Christian', then they are not only wrong, but dangerously wrong, because they are leading others into immorality. Then you must stop them using your pulpit. The Church developed some official doctrines, which nobody was allowed to disagree with, in public at least. These approved teachings were called 'dogmas', from the Greek word for an opinion.

Dogmatic

It is easy for the atheist to make fun of our Christian dogmas. G. K. Chesterton parodied the old proverb about sticks and dogs by suggesting that, for the atheist, 'any stigma will do to beat a dogma!' Yet we have to have official teachings, or everyone is floundering in a quagmire of uncertainty. The danger with dogmas, however, is that they make you dogmatic in your choice of words, and as we have seen, words are quite inadequate to express the truth. You may be surprised to know that most preachers have doubts which they keep to themselves, for fear of disturbing the simple faith of some in the congregation. In the attempt to express ancient truths in a way which will appeal to modern listeners, we may sometimes stray into heresy. I think we should avoid the witch-hunting of the ancient Inquisition. It is right to explore new ground in your thinking, if you admit that it is only a tentative opinion.

Prayer

So I leave you with a prayer by Leslie Weatherhead, which is worth learning by heart:

> From the cowardice which shrinks from new truth,
> From the laziness that is content with half-truths,
> From the arrogance which thinks that it knows all truth,
> O God of truth, deliver us. **Amen.**

Suggested hymns

Come my way, my truth, my life; Tell me the old, old story; Thou art the Way – by thee alone; Twin princes of the courts of heaven.

St Matthias the Apostle   14 May
Assisted Dying, Assisted Living

Isa. 22.15–25 Eliakim replaces Shebna; Ps. 15 Who shall dwell in your house?; Acts 1.15–26 Matthias replaces Judas (*if the Acts reading is used instead of the Old Testament reading, the New Testament reading is* 1 Cor. 4.1–7 Stewards of God's mysteries); John 15.9–17 I have appointed you

> 'Falling headlong, [Judas Iscariot] burst open in the middle and all his bowels gushed out.' Acts 1.18

Suicide

Poor Matthias! He was appointed to fill the vacancy in the Twelve caused by the death of Judas Iscariot. Otherwise we know nothing about him, and on this day there is little a preacher can do but preach about Judas. The Acts of the Apostles says that Judas died when he 'fell headlong'; but St Matthew's Gospel says he hanged himself. The Church *used* to say that this was the sin of despair: all other sins can be forgiven, we said, but by committing suicide you put yourself beyond the reach of even God's forgiveness. That is what we used to say; but now that we have a better understanding of clinical depression, most Christians would say that when 'the balance of [one's] mind is disturbed', nobody can be blamed. Yet there is still a puzzling question: if life is God's gift, surely only God has the right to say when life should end? This difficulty has become more acute since the debate arose about 'assisted dying'.

Assisted dying

It is illegal in this country to help someone to kill themselves. The reason for this is that greedy heirs, wanting to get their hands on their inheritance, might excuse murdering an elderly relative by saying that they were only granting his or her wish to die. So desperate people go to Switzerland, where they can be given a glass of barbiturates which ensure a rapid and relatively painless death. People who have studied this say that every case is different. What do you say to someone who is in perpetual and incurable pain, but is not capable of ending their own life? Or the driver trapped in the cab of a blazing vehicle who begs the policeman to shoot him? Knowing that in this country anyone who does what the dying person requests is liable, if not to prosecution, to years of awful guilt.

Assisted living

But greater even than the problem of assisted dying is that of assisted living. Pain and death are God's blessing on his creation. Without pain, we would not know there was anything wrong with us, and without death, there would be no room for the next generation to live in. But in past ages, people who fell ill died quickly; today, we have discovered medical means for keeping sick people alive long after they have decided they would rather die. In the hospices and dedicated hospital wards they have developed 'palliative care', to continue the life of a patient who is probably terminally ill for several months relatively free from pain. Doctors have a Hippocratic oath to preserve life at all costs. But is not assisted living just as much of an intrusion on God's right to choose when a life should end as assisted dying?

319

Talking about death

Death has become a taboo subject. Talking about it endlessly is morbid; but never to mention death is unrealistic. A Christian who believes in life after death ought to be given time to prepare for it, and may even look forward to it. Even those who believe that death is the end should be able to accept with gratitude the time when pain and grief comes to an end. Brian Castle, the Bishop of Tonbridge, has said that everyone needs a midwife at the time of their death, just as at their birth, to help them through what is a perfectly natural, if traumatic, process. And this is something a Christian, ordained or lay, is well qualified to do.

Our responsibility

Yet the difficulty of deciding how long life support should continue lays a clear responsibility on all of us. After discussing it with our families, we must all write a will, with clear instructions under what circumstances we wish life-prolonging treatments to be discontinued. Jesus stands there at the gate of heaven, waiting to welcome us; why should we wish to delay that happy day if there is no longer any work we can do for Jesus in this world?

Suggested hymns

Lord, enthroned in heavenly splendour; Lord, it belongs not to my care; The highest and the holiest place; There's a wideness in God's mercy.

Day of Thanksgiving for the Institution of Holy Communion (Corpus Christi)   26 May
Ritual

Gen. 14.18–20 Melchizedek brought bread and wine;
Ps. 116.10–17 The cup of salvation; 1 Cor. 11.23–26 The Last Supper; John 6.51–58 Living bread

> 'Jesus . . . took a loaf of bread, . . . broke it and said, "This is my body . . . Do this in remembrance of me." . . . He took the cup . . . saying, ". . . Do this . . . in remembrance of me."' 1 Corinthians 11.23–25

Last Supper

At the Last Supper, Jesus did four things:

1 He took bread and wine,
2 gave thanks for them,
3 broke the bread, and
4 gave them to his disciples.

Then he said, 'Do this, as my memorial.' So most churches repeat these actions, on anything from a daily basis to once a quarter, doing the same four things in the same order every time. In this way we are repeating a fixed ritual.

Ritualist

Some people don't like the word 'ritual'. It reminds them too much of a mindless routine, any variation in which is firmly forbidden. Of course, ritualism can go 'over the top', and the rigid ritualist is someone who is more interested in getting the ritual right than in its inner meaning. You may have heard the story of the monks from a remote monastery in the Middle Ages who had the rare opportunity of visiting Rome and attending a papal Mass. They made careful notes of what happened so that they could copy it exactly when they got home. Unfortunately on this day, a stray cat wandered into the basilica and set up a caterwauling, so His Holiness interrupted the service to say, 'Will someone please take that wretched cat outside!' For centuries afterwards in that particular monastery, they always brought a cat, which they kept for the purpose, into the chapel during Mass and prodded it until it howled, so that the celebrant could say the same sacred words as the Pope had uttered, though nobody could remember why!

Blessings of ritual

Yet the regular repetition of a series of actions can have many benefits. A tourist got into a taxi in London and asked the driver how you get to the Royal Festival Hall. The taxi driver replied, 'Practice, lady, practice!' It is true that you can be a mediocre musician on a minimum of practice, but to become a genius you need, as Thomas Edison said, 1 per cent inspiration and 99 per cent perspiration. It is true in music, it is true in sport, and it is true in living.

Aristotle believed that virtue is acquired by constantly repeating virtuous acts. The habit of resisting temptation teaches us self-control. There is no need to be a genius in religion, but the regular practice of prayer makes it second nature. There is actually a scientific reason for this. When you keep on repeating an action, new neural pathways are created in the brain which bypass the slower processes of decision. That is why you never have to think about what you are doing when you clean your teeth.

Sacraments

So the benefits of repeated rituals are both physical and spiritual. Believers in Jesus hold that 'the Word became flesh', combining spiritual and physical in one person. So in the sacraments, those 'outward and visible signs of an inward and spiritual grace', of which Holy Communion is the greatest, we repeat actions over and again which show us visually how much God loves us, and we get the habit of thanking him for his love. What is more, we do it not alone but together with other people. By regular practice we gain the habit of forming a community, to help each other to improve as persons, and to form a body of opinion and of corporate loving action that can change the world. In the public sacraments like baptisms and weddings, we openly make promises to each other and to God which are harder to break because we know so many people have heard them.

Corpus Christi

So on the Thursday after Trinity Sunday we set aside a day called Corpus Christi, which means 'the body of Christ', to thank Jesus for giving himself to us in this, the supreme sacrament. We thank him for giving us a repeated action to do in remembrance of him, knowing that repeated actions can create all sorts of good habits, which together become life-changing. Whether you like an elaborate ceremonial at your eucharistic feasts, or a plain and simple rite, or a bit of each from time to time, today we celebrate the ritual that Jesus gave us, when he said, 'Do this, in remembrance of me.' It is a repeated action which instils in us the habits of prayer and thanksgiving; of communal action and loving service; of daily awareness of the presence of God and the love of Jesus. What a marvellous invention!

Suggested hymns

An Upper Room did our Lord prepare; Hands that have been han-
dling; Strengthen for service, Lord, the hands; Sweet sacrament
divine.

Visit of the Blessed Virgin Mary to Elizabeth   31 May
Elizabeth, the Mother of John the Baptist

Zeph. 3.14–18 Sing, daughter Zion; Ps. 113 Making her a joyous mother; Rom. 12.9–16 Hospitality; Luke 1.39–49 [50–56]
Magnificat

> *'In those days Mary set out and went with haste to a Judaean town*
> *in the hill country, where she entered the house of Zechariah and*
> *greeted Elizabeth. When Elizabeth heard Mary's greeting, the child*
> *leaped in her womb. And Elizabeth was filled with the Holy Spirit*
> *and exclaimed with a loud cry, "Blessed are you among women,*
> *and blessed is the fruit of your womb . . . And blessed is she who*
> *believed that there would be a fulfilment of what was spoken to*
> *her by the Lord."' Luke 1.39–42, 45*

Elizabeth's story

Elizabeth was getting on in years; she lived with her husband
Zechariah somewhere in the 'hill country of Judaea'; the place shown
to pilgrims today is named Ein Karem. The main purpose of marriage in those days was so that the wife could present her husband
with a son, who could take over as soon as he was old enough as the
principal wage-earner in the family, and earn enough to support his
parents in their old age – there was no old-age pension at that time.
Elizabeth was approaching the menopause, after which women
are not able to conceive a baby in their womb, and she was still
childless. This was a great shame to a woman, who was regarded
as having fallen short in her most important duty; and Elizabeth's
neighbours let her know what they thought of her, as neighbours
will. Zechariah and Elizabeth were both from priestly families, and
because Zechariah had doubted the message that an angel gave
him when it was his week for duty in the Jerusalem Temple, he
had been struck dumb. The angel had said that he and Elizabeth
would have a son who would prepare the way for the Messiah, and

were to call him John; we know him as John the Baptist. But sure enough, Elizabeth became pregnant, and rejoiced that she would no longer be a figure of scorn. She said, 'This is what the Lord has done for me when he looked favourably on me, and took away the disgrace I have endured among my people.' An expectant mother and a speechless father, shunned by their relations and their neighbours, must have made a difficult household. Elizabeth had a cousin, Mary, who lived in Nazareth in the Province of Galilee, and she was not ashamed to be seen speaking to the elderly mother-to-be. When Mary discovered that she too was expecting a child, whom an angel had told her to call Jesus, although she was not married, she too became a disgrace in the neighbourhood. She travelled all the way to Ein Karem, a long and difficult journey for a woman in her condition. This was so that she could visit her cousin, who she knew was also pregnant, so that they could swop their stories, compare notes, support each other and be happy together. When Mary came into the house, Elizabeth was so excited that, as she put it, her child jumped up and down in her womb. Elizabeth was possibly the first person after Joseph to recognize Mary as the mother of the future Lord, and she welcomed her cousin hospitably to her home. Mary sang what we call the Magnificat, and after a while returned to Nazareth. Elizabeth's baby was born, a boy, and everyone expected he would be named after one of his relations. But Elizabeth insisted that he should be called John, a name which nobody in the family bore. The neighbours were astonished, and signalled to Zechariah to give his reaction; he wrote down on a wax tablet, 'His name is John.' And at that moment he regained the power of speech and sang the song we call the Benedictus. We hear nothing of Elizabeth after this, but what a story of God's mercy she must have been able to tell baby John as he grew up. Sadly, she probably did not live long enough to see him take up the prophetic role that the angel had predicted.

Lessons to learn

From Elizabeth, then, we can learn that nobody is too old to be given a task by God, for nothing is impossible to God. She showed the virtue of showing hospitality to her cousin; tender care to her disabled husband; strong faith that everything would be all right if she did what God had told her; and obedience to God in the details as well as the important things of life. We also learn from her not to gossip, and not to pay any attention to what the neighbours say!

Suggested hymns

Brother, sister, let me serve you; Long ago, prophets knew; Tell out, my soul, the greatness of the Lord; Ye watchers and ye holy ones.

St Barnabas the Apostle   11 June
A Levite

Job 29.11–16 Like one who comforts; Ps. 112 Generous; Acts 11.19–30 Barnabas encourages Saul (*if the Acts reading is used instead of the Old Testament reading, the New Testament reading is* Gal. 2.1–10 Barnabas and me); John 15.12–17 Love one another

> '[Jesus said,] "This is my commandment, that you love one another as I have loved you."' John 15.12

Levite

There are at least ten places in the New Testament where St Barnabas is mentioned. I claim the privilege in the coming years to preach on any of them, not only on the ones that are recommended for today in the lectionary. The first is in chapter 4 of the Acts of the Apostles, beginning at verse 36:

> With great power the apostles gave their testimony to the resurrection of the Lord Jesus, and great grace was upon them all. There was not a needy person among them, for as many as owned lands or houses sold them and brought the proceeds of what was sold. They laid it at the apostles' feet, and it was distributed to each as any had need. There was a Levite, a native of Cyprus, Joseph, to whom the apostles gave the name Barnabas (which means 'son of encouragement'). He sold a field that belonged to him, then brought the money, and laid it at the apostles' feet.

So the first thing we learn about Barnabas is that he was a Levite. The Levites were the descendants of Levi, one of the 12 tribes of Israel. But, unlike the other tribes, they had no land of their own. The book of Joshua lists 48 cities which were given to the Levites to live in, but archaeologists have shown that these towns were not built until after the return from exile about 500 BC, so this must have been a late development. The Levites seem to have been in charge of Jewish worship, offering sacrifices to God in each of the cities and shrines, until, when the northern kingdom of Israel split from the southern kingdom of Judah, they concentrated on the northern temples of Dan, Bethel and Shiloh. Then, when the northern kingdom was destroyed by the Assyrians, they fled to Jerusalem and became assistants to the descendants of Aaron, who were priests to the Temple there. The Levites were teachers of the law, singers and gatekeepers. It is one of these that Jesus describes, in the parable of the good Samaritan, as being too concerned with his own purity to touch the (possibly dead) body of the man who fell among thieves, which would have disqualified him from entering the Temple.

Cyprus

But Barnabas was a Levite from Cyprus; it is very unlikely that he travelled regularly to Jerusalem to do duty in the Temple. So perhaps, outside Judaea, the Levites had become secularized. The descendants of Levi might have become rabbis, and their opinion on the interpretation of the Jewish law would be valued. Like other Jews dispersed around the Roman Empire, Barnabas may have gone up to Jerusalem for Passover once a year, and learnt to read Hebrew in the synagogue; but his native language will have been Greek. Like St Paul in his letters, Barnabas may have quoted the Scriptures in the Greek translation known as the Septuagint. When he came to believe that Jesus was the Jewish Messiah, he may have still been accepted as a member of the synagogue, and he must have been well known in all the synagogues of Cyprus, for he took Paul on a tour of them. But when some Greek-speakers, in Antioch, came to believe in Jesus, Barnabas was the obvious person to send for to teach them.

Generosity

We learn from this passage in Acts that Barnabas was very generous, selling a field that belonged to him and giving the proceeds to the fledgling Church to feed their poorer members; this may well have left him with a reduced income to live on. We also learn that he was known as the 'son of encouragement' – 'son of' is a Hebrew way of saying that he had a very encouraging character – compare the 'sons of thunder', 'son of Abraham', 'son of Israel' and 'son of the devil'. So Barnabas must have been what we would call nowadays a pastoral counsellor, encouraging many people when they were depressed and had lost hope. A trained counsellor is a godsend, but anyone can help others when they are down, simply by lending them a listening ear. St Barnabas was generous with his money, his learning, his language skills and his time spent listening to others and interpreting the Scriptures to them. Surely there is something in that list that each one of us could learn to imitate, as Barnabas imitated our Saviour. Jesus said, 'This is my commandment, that you love one another as I have loved you.'

Suggested hymns

Disposer supreme, and judge of the earth; How bright these glorious spirits shine; Make me a channel of your peace; The 'Son of Consolation'.

The Birth of John the Baptist   24 June
Faithful in Word and Deed

Isa. 40.1–11 A voice in the wilderness; Ps. 85.7–13 Salvation is at hand; Acts 13.14b–26 A baptism of repentance, *or* Gal. 3.23–29 The law our schoolmaster; Luke 1.57–66, 80 Birth of the Baptist

> '*A voice cries out: "In the wilderness prepare the way of the* LORD, *make straight in the desert a highway for our God."'* Isaiah 40.3

A worried king

King Herod Antipas was really worried about John the Baptist. Shakespeare assures us that 'Uneasy lies the head that wears a crown'. And King Herod's head was spinning round in circles. He couldn't sleep, he was grumpy to his family and a tyrant to his courtiers. And all because of this wretched prophet, John the Dunker, or Douser, or whatever he was called. For Herod Antipas claimed to be the King of the Jews; but he knew that this claim rested on pretty rocky foundations. His father, King Herod the Great, hadn't an ounce of Jewish blood in him. He was an Idumean, from the desert country near Gaza, and had been appointed King of Judaea by the

Romans. Herod the Great married ten times; Antipas was his son by, he thought, his father's eighth wife, who was a Samaritan. He had been appointed by the Romans to rule over Galilee Province, to the west of Lake Galilee. His half-brother, Herod Philip the First, had married a woman called Herodias, and they had a daughter called Salome, who married her half-uncle, Herod Philip the Second – the son of Herod the Great and his fifth wife – who now ruled over the quarter of his father's one-time kingdom, which lay in the Golan Heights west of Lake Galilee, called Gaulanitis. But when the first wife of Antipas fled from him, in terror, back to her home in Syria, he visited his brother Philip the First, and persuaded Herodias to divorce Philip and marry Antipas. In the eyes of many people it was illegal to marry your brother's wife, and this prophet John the Plunger had gone round accusing Antipas of incest.

Anointed king

But that wasn't the worst part of what John did. Antipas had ambitions to be the King of the Jews – *all* of the Jews, like his father Herod the Great had been. He could only achieve that if he could persuade the Emperor, and get a Jewish priest to anoint him – and the priests didn't like Antipas. And now John claimed to be preparing the way for a coming 'Messiah', a word which means 'anointed king'. Antipas wasn't going to stand for any rival claiming the title which, he thought, belonged rightfully to him – so he had John arrested and detained in the fortress of Machaerus, on the hills east of the Dead Sea.

Torn

But poor uneasy Antipas was torn in two. He hated the prophet, but he also secretly admired him. John was faithful to the truth, in the words he said, and his actions mirrored his words. The Herod clan's lives were a tissue of lies, whereas John's life was honest and open. A couple of lines in Psalm 145, which are there in the version among the Dead Sea Scrolls, and in the Greek and Syrian translations, but not in the later, official Hebrew text, read:

> The LORD is faithful in all his words,
> and gracious in all his deeds.

John the Baptist, to give him his proper name, was faithful in word and deed, even Antipas had to admit that. So the king tried to question the prophet; but John wasn't talking to him. Then his trollop of a stepdaughter, Salome, wangled a promise out of him in return for a lewd dance she did at one of his parties, and Antipas found that, to be true to his word, he had to commit the wicked deed of putting God's prophet to death.

Jesus

John never let on who the anointed Messiah was. But putting two and two together, Antipas worked out it was Jesus of Nazareth. His trusted lieutenant Chuza, and Chuza's wife Joanna, were supporters of Jesus, and Herod learnt a lot from them without them realizing it. Then this Jesus was arrested and Herod Antipas got a chance to examine him, and play a part in having his rival put out of harm's way. It didn't do him any good, though: eight years later Antipas petitioned the emperor Caligula to make him King of All Judaea, and Caligula deposed him and exiled him to France, where nothing more was heard of him. But the memories of Jesus the Messiah and John the forerunner live on, because they were faithful in word and deed. And Jesus is King, not only of the Jews, but of all those who will likewise be faithful to him, in word and in deed.

Suggested hymns

God has spoken – by the prophets; Hark, a thrilling voice is sounding; On Jordan's bank the Baptist's cry; When Jesus came to Jordan.

SS Peter and Paul, Apostles   29 June
Peter's First Letter
Zech. 4.1–6a, 10b–14 Two anointed ones; Ps. 125 Stand fast forever; Acts 12.1–11 Peter released from prison (*if the Acts reading is used instead of the Old Testament reading, the New Testament reading is* 2 Tim. 4.6–8, 17–18 Poured out); Matt. 16.13–19 Peter recognizes the Messiah; *or for Peter alone*: Ezek. 3.22–27 Preaching to his own; Ps. 125; Acts 12.1–11 (*if the Acts reading is used instead of the Old Testament reading, the New Testament reading is* 1 Peter 2.19–25 Suffering for God); Matt. 16.13–19

'Peter . . . said, "Now I am sure that the Lord has sent his angel and rescued me from the hands of Herod and from all that the Jewish people were expecting."' Acts 12.11

To where?

There are two letters in the New Testament that bear the name of Peter. Today I want to concentrate on Peter's first letter. It has been described as the most beautifully phrased, warm and tender book in the whole of the New Testament. Unlike the letters of Paul, it was not written to the Church in a particular place, or to a particular individual. It begins,

> Peter, an apostle of Jesus Christ, to the exiles of the Dispersion in Pontus, Galatia, Cappadocia, Asia, and Bithynia . . .

These were provinces of the Roman Empire in the north-west of what we now call Turkey. It is generally assumed that St Peter, one of the 12 apostles, became the Bishop of Rome, and heard how the Christians in that area were being persecuted; so he wrote a circular letter, to be carried by sea and then on a tour of the churches in that area, whom he had never met. But it is possible that, at the time of writing, Peter had not yet reached Rome, and wrote from somewhere like Ephesus, on the west coast of Turkey, a letter to be carried round the provinces to the north and east of him.

By whom?

Yet there are some people who think that it was not written by Peter. The main pointers in that direction are that the letter is written in excellent literary Greek, which would be unlikely in a Galilean fisherman; that there is a close resemblance between the language of 1 Peter and that of Paul's Letter to the Ephesians; and that the persecutions described in 1 Peter didn't become that bad until long after St Peter had died. But most of those objections are met when we see that Peter says that he is sending it 'through Sylvanus', which probably means he was not just the messenger boy, or the scribe who took down Peter's dictation, but had played a full part in the writing. St Peter's situation has been compared to that of a missionary in a foreign land, who has learnt to speak the local language but is not yet very good at writing it. The missionary may then call a native speaker of the language to take his crude jottings and re-express them in the way a local writer would have done. And Sylvanus is mentioned in the Acts of the Apostles, where he is called Silas, as a well-educated man, a leader in the early Church, and the companion on several of his journeys with St Paul, who speaks of him in terms of equality. He may well have played a part in putting the fisherman's rough Greek into fluent and beautiful language.

To whom?

What sort of people, then, was Peter writing to? He addresses them by a word that means 'household slaves'. Almost 80 per cent of the population of the Roman Empire were slaves, and from them the majority of the Christian converts were drawn. Being told that God loves you, and being treated as equals in the weekly shared meals of the Christian community, was in welcome contrast to the way they were treated during the rest of the week. But if the master of the house discovered that his slaves had joined this underground freedom movement, he might well make them suffer for it. The local mob might turn against these traitors, and since the magistrate was sure to be a slave-owner, they may not have got justice from him, either. Persecution came to Rome in AD 64 when Emperor Nero wanted someone else to blame for starting the fire that destroyed much of the city, but it may have come earlier to Ephesus, where St Paul, too, experienced mob-violence. So St Peter reassures his readers that Jesus will come soon to justify the innocent, and that the way they shared in the suffering of Christ on earth guaranteed them a place in heaven. It's a beautiful letter, and I do recommend you to read the First Letter of Peter through carefully when you have a moment.

Suggested hymns

Lord, the light of your life is shining; O Love that will not let me go; Restore, O Lord, the glory of your name; The church of God a kingdom is.

St Thomas the Apostle   3 July
(See page 182.)

St Mary Magdalene   22 July
Mary Magdalene and the New Eden

S. of Sol. 3.1–4 Seeking and finding; Ps. 42.1–10 As deer long for water; 2 Cor. 5.14–17 A new creation; John 20.1–2, 11–18 Go and tell

> *'Jesus said to [Mary Magdalene], "Woman, why are you weeping? Whom are you looking for?" Supposing him to be the gardener, she said to him, "Sir, if you have carried him away, tell me where you have laid him, and I will take him away."' John 20.15*

Hymn

A hymn by the modern author Hilary Greenwood has three verses, each of them beginning with the line, 'Walking in a garden'. In a couple of hymnals it is sung to the French folk tune 'Au clair de la lune'; or sometimes to an old Irish melody. It was originally written for children to sing to the tune of 'Puff the Magic Dragon'. In the first verse, 'at the close of day', Adam meets God in the Garden of Eden, and tries to hide. God calls Adam not to be frightened, but warns him that his sin has 'brought the winter in, made the flowers fade'. The second verse is set in the Garden of Gethsemane, where the disciples 'could not keep awake, while the Lord was kneeling there, praying for their sake'. The third verse focuses on the unnamed garden where Jesus was laid in Joseph of Arimathea's new tomb. The nineteenth chapter of St John's Gospel tells us that 'there was a garden in the place where [Jesus] was crucified, and in the garden there was a new tomb in which no one had ever been laid'. In the following chapter, Mary Magdalene meets the risen Christ, and mistakes him for a gardener. 'Walking in a garden, at the break of day', Jesus turns to Mary, saying, 'Mary, spring is here today, only death is dead.' The beautiful words make me want to cry, and it is a clever idea to link together the three gardens. But it may not have been accidental – maybe the Bible means us to recognize that the garden where Jesus rose was the place where all the harm done in the Garden of Eden was undone, and it became the new Eden, the place of a new creation and a fresh start.

The new Eden

The Bible reveals to us that God created the universe because he, or she, was so loving that God wanted created beings to love, who would be so grateful that they would love God in return. Love cannot be forced, it must be won by wooing, and given as an act of conscious choice. *Homo sapiens* was the first species to evolve that sort of free will. God was guiding the course of evolution, and placed human beings in a world that seemed like a paradise to them; but it was inevitable that as soon as they had the power of choice they would choose to disobey their maker. And that, apparently, destroyed the garden that God had planned for us. That is the meaning of the Genesis story, and it could not be revealed to us in any other way than through a beautiful legend.

Holy Week

In the seven days of Holy Week – following the pattern of the seven days of creation – Jesus taught his disciples, thus creating the sort of community in which people could learn to love and be loved. Then in the Garden of Gethsemane, they deserted their Lord and fled. On the sixth day – Good Friday – Jesus cried in triumph, 'It is finished' – 'it' meaning the loving community of the Church – and rested in the tomb on the seventh day. On the first day of the *next* week, Easter Sunday, the *new* creation, which St Paul wrote about, burst into bloom, when Mary Magdalene recognized the love in the voice of Jesus, and returned it willingly with her own lifelong devotion. And that was humanity as God had originally planned it should be. 'Walking in a garden, at the break of day, Jesus smiled at Mary and said, "Mary, spring is here to stay, only death is dead."'

Poetic

Does that sound complicated? If so, shut down the left side of your brain, the part that wants logical explanations of everything, and open up the poet inside you. What a lovely story that is, the 'Tale of the three gardens'! Did God intend us to see his recreation of paradise in that way? I don't know. Did St John recognize the parallels between the gardens when he wrote his Gospel? Probably. Does it make a difference to the way we love God? You will have to answer that question for yourself.

Suggested hymns

Christ is alive! Let Christians sing; Good Joseph had a garden; Mary, weep not, weep no longer; Walking in a garden.

333

St James the Apostle 25 July
The Holiness Code

Jer. 45.1–5 Seeking greatness; Ps. 126 Sow in tears, harvest in joy; Acts 11.27—12.2 Herod kills James (*if the Acts reading is used instead of the Old Testament reading, the New Testament reading is* 2 Cor. 4.7–15 Treasure in clay pots); Matt. 20.20–28 Seeking greatness

> 'The disciples [in Antioch] determined that according to their ability, each would send relief to the believers living in Judaea; this they did, sending it to the elders by Barnabas and Saul.' Acts 11.29–30

Jameses

There are an awful lot of Jameses in the Bible. Today commemorates 'James the Apostle', sometimes called 'James the Great'. This one and his brother John were the sons of Zebedee whom Jesus chose to be in 'the Twelve'. There was another James who was also one of the Twelve; he is referred to as 'James the Less', or 'Little James'. He is always called 'James the son of Alphaeus', and we normally celebrate him on 1 May, along with Philip the Apostle. A third James was the leader of the church in Jerusalem, whom St Paul calls one of the 'pillars' of the church there and 'the Lord's brother'. He was probably one of the brothers of Jesus who was only converted after the risen Christ appeared to him. But there is no saint's day devoted to him. In today's reading, the cash collected in Antioch was sent to the leaders of the church in Jerusalem, who are called not apostles or bishops, but 'the elders'. Finally there is the author of the book in the New Testament called 'The Epistle – or Letter – of James'. This begins: 'James, a servant of God and of the Lord Jesus Christ, To the twelve tribes in the Dispersion: Greetings.' He describes himself humbly as Christ's servant, yet he writes with authority, as one Jew writing to other Jews. So he was probably the leader of the Jerusalem church, and the brother of Jesus. As this James has no name-day in our calendar, perhaps James the Great will forgive me if I talk today about James the Greatest of All.

Leviticus

His letter is very simple down-to-earth advice on Christian living. He appears to disagree with St Paul's teaching on faith, saying that you cannot boast that you have faith unless you demonstrate it by living a life of goodness and love. Some have suggested that the whole letter is a commentary on the 'Holiness Code' in the book of Leviticus, chapter 19. This a series of commandments, but much more compassionate and less legalistic than many parts of the Old Testament. It begins: 'You shall be holy, for I the LORD your God am holy.' The commandments of the Holiness Code include:

- You shall not strip your vineyard bare, or gather the fallen grapes of your vineyard; you shall leave them for the poor and the foreigner.
- You shall not defraud your neighbour . . . and you shall not keep for yourself the wages of a labourer until morning. You shall not speak evil of the deaf or put a stumbling block before the blind.
- You shall not render an unjust judgement; you shall not be partial to the poor or defer to the great.
- You shall not hate in your heart any of your relations.
- You shall love your neighbour as yourself.
- When a person from another country lives with you in your land, you shall not oppress the foreigner. You must treat the foreigner who lives among you just like your fellow citizens; you shall love the foreigner as yourself, for you were foreigners in the land of Egypt.

Epistle

Now read how the Letter of James interprets that in practice for his own day:

My brothers and sisters, do you with your acts of favouritism really believe in our glorious Lord Jesus Christ? For if a person with gold rings and in fine clothes comes into your assembly, and if a poor person in dirty clothes also comes in, and if you take notice of the one wearing the fine clothes and say, 'Have a seat here, please', while to the one who is poor you say, 'Stand there,' or, 'Sit at my feet,' have you not made distinctions among yourselves, and become judges with evil thoughts? Listen, my beloved brothers and sisters. Has not God chosen the poor in the world to be rich in faith and to be heirs of the kingdom that he has promised to those who love him? But you have dishonoured the poor. Is it not the rich who oppress you? Is it not they who drag you into court? Is it not they who blaspheme the excellent name that was invoked over you? You do well if you really fulfil the royal law according to the scripture, 'You shall love your neighbour as yourself.'

Now that's what I call Christianity.

Suggested hymns

For all thy saints, O Lord; Great God, your love has called us here; Love divine, all loves excelling; When I needed a neighbour.

The Transfiguration of Our Lord   6 August
Finding God's Will

Dan. 7.9–10, 13–14 The Son of Man; Ps. 97 Clouds are around him; 2 Peter 1.16–19 We saw; Luke 9.28–36 The transfiguration

'About eight days after [the conversation in Caesarea Philippi] Jesus took with him Peter and John and James, and went up on the mountain to pray.' Luke 9.28

Omniscience

Because God created the universe, then by definition he must know everything there is to know. We call this 'omniscience'. But when Jesus came down from heaven to earth, he became human, with all the limitations that implies. He surrendered his omniscience at the incarnation: while he lived on earth he no longer knew everything. By the time he was 12, he had realized there was a special relationship between him and the God he called 'Abba', meaning 'Daddy'. When he was baptized the Holy Spirit came upon him, so he was inspired by an inner voice; but he still had a lot to learn. He had to choose a title from the language of the times. 'Messiah' means an anointed king. At his temptation, Jesus grappled with several possible meanings of Messiah: to be an economic reformer, a conqueror or a wonder-worker. He rejected these — although that is what the crowds wanted him to be — in favour of 'Son of Man', which means a human being with a divine purpose. But gradually he was moving to a more profound and challenging understanding of his nature, summed up as 'Son of God'. When the Pharisees rejected this as blasphemous, he realized that his destiny was to be God's 'Suffering Servant'. At Caesarea Philippi, Simon Peter was the first to acclaim Jesus as Son of God; a week later he climbed a high mountain with his closest friends to spend a night in prayer, asking his heavenly Father whether God really wanted Jesus to accept the role of Suffering Servant. So, St Luke tells us, 'About eight days after [the conversation in Caesarea Philippi] Jesus took with him Peter and John and James, and went up on the mountain to pray.'

Transfiguration

This is the background to the story of what we call 'the transfiguration'. But of course that was not how the disciples saw it. It was a deep spiritual experience for them, when they saw Jesus shining with a supernatural light; walking with Moses and Elijah to show that he was the fulfilment of the law and the prophets; and described by God the Father as his 'Beloved Son'. These visions confirmed their dawning understanding that 'Son of God' was the only phrase strong enough to describe the close relationship between the man they saw and the God they believed in. But what of Jesus; what was his experience that night? He never told the disciples outright, but he gave them plenty of hints. From the night of the transfiguration onwards, he kept on repeating to them that 'The Son of Man *must* be handed over to sinners, and be crucified, and on the third day rise again.' Jesus had accepted that his Father's will for him was to follow the way of the cross.

Seeking God's will

Jesus, although he was the Son of God, always asked, 'What does *God* want me to do?' You and I, though we are only human, often ask instead, 'What do *I* want to do?' As though the will of a mere human being mattered compared to the will of God! Jesus spent a whole night in prayer, asking what God wanted. How often do you and I, when we are planning what we are going to do today and in the future, allow the question of what God wants to even cross our minds? But Jesus submitted his wishes to what God had called him to achieve, no matter how much pain it might cause him. Our prayer ought always to be, in the words of Horatius Bonar's great hymn, 'Thy way, not mine, O Lord':

Thy way, not mine, O Lord,
however dark it be!
Lead me by thine own hand;
choose out the path for me.

I dare not choose my lot,
I would not if I might:
choose thou for me, my God,
so shall I walk aright.

Not mine, not mine the choice
in things or great or small;
be thou my guide, my strength,
my wisdom and my all.

To quote the great commentator William Barclay: 'When Jesus had
a problem, he did not seek to solve it only by the power of his own
thought; he did not take it to others for human advice; he took it to
the lonely place, and to God.'

Suggested hymns

*God of mercy, God of grace; Immortal, invisible, God only wise;
Thy way, not mine, O Lord; 'Tis good, Lord, to be here.*

The Blessed Virgin Mary   15 August
Mary's Conception

Isa. 61.10–11 As a bride, *or* Rev. 11.19—12.6, 10 A woman in
heaven; Ps. 45.10–17 You shall have sons; Gal. 4.4–7 Born of a
woman; Luke 1.46–55 Magnificat

> *'When the fullness of time had come, God sent his Son, born of a
> woman, born under the law, in order to redeem those who were
> under the law, so that we might receive adoption as children.'*
> Galatians 4.4–5

Commemorations

In the modern Church of England calendar, six days are set aside
to commemorate the Blessed Virgin Mary: 2 February, which used

to be called the Purification of the Blessed Virgin Mary; 25 March, the Annunciation; 31 May, the Visit of the Blessed Virgin Mary to Elizabeth; 15 August, which is simply called 'the Blessed Virgin Mary'; 8 September, the Birth of the Blessed Virgin Mary, which unlike all the others is not a 'red-letter day'; and, of course, 25 December, Christmas Day. It is good that we should honour the mother of Jesus, an ordinary teenager who was given by almighty God the most colossally responsible task to fulfil, and who carried it out supremely well. And as Jesus was Divine even before he was conceived in Mary's womb, it is right to call her the Mother of God. Even if a preacher is not called on to preach on every one of those days, to think up something fresh to say about Mary each year is quite a challenge. Today, let us look at the subject that is hardly ever preached about, which is Mary's birth.

Infancy Gospel of James

The Bible says nothing of Mary's life before the angel appeared to her. The first account of her birth is included in a book, never included in the holy Scriptures, called the *Infancy Gospel of James*, claiming to be written by the brother of Jesus. The first mention of this book is in the early third century, so it was probably written in the late second century, or at least 150 years after Jesus was born. It tells a charming story of Mary's parents and her childhood. If the story is true, one wonders why it was not mentioned by any of the Bible writers. And while the Bible several times names the brothers and sisters of Jesus, this book for the first time suggests that Mary remained a virgin for the rest of her life, having no further children after Jesus. So these were actually the half-brothers and half-sisters of Jesus – children of Joseph, an elderly widower, by a former marriage. It sounds, then, as though Christianity was becoming contaminated by Manichaeism, a religion that taught that the material world was inherently wicked, and that sex, even within marriage, was sinful. But most of the Christian Church regards the incarnation, in which Jesus the Word of God became flesh, as affirming the goodness of God's physical creation.

Joachim and Anna

This book, then, says that Mary's parents were called Joachim and Anna. Many churches today are dedicated to St Anne, whom the irreverent refer to as 'Blessèd Annie, God's granny'. According to

James, Anne was a childless woman, whose prayers for a child were answered when an angel came to her house to tell her she would give birth, and Anne offered her unborn child 'whether male or female . . . as a gift to the Lord my God'. So Mary was dedicated to God even before she was born. It does not, however, say that Anne was a virgin when Mary was born. When Mary was 12 years old, an angel helped to select St Joseph to become her husband. When Mary gives birth to Jesus, the visit of the midwives, who confirm her virginity, is described. Then the Christ-child is hidden from King Herod in a feeding trough, and Mary remains a virgin until she dies.

Later developments

Devotion to St Anne grew across Europe in the Middle Ages, particularly when Anne of Bohemia married King Richard II of England. But the official status given to such an unsubstantiated figure roused the fury of Martin Luther. After St Augustine's doctrine of original sin was given the status of a dogma, it was widely believed that the sexual act transmitted the sin of Adam to all his descendants. The birth of the Virgin Mary was not a virgin birth, like that of Jesus; nonetheless by a special intervention of God's grace, Mary did not inherit the 'stain' of Adam's sin, although she was born in a normal manner. That is what is meant by the doctrine of Mary's 'immaculate conception'. This did not become a dogma in the Roman Catholic Church until 1854. However, while shunning false teaching about the sinfulness of sex, all Christians can enjoy the legends about the childhood of Mary as just that: quaint stories meant to honour the Mother of our Lord.

Suggested hymns

For Mary, mother of our Lord; Shall we not love thee, Mother dear?; Tell out, my soul, the greatness of the Lord; Ye watchers and ye holy ones.

St Bartholomew the Apostle   24 August
The St Bartholomew's Day Expulsions
Isa. 43.8–13 My witnesses; Ps. 145.1–7 Speak of your wondrous acts; Acts 5.12–16 The apostles heal (*if the Acts reading is used instead of the Old Testament reading, the New Testament*

reading is 1 Cor. 4.9–15 The shame of the apostles);
Luke 22.24–30 Judging the 12 tribes

> '[Jesus asked the Twelve] "Who is greater, the one who is at the
> table or the one who serves? Is it not the one at the table? But I
> am among you as one who serves."' Luke 22.27

Shame

St Bartholomew's Day was the date of two unfortunate events in
the history of the Church. The St Bartholomew's Day Massacres
in 1572 were when Roman Catholics persecuted Protestants. Less
well known are the Great Expulsions on St Bartholomew's Day
1662, a shameful event in English history which reflects badly on
our ancestors in the Church of England. It is good for their descendants to apologize; but guilt is not inherited, so we should not bear
a grudge about past events; rather look to see what lessons we can
learn.

Reformation

The Reformation in Europe began with Martin Luther. To over-
simplify a complicated period, we could say that Luther rejected
the power and corruption of the popes in his day, and for this was
expelled from the Roman Catholic Church. But Protestantism was
developed by Calvin in Geneva, who took a strictly literal interpretation of the Bible in determining the structure of the Church and the
laws of morality. King Henry VIII rejected the authority of the pope
over the laws of England, but retained the bishops and ceremonial
of the Catholic Church. After Henry's death, Archbishop Thomas
Cranmer translated the worship into English, published the Book of
Common Prayer in 1549 and revised it in 1552. Queen Mary martyred Protestants, and Queen Elizabeth martyred Catholics, mainly
from fear that each was trying to overthrow the present monarchy;
but Elizabeth made a half-hearted attempt at compromise between
Puritans, as the Calvinists were now called, and Papists, which was
the new name for Roman Catholics. Then Parliament executed
King Charles I, and Oliver Cromwell gave power to the Puritans,
who regarded the Church of England as 'only halfly reformed'.
They replaced bishops with presbyters, the Book of Common Prayer
with the Westminster Directory, and passed strict laws against

Sabbath-breaking and images. Many clergy suspected of royalist sympathies were forced to retire. With the return of King Charles II, there was a reaction against this, summed up in the Act of Uniformity of 1662.

Act of Uniformity

This Act approved the revised Book of Common Prayer of 1662, which is still admired as a beautiful example of the use of English prose in divine worship. But it restored power to the bishops, and reversed most of what the Puritans regarded as the biblical reforms they had introduced. Some of the greatest saints and finest minds in the Church of England, such as Richard Baxter – who wrote 'Ye holy angels bright' and other well-loved hymns – now called themselves Puritans, and were very unhappy at being required to sign up to every detail of the Prayer Book. Some compromise could probably have been reached, but the returning royalists sought revenge on the Puritans by excluding from any office in Church or State all those who would not sign up to the whole package.

St Bartholomew's Day

The Act of Uniformity came into effect on St Bartholomew's Day, 24 August 1662 – a cruel date to choose, because it was the day on which tithes and rents were due, in arrears, to the clergy. So if any clergy did not conform, they were not paid and were thrown out of their vicarages, often into poverty. Some members of Parliament and Convocation tried to make financial provision for ejected ministers; the King and the Lord Chancellor asked for a compromise. But these votes were all lost by small margins. Altogether, over 1,800 ministers – about 20 per cent of the clergy – were forced to leave the Church of England in 1662. They were not allowed to preach, teach, meet or hold positions in the State. They were fined, and sent to plantations in Virginia for hard labour. It was a shameful episode.

Compromise

When Jesus appointed St Bartholomew and the other apostles, he warned them against seeking power, saying that instead they must be servants. They were to lead the 12 tribes of the New Israel. Just as the 12 sons of Jacob had learnt that, despite their differences, unity between the 12 tribes was essential to the survival of the

342

nation, so the Church must be ready to make compromises in the cause of unity, with no faction claiming to impose their views on any other. The Great Ejection was a sign that the teaching of Jesus about tolerance was being ignored. In the church disputes of today, are we ready yet to learn that lesson?

Suggested hymns

Bind us together, Lord; Blest be the tie that binds; Lord of the Church, we pray for our renewing; Pray that Jerusalem may have.

Holy Cross Day   14 September
The Bronze Serpent

Num. 21.4–9 The bronze serpent; Ps. 22.23–28 All the earth shall turn to the Lord; Phil. 2.6–11 Obedient to death on the cross; John 3.13–17 God so loved the world

> *'Moses made a serpent of bronze, and put it upon a pole; and whenever a serpent bit someone, that person would look at the serpent of bronze and live.' Numbers 21.9*

> *'[Jesus said,] "Just as Moses lifted up the serpent in the wilderness, so must the Son of Man be lifted up, that whoever believes in him may have eternal life."' John 3.14–15*

Lifted up

According to St John's Gospel, Jesus said that he himself must be 'lifted up'. A strange expression, which he used several times. Gradually it dawns on you that he must mean 'lifted up upon the cross'. And perhaps, also, 'lifted up to heaven at the ascension when he returned to his heavenly Father'. Then all who believe him will have eternal life. He compares this with Moses 'lifting up' a serpent in the wilderness. What's this all about?

Snakes

There are more than 3,000 species of snakes, also called serpents, in the world today. Most of them are harmless, but some 300 species

343

are poisonous. They have a sac of venom in the roof of their mouths, and when they bite, the venom is injected into the bloodstream of the victim. It is possible to create an antivenom, and if a patient is injected with this soon enough they can be cured; nevertheless some thirty to forty thousand people die of snakebite every year. Before this treatment was discovered, a cure from snakebite was considered to be only possible by a miracle or by magic. During the Exodus from Egypt, many Israelites were bitten by snakes as they crossed the wilderness, and Moses was instructed to make a model of a serpent in bronze, and raise it up on a pole. Then anyone who was bitten by a snake could look at the bronze serpent, and they would live. Sometimes snakes are shown in ancient art with wings, and called 'fiery serpents', either from the colour of their skin or from the burning sensation in anybody who was bitten by a snake.

Seraphim

Some of these bronze serpents were later taken into the Temple at Jerusalem, where they were called by the Hebrew name of Seraphim. When Isaiah had his vision of the Lord, high and lifted up in the Temple, we read that:

> Seraphs were in attendance above him; each had six wings . . .
> And one called to another and said: 'Holy, holy, holy is the LORD of hosts; the whole earth is full of his glory.'

The word 'holy', repeated three times, reminds Christians of the three persons of the Holy Trinity: God the Father, Jesus the Son and the Holy Spirit. The serpents, however, bring to mind the bronze snakes lifted up by Moses, which gave fresh life to any sick person who looked at them and prayed to God. Similarly, said Jesus, whoever looks at an image of him hanging on the cross and prays, will receive the gift of eternal life.

Paradise

But there is one more metaphor resonating in the air when we mention serpents. And that is in the third chapter of the book of Genesis, where a serpent appears to Adam and Eve in the Garden of Eden and tempts them to eat the forbidden fruit from the tree of the knowledge of good and evil. The tragic thing is that as soon as

344

people know the difference between those two, sooner or later they will choose to do evil, instead of following the path of goodness. A modern scientist might compare this with the evolution of early humans, who first developed the power of choice. So Satan, the Tempter, is sometimes called 'the ancient serpent'. This, then, gives another, deeper meaning to the cross of Christ. He is able, like the bronze serpent that Moses lifted up, to deliver us from physical sickness, in one way or another, when we pray. But, more importantly, he is able to heal us from sin, the deadly disease that comes from yielding to the temptations of the devil, and disobeying God.

Prayer

So whenever you see a cross or crucifix, pray to Jesus Christ to forgive you your sins, and if you sincerely mean it, he will do so at once. Any words will do, for Jesus said, 'Just as Moses lifted up the serpent in the wilderness, so must the Son of Man be lifted up, that whoever believes in him may have eternal life.'

Suggested hymns

Bright the vision that delighted; Hands that have been handling; Holy, holy, holy, Lord God almighty; Immortal, invisible, God only wise.

St Matthew, Apostle and Evangelist   21 September
Pro-law, Anti-Pharisee

Prov. 3.13–18 Wisdom more precious than jewels; Ps. 119.65–72 Better than gold; 2 Cor. 4.1–6 The open statement of the truth; Matt. 9.9–13 The call of Matthew

> *'The law of your mouth is dearer to me*
> *than a hoard of gold and silver.'*
>
> Psalm 119.72 (Common Worship)

Gospels

When there were many people still alive who heard what Jesus said, and saw the things that he did, maybe even hundreds of eyewitnesses, there was no point in writing it down. Particularly as many believers expected him to return to judge the earth any day now. But when he still had not come, and that generation began to die out, at least four people wrote down the story of Jesus's life in what they called 'Gospels'. These four were Matthew, Mark, Luke and John. Nobody can be quite sure when the Gospels were written, but all the signs are that it was either just before or soon after the Romans destroyed the city of Jerusalem in AD 70, 40 years after Jesus died. But they must have been written before the news spread that the Romans had burnt it, because there is no mention of fire in the Gospels. St Matthew, whom we celebrate today, seems to have been writing for a congregation of Jewish Christians, because he can take it for granted that they will recognize the quotations he makes from the Old Testament, and that they will have a very high respect for the Law of Moses. But like the other Gospel-writers, Matthew wrote in Greek, not Hebrew. This can only be explained if they were Jews who lived outside the Holy Land of Judaea. These 'Jews of the Dispersion', as they were called, could read the Scriptures in Hebrew in the synagogues – or at least the men could – but the rest of the time they spoke Greek, like the rest of the multicultural society in which they lived.

Pharisees

Being Jewish, as I said, Matthew's audience were devoted to the law, and could have joyfully echoed the words of the Psalmist: 'The law of your mouth, [O God,] is dearer to me than a hoard of gold and silver.' The leading exponents of this point of view were people called the Pharisees, with whom Jesus crossed swords many times. After the destruction of the Temple, the Pharisees became even more powerful than the priests, and were the leaders of the expatriate Jewish people. No writings of the Pharisees survive, but from the Gospels, the writings of Flavius Josephus and the later rabbis, we know that they regarded themselves as experts in the law, together with a set of traditions of their own; they were interested in 'ritual purity' and tithing, and believed in an afterlife, angels, demons and judgement. St Matthew, like any good teacher, starts where people are, so he speaks favourably of the law. After all, Jesus said that God cares about how we behave and how we treat each other, and taught us to pray that God's will may be done on earth.

Pro-Pharisee

According to Matthew, Jesus said these things in favour of the Pharisees:

- Jesus said, 'For I tell you, unless your righteousness exceeds that of the scribes and Pharisees, you will never enter the kingdom of heaven.'
- Jesus said, 'The scribes and the Pharisees sit on Moses' seat; do whatever they teach you and follow it; but do not do as they do, for they do not practise what they teach.'
- Jesus said, 'Do not think that I have come to abolish the law or the prophets; I have come not to abolish but to fulfil. For truly I tell you, until heaven and earth pass away, not one letter, not one stroke of a letter, will pass from the law until all is accomplished.'
- And he agreed with them about the resurrection, against the Sadducees who taught that when we die that is the end.

Anti-Pharisee

But Jesus also attacked the Pharisees bitterly.

- He said, 'Watch out, and beware of the yeast of the Pharisees and Sadducees . . .' Then they understood that he had not told them to beware of the yeast of bread, but of the teaching of the Pharisees and Sadducees.
- Jesus said, 'Woe to you, scribes and Pharisees, hypocrites! For you lock people out of the kingdom of heaven. For you do not go in yourselves, and when others are going in, you stop them . . . Woe to you, scribes and Pharisees, hypocrites! For you are like whitewashed tombs, which on the outside look beautiful, but inside they are full of the bones of the dead and of all kinds of filth.' (He made five other attacks beginning with the same words). Jesus said, 'You snakes, you brood of vipers! How can you escape being sentenced to hell?'
- And against their pernickety interpretation of the law he went right to the heart of it: 'In everything,' Jesus said, 'do to others as you would have them do to you; for this is the law and the prophets.'
- And: '"You shall love the Lord your God with all your heart, and with all your soul, and with all your mind." This is the greatest

347

and first commandment. And a second is like it: "You shall love your neighbour as yourself." On these two commandments hang all the law and the prophets.'

Ambiguous

Perhaps St Matthew, then, reveals to us the reason for the apparently ambiguous attitude of Jesus towards the Law of Moses. The Jews were chosen to learn that there is only one God. We cannot choose which god to follow and then fight against the followers of other gods. We must restrain our selfish instincts and work together towards a just and caring society. Yet we achieve this not by inventing a law code full of irrelevant regulations, but by learning to love. Many people today think that all that we Christians, like the Pharisees, care about is rules and regulations. We have to tell them, and show them by our lives, that no, like Jesus, what we are chiefly interested in is love. And to do that, we need all the help St Matthew can give us.

Suggested hymns

Blest are the pure in heart; Gracious Spirit, Holy Ghost; The kingdom of God is justice and joy; Will you come and follow me?

St Michael and All Angels 29 September
The Many-Splendoured Thing

Gen. 28.10–17 Jacob's ladder; Ps. 103.19–22 Bless the Lord, you angels; Rev. 12.7–12 Michael fought the dragon (*if the Revelation reading is used instead of the Old Testament reading, the New Testament reading is* Heb. 1.5–14 Higher than the angels); John 1.47–51 Angels descending on the Son of Man

> '[Jesus] said to [Nathanael], "Very truly, I tell you, you will see heaven opened and the angels of God ascending and descending upon the Son of Man."' John 1.51

'Love is a many-splendored thing'

'Love is a many-splendored thing' became a very popular song in the 1950s. It was the theme tune of an American movie with the same

348

title, produced in 1955. The film was very loosely based on an auto-biographical novel, called simply *The Many-Splendoured Thing*, by Han Suyin. It recounted an affair she had in Hong Kong with the married Australian-born correspondent of *The Times*, who was killed when reporting on the Korean War. The title was a phrase, wrenched out of context, from a beautiful poem called 'The Kingdom of God' by Francis Thompson, and I shall return to that in a minute. Han Suyin was the pen-name of a Eurasian doctor, born in China to a Chinese father and a Flemish mother, and her first great novel was *Destination Chungking*, about the period when Mao Dze-Dong was engaged in the Long March against the Chinese Nationalists. Suyin's first husband had died by the time she moved to Hong Kong. She was disgusted at the way the film romanticized her affair with the Australian, whom they transformed into an American. Those who lived in Hong Kong at the time said she accurately represented the tensions between the traditional Chinese and the more westernized Eurasians, and admitted that her writing was very beautiful. But they were disgusted at the intimate details she reported of their affair, while the correspondent's widow was still alive. Then even those who admired her skills as a writer, and as an interpreter of the Chinese mind to people from the West, were upset that she had taken a phrase in a poem by Francis Thompson about angels and applied it to an illicit love-affair.

Francis Thompson

Francis Thompson was born at Preston in Lancashire, where his father, a doctor, had recently converted to Roman Catholicism. He was educated at Ushaw College in Durham, then studied medicine in Manchester. He never practised as a doctor, but moved to London to become a writer. With no income, however, he was reduced to selling newspapers and matches on the roadside near Charing Cross station. He became an opium addict, and was on the verge of suicide until, eventually, he was found by Wilfred and Alice Meynell, who gave him a house and published his poems. They were acclaimed as the work of a genius by many, including J. R. R. Tolkien.

'The Kingdom of God'

'The Kingdom of God' is a mystical poem revealing how heaven is all around us, even on the streets of Charing Cross, although its splendour is unseen by most people. The Jewish patriarch Jacob saw, at Bethel, a ladder or staircase stretching from heaven to earth, with angels carrying prayers as they were going up it and answers to prayer coming down. So Jesus said to Nathanael, 'Very truly, I tell you, you will see heaven opened and the angels of God ascending and descending upon the Son of Man.' Jesus himself was to be the point of contact, and the reference to the angels and Jacob's Ladder is appropriate to the feast of St Michael and All Angels. Let me read the poem to you:

> O world invisible, we view thee,
> O world intangible, we touch thee,
> O world unknowable, we know thee,
> Inapprehensible, we clutch thee!
>
> Does the fish soar to find the ocean,
> the eagle plunge to find the air –
> that we ask of the stars in motion
> if they have rumour of thee there?
>
> Not where the wheeling systems darken,
> and our benumbed conceiving soars! –
> the drift of pinions, would we hearken,
> beats at our own clay-shuttered doors.
>
> The angels keep their ancient places –
> turn but a stone and start a wing!
> 'Tis ye, 'tis your estrangèd faces,
> that miss the many-splendoured thing.
>
> But (when so sad thou canst not sadder)
> cry – and upon thy so sore loss
> shall shine the traffic of Jacob's ladder
> pitched betwixt Heaven and Charing Cross.
>
> Yea, in the night, my Soul, my daughter,
> Cry – clinging Heaven by the hems;
> and lo, Christ walking on the water,
> not of Genesareth, but Thames!

End of poem. So remember that: the angels are always all around us; we may not see them, but if we are willing, we can make ourselves aware of their perpetual presence, which is a great solace and inspiration.

Suggested hymns

Angel-voices, ever singing; Hark, hark my soul, angelic songs are swelling; How shall I sing that majesty?; When Jacob with travel was weary one day.

St Luke the Evangelist   18 October
No Quick Fixes

Isa. 35.3–6 Healing in the new age, *or* Acts 16.6–12a The Macedonian call; Ps. 147.1–7 God heals the brokenhearted; 2 Tim. 4.5–17 Only Luke is with me; Luke 10.1–9 Sending out the seventy

> *'[God] heals the brokenhearted
> and binds up all their wounds.'*
>
> Psalm 147.3 (Common Worship)

Physician

Luke, whom St Paul called 'the beloved physician', met Paul in Troas in Asia, and described, in the Acts of the Apostles, how 'we' travelled together on Paul's first visit to Europe. They were still together when Paul was a prisoner, probably in Rome, near the end of his life. Luke stayed with the apostle through thick and thin, presumably as his private doctor. Yet St Paul suffered from something he called his 'thorn in the flesh'. He wrote to the Corinthians:

> To keep me from being too elated, a thorn was given me in the flesh, a messenger of Satan to torment me, to keep me from being too elated. Three times I appealed to the Lord about this, that it would leave me, but he said to me, 'My grace is sufficient for you, for power is made perfect in weakness.' So, I will boast all the more gladly of my weaknesses, so that the power of Christ may dwell in me.

So, although Paul had great faith, and was cared for by a qualified medic, his prayers for healing were not answered. Nobody can be quite sure what his 'thorn in the flesh' actually was; some have suggested frivolously that it was Paul's ex-wife! But I very much doubt that; this sounds much more like a medical condition that would respond neither to medical treatment nor prayer. But Paul, bless his saintly heart, turned the experience to his own advantage, saying that God gave him the illness to teach him humility, and to remind him that he was entirely dependent on the grace of God. I expect Luke could have told Paul, out of his own years of medical practice, of many patients whom he had treated to the best of his ability, but who nonetheless had not been cured. As far as we know, St Paul's painful condition stayed with him for the rest of his life.

Healing

This is a problem for many people who are involved in the Christian ministry of healing. You will hear some of them say that God has promised healing to all those who pray with faith. If you are not healed, they say, that proves that you haven't enough faith. This is enough to drive some sick people to despair, who have made superhuman efforts to screw their faith up to a supposedly sufficient level, but without success, as no healing followed. This is surely to confuse the meaning of faith. It is neither a question of what you believe, nor an achievement you can create in yourself; St Paul says faith is the gift of God, and the fruit of the Spirit, which grows naturally over the course of time, nurtured by God's grace.

David Sheppard

David Sheppard, the England cricketer and Bishop of Liverpool, gave to his autobiography the title *Steps along Hope Street*; Hope Street is the road that links the Anglican cathedral to the Roman Catholic cathedral in Liverpool. He describes his friendship with several of the growing charismatic movement in England, who laid great emphasis on healing, through the laying on of hands with prayer. But Bishop Sheppard writes that although such miracles do happen, the work of God should also be seen in the progress of medical research which finds new methods of treatment. He quotes one of his Liverpool clergy who was diagnosed with cancer. Many people, including all his parishioners, prayed for him, and he appeared to make a recovery. But it was only a remission, and soon he fell ill again and died, to everyone's disappointment.

Quick fixes

Bishop Sheppard goes on to quote from David Ford's paperback *The Shape of Living*: 'God is not a God of quick fixes, and easy, instantaneous solutions.' He continues that 'signs of hope are given', but what God is really concerned with is love and faithfulness, and 'healing hearts, minds and communities'. Reflecting on these quotations, I think St Paul, and his 'beloved physician' St Luke, would have agreed that we should encourage those who are sick, and those who love them, to pray with deep trust in God's love. Then we should leave God to decide what is best for us; whether it be a return to full physical strength, or death, which is the healing for all earth's ills, and takes us at once to a better life where there is no more pain. There are many forms of sickness, physical or mental, and many forms of healing. As the psalm says:

[God] heals the brokenhearted
and binds up all their wounds.

Suggested hymns

From thee all skill and science flow; Immortal love, for ever full; O, for a thousand tongues to sing; Sometimes a light surprises.

SS Simon and Jude, Apostles 28 October
Simon and Jude
Isa. 28.14–16 A foundation stone; Ps. 119.89–96 I am yours, save me; Eph. 2.19–22 The foundation of the apostles; John 15.17–27 You have been with me

> 'Thus says the Lord God, See, I am laying in Zion a foundation stone, a tested stone, a precious cornerstone, a sure foundation: "One who trusts will not panic." And I will make justice the line, and righteousness the plummet.' Isaiah 28.16–17

Foundations

The 12 sons of Jacob were the foundation of the ancient nation of Israel, so Jesus chose 12 men to be the foundation of the New Israel, which is a name we give to the Christian Church. Some are famous, and their sayings and doings are recorded in the four Gospels. The two apostles whom we celebrate today, Simon and Jude, on the other hand, were quite obscure.

Simon the Terrorist

Several Simons are mentioned in the Gospels: Simon Peter, Simon of Cyrene, Simon the leper, and Simon Iscariot the father of Judas. To distinguish him from the others, Simon the apostle was called Simon the Zealot, or, from the word Ca-na, which is Aramaic for Zealot, he was also called Simon the Cananaean – nothing to do with the land of Canaan or the wedding at Cana. The Zealots were a Jewish nationalist organization, who resisted the Roman occupation. At times they would stab a Roman soldier from behind in a crowded street; so he could be called Simon the Terrorist, or at least the ex-terrorist, a bold choice for an apostle.

Jude

Jude was also a common name, so the one we celebrate today is identified as the Judas who was *not* Judas Iscariot. He may possibly have been Jude the brother of Jesus, or the son (or brother) of James, or the one who wrote the Epistle of Jude, a passionately pro-Jewish letter. He is mentioned in the Gospel of John for a question he asked. The passage reads:

> Judas (not Iscariot) said to [Jesus], 'Lord, how is it that you will reveal yourself to us, and not to the world?' Jesus answered him, 'Those who love me will keep my word, and my Father will love them, and we will come to them and make our home with them. Whoever does not love me does not keep my words; and the word that you hear is not mine, but is from the Father who sent me.'

Faithfulness

What we do know about Saints Simon and Jude was that they were with Jesus at the beginning, and stayed faithful to him until the very end. At some point after the resurrection they left the land of Judaea and travelled around the Near East as missionaries. They both kept their passionate zeal, but transferred their passion away from nationalism into a zeal for building a worldwide Christian Church, which was open to women and men of all nations and races. Legend tells us that they travelled to Libya, then Armenia. Finally they went to Persia, where they were both martyred. Simon was killed by the gruesome means of being sawn in half.

Humility

We need people like Saints Simon and Jude today. First of all for their humility. There are plenty of people, hogging the limelight, and wishing to be celebrities. Yet most of the change for the better that we see around us is brought about by those who are willing to stay in the background. They work hard for good causes, without expecting any thanks or glory, and are the salt of the earth. There are quite a few in this church, but they wouldn't want me to mention their names. Let's just say that they are appreciated, and thank them for what they do.

Passion

Second, we need people with passion and zeal in the service of God. Simon and Jude gave up being passionate nationalists, though I am sure they remained patriotic. But all that energy they had poured into xenophobia was now turned into the power which drove the engine of their service to the Lord. You can't be a half-hearted Christian; love is not a hobby. A Christian has to love Jesus with all their heart, and mind, and soul, and strength; and love their neighbours as passionately as they love themselves. Loving your neighbours means caring passionately about their needs, serving them in practical ways, defending them against those who would oppress them, and letting them know they are important to us. Most important of all, we shall want to share with our neighbours the good news that God loves them. As St Francis of Assisi said, spread the gospel by every means at your disposal, and if you must, use words. Today we honour Saints Simon and Jude as foundations of the Church; let us also seek to follow the example of their zeal.

Suggested hymns

Captains of the saintly band; Christ is made the sure foundation; Disposer supreme, and Judge of the earth; The Church's one foundation.

All Saints' Day   1 November
The Pursuit of Happiness
(If 30 October is not kept as All Saints' Sunday, the readings on page 262 (All Saints' Sunday) are used on 1 November. If

those are used on the Sunday, the following are the readings on 1 November.)
Isa. 56.3–8 My house for all people, or 2 Esd. 2.42–48 Crowned by the Son of God; Ps. 33.1–5 Rejoice, you righteous; Heb. 12.18–24 Come to Zion; Matt. 5.1–12 The Beatitudes

> *'When Jesus saw the crowds, he went up the mountain;*
> *and after he sat down, his disciples came to him.*
> *Then he began to speak, and taught them . . .' Matthew 5.1–2*

USA

The United States Declaration of Independence was drafted by Thomas Jefferson, revised by committees, and accepted by the Second Continental Congress on 4 July 1776. The most famous part of it reads:

> We hold these truths to be self-evident, that all men are created equal, that they are endowed by their Creator with certain unalienable Rights, that among these are Life, Liberty and the pursuit of Happiness.

Jefferson used to say that he followed the ancient philosophy of Epicureanism, founded about 307 BC, which was materialist, had no room for God, and taught that pleasure is the greatest good. However, by pleasure Epicurus meant the absence of pain, a modest life and the search for understanding. In this it differed from 'hedonism', which is commonly understood to mean self-indulgent debauchery. So it all depends on what you mean by happiness.

Happiness

So ask yourself, what do you regard as pleasure? Is it being alone in beautiful countryside, or is it being together with like-minded people at a concert or a football match? Is it a quiet drink with your friends, or getting roaring drunk? What is the most pleasurable moment you can recollect? Did you wish it could have gone on for ever? Probably everyone will give different definitions.

Love

If the word 'love' occurs anywhere in your understanding of happiness, that is good, because it means you are thinking unselfishly. Caring for those we love makes us very happy. So if we have an unalienable right to pursue happiness we are most likely to achieve our aim if we behave with unselfish love. This is quite the opposite of the hedonist philosophy of grabbing all the pleasures for yourself. By this measure, all the saints were happy people, even when they were suffering for the sake of others. And it fits in well with the definition of happiness that Jesus gave. Where did Jesus define happiness, you ask? In the fifth chapter of St Matthew's Gospel is the answer – in the Beatitudes. The translation 'blessed' is quite correct, but in those days happy people were considered to be blessed by God. So let's retranslate them into modern English, and see what guidance they give us in the pursuit of happiness.

The Beatitudes

1 First, the words from the NRSV Bible: *Blessed are the poor in spirit, for theirs is the kingdom of heaven*, translated as: Happy are those who are aware of their utter dependence on God, as the poor are.
2 *Blessed are those who mourn, for they will be comforted*, which means: Happy are those who are sad because of the death of those they love.
3 *Blessed are the meek, for they will inherit the earth*, meaning: The way to be happy is to be humble.
4 *Blessed are those who hunger and thirst for righteousness, for they will be filled*, meaning: Happy are those who long for justice.
5 *Blessed are the merciful, for they will receive mercy*, meaning: Happy, also, are those who are kind and forgiving.
6 *Blessed are the pure in heart, for they will see God*, meaning: Happy are those who are single-minded in their search for God.
7 *Blessed are the peacemakers, for they will be called children of God*, meaning: So are those who bring peace and understanding between those who are arguing or fighting.

357

8 *Blessed are those who are persecuted for righteousness' sake; for theirs is the kingdom of heaven*, meaning: Happy are those who are picked on because they are unselfish.

9 And finally, an application of number 8 to today: *Blessed are you, when people revile you and persecute you and utter all kinds of evil against you falsely on my account*, which is best expressed as: Oh, you *lucky* people, when people insult you because you are a Christian.

All Saints

That is a good description of the character of those we call 'saints'; and it is quite the opposite of what the world believes is a life of pleasure. But we have declared our independence of the world's standards, and though it sounds a daunting job description, following the way of the Beatitudes guarantees that you will enjoy an eternity of happiness.

Suggested hymns

Blest are the pure in heart; In our day of thanksgiving; Let saints on earth in concert sing; Lord, it belongs not to my care.

Commemoration of the Faithful Departed (All Souls' Day)   2 November
Souls

Lam. 3.17–26, 31–33 New every morning, *or* Wisd. 3.1–9 Souls of the righteous; Ps. 23 The Lord is my shepherd, *or* 27.1–6, 16–17 He shall hide me; Rom. 5.5–11 Christ died for us, *or* 1 Peter 1.3–9 Salvation ready to be revealed; John 5.19–25 The dead will hear his voice, *or* John 6.37–40 I will raise them up

> '[Jesus said,] "Very truly, I tell you, anyone who hears my word and believes him who sent me has eternal life, and does not come under judgement, but has passed from death to life."' John 5.24
> Or '[Jesus said,] "This is indeed the will of my Father, that all who see the Son and believe in him may have eternal life; and I will raise them up on the last day."' John 6.40

All Souls

Today is called All Souls' Day. That is because, in the medieval Roman Catholic Church, 1 November was called All Saints, on which we remember those who have lived and died heroically as Christians, and form examples of holiness to us all. 'But what about my late hubby?' people asked. 'He was certainly no saint, but I want to pray for God to be merciful to him.' And official Roman Catholic teaching was that everybody goes to limbo or purgatory when they die, and if the Pope decides, against the advice of the Devil's Advocate, that somebody really was a saint, they are beatified, then canonized, and declared to have gone straight to heaven. The souls of everyone else will have to wait till the Last Judgement for their fate to be decided, taking into account the prayers that were said for them on All Souls' Day. Other churches are more relaxed, and allow people to be declared saints by popular acclaim. But we all like to have a special day of the year to remember those who have died.

Souls

But what do we mean by a soul? That is by no means an easy one to answer. In the Old Testament the Hebrew word *nefesh* is sometimes translated as 'soul', sometimes 'life', sometimes 'breath'; the soul is not an aspect of the person but the whole person as a living being – Jacob had 'seventy souls' in his household. In Genesis, 'The LORD God formed man of the dust of the ground, and breathed into his nostrils the breath of life; and man became a living soul.' But the word is not limited to human beings in the Bible. Non-human creatures are also souls: 'everything in which was the breath of life'. In Greek, *psyche* has a similar range of meanings: 'my soul' is often a poetic way of saying 'I', as in the Magnificat, 'My soul doth magnify the Lord.' The 'rich fool' in the parable was warned, 'This very night your soul' (or in some translations 'your life') 'will be taken from you.'

Human nature

In the fourth century AD, Christianity absorbed the Greek idea of human nature divided into two, an immortal soul and a material body. The soul was often thought of as coming into being at the same time as the body, though this causes problems in the debate about abortion. Most Christians today regard the soul more as the

359

individual personality which can survive death. God gives to this aspect of human nature a spiritual body in the afterlife.

Afterlife

We believe that those who have faith in Christ will be included in the resurrection of the dead following their death, when all injustices on earth will be generously compensated for. We hope that human life will continue out of time into eternity. Traditionally, however, those who receive salvation were believed to enter some form of purgatory until they were ready to enter heaven at the Last Judgement, following the return of Christ. Today, Christians believe that eternity is timeless. All that is sinful in us will be washed away, and we shall dwell with God and with those we love in joy.

Agnostic's prayer

So don't feel that you have to defend a particular division of human nature into body, mind and soul, because then you will have to ask where the flesh and the spirit fit into this. The Bible does not give a single classification, but seems to accept whatever the people of the day believed. Yet we do believe that, although our bodies do not survive death, there is a spiritual aspect to us, which is capable of forming a relationship with God, and survives after death in a better life than this one, and that we should pray for them on All Souls' Day. Perhaps you have heard the tale about the agnostic, who could not make up his mind about religion, and prayed 'O God – if there *is* a God – have mercy on my soul – if I *have* a soul'!

Suggested hymns

And now, O Father, mindful of the love; Meekness and majesty; My God, I love thee – not because; Rock of ages, cleft for me.

Saints and Martyrs of (our own nation)
8 November
Who May Dwell with God?
Isa. 61.4–9 Build up the ancient ruins, *or* Ecclus. (Ben Sira) 44.1–15 Let us now praise famous men; Ps. 15 Who may

dwell in your tabernacle?; Rev. 19.5–10 A great multitude
invited; John 17.18–23 To be with me to see my glory

'Lord, who may dwell in your tabernacle?
Who may rest upon your holy hill?'

Psalm 15.1 (Common Worship)

Extended families

The days of the large extended family with several different generations living together under one roof have almost disappeared.
Still more remote are the country houses of P. G. Wodehouse, with
dozens of retainers, where a relation or friend might arrive for the
weekend and stay for a year or two. Nowadays when we talk about
people 'living together' we usually mean an unmarried couple. But
in the ancient world a king might bestow on one of his subjects
the honour of being allowed to live in his palace permanently, as a
mark of his favour.

The Temple

The Temple in Jerusalem was regarded as God's palace. Some of
the priests and Levites, the singers and the servants, used to live
permanently in the small rooms around the Temple courtyard, and
regarded it as a great honour. They compared themselves to the
favoured recipients of the hospitality of a great king. The Temple
was the successor to the tent or tabernacle – which was God's temporary home as the Israelites wandered through the wilderness; and
it was situated on a holy site at the top of the hill of Sion. So they
sang, in Psalm 15:

Lord, who may dwell in your tabernacle?
Who may rest upon your holy hill?

This was not a privilege to be extended to every Tom, Dick or
Harry; there were certain qualifications, which they proceeded to
list. Actually, they outlined a very high code of morality for those
who were given the privilege of living in God's palace. Anyone who
could live up to those standards would be a well-nigh perfect human
being; in fact they would be a saint.

Heaven

In the New Testament, heaven is compared to God's Temple. Jesus is described as the great High Priest, 'a minister in the sanctuary and the true tent that the Lord, and not any mortal, has set up'. The angel in the book of Revelation says about the souls in heaven:

> These are they who have come out of the great ordeal; they have washed their robes and made them white in the blood of the Lamb. For this reason they are before the throne of God, and worship him day and night within his temple, and the one who is seated on the throne will shelter them.

Saints

So the saints are those privileged to dwell in God's palace in heaven, and we can apply to them the words of the psalm. The amazing thing is that so many of the great saints come very close to the standard that the psalm describes. They were well-nigh perfect human beings. That doesn't mean that they were not human. They had times of doubt and bouts of bad temper, but they resisted these temptations with the grace that God gave them, and so they were victorious. It's good that we should honour these heroes of the faith, and hold them up as an example to emulate.

Fellow citizens

But lest we should think that saints only lived in the distant past, we set aside one day a year, a week after All Saints' Day, a day to commemorate 'Saints and Martyrs of (our own nation)'. Some of them, from before the Reformation, have the word 'Saint' in front of their name; but you will find many more honoured in the calendar of *Common Worship*, almost up to the present day. They remind us that quite ordinary people, like us, and living in the same country as we do, responded well to the challenges that God threw at them, and came near to what many would call sainthood. So we too, imperfect as we are, may aspire to become saints, with God's grace. And the target for us to aim at is that we too should be included among those described as:

> Whoever leads an uncorrupt life
> and does the thing that is right;
> who speaks the truth from the heart

and bears no deceit on the tongue;
who does no evil to a friend
and pours no scorn on a neighbour . . .
Whoever has sworn to a neighbour
and never goes back on that word;
who does not lend money in hope of gain,
nor takes a bribe against the innocent.

There, that is your aim in life! You can make it, if you try.

Suggested hymns

Lord, round the throne a glorious band; O what their joy and their rapture must be; Rejoice in God's saints, today and all days; There is a land of pure delight.

St Andrew the Apostle   30 November
Patron Saint of Bonnie Scotland

Isa. 52.7–10 The messenger who announces peace; Ps. 19.1–6 The heavens declare God's glory; Rom. 10.12–18 God's messengers reconcile Jew and Greek; Matt. 4.18–22 The call of the fishermen

> *'As [Jesus] walked by the Sea of Galilee, he saw two brothers, Simon, who is called Peter, and Andrew his brother, casting a net into the sea – for they were fishermen. And he said to them, "Follow me, and I will make you fish for people." Immediately they left their nets and followed him.' Matthew 4.18–20*

Fishers

Matthew, Mark and Luke say that Andrew was called at the same time as his brother Peter; St John's Gospel says that he was called first, and went to invite his brother to join him as a disciple of Jesus. The brothers were fishermen, and were called to the task of being fishers for people, in other words to make new converts to the Christian faith. First they invited Nicodemus to meet Jesus, and, just before the crucifixion, Andrew, a Jew with a Greek name, invited some Greeks to meet him, showing that his mission had already expanded beyond the Jewish race. After that the historical record is uncertain, though it is said that he evangelized all over Greece, and as far as Istanbul and Kiev. The story did not emerge until the tenth century, of Andrew being martyred on an X-shaped cross, which gives us the saltire cross of the Scottish flag.

Relics

However, the relics of the saints were very important in the early centuries. No church could claim authority over other churches unless it had the bones, a lock of hair or part of the clothing of one of the 12 apostles. In AD 356 or 357 the alleged relics of St Andrew were taken to Istanbul, then called Constantinople, from Patras, in the south of Greece; so it is likely that Patras was where he died. But crusaders captured Constantinople in 1204, and sent Andrew's body to Amalfi; his head was cut off and sent to Rome in 1461, to stay there until Pope Paul VI, in the 1970s, sent it back to Istanbul, as an ecumenical gesture to the Greek Orthodox. But some of the relics remained in Patras, and in the fourth century, according to the legend, a certain monk of Patras, called St Regulus, was told by God to take the remaining relics of St Andrew 'to the ends of the earth'. So he took them to Scotland. Whether or not you think that is the furthest north that civilization had then reached probably depends on whether you were born north or south of the city that became known as St Andrews! A Victorian historian of Scotland declared this legend to be 'so unlikely that it probably contains a germ of truth'!

Arbroath

In 1321 various earls, lords and churchmen sent a petition to Pope John XXII, known as the Declaration of Arbroath, begging him to put a stop to the cruelties inflicted by Edward I of England on the Scottish people – specifically, and I quote, to the 'deeds of cruelty, massacre, violence, pillage, arson, imprisoning prelates, burning down monasteries, robbing and killing monks and nuns, and yet other outrages without number'! Whether or not that is an accurate account of history is a matter of opinion. But it shows that Scottish nationalism, and hatred of the English, has been around for a long time. The Declaration invokes 'the first of [Christ's] apostles – by calling, though second or third in rank – the most gentle St Andrew, the Blessed Peter's brother', chosen by Christ 'to keep the Scottish people under his protection as their patron forever'.

Democracy

It may be stretching a point to call the Declaration of Arbroath a call for democracy. These aristocrats call for the people of Scotland to be free from domination by the King of England, but say nothing about their domination by the Pope of Rome, or indeed by the Scottish nobility. But perhaps it was a step in the right direction. The recent vote has shown a division of opinion on the merits of regional independence, and of submerging some of that independence in the European Union. It is hard to invoke St Andrew on behalf of one side or the other. But perhaps the Jew with a Greek name, who was called to fish for people, and brought Greeks to speak to Jesus, is trying to remind us that whatever political decisions we make, we must remember that all races and nations are brothers and sisters under the skin, because we are all children of our loving heavenly Father.

Suggested hymns

Dear Lord and Father of mankind; Amazing grace (Scottish melody); Spirit of God, unseen as the wind (Skye Boat Song); The Lord's my shepherd (Brother James's Air).

Sermon for Harvest Festival
Thanksgiving

Deut. 26.1–11 First fruits; Ps. 100 Enter his gates with thanks; Phil. 4.4–9 Rejoice!, *or* Rev. 14.14–18 The harvest of souls; John 6.25–35 Work for the food that lasts

> *'Enter [God's] gates with thanksgiving*
> *and his courts with praise;*
> *give thanks to him and bless his name.'*
> *Psalm 100.3 (Common Worship)*

Thanksgiving

Today is our harvest festival, or, as it is sometimes called, Harvest Thanksgiving. St Paul pointed out the importance of thanksgiving. He wrote to the Romans:

Rejoice always,
pray without ceasing,
give thanks *in all circumstances;*
for this is the will of God in Christ Jesus for you.

Whenever Jesus broke bread, to feed the crowds in the desert or at the Last Supper, the Gospels tell us he 'gave thanks'. This wasn't just saying grace, with a polite 'Thank you, Lord, for our food.' The bread was a symbol of the many things that God has done for us, which make life not only possible but enjoyable. We teach children to say, 'Thank you, Mummy', whenever she does something kind – it shows that we don't take her for granted, and we realize that we couldn't manage without her. Similarly, constant thanksgiving to God reminds us of our complete dependence on his love, without which we should have died long ago.

Carothers

Merlin Carothers is the author of several best-selling books which focus on the importance of thanksgiving. An American, he was drafted into the army. Then he was sent to a military jail for absence without leave and stealing a car. In the early days of the charismatic movement he attended a Methodist church and had a life-changing spiritual experience, which charismatics call 'baptism in the Spirit'. It was a deeply emotional feeling that he had given his whole life to God, and that God had filled him with the Holy Spirit and power to teach and heal in God's name. He was ordained, and returned to the same unit where he had been sent to prison, but this time as their chaplain. But life was not easy for him.

Prison to praise

What happened next is described in his own words in his influential book *Prison to Praise*. One evening he began to laugh, and felt, rather than heard, God asking him whether he was glad that Jesus died for his sins. 'Yes, Lord, I'm glad,' he answered. Then God asked whether he was glad that the soldiers drove nails through the feet and hands of Jesus, and a spear into his side. After a long silence, Chaplain Carothers made the answer he thought God was expecting and, without quite understanding what he was saying, he replied that he was very glad about that. God was pleased with this, and told him that from now on, whenever anything happened to him which was not as bad as what happened to Christ, he was to give thanks to God for what had occurred. The first test was the next morning when, as usual, Carothers was sitting on the edge of his bed wishing he didn't have to get up. But the Holy Spirit told him he was supposed to be thankful that it was time to get up, and if he didn't feel thankful, to ask the Spirit to make him feel it. For many years he had suffered from painful headaches, but he managed to thank God that he wasn't as badly off as some people. Then God told him to give thanks *for* the headache. The pain got worse, but he continued to praise God, and suddenly he felt flooded with joy and all the pain had gone never to return. Then he began to travel, healing people by persuading them to praise God for *everything*, including their pain. It's controversial, and hard to put into practice, but that is why his book is called *Prison to Praise*.

Thanksgiving in church

So it is good we meet in church to thank God for the harvest, from which comes all our food, without which we should die. From this we can learn to make a habit of thanking God for all his goodness to us, every day, until we understand our complete dependence on his love. Every time we go to church we shall feel a flood of joy filling our hearts, until our neighbours say, 'You really should try going to that church, everybody there is so *joyful*!' Whether any of us reach the stage that Chaplain Carothers recommends, of thanking God even for the *bad* things that happen to us, remains to be seen; but you might begin by asking God's Holy Spirit to give you the grateful feelings that could never come naturally, until the whole of your life becomes one endless harvest thanksgiving.

All-age worship

Write on a big poster all the things you want to thank God for.

Suggested hymns

Fairest Lord Jesus; Let us, with a gladsome mind; O Lord my God! When I in awesome wonder; We plough the fields and scatter.

Sermon for a Wedding
Traditional Marriage
John 2.1–11

> 'On the third day there was a wedding in Cana of Galilee, and the mother of Jesus was there. Jesus and his disciples had also been invited to the wedding.' John 2.1–2

Gift

Thank you for choosing to come to church for what we all rejoice to call a 'traditional wedding'. Many people say that traditional marriage is under attack these days, or simply being ignored. A high proportion of couples never bother to get married. But while we are agreed that we want to support the traditional understanding of marriage, we need to ask, what exactly is traditional marriage? The *Common Worship* service states that 'Marriage is a gift of God in creation'. But most Christians today regard the story of the Garden of Eden not as a history of what did happen, but as a vision of what should happen. It would be more true to say that sex is God's gift in creation, to draw us to find partners with whom we can share our lives, and then work together towards the goal of that love which Shakespeare called 'the marriage of true minds'.

In the past

Historically, marriage has evolved from tribal polygamy, through the buying and selling of brides as chattels (which Jesus called 'marrying and giving in marriage'), to the slavery of women to child-bearing and -rearing. Many women among my ancestors, if they survived their first pregnancy, went on to give birth to 12 or more children, approximately one every year, until they died of exhaustion; for this they were expected to obey their husbands in all things. Fortunately, the extended family and the local community shared in the upbringing of children, but that is no longer easy to organize.

Time bombs

Into this scandal of 'traditional marriage' both Jesus and St Paul inserted time bombs, the effects of which are only beginning to be understood. To begin with, Jesus reversed the traditional pattern of a woman joining her husband's family and doing what they told her, when he said the intention in Genesis was that 'a *man* shall leave his parents and be joined to his wife'. And St Paul, arguing from the common assumption that wives should obey their husbands, pointed out that the consequence of this was that a married couple should 'be subject to *one another*', and husbands should love their wives 'just as Christ loved the church and *sacrificed himself* for her'.

Partnership

So the target towards which we should be working is an equal partnership of mutual encouragement and self-sacrifice. This is harder to achieve than many couples realize, so it should begin with a service of prayer for the couple to receive God's help. We should see our marriage service as neither a magical 'blessing', ensuring freedom from pain and grief, nor merely a legal contract, which is a useful device for ensuring that abandoned wives and parentless children are supported financially. St Paul wrote that

Love is patient; love is kind;
love is not envious or boastful or arrogant or rude.
It does not insist on its own way; it is not irritable or resentful;
it does not rejoice in wrongdoing, but rejoices in the truth.
It bears all things, believes all things,
hopes all things, endures all things.

Ideal

Think of the married couples you know, and look honestly into your own hearts, and you will see that very few of us have achieved that degree of mutual unselfishness. But for some couples, especially those who choose to be married in church, that is the target they are aiming at. It is difficult, but possible if you work at it, with God's help, to have a relationship in which both partners are patient, kind, not envious or boastful or arrogant or rude. The ideal marriage is one in which neither partner insists on their own way, is irritable or resentful, nor rejoices in wrongdoing, but on the contrary rejoices in the truth. We should try to be wives or husbands who put up with everything, trust their partner absolutely, are always optimistic, and whose love lasts to the very end of our lives. Any couple who try to set an example of *that* sort of love lead us *away* from the traditional misunderstandings of what marriage is, and beyond romantic and erotic love, towards the mutual caring which the Bible describes as the kingdom of God, on earth as it is in heaven. They deserve our gratitude and our prayers.

Suggested hymns

Come down, O love divine; Let there be love shared among us; Love divine, all loves excelling; The Lord's my shepherd, I'll not want.

Sermon for the Baptism of Infants
Baptism Promises

> '[The Ethopian official] said, "Here is some water. What is to keep me from being baptized?" Philip said to him, "You may be baptized if you believe with all your heart." "I do," he answered, "I believe that Jesus Christ is the Son of God." . . . both Philip and the official went down into the water, and Philip baptized him.' Acts 8.36–38 Good News Bible (verse 37 is in a footnote)

Origins

This is a very happy day. Today we welcome a new member into the family. That means their birth family, of course, who are delighted to have a new baby. It also includes the family of God. Anyone who knows that God loves us as his children, and who loves God as their Father, is a member of the Christian Church, the worldwide family of God. This means that your baby now has around 2,000 million brothers and sisters, in every nation in the world. Children become members of their parents' family when they are born; then all their friends and relations gather to greet their new relation. Children become members of God's family at a service called 'christening', which means 'Christianing', making them a Christian. We pour water over them, because this service has its origins in baptism. In the time of Jesus, it was mostly adults who were baptized, by dipping them in a river, as a symbol of washing away any guilty feelings which might be bothering them, before they entered God's family of love.

Questions

In the Bible story which has just been read, a black man from Ethiopia was baptized – no racial barriers hinder anyone from becoming a Christian. A Christian called Philip told him about Jesus, and the Ethiopian asked to be baptized. Philip asked him one simple question, 'Do you believe that Jesus Christ is the Son of God?' and he answered, 'Yes', and was baptized straight away, no fuss. But there is a curious thing about that story: the bit about the question and answer are not in the oldest copies of the Bible. Unfortunately some people were asking to be baptized who didn't believe in anything at all; so Christians resolved to ask baptism candidates searching questions about their faith. They soon decided that the writers of the Bible had forgotten to mention that, so they agreed to add a few words to the original story.

Children

Now, most people believe that from the first, whole families were baptized together. So what did they do about the children, who were too young to understand the questions? They asked the parents, and people they chose as godparents, to make the promises on behalf of the children. That was fine when children obeyed their parents. If parents in those days told their children, 'I made these promises as your proxy', the children would feel bound to do what was promised. Today we encourage children to think for themselves, and if you told them you had promised something on their behalf, they would do the opposite, muttering, 'Nobody's going to tell me what to do!'

Revision

Recently there was a fuss about a new alternative christening service which had been drawn up. Some people protested, 'You can't leave out the question about renouncing the devil and all his works.' And others said, 'The godparents will think we're asking them to believe in a green cartoon character with horns and hooves.' Actually it was a fuss about nothing, which one newspaper pretended was going to split the Church. They were missing the point.

Welby

Shortly before that, Archbishop Welby produced a short film about the christening of Prince George, which caused many people to think again about christening. He said that the task of the parents and godparents is simple: to make sure the child 'knows who this Jesus is. Speak of him, read stories about him. Introduce him in prayer.' Then help the child to 'grow and flourish into the person God has called [them] to be'.

New promises

Perhaps that shows where revision is needed. We should stop asking parents to make impossible promises on behalf of a child. Instead, ask them to do their best to bring up the child in such a way that they can make an informed choice when they are older. Adapting the Archbishop's words, we should ask parents and godparents:

Will you try hard to introduce this child to Jesus by talking about him, reading stories about him, and praying with this child to the loving God that Jesus told us about and called 'Our Father'?

Will you do your best to show in your own life what it means to love God, and to love everyone you meet, in thankfulness for what God has done for us?

To which the answer could be simply, 'I'll try.' Few people would be unable to make an answer like that; and they will take it more seriously than some antiquated words meaning nothing to people of today: God bless you all, and all your children.

Suggested hymns

I want to walk with Jesus Christ; O Jesus, I have promised; Take my life, and let it be; When we walk with the Lord (Trust and obey).

Sermon for a Funeral or Memorial Service
Talk to Each Other
John 20.11–18

> '*Jesus said to [Mary Magdalene], "Do not hold on to me, because I have not yet ascended to the Father. But go to my brothers and say to them, 'I am ascending to my Father and your Father, to my God and your God.'"' John 20.17*

I wish

How often you hear bereaved people say, 'Oh, I wish I had said so-and-so to them', or, 'I wish I had asked them their views about that.' Thank God, it is not always so, and there are some marvellous deathbed conversations. But many times, death comes unexpectedly. Or there comes a mental change over the dying person that makes it hard to communicate with them.

Death

The one thing that is certain in human life is that we all die sometime. We have almost all lost some relative through an unexpected motor accident. So none of us is too young to think about what will happen when we die. We should all write down or at least talk to somebody about what we want done with our belongings, and what sort of funeral we want.

Change

Then people's personalities change as they age. Once a vicar took his aged mother into hospital, when the gerontologist warned him that the last part of the brain to form in a child is the part that deals with social relationships. And it is also the first part to die when we get old. So it may be that someone whom you have known as a sweet elderly woman for years becomes quite short tempered as she approaches death. Which turned out to be very helpful advice in that case. Then there is the terrible problem of dementia when the sick person cannot even remember who you are. So if there is something you want to say to somebody before they die, it is advisable not to leave it too late.

Locked in

Equally distressing is when somebody loses the power of speech in what is called 'locked-in syndrome'. *The Diving Bell and the Butterfly* is a moving film, based on a true story, of a man who lost the power of speech. He could feel emotions and think thoughts, but he couldn't utter a syllable. But he wrote his life story simply by blinking when his daughter pointed to a letter of the alphabet on a card, when she would write it down till the letters formed a word. So when you visit somebody in hospital who cannot speak, don't give up but say what you were going to say, on the assumption that they can hear you.

Rose

Rose – not her real name – was deeply loved by her family, by the staff at the hospital, and by the chaplains who visited her there. For seven years they gradually came to terms with the idea that she would never leave there alive. Often her family asked the chaplain to pray that she would speak again, and he always did, aloud or in his heart. Then he asked God why he was not answering their prayers. He wondered whether perhaps Rose was teaching them a lesson that she could never have put into words. Her family were wonderful, visiting her regularly, and talking to her with the certainty that she could hear and understand. The chaplain used to pray that she might have peace of mind, freedom from pain and faith in God's promises of eternal life, and once at least he swore that Rose murmured a quiet but heartfelt 'Amen'. Her devoted family would often ask her a question, saying, 'Smile at me if you agree', to be rewarded by a broad grin. So there are other ways of talking, beyond audible words.

After death

And we can go on talking to somebody when they die. Maybe at the graveside, or in some place where we have been happy together. But it can be anywhere. Many people say, 'You know, I have a strong feeling that she or he is still with me.' Perhaps Rose was teaching us that we can, and should, talk to people even when we get no audible reply, and that our words may be answered by subtle signs that nobody else is aware of.

Magdalene

In the Bible, Mary Magdalene knew that Jesus was dead, because she was there when they buried him. And yet she heard him call her by her name – a voice from beyond the grave. So she realized that death is not the end, but the beginning of a new and happier life. And those we love have not left us, but are still close to us in love. The first thing Jesus said after he came to life again, was 'Go and talk!' He said to Mary, 'Go to my brothers and say to them, "I am ascending to my Father and your Father, to my God and your God."' So don't feel bad about the things you never said. There is plenty of time to be together and communicate after somebody has died – and when we, also, have been 'promoted to glory', we shall have all the time in the world to talk to each other.

Suggested hymns

Abide with me; Nearer, my God, to thee; On a hill far away; The Lord's my Shepherd.

Acknowledgements of Copyright Sources

Scripture Index to Sermon Texts

Book	Chapter	Verse	Page
	14	28	133
	15	12	250, 325
	15	12–13	275
	16	5, 7	255
	17	20–21	294
	18	37	279
	20	15	332
	20	17	373
	20	27–28	182
	20	29	114
	21	4	119
	21	20, 24	34
Acts	1	1–2	139
	1	18	318
	8	14, 17	41
	8	36–38	370
	10	39–41	109
	11	29–30	334
	12	11	330
Rom.	6	3	43
	8	37	270
	10	12–13	68
	10	17	260
	15	4	258
1 Cor.	4	9	192
	7	17	53
	10	6	196

Book	Chapter	Verse	Page
	10	13	78
	11	23–25	320
	13	4	56
	14	18–19	201
2 Cor.	1	3–4	206
	3	18	61
	4	7	303
	5	19	82
	8	7	211
Gal.	1	1–6	157
	1	16–21	161
	2	16	166
	3	24–26	170
	4	4–5	338
	5	14	175
Eph.	1	3–5, 8–10	37
	4	8	144
Phil.	1	9–10	7
	3	20	73
Col.	1	15	189
	3	9–10	199
	3	12–15	85
	3	16	32
1 Thess.	2	5–6	301
2 Thess.	3	13	272
Titus	3	4–5	25
Philemon	—	15–17	223

Author Index

383

Subject Index

Entries in *italics* are sermon titles

Notes

Notes

Notes

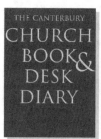

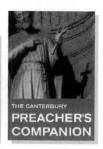

Advance order for the 2017 editions *(available May 2016)*

quantity

Prices are subject to confirmation and may be changed without notice

CANTERBURY CHURCH BOOK & DESK DIARY 2016 *Hardback*   £19.99 + p&p* ....

CANTERBURY CHURCH BOOK & DESK DIARY 2016 *Personal Organiser (loose-leaf)* £19.99 + p&p* ....

CANTERBURY CHURCH BOOK & DESK DIARY 2016 *Personal Organiser (A5)*   £19.99 + p&p* ....

CANTERBURY PREACHER'S COMPANION 2016 *Paperback*   £19.99 + p&p* ....

For details of special discounted prices for purchasing the above in any combinations
or in bulk, please contact the publisher's Norwich office as shown below.

Order additional copies of the 2016 editions

Subject to stock availability

Hardback Diary **£19.99*** ....   Organiser **£19.99*** ....

Preacher's Companion **£19.99*** ....   A5 Personal Organiser **£19.99*** ....

Ask for details of discounted prices for bulk orders of 6+ copies of any individual title when ordered direct from the Publisher.

Sub-total £ ....

*Plus **£2.50** per order to cover post and packing (UK only): £ ....

All orders over £50 are sent POST FREE to any UK address.
Contact the Publishers office for details of overseas carriage.

TOTAL AMOUNT TO PAY: £ ....

I wish to pay by ...

   ... **CHEQUE** for £ .... made payable to **Hymns Ancient and Modern Ltd**

   ... **CREDIT CARD**   All leading credit and debit cards accepted (*not American Express or Diners Club*)
      Your credit card will not be debited until the books are despatched.

Card number: ....   Expiry: ____ / ____

                                    Issue No: ____ Valid from: ____ / ____

                                  Switch or *Maestro* only

Signature of

cardholder: ....   Security code: _____

                                    Last three digits on signature panel

Please PRINT all details below.

Title: .... Name: ....

Delivery address: ....

....

....

.... Post Code: ....

Telephone or e-mail: .... Date: ....

Please ensure you have ordered the edition you require for the correct year. No liability will be accepted for incorrect orders

Return this order form or a photocopy – with details of payment – to

Norwich Books and Music, 13A Hellesdon Park Road, Norwich NR6 5DR

Telephone: 01603 785900   Fax: 01603 785915   Website: www.canterburypress.co.uk